Helen Duffy

A SOLO IN TOM-TOMS

GENE FOWLER

A SOLO
IN
TOM-TOMS

THE VIKING PRESS
NEW YORK   MCMXLVI

FIRST PUBLISHED BY THE VIKING PRESS IN APRIL 1946

PUBLISHED ON THE SAME DAY IN THE DOMINION OF CANADA
BY THE MACMILLAN COMPANY OF CANADA LIMITED

SECOND PRINTING

PRINTED IN THE UNITED STATES OF AMERICA
AMERICAN BOOK–STRATFORD PRESS. INC., NEW YORK

TO

Robert Silliman Hillyer

"*A boy's will is the wind's will,*
And the thoughts of youth are long, long thoughts."

—HENRY WADSWORTH LONGFELLOW

CONTENTS

ix

A SOLO
IN
TOM-TOMS

1

APPOINTMENT IN MANHATTAN

IT HAD been a long quest. Now in 1920 I was to meet my father for the first time. He seemed a fable of a man named Charles Francis Devlan. The world seldom had seen him, nor he the world, during his thirty years of hermitage on the high slope of Squaw Mountain.

This stranger would be fifty-two years old and I, his son, several months past thirty that Indian summer in Manhattan. As I awaited his coming, I remembered my late grandmother's indictments of the man as she sat beside the base-burner stove on distant winter nights in the Rocky Mountain West.

The pioneer grandmother who reared me among the mountains and plains of Colorado said that Charles Devlan was a person of no importance. "He was a stubborn disgrace. A dream-ridden failure, he stayed only long enough to beget you, then forget you, and wander off to the hills."

I had come upon a picture of him among my dead mother's personal effects long ago. The Charles Devlan of the photograph was but twenty-two years old. He had sat for it in 1889, three months before I was born, and one month before his departure into the thirty-year solitude. Our first meeting, I thought, might help clarify the past and provide a lamp for the future.

My philosophies, if any, were a scrambled lot. I lacked the effective weapons of a disciplined intellect. My ambitions were few, my aspirations many. I tossed about on the winds of instinct and caprice, with only an inheritance of faith, together with a sharp eye for the ridiculous, as my balloon and my parachute. Sometimes the balloon collapsed in the sky and the parachute failed to open.

Small questions frequently seemed to be large ones, and the big ones little. Then, in a sudden topsy-turvy mood, I would find the horizon so enchanting that I neglected the proper study of perspective. I would not, or could not, believe in the "vanishing point." I denounced my own eyes as a pair of liars. And when Einstein declared with the serenity of St. Jerome that a straight line was *not* the shortest distance between two points, and that there really were no straight lines, I understood not one symbol among the seer's stupendous formulæ, but I felt the sublimity of his mysticism, the truth of his announcement.

Among the things which I wanted my father to explain was how a quarrel concerning a cup of coffee had sent him to the hills for thirty years. Stubborn absurdities frequently had plunged his son into costly and lasting dilemmas.

I resolved to offer many of my own secrets in exchange for Charles Devlan's confidences. For example, I would reveal to him how confused I had become when three surnames were successively assigned to me before I reached the age of seven. Few persons other than criminals have owned such a profusion of aliases.

At the time of this first meeting with my father I had been a New York newspaper reporter for two years. I was a scared young man. Of what? Of everything. I was pretending not to be scared of the great city. I was making it appear that I had left the West forever behind me. But the fact was, and the fact remains, that I never left the plains and the mountains. Perhaps the late Ring Lardner, who saw beyond anyone's pretenses, had this in mind when he said: "Fowler is the last of the bison."

Certain gallant survivors of Park Row of the twenties accord me the reputation of "a good reporter." If you assume that I am about to undertake a recital of my newspaper exploits, and thereby deflate that legend, then you are the kind of person who believes in the generosity of a roulette wheel. No. I shall wear my fortuitous laurels, hoping the while that some old comrade will not come to grips simultaneously with a bottle and the truth, and speak his real mind while in the presence of discerning moderns.

That year when I met my father, my first child, a son, was three years old. We were occupying a small apartment furnished with some endurable but disheartening oddities from Fra Elbertus Hubbard's East Aurora commune. The apartment house stood on Amsterdam Avenue directly opposite the unfinished Cathedral of St. John the Divine.

The apse and choir chapels of the cathedral had been completed, and the crossing inclosed. Flying buttresses addressed the lateral vaults of the crossing. At night the black and shallow dome, together with the profiled ribs of the arches to which the transepts eventually were to be groined, became the silhouette of a great, crouching cat. The late-hour newspaperman viewed this massive shadow, and knew at once that he was but a mouse. He went indoors, then upstairs to his apartment to kiss his sleeping son, as if to shrive himself for the sins of the day.

That was the year of interviews with Grock, the pantomimic clown; Mary Garden, George M. Cohan, Enrico Caruso. Of a time when the jaunty little bandit, Gordon Fawcett Hamby, went as briskly as a tap-dancer across the death-house floor to sit in the electric chair at Sing Sing prison. . . . The year of the interview on a February Sunday with the Assistant Secretary of the Navy, Franklin D. Roosevelt, then erect and strong and in love with ships. . . . The winter of "the big snow," with traffic stalled and the trees of Central Park bundled in ermine. . . .

The birthday interview with Thomas A. Edison at West Orange, New Jersey, on the subjects of sleep and God. The doughty old wizard enraged a large part of the public by saying that he "had been unable to find any evidence of a deity during the last seventy-three years." Henry Ford confided, "off the record," that his friend Edison actually *did* sleep but four hours at a time, but slept "three times a day." . . . Jack Dempsey, Babe Ruth, John McGraw of the Giants, Otto Kahn, Victor Herbert, James Cardinal Gibbons, Tex Rickard, Charles Dana Gibson, Harrison Fisher, Arthur Brisbane, the Barrymores, Heywood Broun. . . . Prohibition whisky, the League of Nations, Sacco and Vanzetti. . . .

That summer lay upon the city with hot and humid flanks. At night all the flat-wheel streetcars in the world were routed exclusively along Amsterdam Avenue. The black cat cathedral seemed especially menacing. The days became too oppressive for the children to ride their tricycles on a pavement that eventually would underlie the nave and the cathedral façade.

I made an investment that summer, and beyond my means as usual. I purchased a cracker-box cottage for twelve hundred dollars, two hundred dollars down, at Edgemere Beach, among the Rockaways.

The name Far Rockaway always had seemed to me beautiful beyond Shelley. Now at last I was next door to Far Rockaway. Moreover, I had found the sea; and in its presence I felt less scared. During my younger years, I had been told that the waters of Mullen's Mill Ditch eventually reached the sea. And now whenever I went into the ocean at my front door the waters I had seen in childhood, two thousand miles to the west, again seemed with me in this moving vastness.

Each summer day and late into the fall I commuted from my cracker-box beach house to the newspaper office on William Street off the Bowery. A small diary, kept in 1920 and then abandoned—as I abandon most systematic arrangements of living—tells me that Wednesday, September 15, was my day off. I spent that day in the ocean, gathered driftwood, then made a seaside dinner that failed because of sand in the steak. The next morning, says my fragment of a diary, I "took a dip." The day was warm and fair; everything was right with me, except that I needed some immediate money.

I left on an early train for Manhattan to persuade the city editor to grant another advance against my already decimated pay check. Assignment hour on the morning newspaper was at one o'clock in the afternoon. But I arrived at eleven-thirty this morning during the brief forenoon doldrums of the editorial room. I delivered a speech of desperation to the city editor. It was a plea like a mother's to a governor on behalf of a son pining in the death house.

While the generous but wary foreman of the journalists was making up his mind as to whether I was facing ruin or acting as the go-between for a bootlegger, I went to the mailbox. From a cell of this tired honeycomb, I plucked three or four letters addressed to me. One bore a Colorado postmark. I placed these letters in my coat pocket, then retired to my desk, one of the many dilapidated furnitures of the cluttered city room. Meantime, I kept an eye upon the city editor for an inkling as to my financial status.

He was mumbling over the assignment ledger, "God, but news is slow today!" He glared morbidly through thick-lensed spectacles at a portrait of William Randolph Hearst, then added, "Tomorrow's paper will look like a South Dakota farm report."

Between exploratory glances at the editor, I inspected my typewriter. Perhaps, during my day off, some cub reporter had picked the lock of the desk, and banged with two fingers upon the one possession that I never neglected or abused. Then, my eye occasionally cocked toward the city editor, I busied myself among the arthritic drawers of my desk. I kept therein such reportorial treasures as the trial pages of manuscript for the book one always was planning to write; bottles in various degrees of emptiness; playing cards old enough to have served Canfield during his teething time; long-billed scissors probably discarded by Horace Greeley; a pair of overshoes, one of which leaked like the *Hesperus;* dust rags; frayed photographs of Eugene V. Debs, Chauncey M. Depew, Mrs. Fiske, and of the Cudahy kidnaper Pat Crowe; a baseball autographed by Ty Cobb; a paste pot that would require a crowbar to open it; expense-account blanks. . . .

It now was about noon, about a minute before noon as I recall it. I think I am safe in saying that all personal matters, and some others as well, suddenly were blown aside. The invoicing of the desk drawers was interrupted. The problem of my finances was abruptly dismissed. The unopened letters stayed neglected in my pocket. The claptrap building, in which our staff members as well as numerous families of downtown rats were housed, seemed to sneeze gigantically. The dirty windows did the *Danse Macabre.* The portrait of Mr. Hearst listed to starboard. The city editor's jaws commenced to work like a gaffed salmon's. But I now could not hear him or anything else. Then his voice came on like a phonograph's from a standing start as my eardrums returned to the job.

The source of all this confusion was an event now known to history as the Wall Street bomb explosion.

The city editor's nostrils dilated. The thick lenses magnified certain misgivings in his eyes as he said, "Good God! I wish Damon Runyon or Bill Davenport were here!" Then he turned to me resignedly. "Well, get going on the story!"

As I moved in obedience to his command, he called out: "But don't pick up any old women *this* time!"

He had reference to my gallantry during the evening of July 8, 1919. On my way to the office from Carnegie Hall that night, and after reporting the Peace Treaty speech of President Woodrow Wilson, I came upon an old woman lost in the subway station. In physical appearance she reminded me of my grandmother. Instead of attending to my journalistic business, I escorted her to her home in the Bronx. She said that I was "a fine

young man." That was not what the editor said when I came in
late to write of Mr. Wilson.

Thirty persons were killed and one hundred injured by the
Wall Street blast. A horse-drawn vehicle with a cargo of explosives had detonated near the George Washington statue and
the Subtreasury, the site of our first President's inauguration. The
granite of the old Doric structure was pockmarked by the explosion, as was the headquarters of J. P. Morgan & Company across
the narrow canyon of finance.

I had taken a short-cut from the office to avoid the deadlock
of traffic. I had gone to Wall Street by way of an underpass
below the Manhattan terminus of Brooklyn Bridge. The latrinal
odors of that tunnel still were in my nose as I arrived at the place
of the story.

I could see several of my colleagues at work. Their police
cards tucked in their hatbands, they moved with the self-
confidence of great clinicians. I always felt less scared when
among these veterans. Because of their example and their incom-
parable kindness, I had been able to find and hold an exciting
place in the Park Row scene. Several of these men already owned
fame, others were to become famous; some never were to know
the fame they deserved. But to me they possessed, all of them,
greater attributes than renown. They had integrity, and they
knew the high gift of friendship.

The Wall Street explosion had little to do with my father,
except for one thing. As so often happened, I had left the office
with no notepaper in my pockets. Sometimes when on an assignment I had to take notes on the inside covers of matchbooks. It
seems that I never was prepared for anything of practical advantage; and for life least of all.

Today I used the envelopes of my unopened mail for the
recording of names of the dead and dying and for other per-
tinent data. The envelopes soon became overrun with these nota-
tions. I opened the letters to employ their margins and backs
for my scribblings. And now, as I stood on the Subtreasury steps,

and beneath the statue of the Father of our Country, I saw the signature on the short letter from Colorado: "Charles F. Devlan."

As I started down the stone stairs, Police Officer Pat McDonald, champion thrower of the thirty-five-pound weight, commanded me to halt. I was encroaching upon the vicinity of the shattered horse and the wooden confetti that just recently had been a wagon. I soon sped away from that zone.

I moved among the crowd as rapidly as I could toward Trinity churchyard at the head of Wall Street. I went inside the brownstone Gothic church. The noises of the city suddenly became distant and muffled, like the sound made by one's own bloodstream when a conch shell is held to the ear.

I read my father's first letter to me.

Dear son:

I hesitate now, as I long, long have hesitated, to write to you. I am bringing the ashes of my father to Elizabethport, New Jersey, to bury them as he wished me to at the feet of my mother. Would you mind if I called to see you? If you don't want me to, I am sure I wouldn't blame you in any way after all the years I never wrote or did anything for you. But I always have been very proud of you.

Your father,
Charles F. Devlan.

I sat there like a stunned cockerel. Finally I went outside the church. I was still in a wondrous daze when I arrived at the newspaper office. The city editor said he was glad that I had taken "plenty of time getting here."

I amazed him with the announcement: "I just got a letter from my father."

"You don't mean to say! From Lord Chesterfield, no doubt?"

"From my own father," I said. "Isn't it remarkable?"

He studied me through the thick-lensed eyeglasses. "Fowler, sometimes I wonder which one of us is crazy—you or I."

"Thirty years." I said. "I never heard anything like it. Just imagine!"

A long time afterward, I learned from this and other editors that my city-room naïveté not only failed to jeopardize my job but actually saved it on this and many other occasions.

When I replied to my father's letter, I enclosed my home address, my telephone number, and advised him that Wednesday was my day off—whenever I could get a day off from a business as endless as the tides. I wanted to close the letter with "Yours affectionately," but, you see, we were strangers.

I did not hear from him again until October 26. I was covering the gubernatorial campaign of Alfred E. Smith at the time, and on that particular day and night had reported the candidate's speeches in Staten Island and in Brooklyn. When I reached home I found a letter propped against the telephone. This second communication from my father was postmarked Elizabeth, New Jersey.

"Would tomorrow evening be all right?" he wrote. "I believe you said that Wednesday was your day off."

I sent a telegram inviting him to dinner at my apartment the next night. In the morning I went to the South Shore to board up my little beach house against the seasonal nor'easters. I had my last dip of the year in the cold calm water. Then I returned home to wait for the man who for so long a time had seemed a fable.

He did not arrive for dinner; nor did he appear at eight o'clock, or nine. I was becoming concerned about this tardiness. Was he as careless as I in these matters? If he had too many of my faults, I would find it difficult to admire him.

At about nine-thirty, I looked out the front window. A full moon now had risen; it was shining upon the black cat cathedral across Amsterdam Avenue. The flat-wheel streetcars were doing a boiler-maker's business, and someone was throwing light bulbs at a congress of passionate cats assembled in the courtyard of the apartment.

Then the doorbell sounded. I went to the door to open it upon a man who wore a graying Vandyke beard. His eyes were fine and gray, and, as Mark Twain once said of Robert Louis Stevenson, the eyes gave beauty to his face.

We were both wordless for a time. Then, referring to his beard, I said, "So *that's* where you've been hiding all these years?"

This remark contained magic. We shook hands. My father came inside. I offered him an Elbert Hubbard chair. I shut the window against the riot of flat wheels. Then I drew the blind to blot out the silhouette of the cathedral.

My guest seemed uneasy once again. I observed that his hand trembled. It was a strong hand, admirably modeled, but hard as if from toil. He seemed to be waiting for me to speak, yet feeling perhaps that it was his duty to speak first. I perceived that he was not given to much talk.

I remarked that I had expected him to call earlier, as a matter of fact, for dinner. He hesitated, as if turning something over in his mind, then said that he almost had not come at all.

"I am a little backward sometimes," he explained, as if making a self-accusation. "I've been walking the last hour or so around the block."

"That's ridiculous," I said.

"I couldn't make up my mind to come in." He looked at me earnestly, then added, "I was afraid that you might not want to see me."

I offered him a cigarette. He fidgeted, and I asked, "Say, what's wrong?"

"Not a thing." Then he said, "I'd rather have a cigar, if you don't mind?"

"I don't mind," I said. "Why should I mind?"

He brought a cigar from his breast pocket as if handling a contraband weapon. "I was only thinking about your grandmother—"

"What about her?" I asked.

"I mean no criticism of anybody dead," and he paused, "but she was so set against—"

"Oh," I interrupted. "You mean smoking?"

He smiled a little, but said nothing.

"She was against drinking, too," I reminded him. "Shall we have a little drink?"

His self-consciousness left him. A glad fire enlivened his eyes. "Well, now," he said, "I don't do much drinking. But. . . ."

I had gone for the bottle. That bottle held gin presumably concocted from carriage varnish. But we had a drink; and perhaps it was the best drink I ever had or ever shall have.

We talked until late. I asked concerning the cup of coffee. I inquired about matters having to do with his people and mine. It must not be supposed that this first visit revealed all the mysteries that had puzzled me during my long quest for a father. We were to have numerous talks and much correspondence during the next seventeen years.

Now, as I write of my father and of the Rocky Mountain West of long ago, it is as though we again were meeting for the first time. I hear him once more as he speaks of his courtship days, of his friends, his mountain home, his dreams. And I hear him speak without rancor of my grandmother and the cup of coffee that caused the quarrel which sent him into high solitude on Squaw Mountain near Mt. Evans.

Such a small and homely and peasant-like thing seems a cup of coffee. Still, some of us know that nothing really is small, and nothing actually large, but of an entity, and of no dimensions whatsoever except as our imaginations make it seem large or small. For everything is one thing and of one thing. And the thing is not a thing at all, but an idea. Perhaps this idea is both the creator and the created, timeless, endless, and inscrutable.

2

THE APPRENTICE PATTERN-MAKER

AS THE story came down the years to me, it seems that Charlie Devlan left his father's and his stepmother's house for a morning stroll one Sunday in February 1889. This was in Denver, Colorado. He was one month past twenty-one years old. There had been snow; now it was the wind's turn to perform. Devlan paused at the front gate as though to decide which way he should go.

Three small houses stood to the south of Charlie's cottage. They were occupied respectively by a lazy broom-maker, a fragile widow, and an alcoholic teamster. Snowpacks obstructed the front walks of these neighbors, advertising them as procrastinators. The broom-maker was notably lax each winter in putting his own products to outdoor use. The widow was too slack from her washerwoman's labors to clear away the ice or slush from public lanes. As for the drunkard, he neither saw a duty nor heard its call.

Neighbors the other side of the Devlan cottage had been less remiss. Their consciences and their flagstones were reasonably clean. Charlie set out for his exercise along the cleared pathway. He followed a cable-car track that eventually passed a red-brick church to the northward. Ranks of leafless cottonwood trees stood near that small building. Their crooked arms spilled wisps of snow as the winds rehearsed for a March première. Icicles draped the eaves of the meetinghouse with unkempt crystal beards. Whenever the wind or sun barbered this frosty valance, the breaking of the fallen icicles set up a glockenspiel discord.

To Devlan the Methodist church was but a casual landmark. He was not a member of this or of any other congregation; his belief in God as yet was somewhat dim and formless. He took a cross-yard trail made in the snow of the church grounds. His intention was to return home by way of an avenue other than the one that he had just traveled.

As Charlie crossed the churchyard, he saw a carriage horse, blanketed and tied to a post. He noticed that a hitching rein had fouled on a shaft head of the splendid black surrey. The young man freed the rein, then stroked the black mare's poll.

Now the soprano part of an anthem reached him from a narrow memorial window. The voice was sweet and clear and young. This was a fantastic thing, to see no one, yet to hear the unseen one, and feel that she was not a stranger calling to one's heart, stirring it for the first time.

He found himself walking away from the black mare and toward the entrance of the church. He started up a shallow stair-way to the double-leaved door. Then, as the soloist's voice became lost in a choral response, a terrible shyness overcame Devlan. The reedy drone of the organ became a statement of despair to unman a shy and friendless intruder. He retired confusedly to a near-by street corner.

He pretended there to be awaiting the cable car. Each time a foot gong sounded near the intersection, Devlan hastily stepped aside, so as not to seem a prankster or a downright ass. Several cars rumbled past him at intervals. Eventually the congregation sang the doxology: "Praise God from whom all blessings flow. Praise Him, all creatures. . . ."

The doors opened. The miniature thunder of feet sounded

among the pews and aisles. Then the buzzing Methodists began to emerge as from a beehive. The brethren settled their hats solidly against the wind. The women arranged their long, full skirts, holding them discreetly free of the soiled snòw underfoot. The children, bored and hungry, did annoying things to their elders.

The meetinghouse doors closed. The janitor could be heard refueling the fat-bellied stove for Epworth League services. The last of the parishioners boarded a cable car, and the street became a Sabbath emptiness. Devlan walked home slowly, all the time hearing the young voice in his heart.

On Monday he was at his lathe at the Burnham Shops of the Denver & Rio Grande Railroad. He was employed at the machine shops as an apprentice pattern-maker. He earned twelve and one-half cents an hour for ten hours of work each weekday. Sometimes he did additional work on Sunday mornings at the same rate of pay.

When the next Sunday morning arrived, the young man dressed himself in his good suit, a ready-made blue serge bought at Appel's for nine dollars. Then he put on, as an overcoat, a frayed Norfolk jacket, a makeshift to be cast aside when May would bring the columbines to the foothills. The winds of this late February were making up hoarsely for their March debut. The thatches of snow were being stripped from the housetops. The trees went naked in the half-gale.

Charlie set out for the church, unmindful of the seasonal blast from the Great Divide. The branches of the cottonwoods knocked about like the bones of outlaws lynched and obsolete. The wind lashed the winter-shrunk bed of the South Platte River, a placid nonentity until the freshets of spring would flood its low banks. The river lay several squares beyond the small church toward which the gray-eyed young man directed himself.

He arrived late at the church, and once again suddenly became paralyzed in spirit. Devlan retired, as on the previous Sunday, to the street corner. The Rocky Mountain range to the west looked down upon the man and his vacillaton. He felt small and futile and guilty of something as once again he pretended to be awaiting the cable car.

Lost in a welter of daydreams and frustrations, he forgot the cable car. The public conveyance came to a stop. To his astonishment and pleasure, the conductor, a red-faced man with a high voice, was one of Charlie's newly made friends. The two young men recently had been initiated into the Odd Fellows Lodge.

Conductor George Pell took Devlan's fare. "What you doing in the neighborhood of the church?" Then Pell added, "I'm the organist there."

"But you aren't at today's services," Charlie pointed out.

"We're shorthanded," Pell explained. "But I'll be getting my Sundays off pretty soon again."

"You must be acquainted with everyone in the choir," Charlie said. "Do you know the soprano?"

"We have two sopranos," Pell replied. "Birdie, and there's the Wheeler girl. Seventeen. You know the Wheelers?" Devlan shook his head. Pell went on, "Her mother watches her like a hawk. Her name's Dora Grace, but everybody calls her 'Dodie.' Do you sing, Charlie?"

"No," Devlan said. "I can't sing much."

"Well," Pell sighed, "here's hoping the dispatcher won't call me next Sunday."

"I'd like to hear you play sometime," said Devlan.

Pell was delighted. "I'll let you know at lodge meeting when I'm to get back to the organ."

The next Wednesday evening Pell had good news. "I'll be sitting at the organ this Sunday."

"Would it be all right if I come to hear you?" asked Devlan.

"Why, sure, Charlie," Pell said. "Just come right in. We're going to have a wonderful anthem this Sunday. The bass solo is great. One of the Stookey brothers sings it. A big fellow with a big voice. A good carpenter, too."

"Don't the sopranos sing at all this Sunday?" Charlie inquired.

"Sure they do," said Pell. "There's a soprano solo later on in the anthem. Brother Bright, he's the choir leader—and he's got one leg shorter than the other, and wears a kind of iron stilt on it—and he has whiskers that he calls an 'Imperial,' and he's a jeweler. . . . Well, like I started out to say, Brother Bright assigned the Wheeler girl to the soprano solo, what there is of it. You just come hear this Stookey fellow, Charlie, with me at the organ."

When Devlan arrived at the church on Sunday, March 3, 1889, the wind was biting what was left of the icicles from the eaves. Soon spring would complete the thaws, and the wild waters broaden the river.

Devlan was late at church because he had been ordered by his foreman to work at the shops on an emergency project this Sunday morning. He opened the double doors of the vestibule at a time when Organist Pell was playing the offertory. His self-consciousness subsided when he saw the back of the friendly Pell's neck. It was red with exercise as the musician trod the bellows of an old organ placed against the wooden wall panels at the far side of the ministerial platform. Devlan sat looking at the choir, the six women and five men. They occupied pinewood chairs at the left of Pastor Thornton's pulpit.

The newcomer became interested only in the youngest member of the choir. Devlan admired the girl's black hair, the pert curls high over the brow, and the long tresses down her back. The forenoon light was roofed-out and modified by memorial windows. He was too far away to be certain as to the color of the girl's eyes, but they seemed large and dark. Her olive complexion was brightened by a radiance of cheeks and lips. Her garnet-colored turban had a cock's feather on it. She was provocative with girlhood, gracefully enchanting, as she sat clothed in a go-to-meeting dress of dove gray.

Choirmaster Bright stomped into position on his iron foot. The Imperial beard, the frock coat, the black baton, and the weird appearance of the iron foot, gave their possessor a resemblance to the then widely advertised magician, Herman the Great.

Accompanist Pell began to pedal-pump till the back of his neck became redder than before. With one hand he addressed the keys for the prelude of the anthem; with the other, he pulled out the sub-bass and the bass coupler stops as if ringing up fares. And now Mr. Stookey, the huge carpenter, began to sing the solo.

The Wheeler girl had risen with the others, the anthem sheets in her somewhat chubby hands. Devlan was pleased to observe that she was not tall, for he himself was not tall.

After Mr. Stookey's roaring solo was done, the ensemble responded in full chorus. And now the girl began to sing alone. Hers was the voice Devlan had heard that first Sunday outside the memorial window, sweet and clear and young.

After the services, Devlan watched the girl as she joined a purposeful woman of perhaps fifty years, an Irish woman of strong frame. That would be the mother, Mrs. Elizabeth Wheeler, steel-spectacled, clothed in a Paisley shawl and a bustled linsey-woolsey dress. A horseshoe-shaped bonnet sat upon her graying auburn hair, and its black chiffon ties were gathered in a bow beneath the firm chin.

Devlan was looking after the girl and her mother when Pell arrived at his side.

"George," he asked, "how do you go about joining this church?"

3

THE STREETCAR RIDE

AFTER he had arrived home from the church services, young Devlan climbed to the attic, there to rummage among the hodgepodge properties of an old trunk. This chest held the once-prized keepsakes of his mother. She had been dead these ten years in Elizabethport, New Jersey, the place of Charlie's birth in 1868.

As he turned back the lid, the fragrance of camphor, a whisper from the past, addressed the musty garret air. A wedding-dress—the ashes of roses silk split in places where the neglected folds long had lain, a bandbox with a Leghorn bonnet in it, a garland of tiny pink roses framing the inner side of the straw brim; a packet of letters tied with linen thread; a soldier's tunic with chevrons on the wrinkled sleeves, a forage cap; a coin purse of tarnished silver chain, a hair bracelet, a pair of high boots with spool heels, the laces on the inward sides of the dainty shoes. . . . The light from a low window makes a comet tail in which the dust atoms dance and shine. The past has romantic whisperings for one who cares to visit the attic of a house.

Devlan chanced upon a leather-bound diary, his father's, pressed against the stencil-star lining of the old trunk. Charles senior had kept this journal during his period of service as a cavalry sergeant with the Army of the Potomac. As young Devlan opened the pinseal covers of the diary, it occurred to him that it had been written by a man of his own present age, and of his own blood. What kind of youth had his father been? Stern as now? Non-talkative? Had he known love that sustained him on the field of civil war?

Charlie was unable to find among these personal minutes the least reference to emotional attachments, other than the sergeant's fondness for his several horses, and, strangely enough, his friendliness for southern warriors.

In the trunk with the diary, Charlie found that for which he had come, a small Bible with a silver clasp, his mother's Book. He closed the trunk, climbed down from the attic, washed his hands and face at a pump outside the kitchen door, then retired to his own room. He called out to his stepmother that he wanted no dinner. He sat until evening reading his mother's Bible as if for a school examination. A swift perusal of this Book might expedite his membership in the church.

He found some dry rose petals, rusty with age, among the pages of the Psalms. "For a thousand years in thy sight are but as yesterday. . . ."

At sundown Charlie went outside the house for a drink of cool water from the well. As he held the tin dipper to his lips, he looked off toward the snowy range of mountains to the west. He saw the alpenglow behind the silhouette of the massive watershed. He felt spiritually clean and reassured.

Next Sunday the friendly Pell sponsored Charlie for membership in the church. Devlan's quiet deportment and Pell's enthusiastic representations of his friend's virtues lulled the critical faculties of Mrs. Elizabeth Wheeler. She dropped her guard. She permitted her daughter, Dora Grace Wheeler, to "have company" for the first time in the parlor of her house in West Denver. The mother afterward referred to this lapse as "the biggest mistake since Tiberius Caesar named Pontius Pilate governor of Lower Galilee."

How Dora Grace was won, or, to quote Mrs. Wheeler's own word, "lost," to Devlan, seems a miracle, when one considers the difficulties of courtship during a Victorian age. The kerosene lamp was put out by ten o'clock, and with it the suitor. And until curfew time, Mother sat the other side of the portieres, pretending to read or to darn a stocking drawn over a chinaware egg.

The sturdy Mrs. Wheeler had survived the hazards of travel in a covered wagon with her parents, John and Dora Parrott, in 1858. Since that pioneer time, she continuously had challenged poverty and toil. Now she braced herself against the loss of some-one most dear to her. Notwithstanding Mrs. Wheeler's counsels —actually her commands—Dora Grace became headstrong in her purpose to marry Charlie.

The shocked mother wrote to her husband concerning this predicament. Norman Wheeler, absent from home on one of his many silver- and gold-hunting missions among the mountains, replied in a penciled letter:

Nobody is good enough for our Dodie, but if her young man can stand up against you, he deserves the best.

Mrs. Wheeler next appealed by post to her son, Dewey Emmett Wheeler, at this time a reluctant student at Baldwin Theological Seminary in Kansas. He wished to be a surgeon, and was remaining at this Bible school only to please his mother. Dewey Emmett's letter of reply was mostly concerned with his personal need for three dollars.

And so they were married, Charlie Devlan and Dora Grace Wheeler, by the Reverend Thornton on the afternoon of May 21, 1889. They stood on the tomato-color carpet of the pulpit platform in the small church in West Fifth Avenue to recite their promise of a lifelong partnership. Pell, his neck red with happiness and exercise, played a wedding march on the organ.

Then the young couple left on their "honeymoon," a ride

about the city, together with a party of young friends, aboard a chartered streetcar. This four-hour tour had been arranged by Pell at a bargain fee of seventy-five cents a couple. Pell, grains of rice on the crown of his tramway cap and on the shoulders of his uniform, was pleased to donate his services as conductor.

When twilight came, colored flares shone along the topsides of the streetcar "special." Inside it, the wedding party ate sandwiches and cake, drank lemonade, and sang the songs of yesterday.

O, my poor Nelly Gray, they have taken you away, and I'll never see my darling any more. . . .

Mrs. Wheeler did not go on the streetcar ride; she did not approve of frivolous celebrations. She also declined to accept a lift in the Quirke's splendid surrey. She was steadfast in the observance of her first rule of conduct: "to be beholden to no one." Her self-sufficiency, her industry, notwithstanding her liberality in sharing whatever she had of material things, kept her family almost solvent. The men of her house, as those of her father's house, were wanderers, addicted to the pursuit of wild and lonely schemes. Someone had to be the "head" of the family.

The afternoon was still warm and bright when this pioneer woman walked the mile from the church to her home. The floss of the cottonwood trees drifted down on the air; the Platte River was at fast flood.

The emergence of the city from winter is swift and magical. So clear is the atmosphere above the mile-high plateau upon which the city stands that the foothills seem but a short horseback ride to the west. This lens-like quality of the atmosphere deceived Lieutenant Zebulon M. Pike upon his first glimpse of the Rocky Mountains in 1806. The awakening scrub and grass of the nearer hills make the slopes gray-green, the shade and texture of the sackcloth which Paul Gauguin sometimes employed for lack of artist's canvas in Tahiti.

Fifty of the nation's sixty-seven peaks of an altitude of more than fourteen thousand feet rise beyond the foothills. Their long robes of snow recede in May leaving them dressed like Brobdingnagian housemaids, with starched caps and aprons, and skirts of luminous blue. One sees Pikes Peak seventy-five miles to the southwest of the city, hatted by a Gainsborough cloud. Longs Peak, lofty and austere, is a like distance to the northwest. Between these two massive gables, and for a distance of one hundred and fifty miles along the one hundred and seventh meridian of our charted planet, the granite roof extends.

Almost exactly in the center of this great range, and thirty-five miles west of Denver, an ever-white and sprawling eminence, Mt. Evans, commands a group of lesser peaks. Here the glaciers move with slow but powerful patience. Here the blizzards are conceived, the thunders born. Here the waters are held in trust for the continent, immune to panic, politics, or war, to be released in right degree and proper season. We think it a long time, the three and one-half centuries since the Spaniards first saw these mountains. How then shall we reckon the infinite ages they have stood before our coming, and will stand after we have gone?

Mrs. Wheeler entered her home. It was sundown now. She removed her horseshoe bonnet and her shawl, and went to the kitchen to shake the ashes from the cook-stove coals. She put on the teakettle, lighted a kerosene lamp, then sat at the kitchen table, her favorite book, *Imitation of Christ*, upon the white oilcloth cover of the pinewood table.

The teakettle set up a dragon's song. Mrs. Wheeler steeped the tea. She put some milk but no sugar in her cup. Then she returned her eyes and mind to the prose of Thomas à Kempis, whose life had been so secluded and uneventfully pious in the convent of St. Agnes.

THE CUP OF COFFEE

CHARLIE'S family moved to Idaho Springs, a mining and milling town on the south fork of Clear Creek. It was young Devlan's intention to take his wife to live with his people until he could find new employment and then make a home of his own in the mountains.

"No, my dear," said Dodie's mother. "This woolgatherer will strand you on some bare rock. I forbid it."

And so the young couple set themselves up in a room at the house of Mrs. Wheeler.

Dewey Emmett Wheeler arrived home in June of 1889. This rugged young man had shown a greater ability at fist fighting than at theological studies. The doctor of divinity in charge of the Kansas seminary was not an admirer of John L. Sullivan.

In September the woman's prospector husband, Norman Wheeler, returned from the hills. He was burdened with rusty mining tools but with little else. The blizzards and snowslides soon would lock up the mountain passes and ravines. The fifty-one-year-old optimist, once again in the city, would look for winter employment. Perhaps he might promote a grubstake in the spring, a thing he had managed to accomplish several times during the Leadville boom days, when H. A. W. ("Silver Dollar") Tabor had befriended him.

It now was a crowded house.

Norman Wheeler was friendly enough to his son-in-law, perhaps because the prospector was a minority man. Wheeler never was known to side with any majority, no matter from what righteous elements it stemmed. He never had been known to be on the winning side of anything, especially in matters of mining. Three times during his Colorado career he had staked out claims only to find them worthless; but his near neighbors had struck it rich. Twice this had happened right under his nose, and a third time he relinquished a patent on a partly explored mine property only to have a partner of H. A. W. Tabor extend the Wheeler shaft another six yards, and then begin to carry out silver by the ton.

Norman was to have a fourth "dose of the same" in 1891 when working on the north face of Battle Mountain, thirty miles out of Cripple Creek. On July 4 of that year, a middle-aged carpenter, Winfield Scott Stratton, prowling among the decomposed granite of the south side of the mountain, found ore that ran nineteen ounces of gold to the ton. That was the Independence Mine, named for the day of its discovery.

Instead of construing these happenings as reverses, Mr. Wheeler took an opposite view. He advocated the belief that what had happened to Stratton in gold, or to Tabor in silver, could befall anyone "with persistent vision."

On winter evenings or on Sundays, Norman Wheeler would sit in the basement among a great arsenal of picks, shovels, sledges, drills, and miners' candlesticks. There he would munch Bellflower apples, "seconds" obtained for thirty cents the barrel. He pared the specked apples with a huge jackknife as he mulled over a ledger which contained coffin-shaped diagrams of his claims. Then he would consult an array of musty papers drawn up by patent lawyers. Occasionally he would leave the cellar to go outside the house, look off at the mountains, stroke his spade-shaped beard, wave his hand and say, "Wealth for all."

He wore a "pancake hat" encrusted with ore dust. He kept it on his head when indoors, although his wife frequently urged him to remove it.

"Why don't you send that disgraceful hat to the smelter?" Mrs. Wheeler would say. "It probably contains more precious metal than you'll find elsewhere."

"It's not a man's hat that counts," he would reply. "It's what he's got under it."

"Precisely," she would snap.

He wore thick-welted miner's boots, which he kept in repair on a knee-last in the cellar. His array of shoemaker's tools was almost as vast as his collection of mining implements. His wife would wait until the amateur cobbler had a mouthful of shoemaker's tacks, then call down the cellar stairway to ask some tantalizing question.

Although Norman Wheeler lived in a world of tomorrow, and was obdurately optimistic, his past had several sore spots. One of the exasperating reminders concerned his ancestry.

When he chanced to remark that his people "went back beyond the Revolutionary War," his wife said, "Yes, so I understand; they were Hessians. Fought against the Americans."

This implication that Norman's "wrong-sidedness" was an hereditary trait caused him to protest: "My folks were Pennsylvania Dutch, and you know it."

"Indeed, yes," she said. "These so-called Dutch—Germans for the most part—were Hessians, hired by the English to fight us. Paid rascals."

"When you say 'us,' " the husband ventured, "do you mean the kind of Irishmen like your father, who didn't come here till 1834, and ran a saloon?"

Mrs. Wheeler, a foe of the demon rum and of what she regarded as a garbled statement, retorted: "My father, John Par-

rott, and my mother, Dora Parrott, were Irish, God be praised!
From County Cork, to be explicit. Although hemmed in by South
of Ireland papists, they remained God-fearing Wesleyans. They
went from Bandon, Ireland, to Bethel, New Brunswick, Canada,
in 1819. I admit that John Parrott had a tavern there—not a common saloon, mark you. And when he saw one of his little sons
tasting liquor from the glass of a guest at the tavern—not a saloon,
as your Hessian version would have it—my father closed a prosperous business. He then moved with his family to Ohio to become an honest farmer and an exhorter of Roscoe Circuit. John
Parrott preached the Word, and wrote religious poems. He was
not an Englishman, God be praised! And he was not a Hessian!
He had fifteen children, thirteen of whom survived to be edu-
cated at their father's knee. Did your father educate anybody?"

When assailed in this fashion, Mr. Wheeler would retreat to
the cellar, there to examine his rusty tools, eat Bellflower culls,
and study the coffin-shaped diagrams in his ledger. When springtime came, he would gather together his paraphernalia and set
out once again to seek the long-promised wealth in the hills. He
had made ten such pilgrimages, and now was fifty-one years
old, and graying like the hat he wore.

When he crossed the plains in 1858 from Ohio, his objective
had been California; but he had been unable to proceed beyond
Fort Riley, Kansas. The thing that happened to him near that
place was a matter dangerous to mention. Dangerous, that is, for
anyone other than his wife to bring into a conversation.

He had wandered off from the wagon train to attend to a
personal matter. He became lost, and received an arrowhead
wound in the buttock. When he arrived at Fort Riley three days
afterward, he was grievously athirst. The wound had magnified
his hardship.

Mrs. Wheeler maintained that her husband (he was then not
even her fiancé) had been wounded ignobly while fleeing from
Indians. He was hard put to explain among persons of Victorian
speech just *what* he had been doing when wounded. He·would

say: "Well, if I had those old pants here, I could prove there was no hole made in them by an arrow."

While at Fort Riley he became friendly with H. A. W. Tabor, then a farmer and Free Soil advocate. Tabor advised his friend to open a general store, which Wheeler did near a Potawatami Indian reservation not far from Holton, Kansas. He also engaged in cattle- and hog-raising on a minor scale. He slaughtered his animals to sell their meat at his own market place.

Norman and Elizabeth were married in 1863, soon after another man, her first love, had been taken to a madhouse. "Poor Ed Redding," she would say mysteriously, when thinking of that unfortunate man. "The victim of great jealousy."

Norman Wheeler did not like Ed Redding, sane or otherwise. He did not like various other persons, including Indians, any Indians, and never would like them. Possibly his wound had something to do with this prejudice. He learned several tribal dialects, however, for business reasons.

His wife not only liked Indians but spoke in their behalf whenever possible. "Aside from their one vice, the use of tobacco," she would say, "they are an example of dignity and honor. Their women are chaste, and their men keep their word. Can the white treaty-breakers say as much?"

During his Kansas days Wheeler offended the Potawatami Indians, an entire reservation of them. The squaws frequented his small store, so he said, "to steal him blind." The shoplifters would crouch over the cracker barrels, the apple barrels, the potato bins, to shield their crimes with their blankets. "They even got away with cured hams and sides of bacon."

Wheeler brooded about these raids. He complained to the government agency. The officials could do nothing about it, "even if they had cared." Wheeler remonstrated with the tribal leaders, Chief No-Nose and Chief Cut-Flesh. But whenever the pioneer merchant touched upon matters of theft, the sachems pretended that he was speaking to them in the idiom of the ancient Greeks.

Wheeler's was a long-suffering nature, but his temper sometimes played sudden tricks upon him. Then he would become ill with rage. He would stutter and turn pale. During these seizures, he would cry out: "You are a varmint! You are a varmint!" He pronounced the word "are" as if it were spelled "air."

One day he surprised a squaw in the actual performance of a theft. She was making a wigwam of her blanket over a potato bin, while some braves of her tribe looked on stoically. Wheeler asked her in his best and loudest Potawatami to desist. The squaw merely grunted and stayed over the potatoes as if to hatch them.

To his war cry of "You air a varmint!" he added, "Then maybe you'll understand *this!*" He kicked the squaw in the seat of her blanket.

Potatoes and squaw rolled upon the floor. Her fellow-tribesmen began to raise the devil. Other squaws, some with papooses strapped on their backs, commenced to confiscate tobacco and scoops of brown sugar. Wheeler used his fists and boots on all concerned.

That night there was a conference among the townspeople of Holton. It was thought best that Mr. Wheeler take himself and his belongings out of the bleeding state of Kansas. Besides, he now was saddled with a name given him by the Potawatamis, "Man Who Kicks Squaw." He didn't like that.

He wrote to his old friend Tabor, now a backer of prospectors in Colorado mining camps. Tabor wrote in reply that he would grubstake Wheeler if he wanted to come to Colorado to look for silver. Tabor's letter also said that a good market for Wheeler's livestock awaited him in Denver.

In the fall of 1876, Wheeler set out on horseback, driving his sixteen head of steers over the Old Smokey Hills trail. Outside the town of Limon, across the Colorado boundary, he encountered a blizzard and lay for two days and nights in a hollowed out place in the drifts. His cattle perished in the storm, as did his horse.

Far from dismayed by this experience, he wrote to his wife in Kansas, urging her to bring her small son and baby daughter to

Colorado. He had seen Mr. Tabor, he said, and had studied the mountains. Here in these hills there was "wealth for all."

Soon after Wheeler came home from the mountains in the autumn of 1889, he asked his daughter, "Is this fellow you're married to treating you right?"

"Yes," she replied.

"That's all I wanted to know," her father remarked.

He began to search the premises for something that belonged to him. "My leg aches like a tooth," he said. "And I've lost my box of salve. Or somebody's taken it."

The miner frequently bruised himself while working in the hills. He treated all contusions and lacerations with applications of an unguent he made of rendered mutton tallow and shreds of dynamite. His wife feared dynamite. She believed the ointment a hazard, and frequently got rid of it in Mullen's Mill Ditch.

In contrast to Wheeler's enduring optimism concerning "wealth for all," he was equally pessimistic as to matters of health. Other than attacks of pleurisy, an ailment common to the hard-rock miners who frequented the dark, cold, damp holes in the earth, Wheeler was as fit as a bear. True, he sustained cracked bones, bruised legs and arms, and his fingernails were a consistent blue-green from blows when the sledge hammer missed the drill heads; but he was lank, strong, and seasoned.

Still he was forever taking medicines. He would build a small heap of quinine upon a knife blade and swallow the dose with never a wince; and he had frequently been salivated by calomel.

Among the patent-medicine folders in his knapsack was the valuable booklet written by Frederick Humphreys, M.D., patriarch of homeopathic practitioners. The old prospector grew fond of Dr. Humphrey's moist, sweet pills that came in small tube-shaped vials. These pills were numbered instead of named. His favorite was "Humphreys No. 77." What No. 77 cured, I do not know. The prospector also frequented the offices of doctors who advertised their marvels. At the time he first met Devlan, he was trying out the nostrums of a Chinese practitioner known as Gun Wa, who had an office on Larimer Street, once Denver's main business avenue. Gun Wa made a tonic which Wheeler esteemed, a bilious-hued slime said to taste like the gall-bladder fluids of a jackass.

Mrs. Wheeler sat in her rocking chair one night after the supper dishes had been done. She was reading the newspaper. Her husband had coaled the base-burner and was sipping Gun Wa tonic. Mrs. Wheeler's daughter, crocheting a mitten, sat beside her mother's chair. Charlie Devlan, the son-in-law, sat apart, whittling out a small figure from a block of kindling wood.

"Don't get shavings on the carpet, Charlie," said Mrs. Wheeler. Then she turned to her daughter. "The newspaper has something very interesting to say about the well-known and well-liked former jurist, Judge Domer." She creased the newspaper pages, then went on: "Judge Domer has disappeared in thin air. He may be dead." Mrs. Wheeler paused. "The judge's wife says her husband has been a *patient of Gun Wa*. Seems the medicine put him in a kind of trance. She blames *all* their troubles on Gun Wa."

Mrs. Wheeler put down the newspaper with a "There! There you have an example of man's folly and stupidity."

Mr. Wheeler rose, stuttering. He beckoned to Devlan who followed after him. They went to the cellar. Mr. Wheeler lighted a miner's candle, and stuck the sconce spike into the earthen side wall. "Charlie," he said, "I'm a relative, a distant one to be sure, of General Little Joe Wheeler, but I want to say this to you: there's really but one general in our family." The creaking of Mrs. Wheeler's rocking chair could be heard in a masterful rhythm overhead.

One day early in November Mrs. Wheeler said to Dodie, "So that's the way it is, eh? You are going to bring the child of a blunderer into the world?"

From this time until January of 1890, the girl wept a great deal. It was not her nature to weep, that is, to weep for long at a time, but now she was to know a melancholy season. One morning in January Devlan sat alone in the kitchen. If only he had the means, he would insist upon taking his wife, as was his right, to a home of their own. He had proposed that they go live in a small room, notwithstanding their circumstances. But Dodie had pointed out that the coming of the baby would add to their difficulties, and said she thought her mother would feel more kindly disposed when the child arrived. But matters had steadily worsened.

Devlan, sitting today in the kitchen, was troubled by what he believed to be his wife's divided loyalty. It now was time for a test of wills. If Devlan did not win against his mother-in-law in some small measure, no matter what the nature of the test, he felt that he would be lost, and that his love would be lost.

Dodie was in her room. Her mother was with her. In fact, the mother's coming to the room had caused Charles to go to the kitchen. He now sat there, waiting for the coffee to boil, and waiting for the test that he felt must come today, now.

He heard Mrs. Wheeler's footsteps as she left her daughter's room. She came into the kitchen. There were no words for a time. She was humming as she prepared some gruel for her daughter.

Now, Charlie thought, I'll do it. I must do it. I must win over her.

"I want a cup of coffee," he said boldly.

She turned, amazed at his tone, then replied, "Say 'please,' and I'll pour it."

He stared at her defiantly. "I said I wanted a cup of coffee."

She placed her hands on her hips. "Please," she repeated. "Say 'please.'"

"I want a cup of coffee."

"Please."

"A cup of coffee."

"Please."

Neither of the antagonists gave ground. Finally, the young man rose from the table to go to the room where his wife lay in bed. He kissed her. Then he put on his overcoat.

"What is it, Charlie?" she asked. "What's wrong?"

He put on his hat; then he kissed his wife again. "Good luck," he said.

"Charlie!" she exclaimed. "You're not going away?"

He was at the door. Dodie rose from the bed and was putting on her slippers. "I'm no good," he said.

He left the house.

"What have you done, Mother? Charlie's gone."

Mrs. Wheeler put her arms about Dodie, and said, "Good riddance."

5

THREE NAMES IN SEARCH OF A CHILD

IT WAS a tumultuous March 8, 1890, the day I was born, a day and night of wind and snow. The woman, who until now had denounced every aspect of becoming a grandmother, found an extreme and possessive interest in her daughter's newborn child. And when George Pell rang the doorbell to inquire concerning Dodie's health, Mrs. Wheeler said to him, "You may inform your friend that it's a boy; but you may also tell him that it's mine and not his. Is that clear?"

The abating blizzard left white ramparts on the plateau where the city was and in the valleys below timberline of the Continental Divide. And a wreath of snow lay like a memento upon the roof of an old cabin where Charles Devlan now was staying.

It had been his intention to repair this abandoned cabin on Squaw Mountain at once, but time and the winter opposed him. The lone young man had done what seemed his best against the tantara of growing wind and weather. He stuffed newspapers in the chinks where the storms were likely to trespass. He hinged the fire door of the decrepit campstove with baling wire. The small windowpane long ago had been beaten out by hail, so Devlan boarded up the opening in the log wall. When blue skies

35

came again, he would put up a cabin fashioned of logs already
cut but not to be laid until June, a procedure to forestall shrinkage of the wood.

Devlan had found this place during a break in the weather on
a day when he had gone horseback riding eight miles south of
his father's house at Idaho Springs. At a steep dip of the high
trail he had come upon a wilderness of Douglas fir—the "Christmas tree"—slender Engleman spruce, blue spruce with cones three
inches long, towering yellow pine, jack pine, balsam, quaking
aspens, birch, and willows.

Although it now was the season of hibernation, he saw this
locality as the home of abundant wild life: elk, deer, chipmunks,
and Frémont squirrels; bears, weasels, and mountain lions; quail,
grouse, eagles, and harsh-voiced jays; colonies of beaver in the
valleys, and trout in the streams. The spring would unlock this
pale and frozen silence with the resonance of wild bees and the
tumbling songs of liberated streams.

Here the venerable John Evans, second territorial governor
of Colorado, owned a mountain ranch. Beyond that property the
government held a timbered domain. Devlan applied for a homestead site of one hundred and sixty acres of this precipitous public
land.

The young man planned to build his cabin eight hundred and
eighty feet up the south slope of Squaw Mountain. He observed
that falling snows drove across Bear Creek basin to pile up
against a mountain called The Judge. He would make a clearing,
a terrace shielded from the blasts by Old Silver Tooth to the
north of Squaw.

Here a man might enter into a separate world in a cirque hollowed out by mighty movements of ancient glacial ice. The
main bastions of the surrounding wall were Meridian, the Blacks;
the Bishop's Razor, a jagged peak named for the Reverend Frank
Spaulding; Haystack, Old Silver Tooth, The Judge, and Epaulet,
called Sugar Loaf by the natives; and the ever-white Mt. Evans.

Charlie dreamed of establishing here a shelter against his loneliness, a sanctuary for his memories. He would attack the wilderness about him, fell trees and haul the timber to the mines and mills of Clear Creek County. That would be the means of his subsistence. He would do his logging over an early trail where one still might come upon arrowheads of chipped flint and rusty ox-shoes that looked like large iron commas. These shoes had been hand-forged by stragglers of the Mormon migration in the forties.

The now unused trail traversed a ridge ten thousand feet above sea level. Its reclamation would impose hard labor upon Devlan if he were to make it negotiable for a four-horse team and wagon.

He would throw a dam for a sawmill across a narrow gorge, where a garrulous little creek washed the boulders with melted snow. That, too, would mean toil, years of hardy perseverance. He would use as a model the beaver dam that lay on the basin floor eight hundred feet below his homestead.

The young hermit would hunt game and gather wild berries and chokecherries. Eventually he would plant a high garden, with patches of potatoes, onions, and rhubarb. He would purchase a cow and horses on credit. He would build a forge, and the song of his own anvil would announce to him, if to no one else, that he was not a dreaming zero.

And for thirty years to come, he constantly would see Mt. Evans close by. That peak stands 14,260 feet above sea level. At the time of Devlan's arrival there, it was known as Mt. Rosalie, named for the wife of artist Albert Bierstadt, the first man to paint a picture of it. The mountain would be renamed in 1895 for Dr. John Evans, a friend of Abraham Lincoln. Dr. Evans was eighty-one years old when honored by having the peak designated, in a manner of speaking, as his own.

Dr. Evans already had enjoyed many other distinctions. A physician of eminence, he had specialized in mental and nervous diseases before coming to Colorado Territory in Civil War times. The first building of a hospital for the insane in Indiana, at a time when demented persons were kept haphazardly in jails, had been his work. He had served as an outstanding member of the faculty of Rush College in Chicago, and was organizer of its chair of obstetrics. Dr. Evans had attained a reputation as editor of the *Northwestern Medical and Surgical Journal* from 1847 to 1852. This humanitarian also had helped to found what is now known as Mercy Hospital in Chicago. He had studied cholera, and was one of the first men to suggest that the disease was communicable and followed lines of transportation. He recommended quarantine regulations for ports of entry. Upon his retirement from medical practice in 1860, he became a co-founder of Northwestern University, and the college town of Evanston was named for him.

Dr. Evans succeeded in office William Gilpin, the first territorial governor of Colorado. Gilpin had been removed by Mr. Lincoln because of an administrative *faux pas*. During Gilpin's tenure of office, the Confederate flag had been raised one day over a building in Larimer Street. On his own responsibility, Gilpin issued drafts upon the United States Treasury to supply a regiment of volunteers to put down the rebellion. These drafts were not honored at Washington. Mr. Lincoln then asked Dr. Evans to "take charge of Colorado."

Dr. Evans brought extensive personal means with him on the stagecoach journey of thirteen days from Chicago across the upper valley of the Platte and to the mountains and plains of Colorado. He began his duties as a War Governor on May 18, 1862. Then he was forced to resign in 1865 under political fire, as an aftermath of the Sand Creek massacre.

That attack by volunteer cavalrymen upon an encampment of Plains Indians brought about a controversy that still is debated fiercely by old men of Colorado. There had been numerous raids upon the settlers by the Sioux Indians under Chief Little Crow, the Arapahoes under Chief Left Hand, and the Cheyennes led by Black Kettle. With the North and the South engaged in civil war, Washington paid scant attention and lent small military assistance to guard against scalpings and depredations among remote pioneers.

The Utes of the mountain reservation had been persuaded by their statesmanlike leader, Chief Ouray, to stay at peace; but the Plains Indians thought it an advantageous time to put on their battle paint and the bonnets of war. Governor Evans was apprised by friendly tribesmen concerning a secret medicine dance and plans for an assault upon the settlements during August of 1864.

The governor sent representatives to the chiefs for a parley. Left Hand and Black Kettle promised to enter into a treaty. A camp was established for the peace-promising warriors, their squaws and papooses, on Sand Creek northeast of Denver. About seven hundred Indians raised their lodge poles in this mutually designated zone. They displayed both the national banner and a flag of truce over the tepee of Black Kettle.

Governor Evans instructed the Indian Agent to allow no further sale of hunting weapons or ammunition to the tribesmen. He then left Colorado to call in person upon Mr. Lincoln in Washington, to ask the President to send troops to Colorado for the welfare of the territory.

According to the Evans biographer, Edward McMechen, the President greeted Governor Evans as "Commander in Chief of the Army and Navy of Colorado," listened to his complaints, then said: "Well, Governor, you go back to Colorado and handle things as your best judgment dictates during this terrible war, and I will try to handle the situation here."

After the kidnaping of four white women by marauding bands of Indians, Colonel John M. Chivington, commander of the Third Cavalry of volunteers, conferred in September of 1864 with Chieftains White Antelope, Black Kettle, Bull Bear, Heap of Buffalo, and Niva. Relatives of Left Hand also were among the negotiators. The chiefs disowned any connection with the kidnapings, and said they desired peace. They became morosely puzzled, however, because War Department regulations prevented their having personal, firsthand dealings with Governor Evans. The red men could not understand red tape.

It was a time of danger and apprehension. Not only did the parley fail to reassure the frontiersmen, but a swarm of grasshoppers now descended upon their crops. Hunger threatened the communities. The settlers believed that the Sand Creek camp was being misused as a headquarters for kidnapers of white women and raiders of horses and cattle.

During this time of discord and privation, Governor Evans remained on business in Washington. In the executive's absence, Colonel Chivington ordered out the troops of his cavalry command. The mounted soldiers rode out from Denver and Cherry Creek, then crossed the divide between that stream and the Arkansas River, and finally advanced in darkness on the Indian encampment north of Fort Lyon on the Big Sandy.

In civil life Colonel Chivington was a Methodist minister, a tall person with a manner more militant than sacerdotal. He had been appointed to the post of chaplain by Governor Gilpin. Before taking his military oath he had stipulated: "Governor, I will accept a commission from you, but it must be a fighting commission."

Chivington's men surrounded the Indian camp on the night of November 23. They stampeded the ponies of the Indians, then commenced firing at sunrise. Black Kettle and White Antelope, it is said, ran from their tepees, and raised empty hands in capitulation. This gesture was disregarded. According to historians LeRoy and Ann Hafen, White Antelope and about five hundred other braves, squaws, and their children fell beneath the volleys of the cavalrymen. Black Kettle and a remnant of the red colony escaped. There were no casualties among the attacking troops.

Evans's political foes now assailed him for Colonel Chivington's action. A Congressional investigation subsequently fixed the responsibility upon Evans. Then, after Dr. Evans's great friend President Lincoln had been assassinated, Andrew Johnson refused to exonerate the governor. Dr. Evans resigned on August 1, 1865.

The doctor had a beard and a head of hair like the poet Long-fellow's. He was now fifty-five years old as he returned to a life of diversified private enterprise. Dr. Evans became the principal founder of the University of Denver, and had interests in banks, utilities, railroads, and other matters of territorial development.

In 1868 Evans and his family drove in spring wagons for a camping holiday among the mountains. They followed Mt. Ver-non Canyon to a place known as Bergen's Ranch, then drove southwest toward Bear Creek. Dr. Evans rode on alone on horse-back for a distance of four miles to Vance's Park. He decided to purchase three hundred and twenty acres of this picturesque highland.

At the time when Charles Devlan staked out a homestead site northeast of the Evans ranch, the holdings of the venerable gov-ernor had grown to about six thousand acres.

Governor Evans and the old peak named for him both exer-cised a mighty influence upon the life of my father and upon the lives of so many of us who lived in the western world. The white peak became a symbol to all. In its presence, one felt less poor in spirit and more alive to the majesty of time. In my father's eyes, the mountain became a high altar, a place of startling visions during his long solitude. Against the massive slope of the white peak, he twice saw the figure of my mother, her wedding dress fairer than the snow. Both times he became convinced that some important event concerning her was im-pending, and so it proved.

My father eventually confided in me concerning these mani-festations. He did so years after he had left his hermitage among the shining hills, the high lakes at the heads of the glacial valleys, the beaver dams, the mountain meadows, the wilderness of pines. He revealed many things to me when he became certain that I would not ridicule him because of his flight from human relation-ships, or scoff at his mystic excursions.

He had seen the vision for the first time, he said, the evening before Dodie was remarried in 1894. He at once left the mountains, to go down to the city to stay at Pell's house. He was careful to avoid being seen. He now had grown a beard to safeguard his identity.

My father was sleepless and agonized of spirit, he said, and not quite stable in his mind. He remarked that he might have done something desperately alien to his quiet nature, had he not seen a child playing in the front yard of Mrs. Wheeler's house.

It suddenly occurred to Devlan that the child was his own son. The man stood for a while watching the boy playing with a rag doll. Then the tumults and fires of jealousy died, leaving only a dry sorrow inside Devlan's breast. He walked away from the child and away from the house. He started out toward the church where he first had heard the girl's voice. This was her wedding morning. She would not be married in the church this time, but at a house that was to be her own. Devlan had not been able to give her a house. Her new husband could.

At the church he stood outside the memorial window where, almost five years since, he had heard the young singer. The voice that had aroused in him the impulse to meet the girl was not heard today. Not heard, that is, except in his heart. Devlan went back to the mountains.

To me, in 1894, my father seemed only a name, a name seldom mentioned by anyone in the family. I had not known, of course, that he had been standing across the street from me that November day. My grandmother spoke gravely of this occurrence, but I understood little of its significance or of its emotional elements. She said that Charlie Devlan had intended to kidnap me.

Granny did not permit me to go out of her sight during the next several weeks. But she helped me build a snowman, and I thought her very clever, indeed, and more than a match for stealers of children or for any other hazards, including the devil's own machinations.

I did not bear my father's surname, except in one notation, my grandmother's, upon a gilt-bordered page of her huge Bible. Granny soon afterward assigned to me her own family name, that of Wheeler. I bore this label without question for some time. Besides, my mother now had resumed her maiden name of Wheeler.

My first confusions regarding surnames touched me when my mother quite suddenly became Mrs. Fowler. Now I felt that she was slighting me. True, this airy, carefree girl never had seemed a mother to me, quite. She had resigned most of her maternal duties and left the problem of my discipline and guidance to Grandmother. In fact, Granny had usurped those functions.

I called my mother "Dodie." I never became courageous enough to call her "Mother," although I wanted to do so. I spent much time worrying about this. And now a stranger appeared as if from nowhere with the title of "Stepfather." Mysteriously enough, and unjustly I thought, he changed my mother's name to his, but left *my* name out in the cold.

Frank Dennis Fowler was a gay-spirited, adventuresome fellow, a year younger than Dodie. That would mean he was twenty-two years old in 1894. There was nothing paternal about him. He flitted in and out of our everyday lives like a character from *A Midsummer Night's Dream.* How and where he first met my mother I never knew. He had a way of meeting anyone he wished to know and of winning that person's confidence. It took him a longer time than was usual to win mine.

Notwithstanding my brattish attitude toward Frank Fowler, my infantile intolerance of him, my selfish resentment of my mother's defection, her new husband possessed certain talents that seemed even to a prejudiced stepchild to be the attributes of a dashing hero. He was an excellent ballplayer; he was lively on the banjo; he bicycled. At times he exercised sudden generosities, and made gifts to everyone of our circle, and with no apparent motive. He was meticulous, and his way with the ladies was something to be envied.

My elders said that Frank Fowler had a head for business, although given to quixotic risks. His fortunes never remained static, nor did he. Everyone called him Frank, and that is what I myself called him, and without reproval.

I believe that my mother, long tied to the apron strings of pioneer discipline, chose this second marriage as a means of escape into a less circumspect world than that of her mother's house. No matter how rough the West seemed, the homes largely were places of decorum and rectitude. Once across a threshold, one entered into a little scene of Victorian manners. Irish or not, the indoor air of my grandmother's home remained Victorian, although the outdoor air stayed wild western. Granny detested the English, but she conformed to the rules of conduct exemplified by their great queen.

After a single night of residence with Mr. and Mrs. Fowler in their new home at the rear of St. Joseph's Roman Catholic Church, I learned that I could not dramatize myself there as effectively as I had done elsewhere. So I decided to go back to live with Grandmother Wheeler. Granny welcomed this decision. Frank Fowler did not oppose the arrangement. Had I stayed on with my mother, I might have become a considerable burden to her girlhood.

The panic of 1893 had left us in straits more hampering than before, as it had left almost everyone else in the Silver State. The lucklessness of Norman Wheeler, of course, had been persistent. He recently had discovered an especially rich showing of silver near Creede on the headwaters of the Rio Grande.

That was the town described by poet Cy Warman as the place where "It's day all day in the daytime, and there is no night in Creede." It also had been the headquarters of Grandfather's friend, the desperado and confidence man, "Soapy" Smith. Grandfather said that Smith had studied for the priesthood, and that his mother never knew of her son's violent record. In a day when telegrams were indeed expensive, Soapy would send a message to his mother each night after "swindling the tenderfeet." Then he would go to one of the many saloons to announce: "I'm a Georgia gentleman. Does anyone care to dispute it?" and then drink up and gamble away his day's treasury. If memory does not mislead me, my grandfather said that Soapy either killed

Bob Ford, the slayer of Jesse James, or "ran him out of Creede."

Vastly elated by his newest prospects, my grandfather returned from Creede to Denver early in 1893 to promote capital to work his claim, and to say, "I always told you so." That was in April. Then business tightened, and in July the fall of silver was heard all over the world.

My grandmother once described Grandfather's "blow" of 1893 as follows: "After spading up two-thirds of the State of Colorado, your grandfather found 'wealth for all' at exactly the wrong time."

Twenty thousand silver miners were thrown out of employment in 1893. There were soup kitchens in Denver. But Grandfather still had faith in the hills. I heard him say just that to "Silver Dollar" Tabor in later years, and I saw the deposed silver king nod gravely. Tabor had become a prideful though pathetic figure on the streets of our city, or in the Federal Building where he was given the consolation prize of the office of postmaster. Contrary to the Tabor legend, the senator was by no means the blustering dolt of motion-picture and other portrayals of his career of heartbreak. He was a quiet man and a person of sober dignity.

A daughter was born to my mother in 1896. The girl was named after the herald of "wealth for all," and called Normadine. The excitement of having a small sister was rubbed out when I learned that her last name automatically was Fowler. How could this be so? I had a sister, a matter of much satisfaction to me although she lived in a house other than mine, but I couldn't have the same surname as hers. Now I *really* sulked.

I was entered as "Eugene Wheeler" in the first grade at the old Fairmount School. During the first roll call, I behaved like a sullen stowaway, and would not answer to my name when it was called out twice by the teacher.

I arrived home from school that afternoon to find my mother and stepfather calling upon Granny. Uncle Dewey Emmett and his lovely new bride, Aunt Etta, also were present. I was questioned as to my first day's experiences at school. Had I learned anything? If so, what? I put the family in a dither by announcing that I had seen with my own eyes something of the greatest mystical import painted in white at the top border of the blackboard. I wanted my relatives to tell me what the thing meant. This is what I had seen:

I tried to describe these hieroglyphics to my kinsmen, but with no success. I endeavored to reproduce the signs on a piece of paper. No one present could solve the riddle.

"It looks like the handwriting on the wall at the banquet of Belshazzar," my grandmother said. "'*Mene, Mene, Tekel, Upharsin.*'"

I suspected my people of keeping a great secret from me, one that probably had something to do with the end of the world. I insisted upon knowing the meaning of the signs. Some weeks after this, Mrs. Snyder, mother of an arithmetical genius, explained the true meaning of plus, minus, and the rest. But by then I had come to detest arithmetic, permanently. And I have done without the benefits of the numerical science for fifty-six years.

My mentors could do little to improve my arithmetic, but something *had* to be done about my name. I would not let the matter drop. Granny tried to reach a compromise by offering me the name of her own parents, Parrott. She even suggested that I take the name Bateman, her mother's maiden name. She said—on what authority I never knew—that a knight named Sir Giles Bateman had been a favorite of William the Conqueror.

I would not accept these substitutes. So Frank Fowler, somewhat dubious about the procedure, finally agreed to adopt me. Now I had won the surname, my third one, Fowler. It eventually became a worrisome victory.

This damnable mixup of names has dogged me all my life. It

has caused a twitching of strangers' eyebrows and brought the kind of glances that accompany sly thoughts, or even hopes, of the other fellow's bastardy. Passport problems, birth and voting certificates, legal papers, insurance forms, biographical data. . . . Is it any wonder that I became so prejudiced against names in general that I can remember few names in particular with any feeling of certainty or ease? And when some old acquaintance suddenly appears with the challenge: "I bet you don't remember me!" I begin a miserable game of patty cake with my memory, and want to kick myself in the groin.

It may be that my blind spot in regard to names was merely a manifestation of the costly vagueness that always has plagued me in the practical world. It is my habit to dive heart-first, and head-last, into anything of my fancy. Pocketful of posies . . . all fall down. . . .

Grandfather once remarked that I reminded him of "Hazy Austin." I did not know then, nor do I now, if the old prospector drew the analogy from life, from folklore, or from literature.

"Son, you air like Hazy Austin," he said. "Hazy got drunk from a jug while driving his hosses and buckboard out of Telluride one night. He fell asleep in the wagon. When he woke up in the morning, his hosses had been cut loose and wandered off. He looked around, then said: 'If I'm Hazy Austin, I've lost two hosses. If I'm *not* Hazy Austin, I've found a wagon.'"

ONE OF A MILLION

HOW many men of my own present age remain alive? Male Americans who in 1890 were twelve months old or less?

Life insurance actuaries say that 1,566,000 such boys were in the United States that year. Since then 560,000 of our original company have left us; almost twenty thousand stayed but a single winter. For toward the close of the last century various infantile diseases, since arrested, brought bows of white crepe to the doorways everywhere in our land.

Our million male survivors of this class of 1890 saw the twilight of the pioneers. Each of us in his own fashion was an eyewitness to the death of one century and the birth of the next. By means of our collective testimony we can show what manner of men and women lived in our several regions and in our time.

We have had no work that can be looked upon as a faithful history of America. We are too near the events, the prejudices, the political adulterations born of the surge for possession and power, to expect an early interpretation of the national morning. The trustworthy historian, when he comes, will explore the archives with sublime comprehension. At the civil distance of perhaps four or five centuries, he can remove the rust from once-dangerous truths.

Our great relator will undertake an analysis of the chronologies, the dates and arenas of battles, the lists of inventions. He will comment upon the boomerangs of science and philosophy. He will evaluate the tragic effects of such antique and mischievous phenomena as the use and misuse of that which we now know as money. But if he were to resolve only this kind of data, he would become a mere almanac-maker; he would·display to our descendants the dull and labored anatomy of our epoch—never the spirit of a time that was. He will, however, avail himself of the tales and ballads, and thereby create an epic to implement man's faith in himself and in his native land. The early contributors to *Americana*, it then will be seen, wrote not only with validity but with clairvoyance.

Notwithstanding their mighty faults, their hot prejudices, their great quarrels, the frontiersmen everywhere in our land created a legacy of faith, courage, love, and resourcefulness that even now gives America her potency and style.

The American million and I came into the world the year when Frémont the explorer died, and with him a robust era of the West. During our first season Phineas T. Barnum folded his circus tent; James Russell Lowell and Herman Melville forever laid aside their quills, and General Sherman his sword. Walt Whitman and James Greenleaf Whittier left us when we were but two years old; Edwin Booth when we had reached three. Oliver Wendell Holmes died when we were but four years old; Eugene Field when we were five; Harriet Beecher Stowe and Bill Nye when we were six. We had come to the age of seven when Charles A. Dana and Henry George died. Horatio Alger, Evangelist Dwight Moody, and the agnostic Robert Ingersoll passed when we were nine. Across the sea in our youthful time, there lived Johannes Brahms, Pëtr Ilich Tchaikovsky, Lewis Carroll, Queen Victoria, Gladstone, Lord Tennyson. . . .

Great names. But, as I sit during a borrowed hour, I think

mostly of the little people and the little events of that transitional time when the telephone, the electric lamp, and the horseless carriage were new. And the sixteenth-century prophecies of "Mother" Shipton were being studied with excited dread. The airplane, the radio, the motion picture were nonexistent; and, unknown to us, the machine was being arranged both for and against man's felicity.

The little things of the western scene! Grandfather's name tattooed on his lean forearm; the letters etched in blue ink during his time of service with the Kansas militia, when Quantrill was leading the guerrilla raids on the prairie towns. . . . The last of the high, solid-tire bicycles. The wheel club, of which Frank Fowler was a member and its official photographer as well. Women who dared appear in divided skirts as they cycled along the paths. . . .

The Woodmen of the World. Grandfather belonged to Silver State Camp of that lodge. His life was insured in it for one thousand dollars. He made small monthly payments that seemed large to us and ever due. If he were to die untimely, Grandmother assured me in whispers, one of her first acts after the funeral would be to buy me a pony. The old gentleman must have wondered why I inquired so often and so assiduously as to his health as I watched him swallowing his vast assortment of pills or gulping the noxious brews of Gun Wa.

A dark curse in those days attended the child of divorced parents. It is difficult to believe now, in a time when husbands and wives so frequently look upon one another merely as week-end guests, that divorce half a century ago was a disgrace.

I remember the time when I fell in love with Helga, a pigtailed charmer in the first grade of school. Then as afterward I was not a gifted swain, or graced with the art of romantic diplomacy. I suffered over this first passion for perhaps a week before leaving a note on my beloved's desk: "Will you be my girl?"

I could have withstood the anger of an affronted lass, but what Helga gave me was her scorn. When, after long days of agony, I

managed to persuade this young beauty to speak to me, and asked
why she had been offended, she replied with simple finality: "Your
parents are divorced."

Ever since that time I have long hesitated before writing letters
of any sort to the fair. A fevered terror makes my hand tremble
even when holding the pen over such a little thing as a "Thank
you" note. Of course there have been exceptions. . . . *Flow
gently, Sweet Afton.* . . .

Other memories form a montage of vivid musings: The rabid
pug dog, concerning which I wrote in my book about John
Barrymore. . . . Mad Nancy, the witless woman who walked the
streets with a cake of ice on her head. . . . The postman who had
sore gums. . . .

This letter carrier would curse like a wounded troll when the
boys ambushed him to jerk the string attached to a whistle held
between his loose teeth. He was always saying that he would one
day purchase a full set of false teeth for five dollars at Dr. C. B.
Stone's on Curtis Street.

How clever that postman was, Grandfather said. The postoffice
inspectors could not hoodwink *him*. Rightly or not, he had been
suspected of failing to deliver letters that contained money. The
authorities mailed an envelope partly opened; a ten-dollar bill
could be seen inside it. Grandfather's wary friend knew this for
what it was, a decoy.

He delivered the letter, then reported to Mr. Wheeler: "Oh,
it's only somebody out to make a reputation with a whoop-
hurrah."

The G.A.R. conventions and parades of the thousands of veterans whose many great meetings now have become one small
bivouac of centenarians. . . . Train robberies. Masquerade parties.
Confidence men. Grandmother's successive boarders, among them
Bostwick, the tuberculous glass blower, and Joe Shane, who plainly
had an unrequited love for Dodie. Shane announced to me that
the waters of Mullen's Mill Ditch eventually found the great sea.
. . . Toys: the jumping jack, the tin monkey that climbed a string;

crockery marbles, and tops whittled from spools. Homemade wagons, boxing gloves and baseballs fashioned and then demonstrated by Uncle Dewey. . . . Candy pulls and sachet bags and dainty fans. . . .

The sour smells near the saloon door, and the remarkable broad jumps for safety's sake by loafers ejected by the bartender, who once had been Jake Kilrain's sparring partner. . . . The band music at City Park, the snortings and tootlings and drummings rising then falling with the shifting of the wind. And the blows of sooty Blacksmith Bergen's sledge on the anvil of his smithy, as if he too were a member of the park band. . . . The convent of the Home of the Good Shepherd, with the high wall of common red brick surrounding it. . . . The back fence of our own yard, a weathered barrier above which there appeared one day the first terrifying face clearly remembered by me, that of Sis Bilby, her eyes a leering malevolence, and her hair an evil mist. Concerning her, Grandmother said, "The Devil has a sister."

The horse troughs with their mossy-green insides. The smooth and delicate drinking manners of the horses. . . . The arc lights, as large as fish globes, strung from iron arms outthrust from telegraph poles at intersections of the unpaved streets.

The lamp-tender drove a stunted horse and a cart in which he stood on the low tailboard, as if in a chariot. He wore a knapsack of carbons and carried a portable platform, a small podium upon which he set his feet so as to guard himself against shocks while working. He also was equipped with a stick with a hook at one end of it and a stout line at the other. By means of this device he could reach up to release a ring attached to the lanyard of the lamp itself, then lower the globe for the changing of carbons and the polishing or replacement of the glass shield. The ring was anchored high up on the pole and out of reach of young rowdies. But they often shattered a globe with a bombardment of stones.

The stumps of discarded carbon sticks, sheathed with copper, made excellent crayons for sidewalk or fence scribblings. These juvenile news bulletins caused passers-by to look the other way.

The arc light came on at night with a brave spluttering. Then, after it had settled down to the business of illumination, a mighty swarm of flies, moths, and even birds began to swirl about the globe, as if mistaking the zone of brilliance for the aura of a god. . . .

The White sewing machine upon which Granny made many of our garments. My chore was to keep the machine free of dust. The old lady could see a speck of dust at ten paces. As a reward for a good job, I was permitted any one of three privileges: to play locomotive engineer while treadling the machine after the needle and bobbin had been removed; to serve as admiral of a fleet of battleships, six square-stern flatirons on the sea that was the kitchen floor; or to take the supply of buttons from the sewing-machine drawers, to employ them in army or football maneuvers.

These buttons were of several kinds, bone, mother-of-pearl, wood. Once I came upon a metal one with the legend "U.S." on it. This button was taken from me by Granny. She frowned as she snatched it from the heat of a decisive battle. That button, it seems, was an incriminating reminder of mysterious conferences held by Grandfather in the cellar with soldiers off duty from the Fort Logan army post.

Once or twice each year, certain army privates, carrying bundles, would visit the cellar, then quit the premises with no burdens other than a few coins in their pockets and specked apples in their hands. Soon afterward, Grandfather could be seen in a heavy shirt of blue, and wearing muskrat-lined gauntlets and shoes of durable military brand. When he packed for the mountains, there could be found among his gear new suits of long woolen underwear, heavy socks, and other paraphernalia designed for hardy campaigning. Grandmother cleared her conscience by desperately opposing this trafficking in military haberdashery. She decried but did not betray.

So many memories of that far-off time! The bronze statue of a prospector on top of the Mining Exchange Building downtown.

The finest sculpture in all the world! The bearded miner in his rough clothes and crumpled hat, a great nugget in his hand. Except for the nugget, the statue might have been Grandfather's own portrait in bronze.

Indirectly, my admiration of this statue brought me face to face with the foremost of all heroes since Ulysses. My first glimpse of him also brought with it my first disillusionment in respect to demigods.

On the morning of that great day—I think it was late in the spring of 1899—I spent an hour or so in the cellar with Grandfather. I had gone there with a twofold purpose: to inquire as to his health, and to ask him to half-sole my shoes on his knee-last.

The old gentleman was full of specked apples, pills, and new schemes this day. Since the panic of 1893, his prospecting ventures had been curtailed. As a stop-gap necessity, he had gone into the grocery and meat business, first with his son, Dewey Emmett, and then with his son-in-law, Frank Fowler. But his heart and his hopes stayed in the hills. He frequently packed and repacked his rusty tools and the contraband army clothes. He constantly consulted his ledgers and patent papers. He was the best prepared man in Christendom for the riches that never came.

Today, as he carved a half-sole from a slab of cowhide, then fitted it to one of my shoes, he said, "How'd you like to come along with me to the mountains?"

I reeled against the barrel of apples, almost upsetting them in my hysteria. The old man nodded with complete understanding. "It all depends on a talk I'm going to have with Judge Bryce down at the Mining Exchange this afternoon. If things go right, you and me air as good as off to the hills right now."

"But Grandma won't—"

"She's going along," he interrupted. "Maybe Dodie, too, later on. You and me'll go downtown this afternoon to see Judge Bryce; and you can look at the statue on the Mining Exchange."

"Is it a statue of you?" I asked hopefully.

He winked in the manner of one who would not fling aside an

honor accidentally bestowed. His mouth now was full of tacks. He grunted, and the "wealth for all" gleam again had come to his eyes.

Downtown I wanted to remain in the street to look up at the statue; but Grandfather had other things on his mind. We went inside the building and up two flights of stairs to Judge Bryce's headquarters.

It was my first time in a lawyer's office. The fawn-colored books with the gold-lettered paper labels on their spines enchanted me. So also did Judge Bryce. He wore a black patch over one eye, had a black mustache the size of a crow's wings, and looked exactly like a pirate in civilian dress. Chunks of ore served as paperweights to hold down numerous documents on his rolltop desk.

The two men spoke of their late friend, H. A. W. Tabor, and of his death in straitened circumstances at the Windsor Hotel that April. They talked also of William Jennings Bryan. It was obvious from their comments that they regarded the Demosthenes of Nebraska as the savior of silver and of the world.

Notwithstanding my interest in Judge Bryce's eyepatch and pirate's mustache, I became restless. The Judge brought a key from a desk drawer, a key with a lead ingot chained to it. He told me how to find the water closet down the hall.

"Now about financing this venture," the Judge was saying as I went to the hall. "An attorney named Eldridge is my agent in the Clear Creek district. . . ."

I was manipulating the key in the appropriate lock at the end of the corridor when the door was opened from the inside. And now I believe that I dropped dead, and then miraculously was restored to life on the spot. Colonel William F. Cody, Buffalo Bill himself, came out of the very place into which I was preparing to enter!

The tall hero didn't see me. Why should he have? I was but a mortal. He was tidying his long-skirted black coat and giving his pin-striped trousers a tactful touch. Then he made an authoritative readjustment of his Stetson hat on the graying tresses that had earned for him the Indian name, "Pahaska," the long-haired one.

I quit this scene reluctantly but necessarily. When I reappeared from the restroom, my hero had vanished. I ran down the stairs to the foyer of the building. He was not there. My belief in a just Providence was tottering as I went outside the office building.

Buffalo Bill was standing across the street. A group of men, women, and boys surrounded him. He seemed unmindful of his admirers as he looked at the statue on top of the Mining Exchange. I felt at once that he was a man of my own temperament. And in several respects, time has not proved that early opinion to be an erroneous one.

I now forgot all about the trip to the mountains; forgot my grandfather and Judge Bryce. The key with the ingot of lead on it—well, I never knew what became of *that*.

Buffalo Bill set off with long strides. Together with other boys and men, I followed him down the street, studying his every movement. It was said that Colonel Cody cast a longer shadow than did other men, and so it seemed to my eyes. I believed, of course, that the Colonel was en route to a lonely scout's camp somewhere outside of town. I felt certain that, once on the prairie, or perhaps among the cattails and the willows along the banks of the Platte River, he would cast aside the clothes of civilization and put on his pistols and his fringed buckskins. Perhaps he would shoot a buffalo or a hostile Indian with his Winchester rifle, just to keep in practice. Most assuredly he would cook some wild game on a campfire made with flint and tinder, or else by rubbing dry sticks together. If only he would invite me to share that primitive meal! Myself, and perhaps Annie Oakley, as guests of the great man.

I made up my mind to follow the hero anywhere this day, across mountain or plain. And where do you think was "anywhere"? It was the St. James Hotel, and not a camp, a tarpaulin tent, or a tepee. And how do you think Buffalo Bill made a fire for his long cigar as he entered the hotel? Doggone it! He lighted a sulphur match, just as anyone else would. Then he strode majestically into the barroom of the public house.

I almost became a cynic. Nevertheless, I followed after him. Then one of my hero's acquaintances took me by the shoulder, and none too gently pushed me outside the saloon.

"Drinks for the house," the Colonel's voice sounded.

I suppose that I waited for two hours or more in the street near the entrance to the St. James Hotel. I felt that Buffalo Bill would leave this place of frolic decadence and redeem himself somehow. I was still hoping and gawking at the hotel when Grandfather found me. He had been looking for me high and low, he said.

When I described what I had been doing, he said, "What does anybody want to follow old Cody around for? He was only a butcher. Ask Scout Wiggins."

It would be several years until I would ask Scout Wiggins about Buffalo Bill, and it would be ten years till I would become more closely acquainted with Colonel Cody. And in 1917 I would help arrange his burial services on the crest of Lookout Mountain. But right now I was disillusioned.

"Well," Grandfather said on the way home, "we air going up to Clear Creek. That's final. Idaho Springs. Empire. And that's where I mean to strike it rich."

Aboard the streetcar that took us home, George Pell chanced to be the conductor. The loyal friend of Charles Devlan was not in the good graces of the family, although Dodie still liked him, and held long conversations with Pell during choir practice. The purport of these talks never was divulged to anyone, particularly to Granny.

During the ride home, Pell collected Grandfather's nickel. "The boy here," he said as a pleasantry, "soon will be big enough to pay half-fare."

"By that time," my Grandfather replied, "he'll not have to ride the cars. We'll buy him a pony."

What was this he was saying? Did he know of Grandmother's worthy plan to disburse the Woodmen of the World fund, after a proper deduction for the funeral expenses? Pell's next remark set me straight. The pony was to be the result of a mining bonanza rather than that of the post-mortem bounty of the fraternal order.

"I see," Pell said. "Off to the mountains again, eh?"

"We're going to Clear Creek!" I blurted out. "Idaho Springs! Empire! Gee whiz!"

Pell looked off to the west where Mt. Evans stood today like a great white pavilion. "Charlie's done a lot of building and clearing up there near the Springs. He wrote me."

My grandfather was silent for a time. Then he said, "We won't be seeing Charlie."

Pell's neck was red. "Sorry I said anything about it, Mr. Wheeler." Then he left us to attend to his tramway duties elsewhere in the car.

"What did Mr. Pell mean?" I asked Grandfather. "What is my father doing?"

"Now look, son," said Grandfather, "let's not go into that at this time. The main thing is that you air never to tell anybody where you're going on a prospecting trip. No, sir!"

"Why not, Grandpa?"

"Because, when word gets around where *I* go, there's always liable to be a gold rush, or a silver rush. Things like a loose word can start a rush, and a man wants to get there first."

When I arrived home, Grandmother asked, "Why are you so frisky, son? He didn't stuff you with candy, did he?"

"I saw Buffalo Bill," I said.

I was waiting for her to swoon, but she merely nodded. "Then you saw practically nobody. Is that all that happened?"

"No, ma'am. But I can't talk about *that.*"

"You can't? And may I ask why not?"

"It's too big a secret."

"You should have no secrets from your old grandmother. Tell me."

"I shouldn't tell anybody about it," I said. "If I did, it would start a gold rush."

The old lady laughed heartily. "A gold rush in the opposite direction," she said.

Grandfather went on ahead to the mountains. He said he would find a cabin there, or build one if need be, large enough to house us. The old gentleman had been gone two weeks when we received a letter from him. He wrote so seldom to anyone other than patent-medicine firms that it was not to be wondered at when this present letter from Empire bore a pharmaceutical post-script. After advising us to "come on," Grandfather requested us to bring him a new supply of "backache remedy."

The formula for this mixture was set down in his letter: "One ounce compound of sarsparilla, one ounce Tories compound; these to be added to a half pint of rye whisky, and used in table-spoonful doses before each meal and at bedtime. Bottle to be well shaken each time."

Grandfather was not a drinking man as compared with many other toping pioneers and prospectors. Several of his medicines, however, such as the backache remedy, contained enough alcohol to keep him at a comfortable glow.

Granny, who never took any medicine, spiritous or otherwise, would not have on her conscience any part of the procurement of alcoholic prescriptions. She handed the letter to Uncle Dewey, then said, "Do as you see fit about this. He asks for two dozen bottles."

Dewey defended his father's medicinal urges. "Now look, Mother. I admit that he uses up a lot of pills and tonics, but he does it to fight off disease."

The old lady smiled. "I'll say this much for him: here is a man who always meets his diseases more than halfway."

Now we made ready for the journey to the glorious mountains.

7

THE ERUDITE TEA-TASTER

OLD Number Sixty hauled us over a dog-leg course to the foothills. Then we began a four-hour climb on narrow-gauge iron. The stubby locomotive hugged the crags, crossed ravines, became momentarily lost in tunnels, and left furrows of white smoke among the conifer trees.

Old Number Sixty of the Colorado & Southern snaked up the crooked grades at the rate of ten miles an hour or less. A slow-poke pace, you say? You who whiz past everything, and then ask, "Wasn't that a forest?" In an age of slower travel, we had time to observe: "What a remarkable tree that is! Older than Columbus."

The progress of Old Number Sixty and her four wooden coaches seemed brave and fast enough for an elderly century. As the train rolled across the upland plain between the city and the first hills, the whiskers of the prairie dogs twitched with worriment. Upon each hillock of the colony there was to be seen a ground-squirrel sentinel. The stout-bodied warders sat erect on their hind ends while gravely listening to the onrush of an invader so many times greater in size than their accustomed enemies: the coyote, the wild cat, the weasel, the hawk, the rattle-snake.

The underground colonists could deal efficiently with a snake. They would promptly entomb it by packing earth in the steep entrance hole both above and below the marauder. But to outflank and then pin down a snorting python, of which Old Number Sixty was the iron head, would call for a stratagem beyond the powers of these Lilliputians.

The passengers of the train could see the sparse ranches as Old Number Sixty approached the foothills. The cattle grazing on bunch-grass shook their horns as the whistle blew for a crossing. The white faces of new calves seemed daisy-small against the wide greenscape. The pastured horses capered, whinnied, then galloped off from the right of way, where dry tumbleweeds from last season clung like big blond spiders to the barbed-wire fence. A rancher's wife, a red-checked gingham sunbonnet on her head, was strewing grain for the chickens. At Leyden Junction, a signboard in the form of Andrew's Cross warned everyone to "look out for the cars." And in a lone outhouse near the water tower, an old pump-tender sat enshrined like a seedy and forgotten saint. Leyden Junction, then Golden, the bleak doorway to the hills.

Now the train nosed into Clear Creek Canyon. The rails wove among outcroppings of red sandstone, and past gray monoliths sculptured by the waters and the winds.

Swayback snow fences lay along the slopes. Old Number Sixty had a snowplow bolted onto her pilot beam; small avalanches might be encountered even in early summer among the higher regions.

The locomotive wore a spark guard on her stack. This cinder bonnet had been installed just recently. During previous summers, Old Number Sixty and her roundhouse sisters had breathed sparks that frequently set fire to the scrub and dry timber. Complaints by mountaineers went unanswered. Then, on a single day, a shower of sparks set the Silver Mountain Mill ablaze; and a second one caused the Roman Catholic church at Georgetown to go up in flames. Caught between two fires, as it were, the railroad paid

$22,000 in damages, and placed muzzles on the incendiary mouths of Old Number Sixty and her iron colleagues.

Numerous confidence men traveled the scenic route over the Georgetown Loop. They had the dignity and poise of doctors of divinity. They sold mining-stock certificates and other engraved and gilded documents to tourists from the East.

There were, of course, several legally active promoters and salesmen aboard the train today. Perhaps the most agile of them all was the "train butcher." His surest money-getter was a supply of cheaply made smoked-glass spectacles: "To keep the Colorado sun from striking you blind. Only one dollar a pair."

When he tried to sell Granny a set of these glasses, she advised him within the hearing of several customers: "What these good people need is not something to make them less blind, but a device to make them less dumb."

She refused also to purchase the news butcher's scenic postcards, saying, "I prefer to look upon the Lord's own work, mark you, and not the photographer's." Nor would she buy a parcel of fruit and sandwiches for thirty cents. She indicated a Queen Quality shoebox in the baggage rack overhead. It contained our home-packed lunch of fried chicken, sweet pickles, sandwiches, deviled eggs, Concord grapes, and apple pie.

"This generous meal for two," she said to the persistent huckster, "cost a great deal less than thirty cents. Now please run along and cheat the tourists."

In spite of these remarks, the news butcher was doing an excellent business. Then something happened to lessen the popularity of his smoked glasses. The sunny day "that might strike you blind" suddenly turned to putty. Black thunderheads boiled over the mountaintops. Notwithstanding the real greenery of the hillsides, they suddenly put on shrouds. The peaks above timberline became austere and gray.

And now there was played an overture that might have been composed by John Philip Sousa as a march for the mountain kings. Hailstones made a snare drum of the railway coach. Javelins of lightning were hurled against the rocks. A deluge that would have caused Noah himself to pucker his brow came from all quarters of the sky.

The news butcher absolutely refused to exchange other articles of merchandise for the colored glasses he had foisted on the tourists. "This kind of thing," one of the passengers remarked, "gives the state a bad name."

The cloudburst spent itself by the time the train reached Idaho Springs. Clear Creek, flowing parallel to Miner Street, the main avenue of the town, was at full bank. It caroused among the rocks, its waters dun-colored from the mill tailings and the washed-free clay. The valley moraine had turned red-brown from the storm. The wagon trails were burnt-sienna sashes, and a double rainbow became the new millinery of the hills.

The train stopped over for twenty minutes at the small station, the maroon façade of which was trimmed an olive green. The school children of the town came aboard with spool boxes of ore, specimens of quartz studded with iron pyrites which looked like gold to the amateur eye.

Granny now opened the shoebox. "We'll stay right here, son, to enjoy our lunch."

"But I want to get off," I said. "I want to see the engine."

"Never mind the engine," said Granny.

"Why can't I eat with the engineer and fireman?"

The train butcher was walking past our seat as Granny replied: "If you must know, Charlie Devlan's father lives hereabouts. And it might be that Charlie is visiting the old man. Stop fidgeting."

The train butcher paused at the water cooler as if to eavesdrop, slowly drank from the glass, then went outside to the car platform.

"Why don't I ever get to see Charlie Devlan?" I asked.

"Because. Just because. Now here's a nice piece of fried chicken. And try to keep your clothes clean."

She gave me five pennies, and consented to my buying some

caramels. She stipulated, however, that I must not leave the train while seeking the butcher.

I found him casting up his accounts in the coach next to ours. As I selected a cornucopia of caramels from his basket, he asked, "Say, what's that old lady got agin the Devlans?" He held before my eyes a larger cornucopia than the one I had chosen. "Here, sonny," he generously offered, "you can have a ten-cent size, seeing's you're a growing boy. You people know the Devlans?"

"Charlie Devlan's my father," and I hoped that I was saying the proper thing. "But I've never seen him."

"Oho," he said with a grunt of encouragement. "Ain't never seed him, eh? Well, now, you ever seed where your Grandpa Devlan lives?"

I shook my head. "Do you know Charlie Devlan?"

"I know everybody," he replied. "And everybody knows me. Come over to this side, sonny, and look out of this here window."

He directed my attention to the base of a hill north of the town. "That's High Street," he said. "And where Fifteenth Street runs into High, you'll see a clapboard house with a tin pipe sticking out of the brick chimbley. And that's where your Grandpa Devlan lives."

The two-story house stood perhaps sixty feet above the street. Paths led up to it in a zigzag series of ramps on the hillside. Smoke was rising from the chimney. White curtains festooned the windows. Was my father sitting inside that house at a noonday meal in the kitchen? Was he looking out at the train from behind those curtains? These seemed highly probable and stimulating conjectures.

"Now," the train butcher was saying, "you come look out the other side, and up at the trail where Charlie Devlan brings his logs across as props for the mines. It's so steep up there he has to use a tree trunk to brake the wagon, or else it'd roll right down, the four hosses and himself, for a drop of twenty-five hundred feet—maybe even to the Newhouse Tunnel."

My excitement was enormous. I was tempted to leave the train at once, to go to my Grandfather Devlan's home, there to reveal my identity. After the household had been sufficiently impressed, I would consent to become my father's business partner as well as his comrade, and help him bring the logs across the high trail. Would Charlie Devlan be angry because his son's name was Fowler?

The escape of steam, the calls of "all aboard," and the bustle of the returning passengers interrupted this dream. The roar of dynamite at some far-off mine now was heard. Perhaps this same powder blast had been set off by the gallant old prospector now waiting for us at Empire farther on among the hills.

I returned to my place on the rigid, cane-back seat beside Granny. I looked out the window until a great highland had blocked out the town. "How far does Charlie Devlan live from here, Grandma?"

"A million miles, so far as we are concerned," she said with a finality that was hers but not my own. "He's gone and is forgotten."

The great hills closed in from all sides, but Old Number Sixty knew the way out of the labyrinth. And when we had left the train at the small mining settlement that was Empire, a paunchy man with a purple-veined nose and the breath of a malt vat introduced himself as "Mr. Eldridge, attorney-at-law, assessment worker, part owner of the Little Columbine claim, and at your service. . . . Mrs. Wheeler, I take it?"

Mr. Eldridge excused himself temporarily to collect an assortment of crates and bales belonging to Norman Wheeler. These had preceded us by freight the week before. During an examination of the bill of lading, Mr. Eldridge said to the station master: "Judge Bryce has been most generous with Wheeler, I see. And the Judge will never live to regret it."

Then, while Mr. Eldridge was stowing these grubstake supplies in the bed of his spring wagon, he came upon the parcel of backache remedy, a package marked "Handle with Care." He pressed an expert ear against the bundle, shook it a little, then smiled. The veins of his nose dilated as if with glad expectancy.

The several miles that Mr. Eldridge's bay horse wheezed up the trail, then down to a draw at the foot of Red Mountain, were not without incident. It seems that the part owner of the Little Columbine was none too sober even at the beginning of the drive. Had it not been for the homing instinct of the horse, we might have plunged off a trail that had been designed by the local undertaker, or else was meant only for pack animals.

Mr. Eldridge frequently reined in his horse, then got down to reach over the side of the wagon and under the seat board for a jug. Each time he did this he would mutter an "excuse me for a short recess, madam." Then he would go behind a rock or a tree or the braces of a wooden flume, the jug hanging like a briefcase from his freckled hand.

After perhaps the tenth one of these wayside errands, Mr. Eldridge fell asleep while driving. He awakened with a lurch, learned to his own amazement that he was still alive, then apologized with thick phrases for the numerous delays. He got down again from the wagon seat to retire with the jug behind a stump that overlooked a precipice. He wove back to the vehicle to discover that he had been dispossessed. Mrs. Wheeler now was sitting in the driver's place, the reins in her capable hands.

With a senatorial flourish of the jug, the attorney said, "I yield to the lady from the Queen City of the Plains." Then he climbed with some difficulty to the seat Granny just recently had occupied. "I always say . . ." he began, but what he always said was lost in his own personal fog.

"If it does not inconvenience you too much, Mr. Eldridge," Granny observed with mock courtesy, "perhaps you will be good enough to direct me if we come to a fork in this so-called road?"

"At your service," the attorney managed to say. "I'm yours to command."

When we reached the cabin that Grandfather had prepared

opposite Red Mountain, the sun lay low. The old gentleman greeted us calmly, for his was not a demonstrative nature except when hammering or blasting among the hills themselves. There were no embraces. I never saw Grandfather caress anyone other than his only daughter.

Granny had climbed down from the wagon seat, and Grandpa now shepherded Mr. Eldridge to the ground. The attorney insisted upon shaking Mrs. Wheeler's hand again and again, while calling her "the salt of the earth," and "a sight for sore eyes."

Grandmother now learned to her horror that the cargo of the wagon included a shipment of dynamite belonging to the part owner of the Little Columbine. To think that we had been riding all the way from Empire with "Death at our elbow!"

Dynamite was the only thing that ever caused this good woman to show alarm. Her husband's eye would light with a great mischief whenever he was warming dynamite in the oven to dry it. And his wife would go outside the cabin with a swishing of skirts and a medley of prayers.

"He's tempting Providence again," she would say. "One day, mark you, we shall all turn into mincemeat on the other side of the moon."

As Lawyer Eldridge drove off with his jug and his shipment of dynamite, he shouted over his shoulder: "Wheeler, your good wife is a sight for sore eyes! Yes, sir! She is all that, *per se*. Welcome to Red Mountain, madam."

"No one," said my grandmother, "could be a better authority on sore eyes than that drunken sot."

The sun sets early behind the mountains, then the air becomes quite chill. Grandfather had made a brisk wood fire in the sheet-iron stove. Candles were burning in miners' sconces speared into the log walls. There was a brakeman's lantern, unlit, on the table. The butt of a massive revolver, a "side-loader," stuck out from a holster hanging from a peg.

This lantern and this pistol were Grandpa's emergency equipment for skunks. He detested skunks almost as much as he did

Indians. He would rise at any hour of the night to rout a skunk from a place up-wind from the cabin. He did not handle his fire-arm with graceful flourishes, but was an effective marksman. Sometimes when the supply of meat became low, he hunted game with his ancient pistol, and with no regard for any law other than that of his family's hunger.

The cabin itself was large if compared to most prospector's cabins of that day. The walls were of logs. The chinks were caulked with mortar fortified by burro manure, well-aged and mixed with slaked lime and creek sand. The organic ingredient, Grandpa said, encouraged a strong set, prevented frost-cracking, or the shrinkage of mortar away from the logs.

The chimney was merely four sections and an elbow of stove-pipe, badly insulated. The roof was constantly endangered by the hot flue. There was no floor inside this cabin other than a pave-ment formed by several centuries of pine-needle debris hard-packed among the decomposed granite of the valley slope.

There were four bunks, one-over-one, two at either side of the single room. When in use these beds were suspended at their outer sides by means of hand-forged chains anchored to hooks in the ceiling beams. The wall sides of the bunks were attached to hinges. During the day, the bunks were folded sidewise against the log walls, and latched there so as to be out of the way.

This type of miners' bunks had given George Mortimer Pull-man—a seller of hammer handles in Colorado camps in 1859—the idea for his sleeping-car berths. He had offered to share his project with several Colorado friends, but they regarded him as a "woolgatherer." When his Pullman car received world-wide notice after the transportation of President Lincoln's coffin from Washington to Springfield, the inventor's Colorado friends be-came aware of the fact that, to use my grandmother's own phrase, "they really *had* missed the train."

The bed ticking of our bunks contained pine needles, and seemed the most fragrantly restful mattresses in all this world.

And the night music of a near-by tributary to Clear Creek became a part of one's dreams.

A felled log bridged the hustling stream near our cabin. Attorney Eldridge frequently tumbled off this footbridge. Sometimes he "cooned it" across, working his way along on his hands and buttocks, but quite often he would appear at our door, wet and puffing, but gallantly calling out: "Mrs. Wheeler, and may I ask if the lady of the house is in good health today? You are the salt of the earth, you know."

Every day seemed Christmas, with hundreds of thousands of Christmas trees; and every day was 4th of July as well, what with the dynamite salvos from the mines. Smoke would gush from the mountainsides; but the voice of a blast would be delayed for a long time after one saw the white smoke, or so it seemed to the awed watcher and listener. Then a mighty smash of sound would fill the sky. Echoes would rebound across the valley, from hill to hill, as if the gods were exchanging blows among themselves in a great brawl.

I rode burros in this wonderland, among them a lop-eared individualist, the Senator, named in honor of Silver Dollar Tabor. I wrote sketchily concerning that animal in the introduction to a book, *Timber Line*. I now regret that I failed to devote the entire volume to the story of his life, a career in some respects more active than Casanova's.

The place of our home near one of the several "Mormon Roads" across the Great Divide was hardly a settlement, but there were several cabins in the vicinity. Mr. Eldridge was our nearest neighbor, and farther on across the little creek stood the only "real house" within several miles of us. It even had a front porch!

That house was a one-story structure of unpainted boards. There was a conventional floor inside it, and white curtains at the windows of the main room and of two alcoves that were called bedrooms. John H. Blake, an Englishman of early middle age, resided here. He had a French wife and two charming daughters of about my own years.

Mr. Blake was a person of great reserve but of such honorable deportment as to invite the friendly respect of all the miners and prospectors. He seemed to know everything. He told me the names of flowers, herbs, and other objects of nature that hitherto had been regarded by me merely as acquaintances. Now they suddenly took on particularities that enchanted me.

When I learned from Mr. Blake that I had been associating with such botanical wonders as "Kinnikinnick," "Giant Louse-wort," "Pipsissewa," "Purple Saxifrage," "Three-nerve Fleabane," "Sunloving Cat's-paw," "Orchid Beardtongue," "Fiddle-leaf Twin-pod," and "Bastard Toadflax," I belatedly began to realize the importance of living among celebrities. They gave me a kind of reflected honor. I, too, could boast an assortment of names, although not quite as imposing as the ones Mr. Blake recited.

This learned gentleman also informed me that my friends, the prairie dogs of the lower altitudes, never drank water, not a drop of it, but subsisted merely on grass and herbiage. Among other skills, Mr. Blake had the ability to "read" the rings of a felled pine tree, and determine from these testimonies the exact year of a century when there had been a forest fire or damage to the tree trunk by lightning. He found fossil shells on the hillsides, and offered them as evidence that the whole region in an ancient time had been covered by the sea. He told me that certain illnesses were caused by germs that invaded the body; but when I excitedly brought this news home, Grandmother snorted: "Germs? Germs, indeed! Well, I'll believe it when I *see* one."

Mr. Blake had sustained a curious affliction that changed his fortunes and interrupted his career. He had been one of England's foremost professional tea-tasters, an arbiter of tea blends. He had lived in India, China, and Japan, and now was writing a book about tea.

Perhaps the expert's excessive sampling of teas among the go-downs of the Orient or the warehouses of London had drowned his faculties of smell and taste. Or it may have been that chronic sinusitis put an end to his professional activities. Smoking and drinking assuredly had not caused the "catarrh," for Mr. Blake was abstemious.

"A tea-taster," he would say, "must not permit dissipation of any sort, even the partaking of highly spiced foods, to dull his senses. A whole industry depends upon his alert verdicts, judgments so finely drawn as to enable the taster of blends to be able to tell within the fraction of a cent what a tea is worth the pound, and to know without question how old a dried tea leaf is, when it was plucked, in what region, and if it is a first, second, or third picking."

Now, far away from the tea gardens of the world, and as if Mr. Blake were recapturing in nostalgic fashion the prosperous days of his tea umpiring, this man was writing an authoritative book on tea, from seed to leaf, from leaf to cup. And I long remembered the green-covered book with its tea-leaf designs.

Mr. Blake had married a French woman of good family. Then, after his sense of taste had gone into an eclipse, he moved to America to begin life anew. He now was serving as field man for an English syndicate that sought the discovery and development of mining claims. At night his coal-oil lamp burned late as he worked upon the manuscript of his book.

The men and women of the West often had been placed by necessity among scenes of primitive struggle, but they were by no means barbarians or ignoramuses. Their minds were eager enough, their bodies vital, their faith immense. And in a thousand ways, and in several thousand homes, however small, there could be found an affirmation of life and a belief in the validity of the American genesis. Mr. Blake, like Dr. Evans, was but one of the numerous men of character and substance who, without posing as missionaries of culture, helped to refine the crude aspects of the pioneer settlements.

I was unaware of it at the time, but now I know that Mr. Blake was the first of my numerous "candidates" in the quest for a father. I was not looking for paternal affection so much as for guidance in matters that seemed large and grave and important to a boy. In Mr. Blake I found a trustworthy arbiter, one who neither ignored nor ridiculed my questions, and who met my inquiring mind as if he and I were on even terms.

During the years to be, men such as Mr. Blake would appear at times when storm signals were raised in my mind and heart. I learned too little from these friendly mentors, for my disposition was to ride at full gallop, as a mounted cowboy does when picking up his hat from the ground. And sometimes I not only missed the hat but was thrown from the horse as well, and had to return home on foot. But each thing that I did learn from these older men tended to dissuade me from reaching cynical verdicts in respect to the caprices of small men with loud voices.

8

OVER THE HILLS AND FAR AWAY

DODIE came to Red Mountain early in July. She brought with her my three-year-old sister, and a baby brother, Jack, then but a year old. The four bunks of our cabin were taxed indeed.

I slept with Granny in a "lower," Grandpa occupied the "upper," directly overhead; he would make more noise than a jail break whenever he got down to light his lantern, draw on his hobnailed boots, seize the "side-loader," and then go out-of-doors to rout the skunks.

Dodie occupied the "lower" across the room from us. A blanket-lined powder box beside her bed was my brother's bassinet. Our sister slept in the remaining upper, fenced in by a network of stout cords.

Now for the first time, or so it seemed, I could be my mother's real companion. Before this summer, she had lived for the most part in houses other than mine. And before that I had been too young to know of her nearness. Sometimes, it is true, we lived under one roof when Frank Fowler "was doing nicely," as during three of the Spanish-American War months. Then bad times would visit us in a kind of cycle; the moving van would come, and good-bys be said.

Each Sunday when in the city, I had seen my mother at the church where she sang, and occasionally we had Sunday dinner together. But there were so many boarders at Granny's house as to make of a mother-and-son visit a fiasco.

Once Dodie took me to the Golden Eagle store to buy for me a blue-straw hat with a flaring brim. The wind blew it off my head during the streetcar ride home. My mother had not a cent left in her purse, and the streetcar would not wait for us until we could retrieve the hat near the windows of the County Hospital. Someone from behind the bars of the insanity ward frightened us with a sudden wail. We had to walk home, and it was one of Dodie's few times of ill temper. Since that day, I have never liked hats.

Twice each Sunday, I would sit in the church to admire my mother and her musical talent. Just how proficient she was, I had neither the discernment nor the experience to decide. And I do not know now, nor is it important for anyone to know, if she was a vocal artist. I remember that Paul Whiteman's father, the amazing Wilberforce J. Whiteman, described Dodie's ability as "something precious." He invited her to join his choir at Trinity Church; but Granny would not risk her daughter's exposure to a professional career. The mother's influence persisted until long after Dodie's marriage to Frank Fowler.

Dodie sang without affectation. She could be understood, and did not enounce "spring" as "spr-e-e-e-e-nng." I well remember such things as these. I can recall her singing voice so clearly, yet I cannot, much as I would like to do so, bring to mind the sound of her speaking voice.

But I recollect distinctly the times when we walked together in the mountains. There was a corduroy bridge across the creek down by the Mormon Road; but Dodie and I usually crossed upon the felled log near our cabin.

One day my vivacious mother removed her shoes and stockings, and sat on the log to dangle her feet in the cool, clear waters. Her dark curls blowing, her dark eyes fixed upon the dizzying stream, she began to sing. She improvised this little song, I think, for there were no words to it, merely a succession of delightful trills, and a recurring tune obviously borrowed from something other than a solemn hymn. The cascading waters beneath the singer's feet were her accompaniment; it seemed that she was singing of life as a great promise and as a lasting joy for everyone.

Now, quite abruptly, she left off singing. She was seized with confusion. I thought at first that the waters had made her giddy, as happened when one kept an eye fixed for too long a time upon the hypnotizing onrush below one's place on the log.

Mr. Blake was standing on the opposite bank of the creek. He saw at once that he had embarrassed the barefoot young woman. He politely lifted a pork-pie hat from his head. "I had not meant to intrude. Please forgive me." He then turned and walked away.

"Don't mention this to your grandmother," Dodie said to me. "She might think I'd done something immodest."

"You couldn't," I said with all my heart.

She placed her arms about me and kissed me. I would always remember that day, even when the sound of Dodie's spoken words had gone beyond my recollection.

That afternoon, one of Mr. Blake's daughters brought to our cabin a note addressed to Granny. Our family was invited to tea at the Blake house the next afternoon, which would be Sunday.

Perhaps there never was a social event of greater importance than this tea, or the succeeding ones at the Blakes' during the remainder of that mountain summer. Mrs. Blake, slim in a worsted gown with stays and leg-of-mutton sleeves, received us with ceremony. Dodie wore a simple blue frock. Granny's go-to-meeting clothes, alas! had been left in moth-balls in the city; but the old lady's air of self-confidence was her finest garb at any time. She quailed before no one—unless he had dynamite on or near his person.

Mr. Blake produced a zither, and then revealed that his wife played it "for her own pleasure, you know." My mother asked if the hostess would perform for us. I do not remember the tune Mrs. Blake played, some French folk air perhaps, but it sounded sweet. Mrs. Blake then asked if my mother knew any songs that might be found in the repertoire of the zither-player. They finally agreed upon an air called "Over the Hills and Far Away."

After Dodie had sung to the accompaniment of the zither, Mr. Blake was much less stolid than an Englishman was supposed to be, and his wife actually had tears in her eyes. There were encores, then Mrs. Blake and Dodie discussed musical topics over the tea, which had been made with ritualistic care by the expert himself. He used two earthen pots, one for the brewing, and the other for the decanting.

Mr. Blake and Grandmother conversed on tea and various other topics. The gentleman found in the old lady no submissive yielder to his opinions.

In an aside to me she whispered, "Watch me sharpen my claws on this bald-pated Englishman."

She did not hesitate to correct him when he misquoted something about "the vials of wrath" from the Book of Revelation. She was able to tell him the chapter and verse of the scriptural excerpt. He pleasantly consulted a small Bible, then sought to change the subject to a discussion of Mrs. Blake's water-color paintings of the mountains.

"These hills," and Mr. Blake gestured toward a painting of Red Mountain, "seem large in our eyes, Mrs. Wheeler. But the universe is much larger."

Mrs. Wheeler tapped the Bible. "And this, Mr. Blake, is larger still."

The tea authority, an expert on soil, endeavored to retreat from the provinces of Holy Writ with references to "dry farming." Few westerners of that day paid attention to theorists who held that farming could be successfully managed without irrigation.

"We shall all live to see the time, Mrs. Wheeler," Mr. Blake said, "when only the natural precipitation, if conserved, will obtain great results. It takes almost five hundred pounds of water to produce one pound of grain. The procedure will be to store up moisture as it falls. During the fallow season, the ground should be harrowed or stirred after each heavy rain or snow. This forms a dust mulch or blanket, and destroys capillary attraction. Mrs. Wheeler, you were reared on a farm. What do you think of the scientific turning over of fallow ground?"

"I think," replied Mrs. Wheeler, "that the Lord knew what He was about when He left the right side of the soil up."

Mr. Blake simply could not move his guest away from the vicinity of the Lord. He made a last attempt to do so by asking if Norman Wheeler expected to remain in camp during the winter.

Grandfather had not come to the Blake tea. Indeed, it was just as well that he had not. Both he and Mr. Eldridge were under a cloud for supposedly killing a buck out of season. This alleged violation of the game laws had brought a warden from Georgetown to investigate. He was still looking for evidence. The buck, it was said, had not been slain by a shot from a sportsman's rifle, but by a revolver bullet, the kind that *could* have been discharged by a side-loader.

The antlers of the animal, its hooves and hide, had been disposed of in an abandoned mine shaft. There were a number of deserted holes such as this one in the Empire district. For years, since the State had decreed that some wild animals might not be killed in certain seasons, the meat-hungry violators of the game laws disposed of incriminating evidence in an old mine shaft half a mile off the trail and up the draw toward Red Mountain.

When Grandfather and his attorney friend were advised that the game warden was on his way, they visited the abandoned shaft, perhaps to shed the symbols of guilt. Whatever it was they accomplished there, Attorney Eldridge decided to drink from his pocket flask, while pondering the rules that pertained to the *corpus delicti*. Then, to the dismay of both lawyer and client, Mr. Eldridge lost his footing, and plunged, flask and all, into the shaft. The pit was cluttered with an accumulation of antlers from other poaching seasons. These bony branches broke Mr. Eldridge's fall.

There was a bad half-hour of it. Grandpa did some emergency engineering. He set a pair of timbers across the chasm, then "poled" the lawyer out by means of saplings lowered into the pit and thrust solidly at an angle against one side of it. An invoice of Mr. Eldridge's injuries revealed a fractured rib, severe bruises to his back, and numerous punctures in his whole person. The part owner of the Little Columbine looked as if he had been clapperclawed by the devil himself.

At the Eldridge cabin, Grandfather dressed these wounds with dynamite salve. Then he administered a variety of pills and powders, and generously sacrificed a full bottle of backache remedy as well. Mr. Eldridge seemed a staggering pincushion during the next six weeks. He said he had "half a mind to sue the criminal-brained so-and-so who'd left that death trap of a mine in such a careless and illegal condition."

The tea at the Blakes' progressed quite well without the presence of the alleged deerslayers. Several times during the debates between Mr. Blake and Mrs. Wheeler, the hostess attempted to rescue her husband from the scriptural rebuttals. She finally accomplished this by mentioning the possibility that "the ladies might care to see some rather interesting souvenirs from Paris." Dodie was thrilled by this prospect, and even Granny's femininity rose to the surface, as it sometimes did with genuine charm. Mrs. Blake opened a Chinese chest, and from it brought a black velvet bag, tied by means of a gold-colored drawstring.

Now, as we gathered about a table, our eyes wide, she removed some most remarkable objects from the wallet. My present opinion is that they were but trinkets; but in that faraway wilderness, Mrs. Blake's treasures seemed to us as grand and as valuable as anything that might be found in the Tower of London. The little stones on the little rings brought "Ah's" from everyone, including Mrs. Blake herself. Dodie, enchanted by a pair of earrings, held them to her ears as she looked in a small mirror on the wall.

During the several teas to come, the climax to our enjoyment of them was always the moment when Mrs. Blake, to rescue her husband from a conversational impasse with Mrs. Wheeler, opened the chest, brought out the black velvet bag, and displayed the "treasures" of a valentine past.

The days when Granny permitted me to go with Grandpa to the claim were times of glory. The old man would tell his wife a pardonable lie, promising to do no blasting, but merely put in some timber or clear away ore loosened by yesterday's charges.

Did we do any blasting? Enough to make the eardrums dance for the rest of one's life! How brave I thought the old prospector when, for economy's sake, he cut a yellow stick of dynamite in halves, using the same huge jackknife blade as the one from which he took quinine.

"This ain't dangerous at all," he would say of the powder-cutting operation. Then he would prepare a fuse, snipping a proper length from a black coil of inflammable cord. He next would open a round pillbox, then carefully lift from its cotton-packed nest one of several fulminate of mercury caps. Concerning these copper fuse caps, he would say: "These air the little fellows you got to handle like birds' eggs. Blow your head off!"

The cap affixed, he would bed it carefully in the half-stick of explosive. Then he carried this ensemble into the mouth of the tunnel, according his burden the same respect that a mace-bearer shows for the staff of office. He would not permit me to go inside to see him tamp home the charge in the hole he had drilled so patiently in the rock wall.

After he reappeared, we would stand well to one side of the tunnel and behind a spur of rock to witness the miracle. The anticipation of it was almost unbearable. Then, just as it would begin to seem that Grandpa had planted another one of his many sterile hopes, the world would totter. The rocks and debris would burst out as if from a cannon's mouth. Sympathetic slides of rock and shale, loosened by the frost crackings of winter and now shaken free, would spill down the outside slope at the portal. The trees would bend. The chipmunks would cling to the boughs. The echoes would roll and repeat themselves with sublime extravagance along the draw.

Grandpa's eye would shine. "Think we should have a look inside? Might be the real thing *this* time. You never know."

Before we commenced to barrow out the fallen rock, Grandpa would choose several specimens and take them to the sunlight. He would peer at these fragments wordlessly, using a small magnifying glass kept in a hard-rubber shield attached to a brass chain dull with age. On this chain was a small compass that never in its mining-camp career told a true direction, so easily influenced was it by the lodestones in the hills.

Concerning this compass, Grandmother once said: "The only directions it ever seems sure about are those of up or down."

My stay in this paradise was interrupted toward the end of August. I was playing with the Blake girls one morning when their cat carried a kitten from a place underneath the house.

It was my belief that when a cat carried a kitten in its mouth, she was punishing it, or intending to do so. Perhaps I based this conjecture upon an experience of my own when, after I had used a sewing-machine screw driver on the mechanism of Frank Fowler's gold watch; my stepfather seized me by the seat of the breeches and then carried me toward the kindling pile.

I followed after the Blake cat, intending to rescue the kitten. Mr. Blake took this occasion to lecture me upon the habits of cats and their ancient origin. He said that the Egyptians even had honored them with mummification.

He smiled when I remarked, "Granny says a boy never gets too old to learn."

Lest I misinterpret his smile as one of ridicule, he explained, "I do not mean that you are stupid for not knowing about cats. All of us have empty places to be filled. And a man whose own coat is threadbare never should make fun of another man's patches."

The arrival of Granny at the Blake house interrupted this discussion. She was carrying a jar of preserves made of small strawberries gathered from plants which grew wild in the valley meadows. This gift was in return for a squirrel pie that Mr. Blake recently had shared with us. Small lead shot occasionally got caught between one's teeth while one was partaking of the pasty.

While the Blakes were thanking Mrs. Wheeler for her neighborly token, the voice of Attorney Eldridge boomed outside the house. "Three cheers for Mr. Blake, author and world traveler!"

We went to the front porch to find a delegation of prospectors, Grandpa among them, and to see them wave their ore-caked hats and hear them shout three "hurrahs." Mr. Blake stood facing the clearing in which the men were gathered. "Gentlemen, as this is not my birthday, to what circumstance do I owe this honor?"

Lawyer Eldridge, on a dais-like rock, explained in a manner worthy of the Supreme Court. I remember only his opening remark: "Mr. Blake, you are a descendant of Cromwell's great admiral; of that I am sure. Now, if you will but cast bread upon our waters, it will return to you one day in the guise of cupcakes."

The rest of his speech ran about as follows: "For some years past our comrades have been using a community forge for the sharpening of their picks and drills. Now a mishap has occured that well may outrank the loss of the horseshoe nail that cost Napoleon the Battle of Waterloo. A bear, sir, or some other predatory beast, has seen fit to dine upon the leather band of our pair of bellows. The boards also have been split by the careless actions of the vandal. Only the metal ribs and the air nozzle remain intact. . . ."

At this point, an itinerant prospector known to Clear Creek County as "Sawtooth" Joe ambled up on a Jenny. He called out: "Hi, thar! I got sumpthin' fur Mrs. Elizabeth Wheeler."

Lawyer Eldridge turned on his stony rostrum to stare at the intruder. "This is not the time or place, sir, for someone who has had a drop too much to drink."

"Ah, shut up, you old guzzler yoreself!" said Sawtooth Joe. "Whar's Mrs. Wheeler?"

Lawyer Eldridge applied a red bandanna to his hayfevered and rum-inflamed nose, then said: "I hold no brief against an honest drink or two, but we must have moderation in all things. Now, Mr. Blake, we come to you because you are a public-spirited man. . . ."

This time Sawtooth's Jenny caught sight or scent of my burro, the Senator. She set up a lewd braying. Lawyer Eldridge, a veteran of numerous courtroom hecklings by attorneys of shorter ear than yonder Jenny, turned this braying to his own advantage by saying, "Objection overruled."

He skillfully revealed that the pair of bellows was beyond repair, and said that the miners of the district would be content with a secondhand appliance that would cost nine dollars.

"Think of it!" he said. "The lack of a few blasts of air may stand in the way of some one of us becoming a new Croesus. Perhaps my friend Norman Wheeler—and I advisedly call him friend and colleague, my companion in hunting for gold, and in lighter moments for wild game. . . ."

"Tell 'em about them bucks you shoot out of season," called out Sawtooth Joe as he bit off a chew of tobacco.

Lawyer Eldridge winced. Grandpa went serenely to Sawtooth's side, and swept him from his palfrey to the ground. The Jenny, freed of her burden, started off in the direction of the Senator, who now was calling to her with licentious heehaws.

"No violence, please, Friend Wheeler," Lawyer Eldridge admonished his crony. "Let us not dignify this nobody's slanders with the mayhem he so richly deserves."

"Get off my chest!" said Sawtooth to Grandpa. "I got a telegram for your wife."

The word "telegram" electrified everyone but the spokesman

for the miners. Mrs. Wheeler now advanced from the background to say to her husband, "Let him up, Norm."

Grandpa obeyed her, as usual, and he, too, became concerned about the telegram. Sawtooth, still wheezing from his fall, retrieved his relic of a hat, then brought a much-folded paper from the sweatband, a message written in pencil upon a sheet of railroad telegrapher's "flimsy."

"It come over the wire to Empire station yestiddy," Sawtooth announced through a barrier of chewing tobacco. "It's for Mrs. Elizabeth Wheeler."

"But Mr. Blake," Lawyer Eldridge was saying in a frustrated manner, "the bellows . . . the predatory beast that ate the leather . . . the nine silver dollars. . . ."

"The bellows will await Mrs. Wheeler's telegram," Mr. Blake said, turning to the lady to add, "Please read it without delay."

Granny now became more important than the bellows. This was the first telegram we had ever received, here or elsewhere. A telegram was a great event in anyone's life, and a fearful one as well. No one other than capitalists or Soapy Smith ever sent or received telegrams unless there was illness or death in a family.

Mrs. Wheeler adjusted her spectacles, and read the message, her lips moving without sound. Then she announced to the bystanders, "My sister Susan lies at death's door in Kansas. You will please excuse me."

Mr. Blake bowed slightly. "Our profound sympathy and condolences." He waited until Mr. Eldridge had given another Gabriel toot into the bandanna, then said, "I shall be happy to finance a new pair of bellows. Good day, gentlemen."

Granny, Grandpa, and myself returned to our cabin across the creek. There Granny said to her husband, "Your brother Victor has done something horrible."

Victor was Susan's husband. The Wheeler brothers had married two of the several Parrott sisters.

"What do you mean?" asked Grandfather. "Let's see that there telegram."

"It's not the actual message that tells the story. It's what I read between the lines. Vic has shot Susie. And it's murder."

"Now, now!" Norman Wheeler stuttered. "You air jumping at conclusions, Lizzie. Vic never murdered anybody."

"That's *exactly* what he's done," said Granny.

"Oh, now, you air just magnifying," said the old gentleman. "Susie ain't dead yet."

"Not yet," said his wife, "but her life is hanging by a thread." Then, as she began to pack our things, she added: "If Susie dies, I myself will provide the rope for her slayer."

Granny decreed that I accompany her to Denver, where she would stop over only long enough to procure from Frank Fowler the railroad fare to Kansas. I was fearful that we might not arrive in Kansas in time for a deathbed scene. As described to me, these "scenes" not only seemed events of great dramatic import, but a dying pioneer might utter words that were prophetic, or have visions, or sing with the voice of an angel.

Granny's father, John Parrott, died at ninety-one while shouting lines from Charles Wesley's last hymn: "In age and feebleness extreme, who shall a sinful worm redeem?" Then he mounted a white horse, seen exclusively by himself, for a triumphant gallop from Earth to the Pearly Gates. Granny's mother, Dora Parrott, had passed on in a calmer and less equestrian fashion at eighty-nine. Still, she had foretold the "coming of a conflict of nations," and long in advance named a day that almost coincided with that of the declaration of the war with Spain.

All of us except Grandfather set out for Empire in Mr. Eldridge's spring wagon. The part owner of the Little Columbine was not in his jugs today. He seemed genuinely sad at seeing us go. He kept telling Granny that it was "like losing the salt of the earth to have her pull up stakes." She merely wrinkled her fine brow, and said, "Poor dear Susie!"

Now Old Number Sixty came chugging around a highland, and from over the hills and far away.

9

SUNFLOWERS FOR AUNT SUSAN

IN HOLTON, Kansas, the county seat of Jackson County, in almost the exact center of the United States, we found Aunt Susan in her bed. Uncle Victor sat in a far corner of the kitchen, speaking to no one and no one speaking to him.

With the vigilance of childhood, I assembled the facts, then wrote them down in a letter to Mr. Blake. I assured him that I would let him know promptly when Aunt Susan died, if she voiced any prophecies, and if Uncle Victor mounted the gallows. Someone suggested that Aunt Susan write a new will and not mention her husband in it. I felt the injustice of this proposal, and declared in my letter to Mr. Blake that my sympathies lay with Uncle Victor. I then inquired of my mentor if it was "a wrong thing to feel sorry for a man without a friend in the world?"

The letter went on to say that Norman Wheeler's younger brother was one of the surest pistol shots in Kansas. He could ride at full gallop along the margin of a marshland and with his pistol shoot six mud hens in succession as they started up from the reeds. He kept the loaded pistol on his hip by day and beneath his pillow at night in the upstairs bedroom of the small white house. Although she was a pioneer, Aunt Susan's attitude toward a loaded pistol was similar to that of Granny's in respect to dynamite.

One black night Aunt Susan roused her husband with the whispered news that she "heard someone prowling downstairs." Delighted by this opportunity to try his skill on something other than coots, Uncle Victor unpillowed his pistol, admonished Aunt Susan to remain in the featherbed, then added, "Don't worry about *me*."

Uncle Victor tiptoed downstairs to find no burglar there. Then he investigated the premises outside, but could not see or hear a prowler. When he returned indoors, however, he heard someone stirring at the foot of the stairway, but could not see anyone in the darkness.

He shot in the direction of the noise. There was a moan, then the sound made by a falling body. Uncle Victor's two daughters came screaming from their room off the kitchen. They lighted a lamp and saw their mother as the victim.

The doctor said the bullet had "missed the heart by a fraction of an inch." Uncle Victor tossed his pistol into a trash bin, then assigned himself to a place in the kitchen, where he stared all day at a peach tree outside a window. There his meals were served to him apart from the others.

Relatives from the town and from various farms adjacent to it kept watch at Aunt Susan's bedside. She was the most "spiritual" of Granny's relations, and had no words of censure or recrimination to offer against anyone. Granny and I arrived in Holton to find the good woman pale and still.

"The Lord's will be done," she said. "I am ready."

I kept an eye alternately upon Aunt Susan and Uncle Victor, waiting for dramatic happenings. I took time, however, to gather some late-lingering sunflowers to take to Aunt Susan's room, but Granny intervened.

"Good gracious!" said Granny. "What are you doing with all those weeds in the house?"

"For the funeral," I said.

"Oh, you mischievous varmint! That's the Wheeler blood in you. Always doing the wrong thing at the right time. Out with you now!"

I disposed of the sunflowers, but kept a grasshopper that had been hiding in the bouquet. It had short horns, stout yellow thighs, and its mandibles behaved like those of Sawtooth Joe, what with their chewing-tobacco aspects. The grasshopper escaped from my hand and alighted upon Uncle Victor's chest, startling him from his meditations. He seemed helpless and confused. Uncle Victor was not now behaving in the cocky, spirited manner that had made people smile and shake their heads whenever they discussed his pre-Susan days.

The grasshopper incident reminded me of a family legend. I asked Uncle Victor if it was true that he had started a prairie fire in 1874. He winced at this reference to his past. I had been told by Grandpa that Victor had acted with the noblest of motives, intending merely to burn out a swarm of grasshoppers that had been eating the crops. The fire got out of control. I never did learn the full details, although it was said that the jack rabbits didn't stop running until they reached the Missouri State line.

On the day when I gathered sunflowers for Aunt Susan, I waited until all the relatives were upstairs. Then I discreetly informed Uncle Victor that I was ready to help him escape. I imagined that the sheriff and a posse would call upon him the instant Aunt Susan breathed a last prayer. They would, of course, bring a rope.

"If you'll tell me where your pistol is," I confided, "we can shoot our way out of town."

He smiled, as if grateful for my good intention, then resumed his scrutiny of the peach tree.

That night I asked Granny: "What do old men think about when they look off and don't talk?"

"What old men?" she asked shrewdly.

"Lots of old men," I said. "Lots of them just sit and look off at things, the mountains or the trees."

Her reply—a riddle it seemed to me then—stayed on in my mind. "They think of things that will not come again."

Aunt Susan's frail appearance was perhaps the only lie ever associated with her genuinely Christian person. The vitality that had sustained her parents and many of her brothers and sisters was hers as well. Her convalescence was a slow one, but die she would not.

Granny and I went to live on the farm of another sister, Martha, during Aunt Susan's time of recovery. It was a large farm with a sprawling array of buildings bristling with lightning rods. Martha's husband, George Drake, was "an old flame" of Granny's. Uncle George was the most successful member of the vast family. But now he had dropsy and was said to weigh more than four hundred pounds. He looked like a huge twin of the prince who was to become Edward VII of England. His manner was imperial, and the specially built oak chair in which he sat all day, a gray blanket draped across his massive belly and legs, seemed a throne.

George Drake's imperial manner evaporated whenever he was with Granny. It was plain that he admired her and enjoyed her presence. She, however, seemed frigidly distant toward him, and I asked her why she was so reserved.

"One does not call out 'Happy New Year' or the like," she replied, "to a man who has one foot in the grave."

Uncle George familiarly called Granny "Liz," and twitted her about Grandpa's countless dreams. And now I came to a realization of how great was the love she bore the man she had married. It suddenly became plain to me that all her criticisms of Norman Wheeler, the tantalizing remarks that so often sent him stuttering to the cellar, were a sham.

Uncle George's teasing stirred Granny to a fierce defense of her prospector husband. One of her utterances brought about an end to the day's conversation between them. "At any rate," she said, "Norm is not afraid of the steer's mouth."

When we had retired for the night to our own room in the large farmhouse, I inquired as to the meaning of her remark.

"A long time ago," she replied, "George Drake was roping a steer that had gone mad. Then, as he got off his horse to throw and tie the steer, some foam from the animal's mouth fell on George's hand. And ever since that day he has felt sure that he would die of hydrophobia. It's been constantly on his mind for more than twenty-five years. He should know better than to say things about your grandfather to *me*."

On another day, Uncle George mentioned the name of Ed Redding. "You knew, didn't you, Liz, that Ed died a year ago?"

There was a short silence, then Granny replied, "As a married woman, I don't keep track of certain people."

Once again I cross-examined Granny after we had said our evening prayers. She considered my questions for some time. "I've seldom mentioned this," she said at last, "but when I came to Kansas before the Civil War a man named Ed Redding fell in love with me. And so did George Drake."

Delighted by this confidence, I could not help but interrupt, "Did you love them both? And where was Grandpa?"

"Oh, I see," she said reprovingly, "you wouldn't be interested in something that happened so many years ago."

"Please!" I implored. "Tell me. Did they fight over you?"

She turned down the coal-oil lamp wick, then blew out the low flame. "Suppose you go to sleep now, and dream. It's nothing. Just ancient history."

I put my arms about her. I was her great weakness, and I had a villainous knowledge that this was so. One caress from me, and she would cast off the armor which no one else seemed able to break. And besides, I think she longed to speak of her own days of glory.

"Ed Redding was a splendid man," she said. "And George Drake was handsome, as anyone may judge from the tintypes in the album; but he did a terrible thing. He composed a letter to me, copying Ed's hand, and signed Ed's name to it. And the letter made it impossible for me ever to speak or write to Ed again."

"What did the letter say, Granny?"

"You're interrupting again," she warned. "Suffice to say that the letter offended my pride. And it was years afterward that George Drake confessed to me what he had done. And by that time I had married Norm, and poor Ed was in the madhouse."

"On account of you?" I asked.

"Well," she said evasively, "it may be hard to believe now, but I once was considered a rather attractive girl. I had dark auburn hair, as you may have heard. General Lew Wallace once complimented me on my hair. I think that George Drake married Sister Martha because she had auburn hair. But then, mark you, Martha was prettier than I."

"I think you were prettier," I said. "Much prettier."

"Now, now," she said, "that's blarney. Pure blarney. I'll admit that I had rather nice hair, but that was a long time ago." She sighed in the darkness, then whispered, "Now go to sleep."

Aunt Martha and an older sister, Anna, had been the first schoolteachers in Kansas Territory. The capable Martha had borne nine children, and reared seven orphaned ones as well. She was great-hearted, but had stern views as to education and discipline.

"Lizzie," she said to Granny one day, "you simply must not encourage your grandson to miss so much school. What is to become of him? Here he is, poking about, learning nothing when he should be in school."

"We read to each other every night," Granny replied.

"But what else? Nothing. Why, the child only yesterday asked George why the nineteenth century had no nineteens in it, and then insisted stubbornly that it should be called the eighteenth century. George tried to explain the matter, but had to give up."

"I think the lad is right," said Granny.

"You mean to say that the calendar-makers are wrong?"

"Well, Mattie, they have been caught napping at times. Pope Gregory finally corrected Julius Caesar's calendar after fifteen hundred years—a rather long nap. And even now we have a leap-year day sticking out like a sore thumb. Perhaps my grandson one day will give us a calendar that we can depend upon."

"Not until he learns to add two plus two!"

I was entered in the Holton school, and it may be said in all truth that never before in its history had it seen a boy so deficient in arithmetic. Also, I would not, or could not, become proficient in the Spencerian exercise of penmanship.

The teacher complained to Granny: "Your grandson absolutely refuses to use the forearm as a means of restful control."

"I have a son in Denver who writes a copperplate hand," Granny replied. "He doesn't use his forearm. He holds his pen between the first and middle fingers. And, while we are on the subject of forearms, Jehovah wrote with His finger upon the Tablets of Stone on Sinai—*Exodus*, Chapter thirty-one, verse eighteen. And among mortals, I don't think that Raphael painted with his forearm, either."

Aunt Martha was disturbed by my low grades at school. To improve my mind "a little bit," as she put it, she invited Granny and me to attend a lecture given by a visiting doctor of philosophy, the venerable A. S. Dodds, at the Methodist church.

"This is our great chance," Granny said to me, "to astound Aunt Mattie. She doesn't know of our constant reading about Egypt and Persia. And Dr. Dodds is going to speak on this very theme." She winked. "We shall brush up on our facts. Eh?"

The lecture by the elderly scholar was a true delight. He had on view numerous souvenirs of antiquity, among them a part of the winding sheet of Rameses II, and the mummified foot of some unidentified priest of Luxor, and a tempered copper lance that the lecturer said might have been the property of Cambyses, the invader of Egypt. Dr. Dodds, his bald head shining above a selvage of white hair, raised the lance and charged with it along the platform in a portly but dramatic manner.

He paused for wind, then asked, "Does anyone here know who Cambyses was?"

Granny nudged me so solidly that I blurted out, "Yes, sir!" Then, as everyone turned to identify the upstart, I felt unpleasantly dead. Aunt Martha seemed grimly embarrassed, but Granny stood by me. "Tell him!" she coached me in a whisper. "Speak right out, son. You know more about it than he does."

"Well, well, young man," Dr. Dodds was saying, "and who *was* Cambyses?"

"Which one?" I asked. "The father of Cyrus the Great or his son?"

Dr. Dodds twiddled the lance, and I think that Aunt Martha hoped he would hurl it at me. "Cambyses II, young man. Well, who was he, if you *know?*"

"The king of the Medes and Persians," I said with desperate authority.

"Aha! But can you tell us whom he conquered in Egypt?"

"Psammetichus III!" I shouted.

Dr. Dodds had had enough of this. "We shall now proceed with our lecture. I shall tell you of the day when I stood among the ruins of the old Alexandria to see two great obelisks—miscalled 'Cleopatra's Needles'—and of a later day when I saw with my own eyes one of these great monuments rededicated at Central Park. . . ."

At the close of the lecture, Dr. Dodds permitted me to hold the mummified foot as he catechized me on Egyptian history. He shook my hand, then turned to Aunt Martha, obviously taking her to be my nearest ancestor.

"Madam," he said as she squirmed, "you have every reason to be proud of your extraordinary grandson."

On our way home in the surrey, Aunt Martha wouldn't speak to either Granny or me. Inside the farmhouse Granny remarked slyly, "Dr. Dodds doesn't seem to agree with local opinion as to the talents of certain persons."

"Dr. Dodds is an old fool!" Aunt Martha blurted. Then, catching the look of mischief in Granny's eye, Aunt Martha burst out laughing. The sisters put their arms about each other and laughed until they cried.

By this time Aunt Susan was able to sit up to read her Bible. She also found comfort in poems composed by her oldest sister, Lorinda. Her latest poem, actually the last one Lorinda ever was to write, gave solace to Susie:

> *When I shall have come to the brink of the River,*
> *Be silent, loved ones, while I wait for my Guide;*
> *Keep back the vain tears—let not thy lips quiver,*
> *Lest you sadden the spirit that outward doth glide.*

Plans for the revision of Aunt Susan's will were indefinitely postponed. "Besides," said the kindly woman, "what goods and chattels would I have to leave to anyone?"

It was understood that she had reference to Uncle Victor's ruinous wager in 1896 on the outcome of the political campaign of William Jennings Bryan.

One day in November, I received a letter from Mr. Blake. It was a stimulating letter, for he addressed me as if I were a mature person. In regard to my feeling sorry for Uncle Victor, he wrote, "It is a good rule never to sit in judgment on anyone." He recommended that I rely upon my own instincts, adding, "If you have sympathy for your great-uncle, undoubtedly he merits that feeling."

Mr. Blake then asked if I had closely observed the Kansas prairies and how fertile the silty brown loam was. He informed me that much of the deep soil on the western frontal plain had drifted there during the ages from the highlands of Colorado. He wrote also that the pioneers of Kansas were heroic men and women, and had made of their frontier a historic ground. Then he sounded a bugle call that I still can hear:

"Eyes front! You are about to see great things. A new century is less than two months away. Miracles will come to pass. How fortunate that you and I will witness this coming of an age of machines and scientific discovery. I trust that you will be back among us for the great event, to see the new day dawn among the Rockies, in fact, a new daybreak all over the world."

With this letter in my pocket, I felt most important. "Mr. Blake and I are going to see daybreak in the Rockies!" I announced to my teacher. "Will you be there?"

She viewed me with some concern. "No, I shall stay right here. But I am pleased to know that *you* will be *there!*"

10

THE IMPETUOUS CLOCK

GRANDPA was still away at the Empire mining camp when we returned to Denver from Kansas. A letter from him said that Attorney Eldridge had come down with a severe cold.

"He is feeling poorly," Grandpa wrote, "but I have moved him to my own cabin where I can doctor him. The Salter brothers ain't leaving the camp. They have snowshoes and a sledge, in case we got to go to Empire for supplies. So I just think I'll stay on for a spell. The Blakes left a week ago to spend the winter on the Western Slope and put their girls in school. Blake wanted Eldridge to go see a doctor in Georgetown, but my friend don't want to leave the Little Columbine."

Now that I had learned of Mr. Blake's whereabouts, I began a long letter to him. I must have spent a week composing it. I confided several tidbits of information having to do with family affairs. I had no compunctions when writing of such intimate matters to my one correspondent and mentor.

I disclosed, among other things, that Granny and I again were living with Dodie and Frank Fowler in a newly rented house until Grandmother could find a place of her own large enough to accommodate boarders and roomers. I quoted Granny as saying, "This will be a lean Christmas and a lean year. Your Grandfather will see to *that*."

The Fowler house on South Washington Street overlooked a prairie, now snow-covered. There was a big pond about half a mile to the eastward, then known as Smith's Lake. It had a margin of cattail reeds, dank grass, and old cottonwoods. I informed Mr. Blake that the cottonwoods must be fifty years old, a deduction made in the light of his own lecture to me on regional trees. He had pointed out that cottonwoods became rotten in the center at the age of fifty.

I had fished many times in Smith's Lake. There were no gallant trout there, one must admit, but merely a species of runty sunfish. I never had caught any, but it had been an exciting adventure to stray from home or school to meet other boys of my own age.

Ten or twelve shacks lay near by the lake, huts walled and roofed with the metal of tin cans or sealed with tarpaper. Wonderful hermits occupied these shanties. Their stories of a brave past were never to be doubted except by the police.

In one of these hovels there lived a lone woman of incalculable years. She had white hair and a porcelain complexion, and she told fortunes with cards. Cards were not allowed inside our house; they were the Devil's own fan, according to Granny, who depicted Satan waving a gambler's spread of playing cards to keep his fires at high heat.

There was nothing witch-like about old Maggie, the fortune-teller, although a homemade broom of reeds with a willow handle stood in one corner of the tin-walled hut. It was commonly said that Maggie received male callers late at night, men believed to be horse thieves or their like. She also was described as a midwife.

Maggie was soft-spoken and kindly, except when police officers came "looking for gypsies." Chris Krug and I were at Maggie's having our fortunes told free one day. Chris lived across the street from me. His father was a red-whiskered tyrant who beat his son regularly with a teamster's whip. We consulted Maggie to find out, if possible, how soon the hot-tempered old Krug would drop dead. Maggie arranged the cards in a magical circle upon an up-ended crate that served for a table. She called this design "The Wheel of Life."

Maggie was dealing out the last spoke of her wheel when Officer Henry Sellers' high-domed helmet and cowcatcher mustache appeared at the crooked doorway. The policeman gave me a stout whack with his billy club. "Get along home, ye tarrier! You're worrying your grandmother into her grave." Chris darted past the police officer, who shouted after him: "I hope your old man will larrup your backside up around your ears for ye." Then Sellers turned to Maggie. "If I catch ye doing you-know-what, I'll run ye in."

The mild-eyed, porcelain-faced lady now unloosed upon the officer a whole encyclopedia of epithets. His star of authority wobbled on his chest. Then he muttered through his teeth the mysterious word "abortionist!" and went off on other business.

The pond in the prairie to the eastward of Frank Fowler's house now has become Washington Park Lake. There are splendid homes on the site of Maggie's shanty and the huts of the squatters. Hedges and fair lawns landscape the scene. But the mountains that overlook the plain never change, and lads still run away, and policemen send them home again.

In my letter to Mr. Blake, I explained that Frank Fowler had many clever schemes. He intended to set up a factory in which he would make "popcorn crisp." His most recent business venture, the merchandising of a baking preparation, Egg Wonder Powder, had been a failure. Granny said that it turned dough into paving blocks. Also, Frank had been unable to interest a considerable part of the public in his Eureka pants-hangers.

Notwithstanding these reverses, Frank had purchased a fumed-oak piano on the installment plan for my mother. She now was taking vocal lessons from the celebrated Professor Waldemere. He charged her but one dollar a lesson instead of his customary fee of two dollars, "because she was so talented." I went on to explain to Mr. Blake that Dodie was able to pay the dollar because she did her own washing and ironing and that of a neighbor as well.

The Saturday before the Christmas holidays, Granny announced that she and I were going for a streetcar ride. I placed my long letter to Mr. Blake in an old croquet box, where I stored many of my treasures. I used a huge padlock and a chain selected from Grandpa's collection of implements to safeguard my possessions. I fancied that almost anyone might be tempted to make off with such valuable things as the sack of marbles, bits of colored glass, pieces of quartz, shells, tinfoil, a musical top, a mouth organ, an eagle's feather, crayons, kite-twine on a stick, beeswax, fishing tackle, a beanie, some horseshoe nails bent into rings, a Texas steer's horn salvaged from a hat rack, whistles made of willow bark, a defunct stationary engine in miniature, a mason jar half full of stagnant water, a hair from a horse's tail in the fluid. The horsehair was supposed to turn into a serpent if left for six months in the water and in some dark place. . . .

"What rubble!" said Granny. "I think a magpie has made a nest here."

As we set out this Saturday before the Christmas holidays of 1899, Granny confided that we were going to procure a Christmas present for Dodie. "It is a grand tureen made of chinaware."

Granny was carrying a parcel that contained the rust-red wrappers taken from some hundreds of Water White Soap cakes. One might surrender these tokens at the office of the soap company near the stockyards, and choose a premium from among the various kinds of china utensils on display there. Granny had been saving Water White covers for a long time.

I was wearing as galoshes that day strips of burlap sacking held in place by baling wire. Many boys of the neighborhood and of circumstances corresponding to ours had Hooligan puttees such as these; there was no social discredit to be earned by the wearing of them. A boy did not ask himself, "Am I well shod?" but only, "Are my feet dry?"

As we left the streetcar at the end of the line, Granny inquired, "Just why are you writing such a long letter to Mr. Blake?"

"He asked me to keep in touch," I replied.

"Indeed," she said, "and did he, now?"

"Yes, and he wrote me in Holton to keep my 'eyes front' for the new century. Lots of wonderful things are going to happen."

"Yes," she said, "wars, pestilence, troubles. But, mark you, you don't need an Englishman or an old Maggie to tell you what is going to happen. It's all written in the Bible. The Four Horsemen. The prophecies are all there. 'Eyes front,' indeed! Well, John Blake takes a lot upon himself, putting ideas into an American boy's head, such as trout laying eggs, and a lot of other foreign nonsense."

"But trout *do* lay eggs," said I.

We were now at the somewhat ramshackle office of the soap company. The smells from the stockyards and the soap factory filled our frosted nostrils.

"It isn't natural for fish to lay eggs," said Granny. "Fish are created, my boy. Created. Mr. Blake notwithstanding."

On our way up the steps to the office, she remarked, "I'd like very much to read your letter to Mr. Blake."

I was disturbed by this threat to my privacy. I was glad when she turned her attention to the business of the tureen for Dodie. "Stomp your feet," she commanded at the threshold of the office. "We mustn't trail snow inside."

We entered the low frame building to find ourselves surrounded on all sides by chinaware premiums. I never before had seen such a ceramic paradise. There were platters, bowls, trays, gravy boats, cups, saucers . . . well, in after years I was able to stay calm when in the presence of world-famous collections, from Ming to Wedgwood, simply because I had expended all my wonderment that day upon the masterpieces arranged on the counters and shelves of the soap company's office.

Granny herself was stirred by the lavish display. Although she had announced with all sureness that a tureen was her objective, she now seemed to grow uncertain as she stood among the stunning multitude of prizes.

There was but one person other than ourselves in the showroom, a young woman of severe eye and chin. Her muddy-brown hair was drawn back from a wrinkled high forehead and gathered in a "bun." She wore nose glasses, a gold chain attached to one lens and the chain festooned to a clip over her ear. She stood behind a counter scales that had a scoop pan on one side of the balancing mechanism.

"Well," she said, "can I help you, ma'am?"

Granny set down her bundle of soap wrappers beside the scales. A finger to her lip, she turned to examine a dinner service of cream-colored ware decorated with gilt borders and medallion centers with flower and fruit motives.

"I want to make up my mind," Granny said.

"But you came for a tureen," I reminded her.

Granny looked at me reprovingly. "You must learn not to jump at conclusions."

"Take your time," said the young woman. "There are many fine things here, ma'am."

From time to time Granny turned her gaze from the various pieces of chinaware to her bundle of soap wrappers. Finally she came back to her original intention to get a certain tureen with a crinkle-edge cover.

She sighed as she pushed her bundle across the counter. "I believe I'll take this tureen," and she gestured toward her choice as though it were the Holy Grail. "I have six hundred wrappers. I think that is the correct amount, according to your illustrated catalogue."

The young woman untied the bundle but did not count the wrappers. She placed them in the weighing pan. Then she set various counterpoises on the balance pan opposite the scoop, manipulating these brass tellers, rejecting a larger one, then substituting a smaller one as if in a chess game.

Then she looked up to say, "I am afraid that you've miscounted the number of wrappers, ma'am."

"Oh!" said Granny. "You mean there are *more* than six hundred?"

"I mean," and the severe eyes and chin seemed to protrude accusingly, "that you are *short* of the six hundred wrappers."

"But I counted them at least twice over," said Granny. "This is—"

The woman breathed out a short but meaningful puff of doubt from her nostrils. "Perhaps you should have counted them three times."

Irony was not the proper gateway to Granny's good graces. Although a great prize was literally in the balance, she fixed her gray eyes upon the woman, then said with an acidulous serenity peculiarly her own: "And you, young woman, could make yourself somewhat attractive by learning to be more civil."

"I only—" the young woman began, but was interrupted by Granny: "You only were rude. Now count the wrappers. Don't weigh them on that silly contraption. Count them!"

The young woman declined to do this. She struck a schoolteacher's desk bell. The manager appeared in response to the signal. He had a belly like Kris Kringle's, but the upper part of him was alarmingly skinny. As if to carry out this anatomical discord of half-this and half-that, he smiled with only one side of his mouth. The other side was as tight-lipped as a hip pocket, and in the unsmiling side of his mouth he carried a toothpick.

After listening to the problem of the soap wrappers, the man's toothpick moved like a seal's whisker. "Let this lady have the tureen," he ruled. "We'll not quarrel over a slight difference."

"There is no difference," Granny said, "slight or otherwise. I stand by my guns."

The manager himself awarded Granny the tureen with its wonderful lid, then retreated toward the door from which he just recently had come. "And I trust that you will always stand by our fine product."

"No," Granny replied. "Your soap is no better than it should be. In fact, I'm contemplating a change."

The banjo-shaped manager left the room. With an air of victory, Granny watched the young woman wrap the tureen and the lid separately in newspapers. Granny took charge of the bowl part herself, but permitted me to carry the lid. She moved in a queenly way outside the showroom, and I followed after her like a royal page bearing the tureen lid.

The old lady's triumphant mood persisted until my Hooligan puttees caused me to stumble over a culvert near the car line. My bundle fell upon an ice slick. When I lifted the package, a baleful tinkling could be heard.

"Perhaps," Granny said, "you should have kept your 'eyes front' for the culvert instead of for the new century."

After we had reached home with our half-prize, Granny said, "Now may I see what you have been writing to Mr. Blake?"

I unlocked my treasure chest. I voiced no objection to Granny's reading the letter, but I did much thinking. And I wondered then, as I do now, why older persons are not aware of the fact that children do so much concealed thinking.

That evening in the quarters that Granny and I occupied, I found her glowering over my letter to Mr. Blake. She looked up from the scrawled pages. "You must not think of sending such a thing."

"But Mr. Blake's expecting to hear from me," I maintained. "He'll be awfully disappointed."

"He'll survive it," said Granny. Then she got down to cases and let me know that one did not discuss family matters with "an outsider." On this day there was born in my breast a defiance that never has left me, a flaming resistance to censorship of the written word.

I now experienced sudden chills and nausea. Granny suggested that I was having a "tantrum," and I must concede that my record in that respect was not without blemish. The seizure became intensified when she voiced still another opposition to a phrase in my letter concerning Charles Darwin. Mr. Blake had said, "I think it about time for you to read Darwin's *Voyage of the Beagle*."

"What!" Granny now was saying. "Read the works of a learned fool, who claims that man is descended from monkeys?"

She studied my physical contortions, then felt of my forehead. "Good gracious, child! You really *are* ill!"

She sent Frank Fowler for Dr. Calhoun. That practitioner was always the first person to respond to any neighbor's distress, and usually the last to be paid.

The lean and lofty doctor, having arrived in his buggy, brought into the house a cloud of antiseptic odors. The carbolated physician, a slow-talking southerner, had saved me from the wrath of moralists the summer before the one we spent in the mountains. I had come upon a cigar butt left by Uncle Dewey on the edge of a meat block at his store. I went to an outhouse to smoke it. My vision became blurred and my brain a pudding. I staggered up an alley to my house. I was numb everywhere except in the belly, and a mildewed veil settled upon the world.

Dr. Calhoun sniffed my breath, knew I had been smoking, but gallantly protected me by saying, "Mrs. Wheeler, the lad merely has suffered a bilious attack."

And now, in 1899, the trustworthy physician once again peered into my eyes and said, "Too bright," and at my tongue and added, "Strawberry." Then he examined my chest, to find on it the most vividly red sign since the classic advertisement worn by Hester Prynne.

"Scarlet fever," and Dr. Calhoun began to measure out some spirits of niter. "He must be quarantined."

I had looked forward not only to seeing the great new century dawn but to being with my mother during that experience. Now, as on so many occasions, I would be near her, yet once again with a barrier between us.

Granny and I were placed apart from the others, in a third-floor attic bedroom of the Fowler house. I would be compelled to see whatever was seeable of the new century from a dormer window that looked out on a foreground view of Chris Krug's house and a corral in which a young bull was confined. And I could see the yard in which Chris's father regularly beat his son with a teamster's whip. Beyond that yard lay the snow-covered prairie that reached eastward to Smith's Lake. One missed the mountains to the west.

"Now," said Granny in our place of isolation, "you will admit that it is not feasible for you to send your letter to Mr. Blake. The doctor says it might contain germs."

"But you said you never believed in germs. Remember?"

"I said," she fenced, "that I never had *seen* one. Now keep warm."

"Warm!" I exclaimed. "I never was so hot in my life."

The man from the Health Department next day tacked a scarlet-fever card on the front door. The brief but sharp sounds made by his tack hammer beat into my hot head and seemed to say: "No letter to Mr. Blake. No letter to Mr. Blake."

Into the regions of my fever there also penetrated the voice of my mother and the sound of her piano as she accompanied herself in vocal exercises. I dreamed of her as an angel. I thought that my father had come to visit her, and that she was singing for him, and that there never had been a divorce in the family, and that Grandpa had found "wealth for all."

Although my temperature began to recede, Dr. Calhoun informed me that I would have to remain in bed over Christmas. He took the precaution to increase my medication, saying that "Christmas excitement and fever are a bad combination." He shook out a Dover's Powder on my tongue, then said, "You'll try not to become excited about Christmas?"

After I had chased down the powder with some water, I replied, "I'm only excited about the new century."

"Still a little delirious," he whispered to Granny. "But don't worry."

I still felt like Hazy Austin when, two days before Christmas,

Granny said, "Inasmuch as we are marooned in this attic, and you can't write letters to Mr. Blake or sing out all you know to the rest of the world, I've got a treat for you."

"You'll let me sit up at the window and watch Chris Krug play with the bull?"

"No, not yet," she said. "And by the bye, when you get well, you must not tease that bull, either."

The animal to which she referred was just about to enter bullhood. When it was a calf, Chris and I used to let the lively young creature butt us. Now its horns were budding and its sense of humor vanishing. Of late we had been playing in the corral at bullfighting, but we were careful to avoid the charges of the growing beast.

"The surprise I have in store for you," Granny continued, "is just this: I'm going to tell you what everyone is getting for Christmas. But, mark you, it's a great secret."

"What will I get?" I asked.

"Don't be selfish, even in thought," she reproved. "The only thing, other than whisky, that keeps our great country from fulfilling its true destiny is the very question you have asked: 'What do *I* get?'"

"Then what do you get?" I asked, not without mischief.

"I am to receive from Frank and Dodie a new pair of kid gloves and twelve yards of best grade calico at four cents a yard, a real bargain. From Uncle Dewey and Aunt Etta I am getting an order for a pair of Queen Quality shoes, the finest that a dollar and ninety-eight cents can buy."

"And from Grandpa?"

"Dodie has bought in his behalf some black chiffon to retrim my Sunday bonnet, and there will be enough left over for new ties for it." She was silent for a little time, then said, "My husband once bought me a present selected by himself, in person, back in Kansas. A music box that played 'The Last Rose of Summer' and 'Believe Me If All Those Endearing Young Charms.' It was wonderful and sweet. But what do you think happened?

The music box was melted beyond repair by the fire of 1874, the prairie fire that Uncle Victor started. Of all our furniture, we saved only the black-walnut bureau that my parents had brought across the plains. Oh, that Uncle Victor and his grasshoppers, and his fire!"

"I have a present for you," I announced.

"No!" she said somewhat dubiously. "Not really?"

"If someone will only go to Jay Andrews' house and get it."

"We'll have to wait till the quarantine is lifted. Then we can get it, whatever it may be."

I pretended to be casual about a present for someone dear to me. "Jay's father makes handwritten calling cards. And he makes wonderful pictures with his pen; and just because he likes me, he has made a whole dozen calling cards for you, and a dozen for Dodie, and there is a bird drawn in the corner of one card in each dozen."

She embraced me, then began to choke up. "I'm so happy! So happy! I feel just as I did the day Norm brought the little music box home. You have not forgotten me."

I was quick to take advantage of her emotional condition. "Now I've told you what I'm giving you," I said with all cunning. "What am *I* getting for Christmas?"

She straightened, sniffled, then exclaimed, "Oh, no you don't!" Then she warned me: "You'll have to get up very early in the morning to catch your old grandmother napping."

She now proceeded to describe the remarkable present that Frank Fowler had bought for Dodie. It was a clock of black marble with ormolu mountings. It needed winding only every thirtieth day. There were two vase-like sidepieces of bronze that belonged to the clock, a notable group for anyone's mantelshelf. This ensemble lay hidden in a cupboard, although Dodie had peeked at it frequently.

"The only trouble with the clock," Granny said, "is that the gong cannot be depended upon. Frank had the man at the pawnshop overhaul the bell spring, and Frank himself has been tinkering with it on the sly, for he can't get a regular clock man into the house, what with the quarantine. But the magnificent present will delight Dodie, gong or no gong."

There would be toys for Jack and Normadine of course. Then Granny pretended to recollect something. "Oh, yes! Perhaps you would like to know what *you* are to receive?"

My temperature must have risen two degrees at this long-delayed question. "A pony?"

"Hardly that," she replied. "We shall have to wait for certain eventualities before we speak of ponies. Guess again."

"*The Voyage of the Beagle?*"

Her mouth took on tight little wrinkles like the reeding on the edge of a silver dollar. "A remark such as that makes one almost believe that certain persons *are* descended from monkeys after all."

"Then what *do* I get?"

"Some new marbles; ten of them in all."

"Agates?"

"I know nothing of marbles. These seem to be transparent, with pink and green cores."

"Glassies!" I cried out. "That's wonderful!"

"But you must never play 'for keeps,' as you call it; for that is gambling."

"What else do I get?"

"Mr. Blake has sent you a book called *Chatterbox.*"

"I knew he would keep in touch with me!" I shouted. "What is it like?"

"A great deal like Mr. Blake," she replied. "Full of a lot of talk and puzzles and such. It is of good size, has pasteboard covers with a colored picture on the front, and it is thoroughly English."

"You've read it!" I said accusingly.

"Just glanced through it."

"Then let's read it right now!"

"That would be unfair to the spirit of Christmas."

Footsteps now sounded on the attic stair. There was a clinking of dishes, and then a knock, and my mother's voice: "Your lunch tray is ready, Mother. And there's a letter from Pa."

"Dodie, dear," Granny said against the closed door, "would you mind sitting down at your piano and singing 'If All Those Endearing Young Charms'?"

"Not at all, Mother. Just as soon as I get through feeding the children."

Granny waited until Dodie's footsteps indicated that she was beyond our region of contamination. Then the old lady opened the door and brought the tray of food inside the room.

She set my milk and crackers before me, then opened the letter, and read it to herself while neglecting her own lunch. "Your grandfather thanks us for the Christmas turkey and the groceries we shipped to Empire," she said. Then she continued in a grave tone: "They took Mr. Eldridge to Empire finally. Grandpa and one of the Salter brothers went on snowshoes to mark the trail. The other brother drove the sledge, with Eldridge lying on it, all wrapped up in blankets and fur robes. And your grandfather writes that it took all day and into the night for the trip over the snowbound trail, and that Eldridge said, 'Wheeler, I think I am about to get a change of venue.'"

"What's a change of venue, Granny?"

"For Mr. Eldridge, poor lost soul, it means that he now is in another world. And may God forgive him for his follies here on earth."

My mother now could be heard singing the requested song. The old lady restored the letter to its envelope in the manner of a general sheathing a sword after the battle is done. Then she put aside her sandwich, but sipped her tea as she looked out of the dormer window. Her eyes seemed occupied with visions of remembrance. The noonday light played upon the silver of the hair that General Lew Wallace once had praised.

Believe me, if all those endearing young charms. . . . Let thy loveliness fade as it will. . . .

By Christmas Eve Frank Fowler was reported to have repaired the gong of the black marble clock. And on Christmas morning, Granny left the attic doorway part way open for us to hear the lively beating of the leathered hammer on the musical coil when my mother's great present would be "unveiled."

There were early-morning shouts of "Merry Christmas!" up and down the two flights of stairs between the attic and the groundfloor hallway. Dodie called up to announce that Frank had given her a crimson velvet waist, "too beautiful to describe."

"Let us see it!" Granny cried down from our aerie. She then said as though to herself, "That's funny, I hadn't heard of the waist."

"But how can I show it to you?" asked Dodie. "I'd have to come too near the open door."

"Then go outside the house," Granny called, "and stand on a clear space on the front walk. We'll look at your new waist from the window."

Although Dr. Calhoun had insisted that I remain in bed until after Christmas Day, Granny permitted me to go, well-blanketed, to the dormer window "for just a second or two."

We looked out to see my mother, her crimson waist making her seem like some glad flame against the snow. She was waving at us and blowing kisses. I wanted to open the window, but Granny would not permit it. I sent my breath against the pane to free it of frost traceries, and I rubbed a circle on the glass the better to see my gay mother.

The lively scene was interrupted. Chris Krug came screaming from around the corner of his house. His red-bearded father was pursuing him with the blacksnake whip. Chris stumbled in the front yard, and his father began to whiplash him.

I saw my mother turn at Chris's first outcries. She gathered her skirt and was starting across the street, twice sinking almost to her knees in the snowdrifts. She opened the gate and entered the yard. Then, as Frank Fowler appeared in our view to cross the street, I saw Dodie seize the stock of Krug's black whip and stand between the man and the boy. Krug wrested the whip stock from Dodie's small hand, then he raised the lash as if to strike her.

I cried out with rage as I saw this. I shouted something, I knew not what at the time. Then Frank Fowler, by no means as powerful as Krug but an excellent boxer, addressed a neat uppercut to the man's whiskers. The blow did not fell Krug.

Neighbors now intervened; and finally Patrolman Sellers arrived, relieved Krug of the whip, but refused to "arrest anyone on Christmas Day."

I did not leave the window until Dodie had returned to the house and Frank called up to us that all was well. As Granny put me into bed she admonished, "Under no circumstances are you ever again to say or even think what you said at the window." I did not reply, and she continued, "You said you would kill Mr. Krug when you got well. Now isn't that exactly what you said?"

"That's what I mean to do!"

She was deeply shocked. "We must ask God to forgive you. And on Christmas Day! The birthday of the Prince of Peace, who taught forgiveness. I am sad."

That night, after we had read from *Chatterbox*, Granny closed the book. "Now we'll say our prayers. And I want you to promise God that you have forgiven Mr. Krug."

"If I do," I challenged, "will you say in your prayer that you forgive Charlie Devlan?"

She seemed dreadfully hurt, and I at once repented having said what I had. Then she asked, "What in the world made you think of Charlie Devlan?"

"I don't know," I said. "I think of him lots of times, and I think that he wouldn't ever beat me with a whip. And I'm sorry that you don't like my father, and I'm sorry I haven't a father."

"But you have a Father in Heaven," she replied. "We all have a Father in Heaven."

"But I want one here."

She seemed to come to a decision. "I shall say my prayers to-night, and you may listen, for I also must ask God for for-giveness."

Her prayer was somewhat long, as I remember it, and I was anxious to get back to the business of looking at my new marbles before the gaslight was turned out. I recall one thing distinctly: the old lady talked freely but reverently to God, and toward the close of the prayer she said: "Help me, Lord, never to think or say anything against this child's father."

Dr. Calhoun called two days after Christmas to present me with an ointment-box filled with carbolated salve. My skin was be-ginning to itch from the fever's aftermath. I itched inside as well, because of the disadvantage of being pent up in the attic when a new century was just over the hills.

I now recalled to mind that a century plant stood in a brown-glazed jardiniere at the house of a neighbor, old Widow Tuttle. Mrs. Tuttle lived on some sort of pension, and spent all day in a rocking chair near her century plant. She smoked a broken-stem clay pipe, the bowl of which was as dark as her moods.

"Will Widow Tuttle's century plant bloom on New Year's Day?" I asked.

"Nothing ever blossomed within a mile of that pipe-smoking old hussy," was the reply. "Even her husband withered during their first year."

We did a good deal of night-reading while awaiting the com-ing of the new century. My dear old bedfellow would grow progressively weary as she held a book. Her spectacles were a perfect barometer of her state of fatigue. The sleepier she be-came, the farther down her nose the spectacles would travel. I watched these descending glasses, and when they reached the tip of her nose, I would prod Granny. Then she would awaken with a little exclamation, adjust the spectacles, find the place in the book or sometimes repeat a paragraph or so, and continue reading until the glasses once again commenced to slide and her voice dissolve into the dronings of sleepy martyrdom. Then, when even my elbow failed to arouse her for perhaps the sixth time, I would take from her lovely hands the book, lift the spectacles from the tip of her nose, kiss her forehead, and turn out the gaslight.

Eventually I was permitted to rise from bed to play with my new marbles on the hook rug. My skin was so permeated by then with Dr. Calhoun's carbolated ointment, my hands so oily, that my technique in shooting the glassies became deficient. And besides, indoor practice of this sort never is quite satisfactory. Marbles roll too slowly on a rug, and then too rapidly on the floor boards beyond it. They are forever going into corners or under the bed or the chairs.

To my pleased amazement, Granny became interested in shooting the marbles. Notwithstanding the rheumatism in her knees, she got down beside me on the rug and began to practice. She grimaced when she missed a shot, and chuckled when she hit a target.

Considering that she now was nearing sixty years and was a woman, her talent for migs seemed remarkable. She insisted, however, upon using the unorthodox method of holding a shooter between the ball of her forefinger and the nail of the thumb. This novice's position had a name accorded it by derisive male experts, who described it with a short Anglo-Saxon word that is seldom seen in print except in the novels of some of our great realists. The marble-players' epithet, the forbidden term, was followed by a most proper word, knuckle.

Naturally, I did not advise Granny concerning the kind of knuckling she was doing. I attempted, however, to prevail upon her to hold the marble against the thumb knuckle instead of against the thumbnail, for the sake of speed, accuracy, spin, and other controls.

But the purposeful old pioneer said, "No, son, I think I can do it better my own way." And she really shot quite well. She enjoyed learning the idiom of the game, such as "vent," "going fat," and "taw."

We played round-ring, using the center ellipse of the hook rug for the boundary. We also played big-ring, with the whole rug as the arena. And I informed her that there were many other kinds of marble games, square-ring or Hoboken, and that we had a rhyme, "Play Hoboken, go home broken."

"You must never play Hoboken then," she said. "It is gambling when you play for keeps."

The gong on Dodie's clock suddenly ceased functioning the day before New Year's. Then that night, as I stayed awake for the midnight miracle of the century's arrival, the gong quite unaccountably came to life ten minutes before twelve o'clock. The clock suddenly began to strike.

It not only struck, but it kept right on striking. Frank Fowler, according to word shouted up to us, was trying vainly to shut off the mechanism. But the clock, or so I believed, was striking a hundred notes of requiem for the death of an old monarch.

"That clock!" Granny said. "It's gone completely daft. Can't even wait for the New Year."

"It's striking all the years of the old century," I said. "It's the first of the miracles that will happen in the new one."

"A miracle if Frank Fowler doesn't get angry and hit the clock with one of those bronze vases."

The clock kept right on chiming until overwhelmed by a greater din from all the city's 133,000 witnesses to the birth of the century. Factory whistles blew. Men went outside their homes to fire their six-shooters. Bells were rung in the church towers. Neighbors beat upon dishpans and boiler lids with pieces of kindling wood.

Long after the clock gong as well as the spirits of the neighbors had run down, I fell asleep. The next morning when I awakened, all that I could see of the first day of the new century was framed by the dormer window. Instead of any blinding miracles, the morning outside my high cell seemed particularly calm. Calm, that is, until Mr. Krug came out-of-doors with a pan of grain to feed his chickens and to look after the young bull in the corral.

The pan of grain slipped from his hands to a snowbank, but stayed right side up. Little of the grain was lost. The man leaned over to recover the feed pan, and then something happened in one power-packed moment.

The bullock, vapor spurting from its nostrils, charged upon the bent-over Mr. Krug. The pan sailed away like a discus with a tail of corn. Mr. Krug lay almost buried, head down, in the drift. The bullock was preparing to gore him with short horns, but Chris came to his father's assistance. The boy waved a gunny sack to draw the attention of the animal away from the imperiled teamster. When Krug was free of the drift, his red beard had become white with snow. His bushy red hair was white, as if sudden tragedy had bleached it.

Chris kept the bull's attention diverted until Mr. Krug managed to limp out of the corral. Then the son rejoined his father, and the man leaned upon the boy for support as they went to the house. We saw Mr. Krug pat Chris on the back, the only time the boy ever was known to have received from his parent anything lighter than a blow.

"You see?" Granny said of the whole incident, "The Lord knew what he was saying when he said: 'Vengeance belongeth unto me. . . .'"

11

THE MULBERRY TREE

SOON after the attic convalescence, Granny and I returned to our old neighborhood in West Denver. Grandpa had come home from the hills "with a touch of pleurisy" and a chunk of quartz that Mr. Eldridge had left him in his will. This beautiful specimen weighed perhaps fifteen pounds; it had rounded, cloudy crystals and mica scales, and was said to contain gold. Grandpa stowed it carefully in an army blouse among his basement treasures.

A mulberry tree, leafless except for a few ragtags from last autumn, stood in the backyard of the house to which we had come. Once again I could hear the anvil and sledge hammer of blacksmith Bergen, and on Sundays the bells of St. Joseph's Roman Catholic Church.

The first boarder to appear at the gray house in the gray month of February 1900 was Joe Shane. The sandy-complexioned salesman was "waiting until a misunderstanding died down" before going on the road again.

During the New Year celebration—a new century celebration it was—in Hastings, Nebraska, Mr. Shane lost both his wallet and his railroad pass. Stranded north of the Republican River, Mr.

Shane became acquainted with a troupe of itinerant actors. These artists were members of a languished *Uncle Tom's Cabin* company. Their manager and two veteran bloodhounds had escaped the sheriff, but Little Eva and the others stayed behind.

The merchants of Hastings declined to finance Mr. Shane beyond the first week. The marooned drummer sent appeals to his lodge brothers, the Eagles, as well as to the Travelers' Protective Association, in Denver. During one of his calls at the post-office Mr. Shane and Little Eva became friends.

Mr. Shane had been "in wholesale groceries," as the saying was. He kept two large sample cases packed with specimens of his wares in his hotel room. Little Eva, a young woman of extensive appetite, prevailed upon Shane to open his firm's various tins of sardines, peas, tomatoes, and succotash. The salesman and the actress thus avoided malnutrition; but Mr. Shane lost his position because of a betrayal of trust.

Now back in Denver, Shane confided to Uncle Dewey: "When the last crumb of my stock was consumed, that chippy flew the coop with a hypnotist who'd played the Opera House for a one-night stand."

The second boarder at Granny's table was Dr. Oswald A. Parr. He was brought to our house and vouched for by Grandpa himself, one of the doctor's "special patients." The mannerly newcomer wore side whiskers like Chester A. Arthur's, and was said to be a man of means.

Dr. Parr was introducing to the public an evil-smelling preparation, Magico-Sulpho. He offered this cure-all at a special price of twenty-five cents. Whenever the contents of a phial was spilled into a hot-water bath, a fuming inferno was liberated. The rotten-egg vapors reached all the rooms of the house, and the portieres and sofa pillows captured and then slowly released the singularly hideous effluvium.

Dr. Parr set out after breakfast each morning with a brown Gladstone bag stocked with Magico-Sulpho bottles. He seldom partook of a midday meal at our table except on Sunday. Not-

withstanding this loss of six repasts each week, Dr. Parr paid
Granny her full fee of three dollars a week, and without quibbling. The doctor's generosity, as well as the fact that he neither
smoked nor drank, modified Granny's first opinion of him:
"Here's another fake unearthed by your Grandpa."

Dr. Parr stood six feet four inches, "about the size and disposition of George Washington," as he described himself. He
wore chocolate-brown suits, brown scarves, a brown derby hat,
and square-toe tan boots. He also had a sepian innocence of eye
and a manner that charmed almost everyone. Even the new pastor,
the Reverend Collins, was impressed by Dr. Parr. The man in
brown not only gave the minister a month's supply of Magico-
Sulpho, but also conversed with him on the Holy Land and discussed matters of art, particularly etchings and engravings.

Whenever I was subjected to a bath in a wooden washtub
charged with Magico-Sulpho, and as I began to suffocate in
the foul fog, Dr. Parr would say, "But think how healthy you
will be, my boy, fifty years from now; and all because of one
small discomfort at the present moment. Health is wealth. That's
Dr. Parr's golden rule."

A middle-aged couple, the Raffertys, also came to live at our
house. The Raffertys were aloof of manner, as if tarrying among
peasants. They were chronic complainers, slow payers, and refused to accept from Dr. Parr a vial of Magico-Sulpho.

The fifth paying member at our table was Bostwick, a tuberculous glass blower. He slept most of the day and worked most
of the night at a glassworks. Bostwick was a thin, rangy fellow.
He drank a great deal, it was said, but partook of his whisky
when away from Granny's household. Bostwick told me that
he had played end for the University of Michigan; he exhibited
a lump on a mended collarbone to substantiate this claim. Indeed,
he was a remarkable punter, even when kicking the small-size
football Uncle Dewey had given me for my tenth birthday. And
his ability to inflate the football bladder without the aid of a
bicycle pump was that of a wind-blowing artist.

The glass blower always seemed a little sad, as if his life had been spent in gloomy songs and dances. He first appeared at our house with a Mexican hairless dog under one arm and a paper-wrapped object under the other. He was persuaded to rid the premises of both the dog and the package before Granny would permit him to become her paying guest. He went off with his naked dog to quarter it at the glassworks. As for the parcel, it had quite another fate.

That paper-wrapped object, as Granny soon ascertained, was an urn in which the ashes of Bostwick's late wife reposed. Bostwick seemed deeply attached to this memento, but agreed to take it elsewhere. He went downtown with the urn, got drunk, lost the funeral vase, then afterward spent his days off among the saloons trying to locate it. Eventually he suffered a pulmonary hemorrhage, either from blowing bottles or sucking at them. He died at the glassworks.

His last words, as reported by a fellow glass blower, were: "Put my ashes along with my wife's—if you can find the urn— and give the dog to the big-eared kid."

"Indeed we'll not have such a nasty thing as *that* in our house!" Granny exclaimed. "You already have a poll parrot. Isn't that enough?" But she relented, and the Mexican hairless dog became mine. His name was Maximilian.

The thick-witted Raffertys pretended to find comic implications in Maximilian's dark nudity, a beggarly character in his bat-like ears and rat's tail, where meager fringes of gray hair accentuated his general baldness. But I recognized Max's real dignity. He had the grand manner; he carried a bone as though it were a scepter, and his slightly protruding underjaw gave him a Hapsburg lip. He was regally proficient at intrigue. Even his amours strengthened a suggestion that Maximilian somehow was a descendant of Guntram the Rich, or John the Parricide.

Max was ill-armored against attack by fur-bearing rivals. Fore-most among his hecklers was a huge mongrel, Curly, a dog belonging to Mr. Bond, the feed-and-grain merchant. But Max

tried his best to avoid common brawls. He adhered to the Hapsburg adage: "Let others wage war; do you, Austria, marry."

Max, like his late master the glass blower, slept most of the
day, then went out at night. Soon an incredible tribe of puppies
began to appear all over the West Side. Some of them wore lion's
manes and had the bodies of skinned minks. Others looked like
gargoyles. Still others were equipped with shaggy leggings, like
the chaps of cowboys, or had Capuchin tonsures.

Maximilian wore a complacent smirk as he dreamed beside the
base-burner stove on the cool days of early spring. On Sundays,
he displayed a deep interest in the bells of St. Joseph's. He would
listen attentively, his proud head lowered a trifle, as if he had
been brought up to respect good Catholic chimes.

Although he usually was worsted in battle, Max eventually won
a victory over Curly. Mr. Bond's huge dog was well known for
a somewhat amazing eccentricity. He would retrieve tin cans
flattened by the iron-tired wheels of passing teamsters' wagons,
and carry one of these rusty treasures edgewise between his jaws.
The tin-can fetishist would go for hours with such a prize wedged
behind his back teeth. Sometimes he would suffer a kind of
lockjaw, and then it became necessary for Mr. Bond or other
Samaritans to wrest the tin from Curly's mouth.

Curly gave Max a sound drubbing one day in April. My dog's
wounds were not severe enough, however, to cause him to cancel
the next evening's social engagement, a royal call upon a Dalmatian bitch, the mascot of the Third Avenue fire house. Max
was setting out at sundown, for he was a bit impatient this evening, and could not wait for a darker hour. Then suddenly Curly
crossed the path of yesterday's loser.

There was a flat tin can in Curly's mouth, a rusty wedge that
may have been there for several hours; and it muted Curly's
growls. Taking advantage of Curly's lockjaw, the crafty Max
gave the bully such a nipping that he ran into the feed-and-grain
store, his tail between his legs. He never again attacked a Hapsburg.

My parrot, Molly, was not afraid of Maximilian; nor did she have the good manners to let him sleep in kingly serenity. She would suddenly cry out like a revolutionist. Max would awaken with a start, rise, look about apprehensively as if for an assassin, twitch his lip, turn around three times, and then lie down again. He kept one eye open until peace was restored to the realm.

The parrot had been given me by Uncle Dewey, who had procured her from a source unknown to Granny. Dewey Wheeler now was operating a meat market and grocery store in partnership with his brother-in-law, Herman McCready. Herman had come from the Klondike, where he had found a small fortune among the gold-bearing gravels of Bonanza Creek. The store, called The Grand National Market, was situated among the pawnshops and wineries of Larimer Street, the alleyway of which paralleled the red-light district of Market Street.

Many patrons of The Grand National were habitués of the houses of ill-fame; they ate the best food and paid the best prices without hesitation. A season of misfortune, however, came upon one of the women customers of the Grand National, French Marguerite. Her lover deserted both the woman and her parrot. Then a series of health accidents interfered with French Marguerite's practice, and her clients left her. Uncle Dewey, whose heart was large and warm, did not press Marguerite for the payment of her grocery bill.

One day the police ambulance arrived at Marguerite's door, upon which there was painted her name, and above it, like a heraldic crest, a faded red heart. On the way to the County Hospital, Police Surgeon McGillivray put aside his stomach pump, then called out to the ambulance driver: "We'll go on to the morgue instead."

The parrot was left to Uncle Dewey. He had a small aviary and zoo in the back of his store, where the more timid "girls" did their shopping so as not to be seen by critics. There one could see among other things a pair of owls, a pet goose, a bull terrier named Prince, and a lethargic alligator five and one-half feet long, a reptile confined to a shallow tank fenced in by chicken wire.

Uncle Dewey decided to take the parrot and the bull terrier to his home. Molly became jealous of Dewey's baby daughter. The bird not only began to sulk when with Uncle Dewey, but she bit Aunt Etta's nose as that lovely lady leaned over a pan of gingerbread on the kitchen table.

"You darned fool!" cried Aunt Etta, holding an apron to her pretty nose. "You darned old fool, you!"

"Come on in, kid!" screamed the bird. "Don't forget your hat, dearie!"

It was a great day for me when Uncle Dewey placed Molly in my keeping. Now I had a pet that could talk to me and, almost as important, I could confide in her. She called me "Pretty boy," a slight overstatement, but she seemed so sincere whenever she uttered it.

Molly would sit upon my shoulder even when I bicycled. Then she would spread her wings, cry out in what seemed to be a foreign language, then hook her upper mandible to my collar and hold onto my shoulder with claws so needle-sharp as to necessitate an occasional manicure. To snip the needle points of a parrot's eight toes is a task more arduous than shoeing a wild horse.

Granny would listen to Molly's glad cries of "Pretty boy!" "Come in, kid," and the foreign phrases. Then the old lady would say to Dewey, "Now where on earth did you get such a thing? And what is this gibberish she is spouting?"

"The bird was raised in a convent, Mother," her son would reply. "Belonged to one of the schoolgirls."

Molly detested Granny. The old lady had tried to subdue the parrot with a washrag, and then with a broom, the first day the bird came into my possession. The feud between my two admirers was a lasting one. Molly also did not like Mrs. Rafferty. The woman boarder listened shrewdly to the bird's alien whoopings, then intimated that Molly was cursing in the French idiom.

The bird was fond of Dr. Parr, although the vapors of the Saturday night baths caused her to sing in a strangled manner.

Joe Shane, the traveling salesman, upon first seeing and hearing Molly at our house, appeared startled and embarrassed. An unexplained, nostalgic glint came into his eye. He smoothed down his mustache, got out a gold-handled toothquill, then sighed, as if recalling a barbecue or a convention of the Fraternal Order of Eagles.

"Nice bird," he said eventually. "Yes, sir. A mighty nice bird. They like fruit."

Mr. and Mrs. Rafferty voiced an ultimatum one day, saying to Granny that the parrot, as well as Dr. Parr and his evil-smelling essences, must leave the house; otherwise they themselves would go. Granny already had lost one paying guest, Bostwick, by an act of God. It was a melancholy prospect indeed to be threatened with another lessening of her income. But she replied to the Raffertys' threat: "I cannot say that I myself relish these medicinal stenches. Nor am I overfond of the parrot. But no one ever has ordered me about in my own house, mark you, and no one ever will."

The Raffertys left our establishment. Their noses upturned, they drove off with their trunks stowed behind them in Mr. Holford's express wagon. And Molly called out to them as if wishing them the opposite of bon voyage.

When the first mulberries were ripe in summer, I would climb high in the tree. As I sat aloft on peach-crate saddles nailed to the crotches of the tree, I could see and hear much that occurred in neighboring backyards. Each sight, each sound, seemed a new experience, happening for the first time to anyone, anywhere.

And high in the sky each Saturday and Sunday afternoon, one might see Ivy Baldwin's balloon. It floated far overhead, having come from Elitch's Gardens. The figure of Ivy Baldwin seemed toy-small as the celebrated daredevil hung by his toes from a trapeze. Then the balloon would sag and smoke would pour from its funnel, and below it a parachute would blossom, with the toy figure clinging to the shrouds.

There were miracles everywhere. The shadow of the mulberry tree was a rug of enchantment. Within the slow-wheeling shade, deep in siesta, Maximilian lay indifferent to the flies that skirmished like busy lawyers about his flanks.

Molly sat upon my shoulder, or else got down to climb among the branches of the wonderful tree. She sang in a bagpipe tone, and gathered mulberries. She would indulge in gymnastics, and hang head down from the lower branches to perplex the occupants of a poultry pen next door. Her lewd crowings made the hens cackle apprehensively. The squire-like Buff Cochin and Leghorn cocks did not know just what to do to offset the calls of the green and yellow Jezebel. Molly's finery, her worldly air, her masculine imitations, bewildered the virtuous and provincial hens and caused them to molt before their season.

The skies ordinarily were clear in this Rocky Mountain June, but an occasional haze obscured the yards and distorted the small houses. Then I would feel that the magic tree had taken wing. I pretended that I was not of this world. And I felt that somehow I might fly off toward Mt. Evans, there to pay a call upon my father. I thought of him as being the Count of Monte-Cristo, waiting at the château; and I felt that he would escape at the right time to settle old scores.

Sometimes, as I sat in the tree on a hazy day, an inexplicable terror seized me. A confusion of faculties made me feel uncertain as to which was the reality: the life to be seen all about me or the dream. These speculations plunged me into a vortex, nebulous and vast. Then I would return almost breathlessly from the make-believe world, thinking to myself, "Maybe I'd better not go there again."

The small winds stirred away the haze. Then the cosmos of yards, ashpits, and hen coops once more would seem actual enough. Molly, her food pouch fat with mulberries, her beak stained a Tyrian purple, would come waddling along a branch toward me. She propelled her bill in wheelbarrow fashion along the bough, and sometimes she brought me a mulberry. Her head cocked like a confessor's, she would inspect me with one eye, the iris of it contracting until the eye became a bead of fire. She watched over me as if I were her lover, or a dearest child, and she cooed dove-like into my ear.

I sometimes looked down through the swaying patterns of the leaves to glimpse my grandmother laboring all day for the boarders and roomers. There were baking days, cleaning days, and washdays. Strong, starched, and pious, she walked along the clay lanes of the lettuce beds and beneath the laundry lines. A wicker basket, heavy with newly wrung garments, seemed no burden at all for this woman. Weathered clothespins protruded from her mouth like the pipes of Pan. As purposeful as an admiral, she unfurled the Monday wash on the hempen lanyards.

If water chanced to drip on Maximilian's hide, he would rise like an affronted Moor, to glance with cynical reproach at Grandmother. His bar association of flies following after him, Maximilian would retire to the lee of the ashpit, a small Vesuvius which fumed sourly and long.

Noises and tumults shook the air on these summer days. There were the cries of the ragman and the clangors of his rusty cow bell strung on bailing wire between the hame knobs of the horse's collar. Next there sounded, ominous and loud, the pistol-crack salute of a whip in the hand of Doyle, the obese ash-hauler. That grayest of dusty men laid his blacksnake lash athwart the rumps of his plodding mares. He called down the curses of Adam, Noah, Jacob, and Abraham on the beasts. He threatened them with swift excommunication from all churches, including the Mohammedan, if they did not stir their cannon bones.

Then suddenly the explosions of Doyle's goad ceased. He would leave off uttering his oaths, and dislodge his dropsical hips from the buckboard seat. His belly was so big that he could not see the hub step. He would sag like Ivy Baldwin's balloon until he found a footing.

I never saw another man who looked so like his own trade. When Doyle was at work, it seemed as if one ashpit were visiting another.

After Doyle had gone, the Italian vegetable peddler would appear in the alley. The smell of onions, apples, and parsley came with him. He cried his wares as if singing an accelerated Gregorian chant. His scale pans rattled like cymbals. His horse was prodigiously gassy.

There were also to be heard the glad cries of children playing Duck-on-the-Rock, the ringing of farrier Bergen's sledge and anvil, the trilling of the loose-toothed postman's whistle, the asthmatic chugging of "Uncle Sam," a small locomotive of the Circle Railroad that joined Fort Logan and the city, and occasionally the swift commotion as a bar fly was being propelled from the backdoor of McGrath's saloon.

But the most authoritative, the most commanding sound of all was the beating of the alarm bell at the Third Avenue fire house. After the first, swift-carrying reverberations, there would be a tornado of hooves as massive horses charged from their stalls to stand beneath the descending harness racks. And then, with a brave, outward swing of high doors, as reflections of the sun bombarded the polished accouterments and during a crescendo of brass bells, the wagons catapulted into the street. The Dalmatian bitch and Uncle Dewey's dog Prince ran close to the horses' heels, barking joyously.

What enviable good fortune to be high in a mulberry tree to witness this excellent charge of the fire brigade! To see the sleek red sides of the hook-and-ladder, its helmsman perched at the tiller, aft, his body wrenching and straining at the wheel! The cream-colored hose cart, its burnished nozzles and chemical tanks flashing. Then, mightiest of all, the steamer, drawn by three valiant horses hitched abreast.

Deputy Chief Moses, his blond mustaches flying like banners, assumed the place of honor in this swift cavalcade. His voice rose in orders. His cap was grimly set on his head. His hands in the holdback loops of the reins, he would begin to sway like an oarsman to regulate the lope of his bay Hambletonian.

Even Maximilian, usually indifferent to the busier phases of northern culture, would rise from his siesta when the fire bells pealed. He would sniff, cock a fringed ear, and reply in a vibrating tenor to the barkings of Prince and the Dalmatian mascot. Molly would bridle, begin to shout and sing, and crane her neck until she looked like St. Patrick's own swan.

Then the bells became far-off sounds, liquid echoes, dying. And when one turned an eye back to the world-in-little of alleys, streets, and yards, the scene at hand seemed part of an anticlimax.

One evening in mid-July, Dr. Parr and his Gladstone bag did not return to the house. Granny placed the doctor's supper in the oven to keep it warm, but the boarder did not come home. At about nine o'clock, there was a ringing of the door gong. Two men were outside on the front porch. Officer Henry Sellers was one of them.

"Come inside," said Granny with some concern. Then Grandpa joined the group in the hallway.

Officer Sellers waved me aside. "Run along, ye tarrier. This doesn't concern ye this time."

As the group went to the parlor, I heard Officer Seller's voice: "Mr. and Mrs. Wheeler, this is Mr. Belcher of the United States Secret Service."

"What's it about, Henry?" Grandpa inquired. "Secret Service, did you say?"

"It's about one of your boarders," said Mr. Belcher. Then he asked, "Does a man named Perry, or Pelham, or Dickinson, or Parr board and room with you people?"

"Dr. Parr," I heard my grandfather stuttering, "is a fine citizen, and a man of money."

"Man of money is right!" blurted Sellers. "Show them what ye got, Mr. Belcher."

I peered past the portieres to see my grandparents examining some papers. "Take a look at these pictures," Mr. Belcher was saying to his worried hosts. "Ever seen him?"

Grandpa looked up from the papers to ask Granny, "What do you think, Lizzie?"

Granny turned to Mr. Belcher. "I am not in the habit of betraying people."

"I know it's the same man," Officer Sellers was saying. "I've seen him go in and out of here."

Granny turned to him: "Then why do you ask me these questions?"

Mr. Belcher ruffled the papers. "Because, Mrs. Wheeler, this man's a criminal. These pictures don't have side whiskers, I'll admit; but this man's a notorious counterfeiter. Been in lots of prisons. This so-called Dr. Parr has grown a fancy beard, and he has copper plates hid somewhere. He's been passing no-good five-dollar bills for the last two months."

"Copper plates?" Granny inquired. "Come to think of it, Dr. Parr does seem to be a connoisseur of engravings."

Granny reluctantly permitted Mr. Belcher to search Dr. Parr's room without a warrant and to remain on the premises in the event of the boarder's return. The secret service operative waited there until a late hour. When I attempted to obtain his views on Jesse James and other heroes of mine, he was noncommittal. He finally dozed off in Granny's rocking chair.

We retired to our room, and when Granny fell asleep, I got carefully out of bed, found some matches, then went to Dr. Parr's room to see for myself if great heaps of money had been overlooked by Mr. Belcher. I was about to strike a match to light the gas jet when the door suddenly opened. The unlighted match fell from my hands. The silhouette of Mr. Belcher called from the doorway: "You're covered, Parr! Don't make a move!"

"Hey!" I cried out, thinking at once of Aunt Susan's fate. "Hey! It's me!"

Mr. Belcher disgustedly lighted a match, saw for himself that I had no Chester A. Arthur side whiskers, then said, "Oh, hell!"

There were no more Magico-Sulpho baths at our house. And I never knew what became of Dr. Parr. Perhaps he went into politics.

Joe Shane again left for the road, this time "in textiles," and now we had lost all our boarders. Then it came time for Grandpa to do certain assessment work on his Red Mountain claim, or else lose title to it.

On the Saturday morning when Grandpa was to set out for the hills, word traveled from neighbor to neighbor that the dog-catcher was making his rounds. I had been in the basement, helping Grandpa select some tools, when the warning reached me. I hastened up the cellar stairs to find that Max was not sleeping in the shade of the mulberry tree. He was nowhere to be seen.

I went to the street as the dog-catcher's unfair assistant, a bitch in season, came up the dusty road followed by an array of potential victims. Max was among the others, fighting them off as best he could. I called out to Max, but today he had no ears.

And now the dog-catcher himself, a stringy fellow with a badge on his jumper bib, pounced upon the pack. He settled a wire loop about Max's neck. As he dragged Max toward the dog-wagon cage, I began to plead with the man to give me back my pet. He made no reply, but placed Max in the cage among some ten or eleven other dogs of various breeds and sizes. He closed the cage door and clicked a padlock against the hasp. Then he went off to choose another culprit from among the pack that now was moving out of view around the corner.

I was howling beside the cage when Grandpa, a crowbar in his hands, arrived. "Stand aside, son," he said, "till I get a good purchase on that padlock."

As calmly as you please, he began to demonstrate one of the laws of Archimedes. The door and part of the cage as well burst open, and all the dogs scampered out.

Max was of a mind to go back to the very same scene of his predicament, but I restrained him. And now the enraged dog-catcher, dragging another victim, came on the run toward the wagon.

"Hey! What you think you're doing?" he shouted at Grandpa.

"I already done it," said Grandpa.

The old gentleman was leaning upon the crowbar, like a bishop on a crosier. And his manner was cool, certain, serene.

"You'll hear plenty about this," the dog-catcher threatened. "Interferin' with an officer of the pound! Destroyin' property!"

"Come along, son," said Grandpa. "Let's finish our packing."

Officer Sellers called at our house toward sundown. He hinted at Grandpa's arrest. When told that Mr. Wheeler had gone to Empire, Sellers smiled.

"Well, I guess that's a little ways off my beat."

Now in our empty house, Granny said to me, "We don't want to depend on Uncle Dewey for support, although he'd be glad enough to help us. And Frank needs all that he earns at present. I'm afraid, son, that you will have to get a little job. Do you mind?"

I had never thought about a job. "I want to help all I can," I said, "and someday I'll get you everything."

I went to the backyard to find that my personal playground had taken on a new character. It no longer seemed a private place, for a hand was reaching into it to take from it a boy, and lead him into a world of men.

12

THE BIRDS AND THE BEASTS WERE THERE

OURS was a poor neighborhood, but not a slum. There is never a slum where sunlight brings a flower to bloom, where a bird sings in a tree, or a child dreams. But now the dream was to be modified.

I accompanied Uncle Dewey to a taxidermist's place, there to find employment as an errand boy. The bird- and beast-stuffer, an aproned man with a glass eye, studied me as if I were about to become one of his exhibits. Taxidermist Simmons was one of Uncle Dewey's many friends. Whenever an inmate of Uncle Dewey's small zoo expired, Mr. Simmons preserved it so that my uncle might remember the pet as in life. Mr. Simmons had neuralgic hips, and used a cane to get about, tapping the floor like Old Pew.

Dewey surrendered me to the glass-eyed stranger, and left me among motionless geese, deers' heads thrust out from the walls, mountain lions with arrested grimaces, fish set against varnished plaques, and a rattlesnake coiled like a dusty spring in a glass case that also contained prairie dogs and other small mammals. In the center of the floor stood a platform on casters; upon this portable dais a toothy black bear embraced a tree stump.

Mr. Simmons appeared so still and forbidding as momentarily to seem a member of his own dead world. A pair of elk's antlers fixed to a wall cabinet behind his head turned Mr. Simmons into the forest demon pictured in *Chatterbox*.

Mr. Simmons now came to life, shed his antlers as it were, then limped sciatically toward the rear of the establishment. "You can do some odd jobs in the back room till you get the feel of the place. Come along."

I already had the "feel" of the place as I followed him to the back room. There I observed three men at work beside benches or at tanning vats. A devastating smell occupied my attention. Then I noticed several animal hides being salted, cured, stretched, or fitted.

The carcass of a St. Bernard dog lay with ungainly rigidity in one corner of the room. Elsewhere I saw birds with pins protruding from their plumage, a defunct beaver, three cats; a reconstructed deer, its belly and legs sewn with a kind of baseball stitch, an iron rod propping up its middle. The deer stood with grotesque docility while one of the workers cemented eyes into the sockets of its skull. A drawerful of artificial eyes lay part way open beneath a workbench. Perhaps Mr. Simmons had chosen an eye for himself from this drawer.

The mass display of death in this room was repellent to one who thought of animals as live personalities, and never as dead dumb brutes. To see them dissected, flayed, fleshed, their insides exposed, or their forms counterfeited and refurred, their natural bodies degraded into excelsior, sawdust, burlap waddings—this became a nightmare scene.

"Here, Eric," Mr. Simmons was saying to a fat man who had a yellow tape measure draped about his neck. "Here, Eric, put this kid to work. How's Mr. Londoner's bear rug coming along?"

"We're out of Kodiak teeth," Eric responded.

"Then put in polar bear teeth. He'll never know the difference."

Eric took hold of the tape measure with either hand, as if about to skip rope. "We're out of polar bear teeth, too."

"Well, then," said Mr. Simmons, "give 'em grizzly teeth. Don't tell me you ain't got grizzly teeth?"

"We got grizzly," Eric replied.

"Good," said Mr. Simmons, and he rubbed at the corner of his glass eye. "The kid here is related to Dewey Wheeler."

After Mr. Simmons had tap-tapped his way out of the room, Eric turned to me. "Right now I'll let you watch me skin that there St. Bernard." Eric put on a soiled apron and selected a skinning knife from a row of other tools thrust in the loops of a leather band nailed to a bench. He called out to one of the other men: "Hey, Bruce! Will you gimme a hand with the St. Bernard?"

Bruce had been applying paint with a small brush to the feathers of a stoical quail. He held the brush in his teeth as he assisted Eric in rolling the St. Bernard over and onto a tarpaulin.

As Eric began to slash an underbelly incision from throat to tail-end, he looked up to ask me, "What's the matter?"

My lips moved to say, "Nothing," but no sound came.

"Hey," and Eric waved the knife to invite his colleagues' attention. "He's turning green." The other men laughed. "Wait till he sees us skin the Pelionqwee," Eric continued gravely. "Hah! That'll be something."

During the skinning of the St. Bernard, Eric and his fellows continued to discuss the Pelionqwee. "We keep him chained up in that closet," and Eric pointed his blade toward a locked cupboard. "It comes to life once in a while, and we got to be mighty careful."

I had chills, goose pimples, and numbness of the limbs. "Ever see a Pelionqwee?" Eric asked.

"No, sir," I managed to say.

"Of course you ain't," Eric snorted. Then he called out to Bruce: "Hey, how many Pelionqwees are they, Bruce?"

"One," replied Bruce. "Only one; and we got it locked up."

"Yes, sir," said Eric. "And it's a lalapalooza. It's got a human nose and ears. But the rest of it is a cross between a crocodile and a rhinoceros. Hah! And it wears teats all over its whole back. But you'll see it for yourself when we skin it."

As I swept the floor at the close of that day, that long, malignant day, I gingerly pushed the broom past the cupboard wherein the Pelionqwee was said to be chained. I went at last to the front room, there to sweep the floor and apply a feather-duster to the showcases. But now a new terror descended.

Mr. Simmons had gone. The front door was locked. The sundown light from the windows made a jungle of shadows in the showroom. Alone among the stuffed, silent animals, I believed them to be crowding in upon me, planning to devour me. The many staring glass eyes announced my doom.

That night I ate but little, and of the meat none at all. After a week among the stuffed animals and birds, I reported for work one Monday morning to find Eric gazing at me in a stupid way. His cigar butt fell from his lips.

"Get the hell outa here!" he cried as he backed away, and behaved as though I were the Pelionqwee itself. "Don't go near him," he called out to the others, "if you ain't never had the mumps. Mumps is something awful to catch when you get past being just a kid."

The tap-tapping of the Old Pew cane sounded. Mr. Simmons now joined the group to give me a one-eyed inspection. "You better go on home." He turned to Eric. "That's funny. I thought everybody'd got past having the mumps by your time of life."

"It's something awful for a growed man to catch 'em," Eric observed of the malady. "They say it's pure agony. Order him outa here quick, Mr. Simmons!"

As I retired from the back room, Eric began to lave his hands and face with alcohol used to degrease the hides. Mr. Simmons, his antlers again on his head, stood in front of the wall cabinet, and his one eye followed me to the door.

I was glad to stay home, beyond the reach of the dreadful Pelionqwee and the sound of Old Pew's cane. While still swollen with the welcome disease, I received a letter from Mr. Blake. Grandpa had informed my learned friend that I now was working "like a little man" for a kindly taxidermist. Mr. Blake's letter urged me to observe all that I possibly could in regard to the anatomy of Mr. Simmons' dead animals.

I felt somewhat disappointed that Mr. Blake showed no sorrow at the passing of these creatures. Then I made up my mind to return to the charnel house, and not let Mr. Blake down.

Uncle Dewey saved me from carrying out this resolution. He found a job for me with the Merchants Publishing Company. I was to be a printer's devil in the pressroom, and would receive fifty cents more than the two dollars a week I had been earning in Mr. Simmons' service. One might buy five pounds of shoulder beef for fifty cents.

A new world, a remarkable one of great machines and capable men, now became mine. I felt in immediate accord with the presses, the type fonts, and the printers' ink, the stimulating smell of which never leaves the nose.

I became wonder-struck by this clamorous world, my excitement untouched by dread. The men in this plant, to be sure, played their own vocational jokes, such as sending a boy for the paper-stretcher, but these jests were uncharged with terrorizing thoughts or gritty consequences. These men were hearty human beings, not soft, yet amiable underneath their smears of ink, as I since have found most printers to be.

In days of maturity I would come to know the world's largest Hoe presses. I eventually would see machines great enough to drive battleships. But as a boy at the beginning of the century, I found in the two flat-bed presses of the Merchants Publishing Company the ultimate expression of mechanical power. And, as was my custom, I accorded each machine a personality and a living spirit.

Was not a printing press animate, indeed? And did it not give out words from the thunders of its jaws? This and many other things I thought of as I pushed the broad floor-broom along the stone pavement of the aisles separating the vociferous machines.

Sometimes I was "loaned out" by Mac, the foreman of the press-room, to run errands for other departments, such as getting pails of beer at the Silver Dollar Saloon for the Dutchman in the bind-ery department upstairs. I was permitted to operate and ride the freight elevator, the pails of beer as my cargo. Sometimes I took a sip of the beer, but it tasted like Gun Wa's tonic.

I worked at the publishing company until October, and then one evening Patrolman Sellers called at our house. "Mrs. Wheeler, the truant officer is investigating why your boy ain't in school."

"We need him elsewhere," said Granny. "He gets schooling at home."

"I know," replied Sellers, "but ye'll have to send him back to school. Just a friendly warning."

This meant good-by to the pressroom, the composing-room, the Dutchman and his helpers upstairs, farewell to Mac and his hale fellows. It was not the same thing to erase or sponge chalk from a blackboard as to keep the ink disks of the job presses clean. To return to school was a demotion from the world of men. Of course, if Mr. Blake had been in charge of the class. . . .

As I sat in the fourth-grade schoolroom, I suddenly knew why the windows of these chambers were placed so high from the floors: to keep children from looking out at the world.

One afternoon when I returned home from school, Granny said, "Now I want you to stay calm."

"Something wrong with Dodie?"

"No," said the old lady. "It's Max."

"But the dog-catcher never comes this time of year," said I. "Where is he? Where's Max?"

"It's not the dog-catcher, my boy. Max has been very ill all day."

I looked about the kitchen. "Then why isn't he here where it's warm?" I went to the back door to cry out, "Max! Max!"

Granny followed me outside. She pointed to a gunny sack that covered something. When I removed the sack, I found that my pet was dead.

"Somebody poisoned Max," Granny explained. Then, as I hid my face against the wall, she went on, "The person who poisons a dog is not a person at all, but a fiend. Come indoors, son; Grandpa will take Max away."

"Nobody will take Max away," I said. "I'll bury him myself under the mulberry tree."

Uncle Dewey offered from the goodness of his heart to take Max to Mr. Simmons' place to be mounted. He did not quite understand my expression of horror at this suggestion.

I buried Max beneath the tree where so often he had lazed on warm days. Then I looked about for a monument. I found one: the prized quartz specimen that Grandpa kept so carefully wrapped in the army blouse in the basement.

When the old prospector learned to what use I had put Mr. Eldridge's bequest, he was less than pleased. He grumbled as he lifted the rock from the mound. Then, as he looked up from the beautiful, cloudy crystals of the rock, the mica flecks, he said, "You air a handful, son."

He replaced the tombstone on the earth, and then left me alone in the backyard.

There was a brief visit to the mountains late next summer. But somehow the scene lacked certain elements of familiar charm. Dodie was not there with her songs and laughter. Mr. Blake had gone to England to consult with his business partners. And I missed the unsteady presence of Mr. Eldridge, his daily calls at our doorway to pester "the lady of the house" with his thick but courtly cries of "You are the salt of the earth, Mrs. Wheeler."

When Granny and I returned from Red Mountain on September 19, 1901, the flags stood at half-staff on the buildings of Denver. A procession was forming near the Union Depot at the foot of Seventeenth Street. A band was playing "Nearer My God to Thee." Soldiers from three wars assembled behind a gun carriage

festooned in black. On the caisson a black coffin rested, a flag
upon its lid.

We set down our grips on the sidewalk. "It's in honor of the
martyred President McKinley," Granny explained. "The real
funeral is being held in Canton, Ohio. This coffin is empty. . . .
I was born in Ohio."

The symbolism of a mock funeral lay beyond my comprehension. As the mourners marked time, Granny pointed out Major
Oliver P. Wiggins among them. The former Indian fighter and
protégé of the late Kit Carson was serving as one of the marshals
of the day, a black brassard on the left sleeve of his Mexican War
tunic.

"You are looking at history," Granny announced solemnly.

"There's nobody in the coffin," I reminded her.

"It's not the coffin I'm referring to," said she. "I am speaking
of Scout Wiggins, a man of history."

"Where's Buffalo Bill?" I inquired. "I'd like to see Buffalo Bill
Cody."

"Indeed," she remarked with fine irony, "people will pay fifty
cents or even a dollar to see a long-haired fellow on horseback
shooting at silly glass balls. Yet every day they pass Scout Wiggins on the streets. We have several modest prophets without
honor in our midst." She motioned for me to pick up one of the
grips. "Let's have a closer view of Scout Wiggins." We boarded
one of several stalled streetcars, there to sit as if in a grandstand.
"Scout Wiggins," Granny continued, "is worth ten Buffalo Bills."

"Did Scout Wiggins run away from home when he was a boy?"

"Who told you such tommyrot?" and she flared. "Certain
grown persons I could mention do a lot of traipsing off to the
hills." She looked toward the mountains, then composed herself.
"Scout Wiggins married pretty Martha Wardell nearly fifty years
ago. They've been together on the trails, and sat beside the many
campfires. Major Wiggins and his friend, Scout Baker, built the
first real house in Denver."

"Did Scout Baker marry two squaws?"

She squirmed. "I decline to be a party to ancient gossip." Then she went on to say, "Scout Baker, mark you, was a great frontiersman, and Major Wiggins served as chief of scouts and guide for General Heath during the Mexican War."

"Buffalo Bill," I said, "was the greatest scout that ever lived."

"Oh, Buffalo Bill my left foot!"

"But he killed Chief Yellow Hand," I said loyally.

"Let me tell you the facts of the case," she snorted. "Poor Yellow Hand had consumption. He already had one moccasin in the grave when Bill Cody jumped upon him! Hah! Scout Wiggins is worth ten of Cody. Why he was with Kit Carson's famous band of '46. A trail blazer. Went with Carson and Frémont on the Pathfinder's first journey West. Even if he did run away from home when he was a boy, and I doubt it, he returned one day to give his mother the first four hundred Mexican dollars he ever earned. Nobody ever brought me four hundred dollars, Mexican or otherwise."

"Just you wait till Grandpa strikes it rich."

"Even Methuselah couldn't wait that long."

"Grandpa says that he lives in the future."

The old lady bridled. "Did someone intimate that *I* am living in the past? Did he?"

"No, ma'am."

She gazed at me in a manner that made me feel surrounded and outnumbered. "Living in the past, eh? Well, the past needs little defense. Without the past we would have a sorry present, mark you, and no future whatsoever. I am not exactly a fool, no matter what your grandfather says. . . ."

"He didn't say anything," I interrupted.

"Or what your opinionated Mr. Blake says."

"Oh, Mr. Blake thinks you're wonderful."

"What he thinks is a matter of little consequence," she said. "I am well aware that the world changes, and it should. Let the dead past bury its dead, as the poet says. But it can't bury the deeds of the pioneers. Scout Wiggins, for example. We need not forget the original things accomplished by the men of the past. And you are at liberty to inform my mysterious critic, whoever he may be, that I do not live in the past. The past lives in me."

"Yes, ma'am," I replied, then confided, "My kidneys want to act."

"Well," she advised, "don't get lost in the crowd, and hurry back. The cars are apt to start out any minute now."

I left Granny to go down the street to the waiting room of the depot. On my way back, I passed Tourney's saloon at the intersection of Seventeenth and Wazee Streets. There I saw two men standing beside a huge barrel open at the top. One of them was a narrow-eyed fellow in a frayed brown surtout. His companion, a person of saintly aspect, was an unusually short man, bearded, and meticulously clad in a swallow-tail coat and pin-stripe trousers. He was holding in his hands an ecclesiastical black hat out of respect for President McKinley.

The bearded man did not change his saintly expression as he suddenly said to me, "Get away from that barrel, you nosy little bastard!"

I stepped back a pace, but not before I had looked inside the barrel. "Why have you got 'em in there?"

The saintly man was looking toward the depot as if expecting someone. Without turning his kindly eyes in my direction, he rasped: "If you don't get away from that barrel, I'll knock your second teeth out. You don't grow a third set, in case you want to know. Now, get!"

"You better mosey along, kid," the man in the brown surtout advised me. "The Deacon here gets upset mighty easy."

Deacon Green was a confidence man. On the day of the mock funeral, he and his narrow-eyed accomplice were awaiting the arrival of a Rock Island train with its usual complement of Kansas farmers on holiday from the cornfields. These thrifty agriculturists customarily got off the train with telescope canvas valises in their hands and currency safety-pinned inside the linings of their vests. On their way from the Union Depot to the lower Sev-

enteenth Street hotels, they necessarily passed Tourney's saloon.
They were bound to see the Deacon standing beside the large barrel and hear him loudly denouncing his narrow-eyed ally.

"I do not care a fig what you are doing, or why?" the Deacon
would shout to his confederate. "I am a stranger here, it is true;
but surely the authorities will pay attention when I inform them
of the strange cruelty you are practicing. If you do not have this
barrel off the street by the time I return from an important mission, I shall then summon the police."

By this time the valise-carrying stranger himself would be peering inside the barrel to see therein a rattlesnake and a pair of
horned toads. The Deacon now would appeal to the newcomer:

"I can see at first glance that you are a just and humane person
like myself. I must explain that I have just demanded of this cal-
lous fellow that he spare these poor horned toads from the heart-
less serpent."

The Deacon then would take the stranger by the arm and propel him up Seventeenth Street, the Deacon pausing to call over
his shoulder to the confederate at the barrel: "See that you abide
by the laws of human decency!"

And now the Deacon would confide in his "chance" acquaintance that he himself had just arrived in the city "to befriend an
old schoolmate from the theological seminary of Scranton, a
worthy, God-fearing man, now penniless in fact, but about to
gather a sudden bright fortune."

"Of course," the Deacon would go on to say, "I have only a
thousand dollars here in my pocket; but the integrity of my
friend is so deep and his fortune so assured that he can have the
last red cent I possess. He actually needs eleven hundred, but a
thousand is all I can muster."

The various suckers, with astounding enthusiasm, would volunteer the needed hundred. The Deacon "would not think of taking
your money, even though you would net at least $10,000 in sud-
den dividends." But when a stranger almost clubbed his way into
the scheme, the Deacon would relent. The new friends then

would repair to a hotel lobby where a "broker" gave them a receipt for their investment.

The Deacon, the confederates, the barrel, the snake, the horned toads then would disappear until after a victim left town.

The parade now had begun to move up Seventeenth Street. By the time I returned to the place where I had left Granny, the streetcars were crawling along in the wake of the marchers. Annoyed by my delay, Granny had got off the car and was standing guard over our grips.

"I wish the good Lord had found it convenient to dispense with a boy's kidneys," she remarked, "and with Deacon Green's snake barrel as well. Here, take one of these grips. We'll walk over to Sixteenth and Lawrence. We'll have a better chance there of getting a seat on a car home."

As we started up the street I heard the Deacon's voice raised in righteous exasperation above the brassy music of the disappearing band. I turned to see him denouncing his narrow-eyed confederate: "I do not care a fig what you are doing, or why. . . ."

The Rock Island train had arrived to discharge its passengers. A gawking newcomer, a telescope canvas bag in his hand, was approaching the barrel to look inside it.

As we trudged past the corner of Sixteenth and Larimer Streets, one square short of our streetcar goal, Granny pointed out a three-story brick building. "I well remember a brilliant man who worked in the rear of yonder place in the early eighties. He had a pleasant nod for everyone, and he was much beloved. His name was Eugene Field, and he wrote lovely verses in this very same building, before *The Tribune* was merged with *The Republican*. Wouldn't you like to be a great poet some day?"

"No, ma'am," I said.

"Then what would you like to be?"

"I'd like to own a pair of horned toads, a snake, and a barrel."

"You varmint, you!" she exclaimed. "You and Deacon Green and Buffalo Bill!"

13

A KISS THROUGH THE VEIL

ONE morning late in February of 1903, Dodie called upon us while on her way to see Mrs. Phila Dungan, a long-time friend. Mrs. Dungan was making a cream-colored satin dress for Dodie to wear at Professor Whiteman's Spring Music Festival. This was to be the young woman's first appearance among the city's foremost singers at Trinity Church. With Granny's slow consent, Mr. Whiteman had assigned her to a place among his own soloists.

"Now I must hurry along," said my mother, "or I'll be late for my fitting."

She was wearing a black polka-dot veil that day. When she kissed me good-by, I felt the small, dry threads of the mesh against my lips. She remarked that I had "shot up like a weed" to be much taller than herself.

"I'll drop in again," Dodie promised, "after my fitting at Mrs. Dungan's."

That afternoon Frank Fowler stopped in at our house to say that Dodie quite suddenly had fallen ill, and that he was on his way to call a doctor. Would Granny meantime stay with Dodie and look after the children? We went at once to Dodie's house and found her in distress. Her chief concern, however, was the likelihood of missing Professor Whiteman's Festival.

Dr. I. B. Perkins, the celebrated surgeon, arrived to diagnose Dodie's ailment. The doctor came out of the bedroom to confer with Frank and Granny. "She must be removed at once to the hospital for an operation," the surgeon said.

"I don't believe in the knife," Granny objected. "Surely something else might be tried."

"Madam," said Dr. Perkins, "I can't answer for her recovery if we don't operate."

"Will you answer for it if you do?" inquired the old lady.

"The doctor here knows what to do," Frank said.

"There's a great deal of needless cutting and sewing up of people these days," Granny declared. She observed the effect of her remark upon the dignified surgeon. "I am in the habit of speaking my mind, Doctor."

"So I gather," replied the surgeon. He turned to Frank. "The decision rests with you."

"Whatever you say," Frank said to Dr. Perkins. "You're the best judge."

Having overheard this conference, I slipped into the bedroom to look at my mother. Her long hair seemed especially black against the pillow; one hand lay like a fallen leaf upon the coverlet, the palm turned upward, the fingers still.

The doctor and Frank now entered the room. Dr. Perkins affected a cheery manner. "Well, now. We'll just have a little trip to St. Joseph's Hospital, where you'll be taken care of in a jiffy."

Dodie seldom had been ill. The mention of the hospital frightened her. She looked up at the doctor and at Frank. "Is it that bad?"

I was standing at the foot of the bed, thinking of Granny's remark about "sewing up of people." I had the childish tactlessness to inquire, "How many stitches will they make?"

Dodie began to weep. "I don't want to die." Frank led me out of the room. I was not permitted to kiss Dodie good-by. After the horse-drawn ambulance had gone, I had a foreboding that I never again would see my mother alive.

Granny was changing the bedclothes. "Go on home and your grandfather will cook supper for you. Tell him I'll stay here to look after the children and . . ." She paused, got some freshly laundered pillow-cases and a sheet from a chest of drawers, then continued, "to look after the children, and wait for word."

A premonition much more graphic than mine was Charles Devlan's that same evening. I learned from him many years afterward that a feeling of uneasiness had been his as he did his final chores of that day on Squaw Mountain. Then, as night came, he looked out the cabin window that framed Mt. Evans in the moonlight. And now he thought that he saw the figure of my mother against the great hill.

Early the next morning, Devlan asked Gus, a neighboring homesteader, to look after the livestock and poultry. He explained that he "had some business in Denver," but mentioned nothing about his forebodings. Then Devlan set out on snowshoes across the high trail to Idaho Springs, to wait there for a train to the city. In Denver he went to George Pell's house, and verified his presentiment that Dodie was gravely ill.

On March 1 of the year 1903 the mulberry tree stood bare; ice staled with chimney drift lay in its crotches. I climbed the leafless tree, knocked a slab of ice from a peach-crate saddle, then sat looking at the cloud racks of the gray overcast and out upon the wind-swept world. I stayed there until Granny and Grandpa returned from St. Joseph's hospital.

Toward afternoon the old persons came home. Granny arrived first, bonneted and shawled, and went into the house by way of the back door. And now, walking as one beneath a burden, Grandpa appeared in my view. I got down from the tree to go to him. I felt that he did not see me, did not see anything. In the eyes that always had held great dreams, I now observed a blue vacancy. I never would see another face so empty of hope.

After we had sat wordlessly indoors for a long time, Grandpa said, "Maybe you should go lay down, Lizzie."

"No," replied the old woman. "I was up at work the next day after little Dodie was born. I shall stay up now until she is buried."

Dodie lay in a white coffin in her house, a white lace canopy overhead. The cream-colored satin dress made for the Spring Festival was her shroud.

The next morning was gray again, grayer than yesterday. Dodie's friends, young and old, gathered together at the small church. There was one vacant chair on the pulpit platform where the choir members sat as Pell played "Abide with Me," repeating it again and again on the old organ. A wide black ribbon draped the empty choir chair. Among the flowers was a wreath from Professor Whiteman. There also was to be seen a spray of red carnations, but it bore no card to identify the sender.

A catalogue of random thoughts comes to the mind of a child when on his way to the burial of his mother. The last kiss through a veil. . . . This is my first ride in a closed carriage. . . . The gay young woman who dangled her bare feet in the waters of the creek. . . . The red-haired Reverend Collins riding with the Quirkes in their splendid surrey. . . . The time Dodie held the earrings to her ears as she looked into the mirror during the tea at the Blakes'. . . .

At Fairmont Cemetery the mourners who had arrived beforehand were waiting. Sleet began to fall from the cloud racks. At a remote place in the cemetery, Charles Devlan stood unseen by the others. Then, after the words "Dust to dust," George Pell made an excuse to stay behind. He joined his old friend, and they went to the place where the earth was being returned. Charles Devlan took a red carnation from the spray that had on it no card, and which lay among the flowers brought from the church. He stood looking into the half-filled grave.

The sleet-drenched shovelers paused briefly in their labors to permit this interruption.

He had belonged to one woman. Rather, he had belonged to the idea of her, a dream fourteen years long. Now that she was dead, would his dream of her also die?

Charles Devlan thought of this all the way home to his lonely hill. It was the next afternoon, and a threnody of wind was blowing across the Bishop's Razor and the Blacks. Slicks of snow and ice lay among the clearings. Smoke from the cabin chimney trailed low in the persistent wind. Devlan thanked Gus for having looked after the horses and the Jersey cow.

"Did you get your business done in Denver?" Gus asked.

"Yes. All done."

"Have you et?"

"Later on, maybe."

"Then I'll be going down the hill," Gus said. "I left some coffee on the stove."

Gus started off down Squaw Mountain. Devlan went inside his cabin. He stood at the window, to look out at Mt. Evans, great and white. A wool-pack cloud seemed a reflection of the peak itself in a vast mirror.

Would the dream die?

The snows of Mt. Evans become glacial fingers. The fingertips shake off the waters that go to the creeks and freshets and reach the rivers, then travel to the far-off sea. The glaciers move with God's slow patience, but their snows melt in time. New snows come to the mountain, but the granite pile itself is fixed in time and space, exempt from life and from death as well.

The peak always had inspired him; but on this day it sat upon his heart. How monstrously heavy sat the mountain upon the heart! Could Faith move this mountain of sorrow and loss? The sun lay upon the deathbed of the hills.

Devlan cried out. He went from his cabin to cry out with passionate lament, to shake his fist at the mountain. Now he felt something hot and wet upon his arm. He was holding the pot of coffee. He had seized it without knowing what he had been doing, and splashed the coffee on himself.

The conifer trees were stiffly bending like hearse plumes in the coronach of wind from across the Bishop's Razor and the Blacks. The rumbling of a far-off snowslide seemed the response of a ghostly congregation, the Apostles' Creed recited in the cathedral of the mountains.

The man set his jaws and was silent. For fourteen years he had been part of the silence of the hills. Now he thought of the one he had cherished, and of the dream. He thought of the flowers they had gathered during their brief season together; flowers gone to dust, and to gray dust their green stems; the grave a dust-bin, death a broom.

The last song he had heard her sing was "Beautiful Isle of Somewhere." Does a dream die? In her hair has my dearest a flower. . . .

For fourteen years the recluse had fed upon the poppies of hope. Hope for what? A message? A glimpse of her during one of his few returns to the city of his defeat?

Sometimes the loneliness had become almost insupportable to a man in the fullness of his young flesh. Then, after a night of torturing hunger, a man may eat his own heart. He turns his eyes to the dream, mirage though it be, works with all violence at his sawmill or his forge. He brings down the great yellow pine trees with his ax; he beats the cherry-red horseshoes on the anvil. His teeth are clenched, and the lips set tightly over them to stifle the outcries.

The fourteen years had been a long drudgery of mind, but now the recollection of those years took but an instant. How to bring all the sorrows, the heartaches, the yearnings into one view? Death brings them all into one view, exhibiting each thing in relation to its surrounding fate, a finished painting set upon an easel.

The years reverberate in memory. Memory, a kettledrum. Years, the drum beats; and trumpets sound from afar, "It might have been."

What was the rhyme the old trapper made? The stinking old outlaw who poached beaver in the valley pocket below Squaw Mountain? Oh, yes, the frowsy trapper always cackled over his four-word rhyme. He called it *The Poem of All of Us:* "Boom, womb, doom, tomb."

The coffee pot in his hand, the spilled coffee now coldly seeping through his sleeve and jacket front, Devlan stood thinking. He was calmer now. He spoke within himself, announcing to his lonely self that he would cherish the dream.

"I was twenty-two when I left," he said to himself. "Now I am thirty-five. My son is thirteen."

Gus had come back and stood appraising the man who was holding the coffee pot and staring off at Mt. Evans. "I was down in the draw," Gus said, "and I thought I heard you holler out, Charlie."

Devlan turned to him. "It must have been the wind."

14

A FLIGHT FROM INNOCENCE

FABLE changed into fact whenever Ivy Baldwin's balloon appeared overhead. The man in the sky could rise at will to enjoy the status of an angel. However, he did not remain off the ground for too long a time; hopes lived in heaven, but strength came from the earth. Ivy Baldwin both made and sailed his muslin bags, and by so doing seemed to be creating and ordering his own destiny, a playmate of the stars.

The young onlooker, himself a stranger to the riddles of adult experience, now felt that one might approach life by a surer means than that of reverie. Men and women spoke frequently of their struggles to keep body and soul together. Perhaps if each toiler earnestly were to set out in his own kind of balloon, he might keep soul and body apart, and thereby avoid confusion and defeat.

It was Granny's verdict that Ivy Baldwin desecrated each Sabbath day that found him in mid-air advertising an amusement park. She admonished me not to look upon the sacrilege.

During Ivy Baldwin's performances against the blue roof of the world, he rode a trapeze attached to a parachute suspended in turn from the four rib lines of the bag. Sometimes the adventuresome man would swing at the end of a drag rope perhaps thirty feet beneath the trapeze, then climb hand-over-hand to straddle the bar, stand upon his head, hang by his toes, or enact other hazardous gymnastics.

The balloon eventually listed and smoke issued from it. The parachute opened, and Baldwin floated off toward the horizon. I longed to follow after the balloon, to seek the wilted bag among the sword-plants, milkweeds, the sagebrush of the prairie, or draped upon the willows of the South Platte River banks. There was a five-dollar reward for its discovery. I was not permitted to leave the house or the backyard until time for services at a church where now there rose no young voice to stir the heart.

One Sunday Baldwin did not reappear in the sky. An eccentric wind had dashed him against a tree at Elitch's Gardens, fracturing his jaw and both arms. The aeronaut's principal complaint, Dr. Calhoun reported, was that he could not persuade the sisters of charity at St. Anthony's Hospital to roll cigarettes for him.

I wrote to Mr. Blake concerning the interrupted balloon ascensions. He had returned from England, he explained in a note accompanying an autographed copy of his book on tea. Mr. Blake's encyclopedia counseled the reader to store tea leaves in an isolated canister to prevent contamination. The tea-brewer was cautioned to use the softest water in the cleanest of earthenware pots to safeguard the beverage against "piquancy, pungency, harsh, metallic, soapy, fishy, smoky, acrid, or puckery intrusions."

"Indeed!" Granny exclaimed. "I have steeped tea quite well, mark you, during half a century, and in an iron kettle, too." She gestured resignedly. "But the sun never sets on an Englishman's opinions."

In emulation of Ivy Baldwin, I attempted a parachute leap from the mulberry tree. Dr. Calhoun dressed my sprained ankle, but Granny's umbrella was wrecked beyond repair. Frank Fowler, again "in funds," this time as a real estate agent, replaced the umbrella with a smart new parasol of shiny gray material edged with black. My stepfather also gave me a splendid blue bicycle. No

longer need I borrow the cycles of playmates for my rides with
Molly on my shoulder.

This Rambler bicycle widened the world. I now could travel
swiftly to and from many places, chase the fire wagons, and find
adventures with many new friends of my own age. The bicycle
was an emblem of fraternity; all cyclists were potential comrades.
I even received nods from a Civil War hero, Captain Williamson,
pioneer engraver and publisher of Mr. Blake's book.

The gray-bearded Captain was not the kind of man to "pick
up" with just anyone. Captain Williamson enjoyed a high social
standing, although he had to maintain it upon one good leg, the
other being artificial. The old gentleman would propel his bicycle
lopsidedly along the walks, and career toward gateposts, trees,
and pedestrians. His dashing nature, however, saw him through all
perils; and whenever we almost collided, the Captain would nod
confidently. If we chanced to meet on foot, however, he passed
me by with martial hauteur.

The Captain resided next door to the best of all my bicycling
friends, indeed one of the best of my lifelong friends, Edward
Killian Sullivan. I first met Ed Sullivan after prowling among the
parochial schoolrooms in the basement of St. Joseph's Roman
Catholic Church. I had stood my bicycle against the wall near the
school entrance this day. I returned to find Ed comparing his
bicycle with mine. His had no coaster brake, but otherwise was
similar to mine in make and color.

He sized me up, to decide whether he could trounce me or, if
not, lure me to his house, where his quiet-mannered but lethal
eldest brother, Art, frequently attended to rough challengers.

"Nice bike you got," Ed remarked.

I replied in a manner that astonished him: "Sir, I perceive you
are a vile Whig."

He could not know that I had been reading Boswell's *Life of
Johnson* and fancied at times that I was living in the actual pres-
ence of the learned Doctor and his great compeers: Goldsmith,
Garrick, and Sir Joshua.

"Nice bike," repeated Sullivan uncertainly. "What you been doing in our school?"

"Looking for a rifle," I replied. "And take your hands off my bicycle, sir."

"A rifle?" and Sullivan became interested. "A rifle around *here?*"

"Hundreds of them. And maybe a cannon."

"Who says?" Ed asked with a suspicious leer.

"My grandmother," I answered, then confided, "The Catholics are getting ready to murder everyone."

Sullivan seemed unimpressed by the homicidal phase of my statement. "Let's both go look around the place; I'd like to get a real rifle for myself."

We were unable, oddly enough, to locate the secret arsenal. On our way back to our bicycles, Ed saw the parish priest.

"Let's get out of here in a hurry," and Ed prepared to mount his bicycle. "He's a real Whig."

The Reverend Father Edward Killian Cantwell, from whom Sullivan had taken his own confirmation name, called out: "Just a moment, Edward. I'd like to have a word with you, my son."

The slender, personable priest sternly began to lecture us, presumably mistaking me for a Roman visitor from St. Leo's or some other West Side parish. "Boys," he said, "I understand that some of you have been at work cleaning the bricks of a certain dismantled building. And I am forbidding you to do it."

Father Cantwell had reference to a structure that just recently had housed the *Denver Catholic Register*, a denominational newspaper. The *Register* had moved to more commodious quarters, and the old building been sold. After transferring the deed, the church authorities belatedly learned that the actual purchasers of the property were Mormons. Moreover, these Latter-day Saints were preparing to set up a tabernacle of bricks salvaged from the recent home of the *Catholic Register*.

As if this dismaying circumstance were not enough, Father Cantwell ascertained that certain pupils of St. Joseph's school were accepting fifty cents the hundred for knocking mortar from former Catholic bricks, and at the behest of local admirers of Brigham Young.

"Edward, my son," Father Cantwell was saying, "we expect you as a soloist in our choir and captain of the parish cadet corps to set a proper example. We do not deny the Mormons or anyone else the right to worship in their own fashion. But no more brick-cleaning in their behalf! Do I make myself clear?"

"Yes, Father," said the rebuked soloist and cadet corps captain.

Father Cantwell turned to go to the rectory across the alley-way, saying to me as he passed: "And see to it, young man, that you also be a credit to your own parish and to your good Catholic parents."

After I had recovered from the sudden honor of being received, as it were, into the Church, I remarked to Sullivan, "If you're a cadet, you must have a rifle."

"No," he replied. "A sword."

"But the other cadets?"

"They have wooden guns."

Having thus confirmed Granny's report that the Catholics were armed and ready, I asked Sullivan, "Think I could join the cadet corps?"

"I don't know," my new friend replied. "We don't take in everybody."

My thoughts now turned to another possibility. "Do you really get fifty cents for cleaning the bricks?"

"You just heard what Father Cantwell said."

"Then, sir," and I resumed the role of Dr. Johnson, "let us visit the brick pile to earn a few pence."

"I was on my way to do just that," Sullivan said happily. "Come on. But you better not call the other fellows 'sir.' Some of 'em are kind of tough."

After we had cleaned fifty bricks for the Mormons and spent the money at Rust's bakery and candy store, Ed invited me to his home. We found Papa Sullivan mumbling to himself as he worked upon a letter. Finally he put his indelible pencil in an upper vest pocket.

"Edward," he announced, "I've just canceled my subscription to *The Republican*. That newspaper has the gall to refer to Corporal Whitcombe as the youngest Civil War veteran. It's a contemptible lie! Everyone knows that I am the youngest." He brandished the letter. "I've written to Editor Stapleton." He shook hands with me. "How do you do, young man? And were any of your people soldiers of the North?"

"One of my grandfathers," I replied.

Mr. Sullivan eyed me shrewdly. "And how old was your grandfather when he enlisted?"

"Seventeen, I think."

Ed's parent now became most cordial. "Good! Good! A young age, seventeen. I had just turned eleven myself when I carried the drum into battle. Stay for supper; we're having tapioca pudding."

Always on the alert for a substitute father, I set Mr. Sullivan down as a suitable one *pro tem*. There were these seeming advantages in not being a blood-son of my various paternal candidates: I didn't have to obey them, nor did I need become an apprentice to their respective trades or professions because of family tradition and against my own preferences.

Payment must be made, however, for absence of early masculine discipline. And the years bring with them their duebills. But we are not speaking of later years, and this is not a book of confession, but the story of a quest and of things as seen through the eyes of a child among the mountains and plains, a spectator in search of heroes, rather than a hero seeking an audience. Buffalo Bill was one of my heroes because of his gallant deeds; Mr. Blake because of his generosity of mind; Mr. Sullivan for his bigness of heart. It is said that when a boy is looking for a father, he is seeking God.

James Eugene Sullivan was a traveling man, reverenced by others of his calling as the "Dean of the Road." As a plumbing supply salesman, he was in his own fashion a pioneer. He introduced to the West the latest sanitary comforts, not the least among them a bathroom utensil known as the Silentflow. Mr. Sullivan decried frontier outhouses, and also was a crusading opponent of the Vogel seat. That seat released a sudden, revolving Niagara when in use. Attached to the wall side of the contrivance, a large cylindrical weight hung as a counterbalance to stay the whirlpool as a person rose from privacy. The seat would spring up, like a bear trap working in reverse, to put a man out of commission if struck in some vital place.

Mr. Sullivan had two worries, both having to do with his obituary. He anticipated that some dolt of a newspaper writer might neglect to credit him with properly piping and fauceting the West, or deny him posthumously his historic place as the youngest soldier of the Grand Army. To forestall these injustices, Papa Sullivan compiled a true account of his career and kept that journal in a suitcase which also contained his burial wardrobe.

The coat of these farewell garments was the Prince Albert he had worn when initiated into the Knights of Columbus lodge. The shoes, black Congressionals long treasured, never had been used. There also might be seen among the funeral clothes a suit of long woolen underwear and a white waistcoat.

Papa Sullivan's memoir revealed that his surname originally had been O'Sullivan. His French wife had little use for the Irish, and before accepting him as a husband stipulated that he strike the Celtic "O" from his name.

On the afternoon of our first meeting, Mr. Sullivan inveighed against all claimants to his title as he washed his hands and face at the most modern of basins and combed his hair. Papa Sullivan's hair actually was white, as was his mustache; but I did not know of that at the time. At first glance his hair and lip adornment seemed glossy black. I afterward observed that his locks took on startling variations of hue. A hardware dealer in Santa Fe, one of Mr. Sullivan's customers, had given him a special comb which had hollow teeth. The handle, also hollow, contained a dismal-colored fluid that fed down through the teeth of the comb.

The chemical in the comb's reservoir apparently had a close affinity for the lead of Mr. Sullivan's indelible pencils. He had the habit of occasionally stroking his hair or mustache with his pencil when taking orders for the Silentflow or other catalogue numbers. It is unlikely that Mr. Sullivan was color-blind; still he never seemed to realize that his doctored hair gained more attention than did his stories of beating the drum during Sherman's march to the sea or of playing the fiddle with Bodle Collier after the Battle of Atlanta.

Papa Sullivan excused himself to go to the corner mailbox to post his denunciatory letter to Editor Stapleton. On his way back to the house he was almost run over by the one-legged cyclist, Captain Williamson, his next-door neighbor on Pearl Street.

"Well! Well, sir!" exclaimed Mr. Sullivan.

"Well! Well, yourself, sir!" echoed the Captain.

This exchange of sarcasms indicated that the two gentlemen were not on the best of terms. Ed Sullivan explained to me that his father and the Captain had been restrainedly chill toward each other during several years past, and for reasons that neither man saw fit to advertise. Their mutual frostiness may have come about when the Captain, as commander, neglected to invite Mr. Sullivan to join the George Washington Post of the Grand Army. Then again, Captain Williamson was an influential Methodist, oftentimes the host of Chancellor Buchtel of Denver University. Mr. Sullivan, a Roman Catholic, played High Five and other sociable games of cards with priests.

Whenever Mr. Sullivan eavesdropped on the Saturday night fife-and-drum rallies at Captain Williamson's next door, he kept time with his foot and voiced comments such as: "Those old fogies are tearing 'The Mocking Bird' to shreds."

Some weeks before I met the Sullivans, violent labor disputes had come to the gold camps of the state. There were strikes in the Cripple Creek district and elsewhere. A strike in seven large mines of Clear Creek County, the territory in which Grandpa had been prospecting of late years, was a matter of nearest importance to us. The miners were demanding an eight-hour day at the same wages they had been receiving for a nine-hour shift.

Although Grandpa was primarily a prospector, he drew occasional wages as a hard-rock mining employee to help finance his own explorations. As a mine worker, regularly situated or not, he gave allegiance to the Western Federation of Miners. He had no religion other than loyalty to his friends and to their causes.

The mine owners looked upon Grandpa's economy of speech, his unsmiling silence, as a symptom of dangerous thoughts. When he quoted his wife's description of Governor Peabody as "Governor Nobody," the Clear Creek magnates set him down as an "agitator." When the Governor ordered out the militia and encouraged deputy sheriffs to deport the strikers, Grandpa said, "Well, let 'em come. I got a mighty fine side-winder pistol."

Grandpa's recent backer, Judge Bryce, had died during the past winter. Uncle Dewey and Frank Fowler arranged to support Granny and me during Grandpa's annual pilgrimage to the mountains in the spring of 1903. It was inexpedient, however, for them to finance the goldseeker beyond paying for his railroad ticket. The old prospector decided to work at the Sun and Moon gold mine in the Clear Creek district until such a time as he could afford powder and supplies for his own private ventures at Red Mountain.

In May the one hundred and fifty miners at the Sun and Moon declared a strike. When the mine operators asked Grandpa if he were walking out with the others, he said what he usually said in times of trouble—nothing. He packed up his belongings, was promptly blacklisted, and went home. An attack of pleurisy kept him indoors until an itinerant quack outfitted him with an "electric belt" which "did wonders" for him.

The old gentleman sat in the cellar, reading the strike news in the papers and adjusting his electric belt. He celebrated his convalescence early in July by assisting strikers at the Grant smelter and the Globe smelter in North Denver to extinguish the furnace fires in both plants. Then he returned to the cellar to repair his boots, eat specked apples, and read the newspapers.

On July 28 some kegs of powder rolled down the hillside of the Sun and Moon mine. The explosion wrecked the transformer house. The blast killed Phil Fire, an Italian miner. Five hundred citizens of Idaho Springs, led by Lafayette Hanchette (Grandpa had an interesting but indelicate pun for this man's surname), marched to the jail where fourteen striking miners were awaiting trial. The citizens seized the keys to the calaboose, then escorted the prisoners to the limits of the town, threatened them with the hemp, and warned them never to come back.

"I'll not stand for this!" said Grandpa, frowning like Ajax.

When he subsequently read the decision of District Judge Frank W. Owers of Georgetown, the old prospector rose from his cobbler's bench in the cellar to lead himself in a cheer.

The Judge had ruled: "The action of the Idaho Springs mob— I take pains to use the accurate term—in running out of town, with threats of violence, the officials of the miners' union, was sheer anarchy, an outrageous violation of the rights guaranteed by the Constitution to the humblest person."

The spectacle of the usually quiet Mr. Wheeler waving his newspaper and cheering in the cellar seemed most impressive. "Hooray for the humblest person!" he shouted.

He did not go again to the hills that summer. Uncle Dewey made a place for him at the Grand National Market.

Granny received word that her sister Martha lay dying in Kansas. Granny dried her eyes. "Our large family is narrowing." She now spoke of her several brothers and sisters who had "crossed over Jordan," among them Robert Parrott, her favorite. "Robert," she said, "stubbornly declined to fight against the South." Then she added, "The war between the North and the South was a monstrous error. It really should have been fought, if at all, between the East and the West."

The dissenting Robert, she continued, had gone in Civil War days from Kansas to Montana, there to discover one of the largest copper fields in the world. "The Parrott mine still bears his name. He sold this property to Marcus Daly for ten thousand dollars and the Parrott mine became the foundation of that copper king's vast fortune. My brother soon lost the ten thousand but," and she spoke as if in his defense, "he became a brilliant lawyer."

As Granny went on to canonize Robert and her numerous other kinsmen, I interrupted mischievously, "How about Uncle John?"

"You varmint!" she exclaimed.

This eldest brother had embarrassed the Parrott survivors by taking a third wife at his then age of eighty-six years. "John and Robert became estranged," and Granny tried to divert my attention from John's romantic didos, "because they held contrary views regarding the Civil War."

I had but a misty memory of Uncle John, but as I now chance upon a tintype of Granny's eldest brother in a long-neglected album, my recollection of him is suddenly amplified. I see a tall man of keen eye, his hair worn long like a music master's or Buffalo Bill's. He is carrying, sword-fashion, a blackthorn stick. Old Uncle John has on a Civil War hat and a blue military tunic decked with celluloid buttons bearing slogans political and otherwise. He sits in the sun on a bench in a small park, and scatters breadcrumbs to the birds. Uncle John rises to tip his hat to young ladies who seem to find him attractive notwithstanding his many celluloid buttons and his many years.

"How old is Uncle John's new wife?" I asked.

"John," Granny sighed, "always has been a victim of petticoats. Strong in every respect until a pretty face catches his eye; then he turns into curds and whey. Never mind how old his wife is. Old enough to know better." She shook her head, then continued: "During the great war he fell asleep while on sentry duty. He would have been shot for that, had not our mother written to President Lincoln." She paused. "If a pretty hussy had passed the

ramparts that early morning, Petticoats John would have awakened with all alacrity." The old woman began to hum "When the
Roll Is Called Up Yonder I'll Be There."

Granny departed for Holton, and left me in Grandpa's keeping.
During her absence, I entered upon a helter-skelter holiday of
mischief.

One day turned out to be especially rampageous for several
companions and myself. We had stolen, for no practical reason
it would seem, a basket of cucumbers and a crate of tomatoes
from a vegetable wagon. As we lurked in an alley off South
Broadway we saw a spectacle that invited uproarious action. A
young man of athletic build, and dressed in a fabulous manner,
was carrying a cub bear and leading a crow-bait white horse
northward along Broadway. The man had on a resplendent military uniform with fringed epaulets, and a black patent-leather
chapeau weighed down with gold braid. A sword and scabbard
clanked at his side.

The horse kept pulling at the reins, shying and snorting because of the bear. We now began to bombard the trudging
dragoon with our vegetables. The horse got away, but the man
clung to the bear, meantime threatening us with mutilation and
death itself. Officer Henry Sellers bicycled into the scene to
interrupt our attack. We scattered fast. The dragoon and his bear
retreated, shaking off tomato juice and cucumber remnants.

The dragoon, an actor on tour, arrived at the Tabor Grand
Theatre with his bear just in time to play his minor military part
on the stage. The beast subsequently chewed the key clerk's arm
and then bit the elevator boy at the hotel where the actor was
residing. The animal fell asleep in bed with its master.

Next day the hotel management advised the theatrical dragoon to rid the place of the "stinking, vicious cub." The actor
took his beast to the zoo at Elitch's Gardens, to present it to
the keeper. While there he heard the playing of symphonic music
at the Gardens theater. The actor went into the theater auditorium to find an orchestra rehearsing under the direction of Signor

Rafaello Cavallo. When he returned to his hotel, he was of a mind to quit the drama and become a composer. He afterward composed music, and became a painter and an etcher as well, but the theatrical world was to yield him his largest fame.

During a conversation with Lionel Barrymore in 1943, I chanced to mention the episode of the vegetable bombardment of the dragoon on the streets of Denver. This reference had a galvanic effect upon my eminent friend.

"So!" shouted Mr. Barrymore. "*You* were one of those little bastards who caused me so much trouble that day forty years ago!" After this revelation that he had been my target, he went on to explain: "I had been drinking with some soldiers from Fort Logan after a morning dress rehearsal with Uncle Jack Drew at the Tabor Grand Theatre. The hospitable soldiers invited me to visit their post. I decided out of military courtesy to remain in my theatrical dragoon's uniform. The soldiers procured for me a two-dollar mustang at the city pound, and then we set out for Fort Logan. Along the way we became interested in a dice game at a saloon. We lost all our cash, but I won the bear on the last throw. Four was my point, as I recall it."

Mr. Barrymore glared at me, then continued: "It was getting on toward curtain time, so instead of proceeding to the Fort I turned back toward town. The horse and bear took a silly dislike to each other. Then suddenly vegetables began to fall upon me. That evening at the theater, when Uncle Jack observed the condition of my uniform, he asked, 'What part are you playing tonight, Lionel? A garbage collector?' I shall never forget the fair city of Denver or its foul young citizens."

On that same evening of the long-ago bombardment of Lionel, I went with Ed Sullivan and several other cronies to a drugstore owned by the uncle of a boy named Lucian. The nephew somehow had procured the key to his relative's pharmacy. Lucian drew the blinds, lighted a gas jet in the back room, then pointed out three casks of wine cradled on a shallow platform.

Lucian found rubber tubes to siphon off the wine. Between

turns at the cask bungs, we visited the showcases and cubbyholes to collect an assortment of souvenirs: shaving brushes, razors, cough drops, hairbrushes, bottles of patent medicine, clinical thermometers, and a magnificent stock of syringes and bulbs.

My last dimly lighted journey from showcase and counter to the back room became a peculiarly hazardous climb. Not only did the floor suddenly take on the aspect of a steep hill, but it began to spin as one struggled upgrade. Then the treacherous hill decided to change its position from up to down. The teetering of this world of showcases, shelves, bottles, casks, and bins contradicted all the laws of Sir Isaac. Ed Sullivan was announcing his intention to fly over the scene, a brilliant attempt which, if achieved, would antedate the feat of the Wright brothers by several months.

The first electric thrust of alcohol. . . . Ride a cockeyed horse to Banbury Cross . . . shall have a new master. . . . Sir, I perceive you are a vile Whig, a vile Populist, a vile Republican, a vile Democrat, a vile vial, violin, villain, village, vill . . . vill . . . anvil . . . hammer on the anvil, beating on a heart. . . . Will you be my girl? . . . Your parents are ·divorced. . . . Three names. . . . Dodie is dead. . . .

The seven or eight of us succumbed at last as though on a battlefield. We awakened at daylight to find the floor flooded with wine. We ourselves were sticky and wet with wine, inside and out. Someone had neglected, after sucking at a siphon tube, to remove it from the bung.

I turned on a water faucet. The stream did not slake my thirst, but instead spoke hissingly of the wages of sin.

"Father Cantwell will sure fix me," Sullivan was saying.

I reached home to find that Grandpa had gone to his day's work. And to my muddled dismay, I found that I had left my parrot out-of-doors all night. Always, until now, I had taken the cage indoors at sundown and covered it carefully with a calico cloth to shield Molly from drafts.

When Grandpa returned home that evening, he wordlessly

began to cook our supper, sour-dough biscuits and salt pork. I played tug-of-war with this stubborn food, and was about to go to my room when the old gentleman remarked in a matter-of-fact tone: "Your grandmother has a saying, 'There are three kinds of people who can't handle strong drink: the Indians, the Irish— and everybody else.'"

At what age do we begin to learn from experience and take warning? At about one hundred and seventy-six, I should imagine.

After a night of melancholy reflections, I merrily returned next day to a rendezvous with my cronies. They had confiscated a supply of saltpeter and sulphur from the drugstore to make an explosive mixture which we strewed upon the streetcar tracks. This time Henry Sellers captured three of our number. The police officer whacked us with his billy, then took us to Judge Ben B. Lindsey's Juvenile Court, where another tramway case, similar to our own, was to be heard.

We found perhaps twenty boys waiting to go before "The Kids' Judge" on various charges. I was well acquainted with two of these culprits: Red Rothwell, cousin of Young Corbett, world featherweight champion; and Paul Whiteman, son of Professor Wilberforce J. Whiteman.

Rothwell seemed nervous, but his co-defendant, Paul, appeared as calm as you please. In fact, the young musician was taking a nap in his chair as my cronies and I arrived at the courthouse. When Rothwell learned that I was "a tramway case," he awakened Paul to say, "Hey, they're in the same boat as us!"

Paul and Red were charged, among other things, with having applied butter to the car tracks on a hill at Eleventh and Sherman. They had committed this slippery deed a short time before the last trolley was due to pass at midnight on the way to the barns. Three passengers were aboard the car, but fortunately escaped harm during the frantic slide down the buttered iron.

Young Whiteman was happy to learn that I was a tramway case. "I can't think of anyone I'd rather have as a pal at the reform school."

Red Rothwell became panic-stricken at this reference to the reform school. "It's our tenth offense," he said. "I mean we've been accused of nine other little things."

"Little things?" Whiteman said with meaningful irony.

I myself was unable to feel at ease over the reform school prospect. "We're goners, eh?"

"I don't know," Whiteman yawned. "But Judge Lindsey always gives you a fair shake. Only don't tell him a lie."

The door to the Judge's "courtroom" opened. An attendant singled out the tramway cases. Those among us who had sinned against that corporation entered the presence of Judge Lindsey.

I saw in him a small man with a large head and large, widely spaced eyes. The eyes were friendly, but they saw inside you. The Judge sat on no fear-giving high throne, nor was he robed in a black toga. He greeted us cordially, memorized our names, then invited us to sit as a group beside him at the "conference table." There was no one present to take down notes or record testimony. This remarkable man would hold in confidence anything that we might say to him.

Judge Lindsey listened attentively to the charges made by Officer Sellers and the tramway investigator who was appearing against Paul and Red. "Thank you very much, gentlemen," the Judge said to the complainants. "Now you may retire. These boys and I will have a heart-to-heart talk."

After the men had gone, Judge Lindsey turned to Whiteman. "Paul, I am glad to see you again." He then added significantly, "And I believe I am going to see you more often for the next several weeks. Now, tell these boys what Professor Whiteman, your good father, detests most."

"A lie," replied Paul without hesitation.

"A lie and a liar," and the Judge inclined his head. "Now tell them what *I* dislike most."

"Same thing as my old man," Paul answered.

"Exactly," agreed the Judge. "A lie and a liar. And if I were a boy again, I'd never refer to my father as 'the old man.' Just a little courtesy that costs nothing. Now we all are agreed, I think, that we don't care for lies or liars. So, Paul, suppose you tell us what has been happening to you and Red, up to and including the buttering of the car tracks last night."

Paul began a recital that seemed astonishing from the standpoint of frankness and self-incrimination. "Judge, Red and I have been spotting houses where they are having parties. Then we cut the backdoor screen—"

"To help yourselves to the ice cream?" interrupted the Judge.

"Yes, sir. We do it every night."

"But last night," the Judge said, "you took a tub of butter. That mystifies me."

"We made a mistake," Paul volunteered. "The creamery delivered butter instead of ice cream. There wasn't any party there."

"So you took the butter anyway? Why?"

"Just took it," said Paul. "No reason, I guess."

The Judge studied the plump defendant. "You come from an excellent home, Paul. Of that I have personal knowledge. There is plenty of butter at your own house. And besides, you do not look as if you needed an oversupply of ice cream and butter. And just so that you may be reminded of your duties to a fine home and fine parents, I'll ask you to report to me each Friday afternoon during the next two months." He turned his eyes toward Red. "And the same for you."

The Judge then gave attention to me and my companions. After hearing our saltpeter-and-sulphur admissions, he delivered a probationary sentence similar to that accorded Paul and Red.

"By the way," he remarked to my group, "I never ask anyone to snitch, but I'll appoint you three as my deputies to notify all the other members of your crowd to report to me. They will do it of their own free will."

"Judge," I asked with much foreboding, "will you tell my Grandma about this when she gets back from Kansas?"

"Anything that goes on in this room is strictly among us pals," he said. "But you yourself will tell your grandmother all about your own case. And she will understand."

The Friday meetings with Judge Lindsey became events of pleasing importance. This man, himself childless, had for his children all the outcasts of the city, all the waifs, all the growing boys who were wayward. On rare occasions he felt he must send a boy to the reform school. But when he did so, that boy did not go, as in other days, in irons or with a guard. He was put upon his honor not to escape but report to the juvenile prison at Golden as though of his own accord. Seldom was this trust betrayed—three times only, I believe.

Benjamin Barr Lindsey was about thirty-four years old at the time when he heard our tramway cases. Already he had achieved a considerable degree of fame for his dealings with wayward boys and girls, as well as for his crusades in favor of social reforms. A native of Tennessee, he had come penniless to Denver at the age of sixteen. He worked at various manual tasks by day, then studied by night at the law offices of an elderly attorney. He was a brilliant student. In 1899 he became public guardian and administrator of Denver. He at once undertook the revision of court procedures in respect to delinquent children.

Judge Lindsey's readiness to forgive the young transgressor distinguished him from other managers of juvenile conduct. Until this innovator became the champion of the strays, any wayward boy seemed criminal bent. A girl sinned once and was lost forever; there was no road back.

This man spoke truth to adolescent Americans, and from them received truth. He did not bombard them with the thunderclaps of rhetoric or garb them with the sackcloth of the damned. There was a hill of truth, said the Judge. Many roads led to its summit. The Lord advanced to meet the seeker of truth, no matter by which road the pilgrim might come. Many boys strayed, but none should call himself lost. There were places to be avoided, just as a sensible boy thought twice before venturing upon the railroad trestle below Monkey Tree. But if caught when upon that high trestle, as my friend Ed Sullivan once was, and when a Colorado & Southern freight train roared down upon him, he escaped disaster by hanging by his hands over the side of the railway bridge until the cars stormed past. The important thing was to hold on courageously, then climb back to safety and not go on that trestle again.

There is no monument to Judge Ben B. Lindsey in the City of Denver. He needs none.

When Granny returned from Kansas, I hesitated to inform her of the events that had taken me before Judge Lindsey's court. But when the next Friday arrived, I had to supply a reason for my legal journey downtown. She accepted my confession with unexpected serenity.

"You will find that there is one judge you cannot appease or escape. His name is not Judge Lindsey. His name is Conscience."

After I had completed my probationary period, I became uneasy of mind. I had not told Judge Lindsey everything, and I felt that I had betrayed a trust. After weeks of indecision, I called upon the Judge to tell him about the drugstore raid and the experience with the wine casks.

"Oh," he said, "I know all about that."

This amazed me. "You do?"

"Yes, but there was no complaint made by Lucian's uncle. And I felt that you would tell me the whole story eventually. Feel better?"

"Yes, sir," I replied, "only I can't make things square with Molly, my parrot."

"No," the Judge said, "and any punishment I might deal out to you would be as nothing compared to your sorrow over the parrot."

My bird had become wasted and progressively ill since that night I had left her out-of-doors. She no longer sang or called to me. Molly's once bright plumage had lost its green luster. Her body-down was drab and filthy. She sat unsteadily upon her perch. Nor could she swallow the mashed vegetables that I pushed gently inside her two-hinged beak. I kept the bird alive by wrapping her in a piece of canton flannel, then placing her from time to time upon the apron of the warm oven. I used an eye-dropper filled with barley water to wet the small black tongue.

One morning in December Granny called out: "You'd better come here. Molly is flat on her back."

I could not find the courage to go to my pet. Instead, I remained in my room, a coward. Heartbroken and cowardly, I dared not look upon the thing I had done. Eventually I did leave my room to lift the wire-work dome from the cage tray. I wrapped the dead Molly in the canton flannel cloth. I then went out-of-doors to place the small bundle on the snow beneath the mulberry tree. Then I hacked out, with a prospector's pick, a place in the frozen earth beside Max's monument.

15

THE COMING OF SEA HORSES

THERE is always to be found among us a faultfinder, a kill-joy. We had one, a boarder named Mr. Frey, a book-subscription agent. This captious fellow solicited orders for the works of the late Professor O. S. Fowler, whose linen-bound lectures on self-culture and perfection of character, amativeness, matrimony, and phrenology supplied zestful reading to Victorians. So far as I know, Professor Fowler was not a relative of my stepfather, although Frank once paid fifty cents to have his own head examined by a phrenologist.

Mr. Frey received orders, as a side line, for enlarged crayon portraits. In fact, he bartered one of these pastels, a picture of me as a five-year-old, as payment for a week's board and room at Granny's house. I may say that if I at all resembled this portrait, my romantic aspirations were hexed from the beginning.

Mr. Frey not only persuaded the Sullivans to submit photographs of the family for the purpose of enlargement, but also sold Papa Sullivan one of Professor Fowler's most popular books, *Science of Life*. Mr. Sullivan placed this book among the several Civil War volumes in a glass-door secretary.

A broken pediment surmounted the Sullivan cabinet, with a

carved wooden crown instead of the customary urn in the center of the design. Papa Sullivan hid the brass-looped key behind the fluting of this diadem. Whenever Edward and I found an opportunity to do so, we would unlock the secretary and study the anatomical charts in Professor Fowler's book.

We were almost discovered at this research one Sunday morning when Mamma Sullivan's cousin, Mr. Messier, called with his large family of children. Mr. Messier was French, and all his brood spoke French. The good man owned an ice-cream factory on Nineteenth Street. Sometimes after Sunday Mass he would bring a freezer of ice cream to the Sullivans' in a closed delivery wagon. When he unlocked the tail door of the vehicle, the children popped out jabbering like the youngsters of the Old Woman Who Lived in a Shoe.

In the Sullivan parlor, where the ice cream was served, the conversation was carried on in French. Mr. Sullivan understood not a word of French, but pretended that he caught on. He would stay among the guests only long enough to eat the ice cream. Then he would escape the lively, shrugging, gesticulating linguists, saying, "It sounds to me like they're starting a fight." In another part of the house, he would get out his fiddle, tune it, and play Irish melodies.

On one of these Sunday mornings Edward and I had our ice cream in the sitting-room, on the other side of the heavy brown portieres from the babbling Frenchmen in the parlor. We decided to refresh our minds with an inspection of an especially attractive diagram in Professor Fowler's book having to do with the "seventh month after conception."

We were studying this chart like a pair of scientists when Papa Sullivan's boots sounded on the linoleum of the hall. Ed restored the book to its place beside the Civil War commentaries, but did not have time to remove the brass-looped key from the lock.

His ears ringing with Gallic echoes, Papa Sullivan entered the room, his fiddle in his hands. He crossed over to the secretary to open a drawer in which he kept sticks of rosin, cat-gut strings, and other accessories for the violin. He had opened the drawer but halfway when he caught sight of the key in the lock of the door. He removed it, looked at us searchingly, said nothing, then put the key in his vest pocket. As Mr. Sullivan left the room, he plucked at the strings of his fiddle. The next time when we looked for the key it was not in the wooden crown.

Papa Sullivan had one possession that I coveted, a pink mustache glass, with a glass guard bridging the inside brim. Mr. Sullivan kept it on top of a highboy in his bedroom. Several times I hinted to Mr. Sullivan that I would like to own such a treasure, but he said he needed it as a receptacle for pen points. He seldom wrote with a pen, but it was his habit to collect pen points as well as stationery from the many hotel rooms he visited during his sales tours.

The use of mustache cups was beginning to be looked down upon as an archaic practice. Uncle Dewey had put aside his own cup, and also got rid of his mustache. I decided to make a collection of these drinking vessels, so Uncle Dewey gave me his. I managed to accumulate several others from men who wished to belong to a new century and new fashions.

Granny permitted me to house the cups in a trophy cabinet in our parlor. She assigned them to a place on the bottom shelf where lay a chunk of brain coral, a bouquet of artificial daisies, and a box of earth from the Mount of Olives.

Mr. Frey one day examined the group of mustache cups and remarked: "Ah, hah! But have you got a left-handed one?"

This belittling experience warned me never again to display my prizes carelessly. Because of Mr. Frey and others of his quibbling kind, I also learned not to discuss with just anyone the thousand wonders that an adult world regarded as commonplace affairs.

I persuaded Granny to admit to the trophy cabinet yet another of my treasures, a dried sea horse. Mr. Blake had sent it to me in a pasteboard box lined with cotton. Until I saw with my own eyes this small mummy of a sea horse, I had always thought that a gigantic breed of marine stallions and wild mares galloped in the deep, to set up waves and winds. From words uttered by Evangelist Cranston at a revival meeting, I had come to a belief that sea horses actually were the ghosts of Pharaoh's steeds engulfed with their masters in the Red Sea. Perhaps the Chinook wind itself came from Egypt, the land of ancient mysteries.

The cattlemen and the flockmasters of Wyoming, our neighbors to the north, took the Chinook for granted. Perhaps, as I now write this postscript to my youth, I should consult the meteorologists as to the origin and conduct of a wind that arrives without fail in dead winter each year to lick up the snow, skim the ice from the rivers, and draw the frost from the plains, all in the course of hours. But somehow I dread the explicit words of scientists. There surely would be among them a Mr. Frey to ransack my miracle. So I prefer to rely upon the long-remembered words of Mr. Blake.

In a letter pertaining to sea horses and their habits, Mr. Blake satisfied my inquiries as to the Chinook phenomenon. That wind, said he, originated in the far-off Japanese current of the Pacific Ocean. It had been named, however, after the Chinook Indians of the Northwest. Early-day trappers and traders had observed the periodicity of the wind's arrival from the regions explored by Lewis and Clark. At a later time, when drovers brought Texas livestock to the plains east of the Rockies, great blizzards suddenly bore down. The herds strayed, and it was thought they surely would perish. But next spring the settlers were amazed to find their cattle alive and *fat* and the cows calving. The Chinook wind had uncovered the grass at a time of hunger.

The Chinook was vapor-laden when it first reached in from the Pacific to pile against the Cascade Mountains of Oregon, Washington, and British Columbia. The mighty frustration, as the gale beat against the lofty stone, drove the wind to a high altitude, where it became polar cold and drained of moisture. The cyclonic mass then descended as though in a thirsty rage on the other side of the Cascades. The rarefied Chinook, now warm from compression, burst eastward, drinking up the snows along its broad path. Then once again, as if experience had taught it nothing, the Chinook attacked mountains, this time the Rockies. The cavalcade smashed against this second barrier of rock, and once again was hurled sky-high. Thirstier than before, the Chinook raced down the eastern slope of the Rockies to suck up the snowdrifts and uncover the feed grass.

In January of 1904 the Colorado plains shared with the Wyoming ranges in the sudden thaw. The air became warm; there were bird songs as the Chinook paroled the earth from a white asylum. The good weather, so generously lent by Wyoming to Colorado, became a main topic of conversation. Even the war between Russia and Japan seemed a remote event that had little to do with a western world that breathed the gladness of false spring. Mr. Frey's pessimisms lost their effectiveness, although he did manage to exasperate Granny by speaking disparagingly of Theodore Roosevelt's policy in regard to the Panama Canal Zone, adding, "The country is going to the dogs."

"We have dark days and ugly forces sent by Satan to plague us," replied the old lady, "but, mark you well, we always survive them. Mr. Frey, when you have doubts concerning our country, you are thinking like an insect."

There was one controversial matter, however, that even the fair weather did not dispel. Sometime during 1903, a civic meddler had prevailed upon the officials to rename the streets west of Broadway in alphabetical order. The smug innovator had intended to deal in similar fashion with the streets east of Broadway, where dwelt the rich and influential personages of Capitol Hill. However, he dared not molest the avenues that bore the stalwart names of Lincoln, Sherman, Grant, and Logan.

The renominator of streets had his way with the westsiders, who lacked the implements of political favor. We saw new signs take the places of the long-familiar boards along Tremont, Water, Evans, and other thoroughfares. It was as if our part of the town were being remarried to a multitude of stepfathers.

As a person bedeviled by name changes, I may have held a

prejudiced view concerning this event. But many others regarded it as an atrocity. Mr. Sullivan, for example, wrote a letter of protest to Senator Tom Patterson, owner and publisher of the *Rocky Mountain News*.

Grandpa, of course, objected to this tampering with street names. He was infuriated by the fact that most of the new street names were Indian: Acoma, Bannock, Cherokee, Delaware, Elati, Fox, Galapago, Inca. . . .

As long as we remained in this neighborhood, Grandpa declined to recognize the change of our street's name from South Twelfth to Fox. At the polls, he insisted upon being set down as a South Twelfth Street voter. His mail frequently was delayed at the postoffice for readdressing or strayed for weeks.

Not even the fair skies tempered Grandpa's annoyance, though the good weather, as I recollect it, persisted until after Lincoln's birthday anniversary. As always the day was an event at our home. Early in the morning of this Friday, February 12, 1904, Granny read "When Lilacs Last in the Door-yard Bloom'd." Then she washed the dishes and Grandpa went to his day's work at Uncle Dewey's store.

The patrons of the Grand National, the madams and the lesser ladies of the red-light district, did not observe holidays or anniversaries by the reading of poems. They were busier than usual on all such days except Christmas, a time when they became sad and introspective.

After Grandpa had closed the front gate behind him, Granny announced that she was going to dust the parlor furniture. She began to fold a sugar-sack cowl over her head to protect her hair from dust. This pioneer woman now was a month past sixty-three years of age, and but for rheumatic twinges was as sound as Davy Crockett in his prime.

As I watched her wrap the sugar sack about her head, I wondered why she kept her hair sleeked back in such a plain manner; a gesture against worldly vanity, perhaps. Her hair now was quite gray, and whenever she washed it the curls that were its natural property softened her handsome face. But she peeled back the tresses that General Lew Wallace once had found so enchanting, and otherwise hid the charms that most women sought to emphasize.

Her only concession to beauty was to employ an occasional flick of powdered rice upon a skin as unblemished as a child's. No one other than actresses or women of the streets used rouge in that day. Nor did Granny need artificial coloring; like many women of auburn hair, she had been born with apples in her cheeks and cherries on her lips.

As I now remember that little scene of long ago, I suddenly am caught in wonderment concerning the strong white teeth of the woman. She retained them until she died in her eighties, and the only thing she used to cleanse her teeth was a little salt on a brush. For that matter, Grandpa also kept his own teeth, worn down as he grew very old. Notwithstanding the calomel he had consumed, his teeth remained firm and all that he ever did in their behalf was to rinse them at a creek when in the mountains or at the pump when in the city.

"Well," said Granny, as the last pin was placed in the sugar-sack hood that day, "we have work to do."

I had been looking at the pictures in the family Bible, and was struck by the similarity of Granny to Ruth. Ruth seemed much younger, to be sure, and wore no spectacles, but Granny, I thought, resembled her. Grandpa looked like Moses.

I ventured to announce to my grandmother that Grandpa was exactly like Moses, a pioneer and a rugged fellow. Granny patted her dust cap into place. "He resembles Moses in only two respects: he is always beating at rocks and looking at the Promised Land."

I thought this over for a time as I turned the gilt-edged pages of the great black and gold Book. Soon I was absorbed, as always, by the exciting pictures. There were two thousand of these, according to a legend engraved beneath the eye of God, an omniscient eye that looked out at the world from a diamond-shaped device on the broad spine of the Bible.

If this eye were not enough to prompt one's moral repair, then the Book's awesome illustrations would accomplish the reformation. Angels with flaming swords, the homicidal embrace of Cain, Noah cursing Ham, the departure of Lot and his salt-destined wife from blazing Sodom, Jacob in the hammerlock-hold of a winged wrestler, Samson tomahawking the Philistines with the jawbone of an ass, witches at work, kings falling on battlefields, cities toppling, writhing serpents, fiery chariots in the sky, disasters, devils, pits of eternal torment. . . .

I believed that a magic explanation of the gory tableaux lay in the meaning of the word "Selah," as contained in the Psalms. Were a person but to arrive at the meaning of the word, he would possess a charm against all the disasters shown in the Book of Books. Here it seemed was the mystic key that would unlock the secrets of ancient wisdom.

I made several attempts to have the word explained. Mr. Blake believed "the term signified a mere pause in the poems of David." He added that I should consult Granny on all matters of Scripture.

"I've counted all the Selahs," I informed Granny. "There are seventy-four of them."

"Indeed?" and she wrinkled her brow. "All right then, there are seventy-four of them; and if Jehovah wanted us to know what the word meant, He would have told us seventy-four times."

The Reverend Collins said that Selah meant "let the instruments play and the singers stop." I didn't believe him. Nor was I convinced by Revivalist Cranston who said, over a second helping of pie at our board, "Selah was a blast of trumpets by the priests. It may also mean 'Up, my soul.'"

Mr. Frey said, "Selah means Selah," and he winked with outrageous impudence at the family Bible that rested upon the fringed brown velvet throw of an oak stand. I wondered that he was not struck dead, for the golden eye of God saw him.

That Bible weighed fifteen pounds. It was five inches thick, and had cost fifty dollars, a fortune. Mr. Frey had endeavored to persuade Granny that her Bible was "behind the times" in respect to illustrations and reference notes. When he offered to procure for her another and better Bible, and accept seventy-five dollars worth of board and room in return for this courtesy, the old lady said: "Mr. Frey, when you speak slightingly of the Book that rests upon that table before us, you are speaking against the family altar. I shall prepare a sandwich for you to eat while on your way to some other house that is not so particular about its guests."

Mr. Frey went into exile somewhere in South Denver.

Whenever Granny spoke of the Holy Land, which was often, I became convinced that she had been there; not last month or last year, but at the time when the Tablets of the Law went into a second edition on Mount Sinai. She had all the vitality and pride of an eyewitness. It was my belief that she had survived deluge and locust plague to see the temple of Solomon rise. Ageless and privileged, she had stayed on, I fancied, for the Crucifixion. Otherwise, how could her stories of that tragedy be so precise and graphic in every detail, especially her noticing the trembling lips and the repentant blinkings of the Good Thief?

On this Lincoln's birthday anniversary, I ventured to ask, "Why did they have to give Mr. Lincoln the name 'Abraham'?"

"No one *had* to give it to him," she replied. "But he well deserved such a hallowed name."

"I think that the first Abraham was a bad old man," I said with conviction.

This announcement shocked her. "What in the world! Did that fool of a Mr. Frey tell you that?"

"No, ma'am," and I pointed out a picture in the Book. "Here's Abraham getting ready to kill his own son with a hunting knife."

"And supposing he is?"

"A father who'd kill his son can't be any good."

She lifted my hand from the page of pictures, then closed the great Book. "You are young and ignorant." She thrust a cloth in my hand. "Help me clean the furniture."

Granny began to polish the glass door of the trophy cabinet in the parlor, her eyes fixed upon the souvenirs of the past. The last keepsake put upon display was a three-piece tea set; it had been Dodie's most admired possession. Handpainted red roses beautified the teapot, the cream pitcher, the sugar bowl; and the handle of each piece was fired with gold leaf.

Granny permitted me to unlock the glass door of the cabinet and remove the dried sea horse, which lay like a question mark in the shallow, padded box. I was still thinking, however, of the patriarch and of his apparent willingness to slay his son.

"Abraham told a big lie to his boy," I blurted out.

Granny turned to me in a stunned manner. "Will you please explain that remark, and then promptly apologize to God?"

"Abraham told Isaac they were going up a hill to make a sacrifice."

"Which is Gospel truth," she said grimly. Granny always maintained that she permitted free speech in her house, but I think she did so on the premise that if anyone talked long enough he eventually would contradict his own arguments. I was mindful of this pitfall when she added, "Proceed."

"Well," I went on, "when little Isaac asked where was the lamb for the sacrifice? Abraham said, 'Don't worry about that, son, the Lord will have one for us.' "

"And that also is Gospel truth."

"No, ma'am," I insisted. "All the time the old man had a knife in his belt ready to stick Isaac."

"Abraham did this in obedience to God, who spake to him."

I shook my head. "And, besides, Abraham let the little boy carry a big load of wood up the hill; wood for his own burning, after he got stabbed."

"Now, mark you," Granny said, "Abraham obeyed God's command. Secondly, he didn't kill his son, now did he?"

"But he was going to!" I pointed out. "How could Isaac ever

trust him after that? A father that would tie up his son and wave a knife over him—"

She placed a hand over my mouth. "That's enough! And I'll have you know that Abraham didn't tell a lie; for when the Lord spake to stay his hand, there *was* a lamb caught in the bushes for the sacrifice."

I pulled her hand from my mouth to shout, "It wasn't a lamb. It was a ram with horns."

I now was strong enough to ward off her hand, but I did nothing of the sort. After I had exercised enough "free speech" to suit my own feelings, I deliberately restored her hand to my mouth, to give her a physical victory.

She began to chuckle. "You varmint! You mischievous varmint, you!"

And now our attention turned to another matter. We heard the sound of a "whoa" outside the house. Granny parted the ecru lace curtains at the front window. We saw Frank Fowler get down briskly from a buggy seat and drop a round weight attached to the bridle bits of a sorrel gelding.

"He must be doing nicely again," observed Granny.

As Frank entered the front gate, the old lady remarked his new derby hat and the suit of clothes tailored in keeping with New York fashion advertisements.

"Hello, everybody!" Frank cried out as he shook hands with us in the hallway. He explained that he had no time to sit down for a long visit, and announced that he had come to take us for a ride in his new rig.

"I don't see how I can manage to get away," Granny said. "There's a lot of work to do." She turned to me. "The chickens have to be fed."

"But it's a holiday," Frank reminded her.

"The chickens don't know that," she replied.

"I'll go feed them while you put on your Sunday dress," I volunteered. "Please, Granny."

"Well, all right," said she, "but don't waste so much corn this time." She left us, saying, "Excuse me, please, while I put on my best bib and tucker." As she reached the door to her bedroom she added, "My *only* bib and tucker."

Frank waved his derby toward the closed door. "She's the only one in the whole shebang that amounts to beans." He now noticed, for the first time, the sea horse that I was holding in the cotton-filled box. "What's that you got?"

"A dried sea horse."

"A dried *what?*" he asked.

I showed him the bony-ringed wonder. "Did you know that sea horses come out of their father's chests, or maybe from the inner edge of their tails? Mr. Blake sent it to me."

"Look here, son, I never did quite catch onto you." Frank drummed with his fingers on the stiff crown of his hat. "Why don't you buckle down to something that makes sense?"

I had no reply for him. I looked at the sea horse and said nothing to it; and it said nothing to me. But the sea horse and I understood each other perfectly.

"I don't aim to scold," Frank went on to say in a kindly tone, "only you must grow up to be a hustler and amount to something. Mr. Blake, who's he? Who's anybody that keeps his nose in a book?"

"I'd better go feed the chickens," and I carefully restored the sea horse to the cabinet. "Mr. Blake," I remarked, as I turned the key in the cabinet door, "has *written* a book."

Frank followed after me to the feed sack on the back porch. "Written a book, eh? Well," and he put on his derby with a flourish, "I bet it ain't a bank book."

I scooped grain into a pan and soon became the most popular figure in the chicken pen. Above the hungry tumult of the poultry, Frank was saying: "Don't think for a minute that I've lost interest in you just because . . . well, just because there's been a death in the family. What I mean is, you got to pick out something in this man's world and go after it. And don't moon around with sea horses and stuff that don't get you anywhere."

I scattered the last of the corn to the hens. "Did you ever read *Voyage of the Beagle?*"

"Beagle?" he snorted. "Sure. I had a beagle down in Arkansas. At least he was part beagle. But what I mean is, when I was a kid I put business first. Why, I even melted the spots of solder out of the bottoms of tin cans to sell it. I was a hustler from the word go. And when I gave you my name, I did it so's you'd have it to live up to."

I turned to go toward the house. "Do you want your name back?"

He put his hand upon my shoulder. "I don't aim to scold, like I just said, but too many people are failures simply because they just mosey along."

My back was turned to Frank. "I could use one of the other names," I said. "If you don't want me to have yours, maybe Charles Devlan would—"

He turned me about to face him. "We'll just forget all about that fellow. No, I want you to keep my name. I'm not an Indian giver."

As we walked toward the back porch, I looked off at Mt. Evans.

Frank clapped me on the back. "Now take my own case. Here I am building a hotel and cottages in South Boulder Canyon. A summer resort. My ideas will make it the greatest place there is. Promoted the money myself. Did I learn how to do all this in a book? No, siree!"

Granny appeared at the kitchen door in her bonnet, shawl, and Sunday gown. "I'm ready, Frank."

"The boy here," Frank said on our way around the house, "ought to be thinking of something more practical than sea horses."

"Give him time," Granny remarked as we got into the buggy. She smoothed her lace fichu, and spoke as if I were not present at all. "He's inquisitive and credulous, lively, and susceptible to affection. He would have been the first to follow the Pied Piper. Let him cherish his illusions as long as he can."

"Ho! Hum!" and Frank shook the reins to make his horse "hustle." As we drove along, he spoke of the new summer resort which lay in a fabulously beautiful valley pocket twenty-nine miles northwest of Denver. Warm water rose from the floor of the valley; Frank was capturing it in a large swimming pool.

It should not be inferred that Frank Fowler was a grinding money-grubber. Money of itself was not his passion, for many times he risked and lost small fortunes. It was action that he sought, and action that he saw as the mission of Americans. And in his fashion he had dreams and schemes of what he called "progress." His personal theory about his own fortunes was, I think a good one: "If I have money, anybody in the family or my friends can have a piece of it. If I haven't any money, they shouldn't even ask."

As we drove with Frank in his new buggy, he went on to say of his resort: "I'm calling the place Eldorado Springs. The water there contains radium. And I'm building a stairway up the side of Castle Rock."

"What on earth for?" Granny asked. "It sounds crazy."

"Good! Good!" cried Frank. "That's what I'll call it, 'The Crazy Stairs.' I'm stretching a steel cable across South Boulder Canyon, from cliff to cliff; five hundred and eighty-two feet high and six hundred and thirty feet across. The highest wire-walk in the world."

"Who'll walk across it?" I asked, the excitement of the moment crowding out the memory of the lecture on hustling. "Will *you* do it, Frank?"

"No, sir," and he seemed awestruck by his own words. "We're packing in the equipment right now and stretching the wire with burros. There's only one man to walk it; one man only. You've seem him do other great things. You've seen him up in his bal-loon—"

I cried out, interrupting him, "Ivy Baldwin!"

"Nobody else," said Frank. "The man has iron nerves."

I almost fell out of the buggy seat with ecstasy. "Will I see him do it, Frank?"

"We'll think about that later. Maybe so. My brother Fred is going to stand on one of the Twin Peaks the first day, to greet Ivy as he comes across the high wire." Frank's older brother was preparing to resign his position as a dining-car steward to operate the proposed hotel at Eldorado Springs.

As we drew up at a brick house, my remarkable stepfather said, "I'll own this cottage when the money begins to roll in."

"It's a pretty big place for just you and the children," Granny remarked as we got down.

"Come on inside," Frank said. "I want you to see something nice."

"What on earth might it be?" and the old lady permitted Frank to help her across a narrow irrigation ditch, the bank of which formed the sidewalk curb.

"Never you mind," said Frank. "Just come in and see."

There were two surprises in Frank's house. One was a new wife. Granny met her matter-of-factly. The second Mrs. Fowler was an auburn-haired woman of pleasant manner; her first name was Molly, the same as my parrot's had been. When Granny failed to comment adversely upon the marriage, Frank seemed gratefully relieved. He then introduced us to his second surprise, a private telephone on the wall.

"I transact a lot of business over it," Frank said of the instrument. Then he inquired of Granny: "Did you ever make a telephone call?"

"I can't say that I have," she replied.

"Then let's make one now," said Frank. "It's a great thrill."

"No, thanks," said Granny, plainly disconcerted by the prospect of making a first call. "If I have anything to say to a person, I always say it to his face."

"Oh, go ahead," Frank coaxed her. "They allow us two calls a day without charging extra."

"Telephones mean nothing to me," and the old lady fidgeted.

Frank seemed delighted to see the customarily self-sufficient woman twisting her shawl fringe and tapping the floor with her shoe. Perhaps he was thinking of the time when she had found a large mad dog in the chicken pen and fearlessly advanced upon it, waving her apron to occupy the snarling beast's attention till Frank could use his shotgun. Now a telephone on the wall disconcerted her. I had never seen her in such a dither except when exposed to dynamite.

"Are you scared, Granny?" I asked.

She roused to my heckling. "Scared? Why on earth would *I* be scared? And of what, pray?"

"Of the telephone," I said.

"Now let's see," Frank said. "Who should we call up? The Brown Palace Hotel? The Governor?"

"Call up Grandpa at the store," I sang out.

"Great!" Frank agreed. Then, while Granny was muttering, "Never mind, he'll be busy; just forget it, Frank," the capable promoter got the Grand National Market on the wire. He spoke to Uncle Dewey, boasted a bit about Eldorado Springs, asked how business was, then announced: "Somebody here wants to speak to Mr. Norman Wheeler. Never mind who. It's important."

Granny, her shawl askew on her broad shoulders, permitted Frank to place her in the correct position to talk into the instrument. When she heard a voice over the wire, enough of her composure returned to enable her to speak. "Norm? Is that *you,* Norman? Well, I'll declare!"

Her expression was the same as in the attic the time I had scarlet fever and she told me of Norman's gift of the small music box. "Now, now," she was saying into the telephone. "Go along with you! I just happened to drop in on Frank. And. . . ." She turned from the mouthpiece to ask, "Should I mention anything about you being married again?"

"Why not?" Frank replied. "He's hearing everything you say right now over the wire. Molly will say hello to him herself."

Mr. Wheeler obviously *had* heard the asides. To something he asked, Granny replied emphatically, "Oh, no! Nobody ever was as sweet as our little Dodie."

Then she yielded the receiver to Frank Fowler. He failed to introduce Molly over the telephone. As he put the receiver in place, a slight frown shadowed his eyes. Everyone was silent for a time, then Molly said graciously, "I know that your daughter was beautiful and fine, Mrs. Wheeler. Frank showed me her picture, and he said she was fine."

As we drove home, Frank seemed to be worrying about something. Then he said, "I hope you think it's all right?"

Granny pretended not to know what was on his mind. "Eldorado Springs?"

"Me marrying again," he replied. "I waited almost a year."

"It was nice of you to let me speak to Pa," she said.

Frank looked toward our house. "When things shape up right, I'm going to buy you a home all your own, with electric lights in it and a real bathtub."

"We manage to get along, Frank," she remarked.

"And as for you," Frank said to me, "I want you to be my guest at Eldorado Springs next year as soon as school is out. And bring the sea horse with you."

After Frank had driven off, I got out my bicycle and rode to the Sullivans' to spread the great news about Eldorado Springs. I found the household in a condition of excitement. Mother Sullivan was trying to induce her husband to pack his luggage in time to catch a train. Her four sons and two daughters were joining in her entreaties.

The spirited Hibernian was supposed to depart for Pueblo, his first port of call during the springtime sales campaign. "Papa's writing one of his hot-headed letters," Ed explained to me. "Won't budge till he's got it out of his system."

We found Mr. Sullivan at a table beside a huge brass bedstead upon which a grip and a sample case lay open among a welter of shirts, underwear, nozzles, faucets, and catalogues. On the wall at the head of the bedstead a crucifix looked down. On the opposite wall was a colored print of the Virgin and Child. To one side of the bed a picture of St. Joseph was hung. Across from St. Joseph was a huge reproduction in color of a painting of the Battle of Kenesaw Mountain.

Mr. Sullivan, in his shirt sleeves, was at work upon his letter. The indelible pencil was flying over one of many sheets of stationery that carried the names of various hotels. His hair and mustache glowed with Eastertime tints. He paid no attention whatsoever to the frequent warnings of his wife and children that he would miss the train.

"Can I go to Eldorado Springs next summer?" Ed asked his father. Mr. Sullivan held up a sheet of paper, then slapped it sharply with the back of his hand. "Hah! I guess that'll put *her* in her place, and *him* in his."

"How do you do, Mr. Sullivan?" I said. "Can Ed go with me to Eldorado Springs when we graduate from the eighth grade?"

He got up from his chair to look for a stamp in the top drawer of the highboy upon which the pink mustache glass stood.

"Never heard of Eldorado Springs," he remarked as he found a stamp in one of the small tin boxes in the drawer. He returned to the table, then began to address an envelope.

"You'll miss your train," Mrs. Sullivan again called out from downstairs.

"Train?" said Mr. Sullivan, and he licked the gummed flap of the envelope. "As if I'd let a train or anything else interfere with my duty to keep the record straight."

Mr. Sullivan thrust the sealed letter into the pocket of a coat on the bed. Then he commenced the last-moment packing for his commercial journey. "Always *try* to be polite to a lady, boys," he said. "But if they go too far, let 'em have it with both barrels."

He shook a finger at the pocket from which the letter stuck out. "I don't know the woman, only her name and her published address. Don't want to know her, in fact. But her husband died the other day, and she shot off her mouth to the newspaper—and by the way, I'm cancelling my subscription to *The Rocky Mountain News*—and she told them in an interview that her husband was the youngest veteran of the Army of the North."

He sucked in a long breath. "I wrote to this upstart of a widow. I says in my letter, says I to her, 'Madam, your husband may have been brave and all that, but when he bragged to you that he was the youngest veteran, he lied in his teeth.'" Mr. Sullivan caught St. Joseph looking down at him. He hastened to add, "The deceased probably was brave enough. God rest his soul."

Then he gazed at the picture of Kenesaw Mountain, stopped packing, and crossed over to the battle scene to point out a tree that showed above the smoke of cannon fire. "It's unbelievable, boys, but that's the exact spot, that tree, where I stood beating the drum—the youngest of all the Army."

"You'll miss your train!" came from downstairs.

"Oh, yes, yes," said Mr. Sullivan resignedly as he returned to the bedside to strap up his grips.

"Mr. Sullivan," I asked. "Would you do me a big favor?"

"Name it," said he.

"While you're gone, and if I promise to take good care of it, will you let me keep your mustache glass for you?"

"Well," he said, "I don't know. It's breakable."

"I'll keep it locked up with my collection," I said.

"Collection?"

"I collect mustache cups. I haven't got a left-handed one, but if I had a *glass* one. . . ."

"There are some pen points in it," said Mr. Sullivan, "but just empty them out in the drawer and take the glass."

"To keep?"

"It's yours," and he shook hands with me. "To keep."

After Mr. Sullivan had gone, and as I shook the pens from the glass, a brass-looped key fell out. Ed and I exchanged happy glances. Now we could resume our scientific studies of Professor Fowler's informative book. . . . Selah.

16

BETTER THAN A COACH AND SIX

THE possibility of going to Eldorado Springs seldom
left my mind during the remainder of that year and
the beginning of the next. This turmoil of yearning, of
waiting, of wishing, resembled the secret anxieties of a
lover in the throes of an unlikely suit.

I ran errands with uncommon zest. I sprang to fulfill commands.
There were fewer fist fights and no black eyes. My report card
during the final term in grade school showed two amazing im-
provements: I passed in arithmetic for the first time, and my deportment was recorded as "good" by the same teacher who earlier
had described me to Principal Cogswell as "an impetuous dunce."
Notwithstanding these honors, it seemed probable that summer
would find me working at Uncle Dewey's store. The Crazy Stairs,
the magic radium springs, and Ivy Baldwin walking the high wire
above the abyss beset my dreams.

I decided to test the efficacy of prayer. Perhaps this was an
ignoble stratagem, but I had grown desperate. It was well known
that shipwrecked men, when all else failed them, turned to prayer.
I hoped that it would work in my case. One day, when Granny
was cutting some canton flannel material for a nightgown, I inquired if prayer ever missed fire.

188

"Whenever it does," and she guided her scissors expertly, "it's because the one who makes the prayer is unworthy or his cause unjust. God answers every just prayer."

"Even the long ones?"

I had in mind the protracted supplications of Aunt Etta's uncle, the Reverend Harvey Scott. This retired minister wore close-cropped side whiskers the color of faded ginger and a skullcap of black moiré. Occasionally some ailing or weary clergyman invited Uncle Harve to occupy the pulpit for a Sunday. The otherwise gentle ex-pastor exhorted and prayed like a garrulous lion.

"The trouble with many prayers, especially the long ones," said Granny, "is that the seeker for blessings becomes greedy. It is fitting that we pray for exactly what we need, and nothing more. When we ask the Lord to give us this day our daily bread, it is neither fair nor honest to go on from there to demand cake, jam, roast pheasant, or to add: 'O Lord, while You are about it, would You mind sending down a coach and six?' "

It was my intention to enlist her pious influence. "I have been praying a little bit extra myself," I confided.

She began to curve out an arm size in the material for the night-gown sleeve. "Let us hope that your prayers are not selfish ones."

"Should I tell you what they are?"

"Whatever you say to Our Heavenly Father becomes a private matter," she observed somewhat casually, although she lifted a quizzical eyebrow. "When we approach the Mercy Seat, no one eavesdrops on us."

I began to despair of bringing my problem before her under the guise of prayerful discussion. "When Uncle Harve prays," I pointed out, "everyone within a mile knows what he's asking for."

"But only when he's praying for the whole congregation." She shifted the pattern, snipped and sheared it, as if editing one of Uncle Harve's invocations. "His prayers *could* stand a little cur-tailment."

"If you're not interested," I said, "maybe I could get Uncle Harve to do some praying for me."

This threat of taking my business elsewhere caused her to look up from her scissoring. "Oh, I may put in a word for you, provided your request is not a mere whim."

"I wouldn't bother God with something that isn't big."

She weighed this statement. "What is it that means so much to you at the moment?"

"It's not a moment," I said. "It's been a year."

"I've never known you to stick to anything that long. You mean to say you've been praying on one subject for a whole year?"

"Well, I've wanted it almost a year," I said, "but I've only prayed a week."

"It must be something important then."

"It's even better than a coach and six." I borrowed the tones of Deacon Green, the confidence man. "I've asked God to send me to Eldorado Springs this summer."

She fended me off with the shears to forestall a caress. "Now, now! Isn't that precisely what we've been talking about? The praying for a selfish reward?"

"If God will send me to Eldorado Springs," and I kept trying for an opening, "I mean God and you and Frank—"

"Suppose you leave Frank and me out of it," she interrupted. "You are not praying to *us*, mark you."

"But," I persisted, "you and Frank could act as the instruments of God."

"I'm afraid," she said, "that we need you here this summer. Suppose we wait, and then see."

That night I prayed so hard that Heaven must have thought that Uncle Harve had gone to work on the night shift.

At the coal-mining camp of Marshall, in early June, Frank Fowler met the train. The postmaster sorted the mail in the corner of the general store. Then my stepfather and I set out on a pair of saddled burros for Eldorado Springs, a mile or more west by south.

We approached a valley gateway formed by the walls of South Boulder Canyon. Frank pointed out Twin Peaks and the high wire, a spider's bridge strung between a cliff and a massive shoulder of granite. The summer resort lay in the valley beyond this rocky proscenium, and a brisk creek in which Uncle Fred cooled his beer skirted the new hotel and the cottages of the pleasant settlement.

After Molly Fowler welcomed me with a sandwich on the front porch of her summer home, my stepfather selected two envelopes from the mail brought from Marshall. "Would you take these letters to Ivy Baldwin's cottage?" and he nodded toward it. "The one over there by the hotel."

If I die because of an overstimulated heart, I want the coroner to get it through his head that the condition will not have been due to alcohol, tobacco, or wicked nights in the brothels, but because my stepfather asked me in that summer of 1905 to deliver mail to the renowned Ivy Baldwin.

Inside his cottage, the great man sat at a table, his back to the screen door. I stood for a hesitant time, the letters in my hand, and my nose pressed against the wire mesh. A pair of Police and Fireman's suspenders made an X on the hero's back. He was pasting a newspaper clipping in a huge scrapbook. I knocked lightly on the framework of the screen door.

"Come in, Frank," he called out, not looking around. "It ain't hooked."

"It's not Frank," I said as I stepped inside.

He turned on his chair to look at me with widely spaced eyes, squirrel shooter's eyes we called them. Overhanging black brows and a field marshal's mustache accentuated the breadth of his face. "I take it you're Frank's stepson?" He again sized me up, ripped open one of the letters, read it, then frowned. "Hm!" he intoned. "Hm! Hm! Well, that's a holler!" He looked up to ask, "Go to school?"

"I just graduated."

"Ever throw books at the teacher?"

"No, sir."

Ivy Baldwin re-examined the letter, then tossed it beside the scrapbook. "You don't have to call me 'sir.'" He read the other letter, flicked it across the table, then picked up the first one again. "Hm! Hm!" He rose to go to the screen door to look off at the high wire. I observed in him a man of short stature, a compactly fashioned gamecock of superlative grace and strength. Ivy Baldwin was five feet three inches tall, and weighed one hundred and twelve pounds. He then was thirty-nine years old, and quite indifferent to the fact that Death so often breathed upon his neck.

"I got a son named Harry," he said, as if addressing the high wire. "The principal writes me that Harry threw a book at him." The great Ivy seemed puzzled about something. "This here Mr. Twitchell writes that Harry won't be promoted unless I punish him." He turned from the doorway. "Will you hang around till I think up an answer?"

I was happy to stay in the vicinity of the hero but scarcely prepared for his next comments. "There are two things," he suddenly announced, "that almost scare me to death." I gazed unbelievingly. Was he joking?

"I don't see why all this folderol," he went on to say. "Harry's out of school for the summer, and he can't throw books for the next three months." Then he returned to the matter of his phobias. "Yep, two things scare me, and I don't know which scares me the most. One of 'em is I simply can't go down under the earth, like the time they tricked me into a mine elevator at Lead, South Dakota, then dropped me in the ore bucket two thousand feet down the shaft; and the other is when I got to write a letter. Writing a letter makes me shake all over. Nothing ever feazes me except when they put me in an ore bucket or I got to write a letter."

This confession distressed me. "Mr. Baldwin," I offered, "may I write this letter for you?"

"*Would* you?" he asked. "Would you take that bugaboo off my hands?"

"Yes, sir," I replied. "If you'll just tell me what you want to say."

He moved swiftly, lightly, like the best-balanced of all cats, to find pen and ink and a writing tablet. "Set yourself right here, son, and let's get it over with."

Mr. Baldwin, his eye again fixed upon the high wire in the distance, dictated as follows:

Dear Mr. Twitchell:

You say Harry threw a book at you. And you want me to do something about it. What's the matter with you? Ain't you big enough to lick him?

He now seemed in high spirits as he said, "Close it with 'Yours truly,' and I'll sign it. And thanks a lot, young fellow. Just for this, I'll let you peek at my scrapbook."

Ivy Baldwin had begun to compile his scrapbook in the eighties, and it seemed a story written in the skies. Six times around the world he had gone; his luggage a balloon, a balancing pole, green tights, a net, a parachute, camel-hide shoes, and his newspaper clippings. The scrapbook justified Ivy Baldwin's celebrity.

The firsthand reminiscences of the hero became fixed forever in my memory. He was not boastful or given to swaggering. Rather he spoke with a frank exactitude concerning his many feats, neither praising himself nor belittling. A man who walks a slender wire, rides a balloon, or dives from a tower into a net is a realist.

Ivy Baldwin was born in San Antonio, Texas, in 1866. His name then was Willie Ivy. As a boy he carried newspapers on horseback for the *Express* on the Government Hill route. The Express Building, then in West Commerce Street, really was his home, for he slept on paper piled in the basement pressroom. The backyard of the newspaper property extended to the river, and overlooked a swimming hole bordered by pecan and cypress trees. Old St. Mary's College stood on the opposite bank of the waterway. Ivy learned to perform on a trapeze suspended from a tree limb, and to walk a high rope stretched across the river.

He desired more than anything else to be an aerialist, and saved something each week from his earnings to buy green tights and spangles. His funds received a sudden lift one day when a man on horseback gave Willie Ivy ten dollars in gold to carry a message. The horseman was a fugitive from the law, Cole Younger, one of bandit Jesse James' lieutenants.

Willie Ivy purchased green tights. He advertised that he would walk a rope stretched seventy-five feet above the waters of the lake at San Pedro Springs while a band played a waltz. When he had accomplished this feat, the spectators passed the hat. Colonel Augustus Belknap, traction pioneer of San Antonio, sponsored Ivy's second public enterprise, a balloon ascension. The lad soon afterward joined the Thayer & Noyes Circus as an aerialist.

Captain Jenkins, the bareback rider, was the star of this show. When the equestrian failed to appear for a performance one day, Mr. Thayer invited Ivy to ride in the Captain's stead, adding that if he fell from the horse he could pretend to be a clown. The young aerialist was able, by means of his sense of balance and timing, to turn somersaults and stand expertly on the circus horse.

Late in the seventies, the Baldwin brothers, Samuel and Thomas, celebrated aerialists of the day, lost their third partner. They offered Ivy an apprenticeship with the troupe. The boy took the surname of Baldwin, and soon became the mainstay of the trio. Ivy Baldwin became one of the foremost high-wire performers in the world. In certain respects he took greater risks than did the French daredevil Blondin.

The tales of Baldwin's adventures, his escapes from death, were enough to make any lad's eyes pop out. It may be correctly assumed that I kept at his heels like a loyal spaniel. At our first meeting, I spent some time turning the pages of the scrapbook. Several newspaper articles written in foreign languages were pasted in it, among them some Oriental accounts, with line drawings depicting Ivy as he leaped from a high bamboo tower into a net.

"That's when I visited Japan in 1884," and Ivy chuckled. "The Japanese," he went on to say, "are kinda serious-minded, especially about newspaper ads. I was on my first trip around the world, making balloon ascensions and diving into a net from a tower a hundred feet high. When I got to Tokyo, I thought it would be good showmanship to take out ads that I was going to do it from a hundred-and-fifty-foot tower. Well, I went ahead and ordered my regular tower, excepting it was of bamboo and lashed together instead of nailed. When it was all finished, I got a call at my hotel from four polite Japs dressed up in swallow-tail coats and plug hats. They kept sucking in their breaths and bowing, and saying I'd please make my tower higher; and they showed me some newspaper ads that I couldn't read."

Baldwin chuckled again, then continued: "I says to these Jap callers, 'Higher?' I says. 'Do you want me to jump off of the moon?' Well, they put their heads together and bowed to each other and jabbered some more, and then said to me, 'Please, the promise is you jump, not off moon, but a hundred and fifty feet. We measure the tower, and it is, please, only one hundred.' So I had to add fifty feet to the tower. I hoped for the best, and made the jump. Three days later, the same plug-hat Japs called on me with a brown silk kimona, a present from the emperor. It had pictures of my tower embroidered on it and some balloons."

"Did you get hurt when you landed in the net?" I asked the hero.

"There's nothing to it," he replied. "After you fall the first seventy feet the air gets as thick as water, and you can turn yourself any way you want, just like diving into water. But you got to be sure to land on the back of your shoulders, just below the neck. Then you flip over on your back on the net and bounce twenty feet, and land rightside up."

Balance and self-confidence, he said, were the secrets of aerial success. "I think that's true of a whole lot of other things, too," he added. "Balance and self-confidence."

"But you do go to the hospital sometimes," I remarked.

"Oh, sure," he said. "Like the time in 1887 in Wichita Falls, Texas. I was walking a high wire between a livery-stable roof and the opera-house roof, seventy-five feet over the main street. I rigged two guy ropes to the middle of the cable to stay it, and I stationed two fellows down below, each one holding onto a guy rope. Well, I am in the middle of my performance, and the rope-holders are hauling smart against each other to keep the wire steady, when a roaring drunk comes galloping down the street on a horse. He rides into one of my assistants, knocking him loose from a guy rope. The other fellow, not aiming to do it of course, yanks the wire right out from under my feet. I fall seventy-five feet. I get four busted ribs and a busted ankle; but I'd never been bunged up at all if I hadn't landed on a pile of bricks."

A soft-soled shoe such as boxers wear lay beside the scrapbook. I presumed that the little shoe was Ivy's, for he had the smallest feet I ever saw on a man.

"It's got a camel-hide sole," he said of the lone shoe. "It don't get slippery in wet weather."

"Will you walk the wire across the canyon in this?" I asked. "And where's the other one?"

"I'm breaking in a new pair," he replied. "If you want to see the mate to this here shoe, you'll have to look on the bottom of San Francisco Bay."

Ivy Baldwin had made numerous balloon ascensions over the Golden Gate. He also had walked a high wire from the Cliff House to the Seal Rocks. After one of his balloon jumps, he became fouled in the parachute shrouds when in the water. While freeing himself he lost one of his shoes; he kept the other as a souvenir.

During the 1889 summer season at San Francisco, Ivy Baldwin signed a contract with John Elitch, Jr., of Denver. Mr. Elitch was the proprietor of a Larimer Street restaurant and owned an orchard and truck garden in North Denver, which supplied fruit and vegetables for his eating house. Mr. Elitch married one of his restaurant employees, a comely and intelligent young woman, and they prospered. Now he planned to build an amusement park known as Elitch's Gardens on the site of his fruit and vegetable acreage. He established a zoo there, arranged for Signor Satriano to give band concerts, and put up a large wooden theater where the asparagus beds had been. Stock companies of well-known players summered on the premises, and gathered stray asparagus among the petunias near the foundations of the theater.

Mr. Elitch engaged Ivy Baldwin to make balloon ascensions in Denver at five hundred dollars for each performance. The Gardens showed a profit of thirty thousand dollars the first season, but Mr. Elitch died of pneumonia eleven months after the resort was opened to the public in 1890. The property passed into the hands of Mrs. Mary Elitch, the widow.

Colorado pioneers held annual picnics among the pleasant surroundings of the Gardens, and children played there as if in a sanctuary of fairyland. The theater and Ivy Baldwin's daring deeds advertised the Gardens to all the world. Baldwin himself frequently gave exhibitions elsewhere, but he looked upon Elitch's as his headquarters.

As early as 1897 Ivy's mind turned to thoughts of flight in heavier than air machines. Together with Captain Glassford he fashioned, for experimental purposes, a box kite eighteen feet long and ten feet high and ten across. He used two-by-four timbers for the struts, and spans of reinforced muslin for the sail area. A piano-wire cable, paid out from an anchored drum, bridled the kite when aloft. It was a hazardous procedure to ride this huge contrivance, but Ivy decided to do so. One day the Captain and he managed to put the monster into the wind. A drag line trailed the big box as it began to soar free. Ivy climbed this cable hand-over-hand as the kite threshed against the tree-tops. He lifted himself inside the rectangular section, but had time only to unfurl an American flag when the kite made a downward swoop, dashed itself to wreckage, and knocked Ivy unconscious.

Baldwin, assisted by his wife—and afterward by his son Harry —made his own balloons. These envelopes ordinarily had a diameter of twenty-nine feet at the bulge, and a surface of two thousand six hundred and forty-two square feet. It was an enchanting spectacle to observe Mr. and Mrs. Baldwin amid a white sea of Dwight Anchor Brand muslin as they treadled the two sewing machines that stitched the gores.

Other lads of the town envied Baldwin's son his assignment to "dope" the fabric, to make it airtight with a paste composed of molasses, sulphur flour, yellow ochre, and alum. Harry did not regard his duties as anything to be coveted. Whenever a pitcher of molasses appeared beside the pancakes on the Baldwin breakfast table Harry would lose his appetite.

Ivy Baldwin filled his bags with fumes generated in a pit where wood and gasoline were burned. Or else, as in his larger captive balloons, Ivy used hydrogen given off from the chemical reaction of iron filings and sulphuric acid. Once he inflated a bag with commercial gas obtained from a storage plant a mile distant from Elitch's Gardens. A ground crew walked the filled balloon home, while Ivy himself sat aloft upon the trapeze. The six walkers kept the bag in tow at an altitude of forty feet. To get past the telephone and electric wires strung to poles along the way, Ivy directed his men to let go of the ropes one at a time. Then he drew in the lines successively, and dropped them in turn on the other side of the obstruction.

This procedure was tedious as well as expensive, so Ivy decided "to stick to the smoke-pit method." During the process of inflating an envelope, two attendants known as "sparkers" stood, one outside and the other inside the bag, with buckets of water to deal with a fire. The sparker stationed inside the balloon became exceedingly warm as fumes seethed past his head to bell out the muslin dome.

One of Ivy's sparkers, a colored man named Frank Frazer, lived in dread of ever going up in a balloon. He hummed spirituals and kept a suspicious eye on the big bag as it was made ready to lift Ivy Baldwin from the ground. One day, just as Ivy was about to spring to his place on the trapeze bar, the balloon escaped. Frank's foot got caught in a snarl of a dragrope. Upside down the sparker sailed aloft. He plainly was in a panic, and why not?

"Do somethin' quick, Mr. Baldwin!" Frank called out in transit. "I'se scairt!"

It was no sweet chariot that had swung low to carry Frank away. He now was alone some four hundred feet in the air; he began to wriggle like a dazed carp. The people of Denver understandably believed that Frank's performance was intentional as he soared above the city with one foot in a noose. The fact that he was a colored man lent a picturesque aspect to the show.

At about nine hundred feet, Frank decided that it was time to quit walking all over God's Heaven upside down. As a constant spectator of Ivy Baldwin's ascensions, and as one familiar in an academic way with the technique of ballooning, Frank analyzed his predicament. Then, in a manner of speaking, he began to climb his own leg. At fifteen hundred feet he succeeded in lifting himself onto the trapeze. The balloon and Frank eventually came down near the stockyards.

It might be supposed that Frank had a nervous breakdown, or that he boycotted Elitch's Gardens; but such is not the fact. From that time on, Ivy had difficulty in keeping Frank on the ground; he wanted to go up every week—a convert.

Perhaps Ivy Baldwin was the first man to have had a bird's-eye view of Denver. He usually ascended to an altitude of fifteen hundred feet. "If I went higher than that," he said, "no one could see me plain."

The aeronaut reported that the atmosphere was not as cold up there as it was when one climbed a mountain. "There's a warm current over the town, after you get up a thousand feet," he said, "and it stays warm up to fifteen hundred feet."

All these things my hero patiently unfolded to me.

During an ascension in Mexico, Ivy made a parachute leap into cactus country. Indian natives stripped him of his clothes, applied warm tallow to his body, and used a knife blade to scrape off the coating when it hardened, to remove with it the cactus spines from Baldwin's skin.

He had jumped into many other odd places, among them the jungles of Java, where he defended himself with a tree limb against wild apes. At another time, he came down among head-hunters of Borneo. The natives mistook him for a visitor from the spirit world and endeavored to persuade him to remain among them as their high priest.

Three of Ivy Baldwin's balloons exploded or burned when aloft. He had his closest call during the Santos Dumont dirigible craze. He had fashioned a cigar-shaped bag and a gondola for a 4th of July ascension at Elitch's Gardens. While he was consider-ing the problem of powering it, he received a visit from a per-suasive, white-bearded fellow, who introduced himself as "Pro-fessor Starling, physicist and weather forecaster."

"I ain't worried about the weather," Ivy told the Professor. "What I need most is a contraption to run my dirigible."

"Exactly," the Professor said, "and I've got it for you."

"Where is it?"

The Professor said that his machine was of such importance that he must decline to show it to anyone until the evening before the ascension, and then only to Ivy. It was something that would startle the world.

On the night before the 4th of July, the Professor drove an express wagon to Elitch's Gardens. Then, as the Professor drew aside a tarpaulin, Ivy saw an array of electric storage batteries, several lengths of stovepipe, and twelve electric fans.

"Maybe," Ivy said in speaking of the incident, "the contraption could have given me enough power. But the darned thing weighed eleven hundred pounds. The total lifting capacity of my dirigible was only three hundred and fifty pounds."

When informed that his batteries, pipes, and fans were too heavy, the Professor threatened to sue. In recalling the episode, Baldwin added: "He kept hollering, 'You've blasted my reputation as a physicist!' The crowd expected a real dirigible, so, just for the effect, I hooked up two of the batteries to one of the fans and lashed them aft in the gondola. I was up about eight hundred feet when a battery worked loose, and I was afraid it would fall on somebody. When I went aft to make it fast, there was an explosion. The bag caught on fire. I landed in some trees, with severe burns and bruises."

In 1898 Ivy enlisted with the Signal Corps of the United States Army in the war with Spain. He built a captive balloon and went up in its basket during the Battle of Santiago. During a flight over the front lines, the balloon was shot down by small-arms fire.

On the day when I examined Ivy Baldwin's scrapbook at Eldorado Springs, I forgot all about returning to Frank Fowler's house. It was growing dark when Frank entered the Baldwin cottage to say to me, "I was beginning to think the coyotes had got you."

"I was just telling the boy," Ivy said, "how I was making a high-wire walk between two office buildings in Baltimore when I bumped into a city ordinance that—"

"Better save it till some other time, Ivy," Frank interrupted. "Molly is waiting supper."

"Frank," Ivy asked, "did I ever tell you that story, the one about Baltimore?"

"I'm more interested in how many people we'll draw next Saturday," Frank replied. "I've advertised the high-wire stunt all over the state."

My stepfather's indifference to the Baltimore story seemed an appalling circumstance. I have never become quite used to the world's way of withholding its ears as well as its flowers from the living. How can it be that workaday mortals everywhere rub elbows with great men, but not see their mighty qualities?

"Mr. Baldwin," I said, "I'd rather hear what happened in Baltimore than eat."

The hero exchanged glances with Frank, who said good-humoredly, "Seems like you got a steady customer, Ivy." On his way to the door, Frank added, "Send him home if he gets too much for you."

After my stepfather had gone, Ivy Baldwin lighted a kerosene lamp. "I've got a cold chicken here, and we'll boil some coffee on the coal-oil heater."

As he prepared this most wonderful meal, Ivy said: "Oh, that Harry of mine! Harry once picked up a dog that had been run over by a streetcar and nursed it back to health. One day at the fair grounds, while I was getting ready for an ascension, Harry's dog sneaked into the frankfurter concession and gobbled up a lot of wienies. Then he dragged a whole bunch of wienies behind the grandstand. And when I refused to pay for the damage, the fellow at the frankfurter concession made Harry work for him the rest of the week for nothing. And I didn't interfere, because it's a good thing for a kid to learn how to straighten out his own troubles."

"But what happened in Baltimore?" I reminded the hero.

"Oh, yes," and Mr. Baldwin set down two tin cups for the coffee, and said that we would eat the chicken from our hands. "Well, it was the Shriners' convention, and I was booked to walk a wire a hundred and twenty feet over the asphalt street. After I'd made the walk, I got pinched. The cops said there was a city ordinance that forbid any aerial act without a net under it. The judge fined me five dollars and said, 'Don't you try it again.' That night I went to the waterfront and bought me an old fish net. The next morning I laid the net flat on the pavement, and I made another walk. When the cops got ready to pinch me again, I had the haw-haw on 'em. I showed 'em I had a net, even if it wasn't a regular one and even if it lay flat on the pavement."

The day for the great event arrived at last. Ivy Baldwin was to set out upon the record-breaking walk on a cable stretched across South Boulder Canyon. About fifteen hundred persons were there to see the deed, many of them doubting that it could be done.

It was a warm afternoon, almost cloudless, and the sun beat against the rocks of Twin Peaks. Ivy Baldwin was serene. He dressed himself for the performance with all the care of a matador. First he strapped a leather-covered guard between his legs, explaining: "I don't aim to fall, but when a man falls, he must straddle the wire. First you let the balancing pole hit the wire, exactly in the center of the pole. That breaks the fall. Then you let your crotch hit the wire. And if a man's crotch ain't padded, then it's just too bad."

He drew on a tight-fitting union suit, and over it a short-sleeved white shirt, the collar of which he turned inside. Then he stepped into an old pair of trousers, saying, "You expected tights and spangles, eh? Well, that's for circuses. These pants are my lucky ones." The cuffless trouser legs were narrow and cut high above the ankles. Now he put on white cotton socks with no garters. "Can't trust garters," he said. "They might come loose and trip you." Next he took the new camel-hide shoes from a cardboard box, inspected them, flexed the soles, then laid them aside after looping the laces together.

"Stones cut into these shoes," he explained. "I'll put 'em on when I get up on Castle Rock. Then I'll roll the socks down over them." He drew on a pair of old boots, looked out at the wire and at the sky, then said, "Now you go with Fred up Twin Peaks, and be the first to congratulate me as I come across for a new world's record."

There was a cheer as Ivy climbed the Crazy Stairs. He had the manner of a champion, not arrogant, but not too chummy with his admirers. His wire-walking shoes dangling from one hand, he moved like a ballet master. He raised his other hand in a circus-arena salute.

Fred Fowler was climbing Twin Peaks, but no admiring eyes were turned in his direction. Uncle Fred was a big fellow, and his muscles were unaccustomed to any exercise other than standing at the money tills of railroad eating houses or of dining cars. He puffed as he climbed to a place on a rock shelf opposite the cliff where Ivy now was taking off his old boots and putting on the camel-hide shoes.

"I should have brought along a bottle of beer," the perspiring Fred was saying. "It's hotter up here than a Harvey House stove."

Little gusts of wind carried the voices of the spectators up the mountainside. Across the chasm Ivy was lifting the balancing pole, a hickory spar twenty-five feet long and weighing a pound to each foot. The champion was hatless. He stood with the sun beating against his neck and shoulders. Now he grasped the pole, his hands perhaps two feet apart, the palms turned outward from his body. The pole sagged on either side of the man, who carried it belly-low. The pole ends dipped down to wire level, lowering the walker's center of gravity.

There were no cheers as Ivy Baldwin set out upon what he estimated would be a six-minute walk, allowing for pauses midway over the wire for "stunts." There were no cheers, for it is an American courtesy not to disconcert a champion as he risks his neck.

Baldwin did not fix his eyes upon the wire as he set his practiced feet down upon it, but kept his gaze far ahead and to one side of the strand. There was a slow cadence to his movements, a precision and a grace, as he set down his small feet upon the seven-eighths-inch thickness of the woven steel. He occasionally glanced at the two guy wires that formed a long inverted V from the high cable down to anchorages on the canyon floor. Perhaps he was remembering the thing that happened to him in Wichita Falls when the drunkard had ridden in. If he fell today, it would be for five hundred and eighty-two feet.

Suddenly Ivy Baldwin leaned to one side. He actually was leaning against a surge of wind that funneled through the canyon toward the plain. Such flurries as this one came without warning, and lapsed with fickle haste. Only the alacrity of the champion and his long acquaintanceship with the skies permitted him to cheat the eccentric gust.

In the vastness of the scene, he seemed a bead on a string. Halfway across the chasm, Ivy lowered himself and his pole to straddle the wire. Then he almost contemptuously drew himself up again to rest one knee on the cable. Next, he lowered his head, and stood upon it on the wire. The spectators cheered him as he curled himself over to his feet to resume his journey.

The walker had been on the wire for perhaps five and a half minutes, and was about forty feet away from Fred's place on Twin Peaks, when he stopped short with a wavering stance. "Hey, Fred!" he called. "Start counting out loud, and keep right on counting."

"Counting?" the amazed Fred shouted. "Counting what?"

"Start counting 'one, two, three,'" Ivy said, "and keep it up good and loud."

"What in hell's got into you?" Fred inquired. "Are you crazy?"

"I've gone blind," Ivy said in a calm voice.

"For God's sake!" Fred exclaimed. "Are you kidding?"

"Commence counting," Ivy said, "so's I can tell by the sound what direction I'm going."

Fred's concern was great. "One, two, three . . . one, two, three. . . . Are you all right, Ivy? One, two. . . ."

"That's it," Ivy said, and his face showed not a shadow of fear or dread. "How close am I? Fifteen feet?"

"About fifteen, I'd say, Ivy. One, two, three. . . . For God's sake! . . . One, two. . . ."

Ivy was within six or seven feet of his goal now. "Don't grab me careless, Fred," he directed. "Just de sure and get hold of the middle of the pole exactly between my hands. And stand braced."

"One, two, three. . . ."

Ivy was within Fred's reach now. Uncle Fred, shaking in his boots, braced himself. "One, two. . . ."

Fred seized the pole. Ivy sprang from the cable to the rock shelf. "Well," he said, "I never had anything like that happen to me before."

"What the hell went wrong?" Fred asked. "Can't you see anything?"

"The sun," Ivy said, "was mostly to my back, and I hadn't counted on it bothering me. But when I kept looking at the rocks ahead, the reflection blinded me."

"Can you see now?" Fred inquired.

"Only some round zigzags, like green fireworks. Tomorrow I'll put on a pair of smoked glasses."

Fred guided Ivy to the edge of the rock shelf, where the champion gave his circus-arena salute as if nothing out of the ordinary had occurred.

The sun was not Ivy Baldwin's problem on another day. This time it was cloudy, and the champion himself saw storm warnings that should have persuaded him against walking the high wire. But he said that he would not disappoint the spectators.

When he had got halfway across the canyon, a cloudburst descended. The watchers saw Ivy almost blown from the wire. Great sheets of water beat upon him. He hung by his knees for more than twenty minutes. He struggled up at times when the rush of blood to his head became insupportable.

The lightning drove against the rocks as though the devil himself were clapping his hands. Hail followed the lightning and rain. But Ivy finally managed the crossing, although his journey from Castle Rock to Twin Peaks was an hour long.

At this writing, Ivy Baldwin is eighty years old. I last saw him in the springtime two years ago at his home at Marshdale in the Rocky Mountains.

I had returned to Colorado to look upon scenes dear to my youth, to seek out the surviving pioneers, to have last words with my heroes: Lord Ogilvy, of whom I wrote in *Timber Line*, and who said recently at eighty-six that he was "too proud to die"; Colonel Bill Thompson, Silver Dollar Tabor's bellboy in Leadville; and Fire Chief John F. Healy, whose heart only a few months ago grew still.

"Where'd you like to go most of all?" Chief Healy asked.

"To see Ivy Baldwin."

We drove in the Fire Chief's car over splendid roads that had been mere trails when I was a boy. The years fell away. It was as though I were aboard old Number Sixty once again, looking out upon the mile-high plateau; at old farm machinery, rusty and forlorn, like outmoded authors; plow furrows etched in lines, arcs, and chevrons on the contours of the prairie swells; the new alfalfa rugs on the brown earth; silos and barns bearing old and tattered circus posters, hangnail souvenirs of long-ago holidays. Then the arroyos, their sides palisaded; clover and lilacs and columbines; the cattle grazing, heads low, their tails out like pump handles. The foothills. . . .

The thunder comes up fast in May. Dark clouds converge. There are great rolls and crashes, an overture to celebrate one's return to the hills.

When the storm lifted, we were at Ivy Baldwin's home. And across the high meadow Mt. Evans stood in full view.

The little man was in his yard watching his cat chase cottontail rabbits. Their little scuts bobbed like powder puffs among the wild grasses. Ivy was older by forty years since I had seen him walk the Eldorado Springs high wire; older by thirty years than the time I watched him fall with his homemade airplane into Sloan's Lake. Older, yes, but one might know him anywhere; the squirrel shooter's eyes, the shoulders square, the field marshal's mustache fiercely spread above the wide mouth.

"This is a surprise," said Ivy. "I'm kind of holed up these days."

The Chief was examining a coil of wire cable on the ground.

One end of it was looped to a block-and-fall, and the other end fastened eight feet above the earth to a stout fir-tree trunk. An X-shaped brace of undressed pine and a balancing pole lay beside the cable.

"What's all this, Ivy?" the Chief inquired.

"I've been teaching my grandson to walk the wire," Ivy replied. "Care to come inside and set down?"

"No," and the Chief pointed a thumb at me. "I just took time off to deliver this horse thief. I got to get right back in case the city catches on fire."

As the Chief's car went out of view, Ivy said, "Fifty years he's been a fireman; the gamest man I ever saw."

We went to the house. I observed that Ivy's legs were not what they used to be, and he puffed a bit. "They tell me I got arthritis and heart trouble," he said, "and I think they all are a pack of liars. I'm as good as ever."

"Still got the old scrapbook?" I inquired.

"Yep," he replied, "and there'll be a lot more clippings in it soon. I'm going to walk that high wire at Eldorado two more times, no matter what your brother or anyone else says."

My brother Jack, who now owned Eldorado Springs, had told me of Ivy's intention. Baldwin had walked the high wire across the canyon ninety-eight times in all, the last time when he was sixty-five. It was his ambition to accomplish the feat one hundred times, but Jack, as well as Ivy's son Harry, had vetoed it.

"I'd like to humor Ivy," Jack told me, "for I love the old boy as well as anyone. But I don't want to go to prison or be hanged for murder. And he's liable to sneak up here one day and get out on that wire before we can catch him."

I was turning the pages of the old scrapbook when Ivy asked almost timidly, "How'd you like to see me walk the wire out there in the backyard?"

I tried to stay calm, but a great excitement took hold of my insides. I thought of Ivy's age, his arthritis, his heart condition. I did not want to be a party to the death or injury of my long-time hero. What to say? There was a whimsical expression in the squirrel shooter's eyes.

"Yes," I said eventually, "I'd really like to see you walk the wire again."

He did not bother to put on his camel-hide shoes. Perhaps his eagerness to perform before an audience, albeit an audience of one, caused him to neglect the usual preparations. He led the way to the backyard apparatus, refused all assistance as he drew the wire taut by means of the block-and-fall, and then wedged the X-brace, like the bridge of a violin, under the already tightened cable. The wire extended about thirty feet to the tree trunk.

"Can't use a ladder to get up," he explained, as he picked up a balancing pole. "I'm too stiff in the joints to climb ladders. I'll have to walk up the stays."

He held a short hickory pole today, with pieces of lead pipe battened on either end to give it weight. And now he began the climb up the hemp lines of the block-and-fall to the crossing of the timber X. I wondered how he would manage to get past this barrier and onto the wire.

All stiffness suddenly left him. He threw a small foot in an expertly graceful arc over the obstruction, then followed with the other foot. And now he began the walk, and I forgot my concern for his safety. Memories of his great exhibitions at Eldorado returned to me, and perhaps came back also to the old champion. His performance was flawless.

When he reached the tree at the end of the wire, I felt relieved. I was wondering how he would get down and if it would be tactful to offer a hand. Then he suddenly began to return to the X-timbers, and I almost had a heart attack myself. Now he was walking *backward!*

When he had completed this fine exhibition, and had come down the block-and-tackle hemp, I began to applaud. The champion was delighted to hear the clapping of hands, the noise of which was magnified by the hills, by Mt. Evans, white and massive in the near background.

17

AND SOME IN VELVET GOWNS

JUST recently I decided to consult several of my old jilters, belatedly to explore a question that once stood like a scarecrow in my mind. Except for a devastating timidity when in the presence of women whom I have admired, I have not been able to account for my romantic bunglings of long ago.

"You are wrong in thinking I did not like you," said a grandmother who, at a time now remote, had all but driven me to suicide. "But you were always eating something. Carried pieces of dry toast in your pockets."

"Gene, dear," said another, a spinster, who forty years ago had sonnets instead of lips, "how was I to know that you cared? Why, one night when we were sitting out a dance at Cotillion Hall, you suddenly remarked above the music, 'I wonder if a horse's legs ever go to sleep?' Naturally, that kind of talk. . . ."

She kissed me good-by, an act that, forty years ago or even thirty, would have lifted me to the heavens. I decided not to proceed further with my canvassing of old loves. And I now leave it to the big-eyed psychologists to determine—if it be important—why I stayed out of the trees of Adam's orchard until after I had reached the age of twenty-three.

After the Eldorado Springs holiday of the summer of 1905 I entered high school, but an attack of erysipelas soon interrupted my first term. Upon my recovery, I did not return to school at once but went to work as a delivery boy at Uncle Dewey's store instead. It became a year of paradoxes in respect to the life lived inside oneself and that which one showed to the world.

The Grand National Market supplied meats and groceries to houses of ill-fame, large and small. I had daily contact in the red-light district with the people of a forbidden world. Alive as I was to the savage hungers of adolescence, I escaped seduction in the brothels, a fact that makes my experience unlike the adventures of such writers as stand naked in their inkwells. In the years to follow I would undergo seasons of amorous waywardness, but not now.

The inmates of the cribs and parlor houses may have had much to do with my youthful continence. Contrary to legend, these women were not the cunning agents of a boy's depravity. I believe that any man's vice is of his own making, be he young in blood or an old rake flying the remnants of his passion like a riddled banner.

The Grand National Market seemed to me to have been transported from Bagdad. Its shelves held merchandise seldom heard of by ordinary Westerners, or tasted by them. These expensive goods were imported for the epicureans of the red-light district, many of whom were continental Europeans. The panders of "The Row" spared no expense on self-indulgence in wine cellar, wardrobe, or at table. I have long observed that the worse off a man's morals are, the better he dines, drinks, and clothes himself.

The chief employee of the Grand National, Mr. Ott, behaved as if this market and all its assets were his own. Mr. Ott was a Rhinelander. He wore a militaristic mustache in the Hohenzollern fashion and was supposed to look like Kaiser Wilhelm. He treated the rest of us, Henry the butcher, Carl the clerk, and myself, as if we were his subjects or his troops. The stern Rhinelander was the best grocer I ever knew. His thrifty ways with the merchandise offset the losses incurred by Uncle Dewey's generosity, Grandpa's carelessness at the scales, and my huge appetite.

Among other skills, Mr. Ott could manipulate a crate of strawberries fresh from the wholesale market, turn out the fruit on a clean paper, then rearrange the berries so artfully that there would be enough left over for an extra box; and all the other boxes would seem fuller than before. Mr. Ott heaped the berries with an air space underlying the top layer of each container, explaining that this procedure "involved the principle of the arch." He would hold a large berry before his eyes, saying, "Dis is my keystone. Yah!"

Nothing that ever occurred at the Grand National escaped Mr. Ott's eye; he would have made an excellent prison guard. It was his habit to inspect everything and everyone "like they do in the Old Country." Whenever he held one of his ear lobes with thumb and forefinger and fixed you with his small eyes, you were aware at once that a reprimand, as well as a lecture on discipline, was forthcoming.

Uncle Dewey didn't care how much I ate from the stock, but Mr. Ott would upbraid me for my continual nibbling. I carried in my pockets enough prunes, raisins, crackers, and bars of chocolate to support a soldier two weeks in the field. When I began to educate my palate to such imported dainties as caviar, anchovies, pâté de foie gras, or smoked sturgeon, Mr. Ott glowered and barked out, "Dis is going too far. Yah!"

Mr. Ott was an apostle of cleanliness. It also was Uncle Dewey's nature to be meticulous, and Henry the butcher wore aprons worthy of a chief surgeon. There was one discordant note, however, and one person over whom Mr. Ott could exercise no control. I refer to Grandpa. Not only did the old prospector look like nothing that belonged to a grocery store and meat market, but he insisted upon wearing corduroy trousers tucked in at the tops of unshined boots and keeping on his old miner's hat, the pancake relic of the hills with its ore dust and stains. The only concession the man of the mines made to business was a penny pencil thrust beneath the sweatband of his hat and in front of his right ear. Sometimes he absent-mindedly forgot to remove the pencil at the close of day. Then, when on his way home on the streetcar, he would discover the pencil and pluck it from its place as if it were an advertisement of a prospector's demotion.

The women of the red-light district seemed genuinely fond of Grandpa; they called him "Dad." He would not, however, permit the men customers to call him that. Whenever one of the male habitués of Market Street became so familiar as to address him as "Dad," the old gentleman would say frigidly, "The name is Wheeler."

It was not openly declared, yet I soon came to understand that I was not to reveal to Granny the full facts of my exposure to the regions of carnal events. The usually sagacious woman stayed as ignorant of my delivery-boy adventures as she had been of the sporting-house upbringing of the late Molly, the parrot.

I was going to my place of work one day on a streetcar of which George Pell was the conductor. I had not seen Mr. Pell since Dodie's funeral, for he soon thereafter had left his place as organist at the church. Mr. Pell, I thought, asked too many personal questions today. I did not know until long afterward that he was maintaining a loyal correspondence with Charles Devlan. He asked me this day why I did not write a letter to my father.

"He never writes to me," I said.

"Your father is a mighty fine man."

I did not reply to this, although I was pleased to hear a good word spoken in behalf of one to whom my thoughts often turned.

"He never loved anyone but your mother," Pell continued. "And naturally he'd be interested in anything you do."

"How do you know he would?" I inquired.

There was a swishing sound overhead, and the car faltered on a curve. "The darned trolley has slipped off again," Pell said on his way to the rear end of the car to take care of the trouble.

The car started up again, and Pell, puffing from his efforts with the trolley rope, returned to ask, "Where do you get off?"

"Nineteenth Street," I answered him. "I'm working at Uncle Dewey's store."

Pell seemed stunned. "Ain't that kind of a bad neighborhood?"

"I deliver groceries in the red-light district," I replied with an air of worldly superiority.

"You mean you see and talk to those women?" he asked.

"They're all nice to me," I replied. "Mighty nice."

Pell's eyes were wide. "And your grandmother permits it?"

"Uncle Dewey and Grandpa are there, too," I said.

"Powers above!" Pell exclaimed. "The old lady must be daft."

"Why don't you tell that to her?" I asked.

"Oh, no!" and he quailed. "Nobody can tell her anything. No, sir!"

Pell soon afterward called upon Uncle Dewey at the store. I heard only part of their conversation as I brought in the empty baskets from the wagon in the alley.

"George," Uncle Dewey was saying, "you mean well, but it's none of your business, and it's none of Charlie's business. I keep an eye on the boy."

"But," Pell objected, "he's bound to see and hear things."

"He'll see and hear less around here," Dewey said, "than he would running the streets. Moreover, these girls are looking for dollars, not delivery boys."

"Well," said the worried conductor, "I suppose Charlie ain't got any rights in the matter."

"None at all," Dewey replied. "And if Charlie moved his backside off that mountain and came down to Market Street once in a while maybe he'd not be in such a crazy stew."

"That ain't fair," Pell said.

"But it's the way a man's made," Dewey said. "You can't hold off year after year and not. . . ."

A commotion at the front part of the store interrupted the conversation. "It's Pa again," Dewey said resignedly. He hastened to the grocery department to find Grandpa hurling cans of French peas and crocks of goose liver at a male customer, then grappling with him. My sixty-six-year-old grandfather was fighting fiercely, but not according to the rules of boxing as formulated by the Marquis of Queensberry. Grandpa's antagonist was a procurer known as Diamond Louie, so called because of the numerous gems he wore, including a diamond set into an upper front tooth.

"Here, now," said Uncle Dewey, "what's going on?"

"I'm beating the hell out of this pimp," Grandpa said from a clinch. "That's what's going on."

Diamond Louie was yelling, "Get this crazy old bastard off of me!"

"Break, Pa!" Uncle Dewey commanded as he went between the men. Then, as Mr. Ott, Henry the butcher, and Uncle Herman restrained Grandpa, Diamond Louie straightened his coat, took an invoice of his gems, felt of his jeweled tooth, then announced: "From now on I'm trading some place else. See?"

"I see," Uncle Dewey replied. "And you're dead right, Louie, because your teeth might come loose around here."

As Diamond Louie left the store, Grandpa called after him, "I don't like pimps and pimps don't like me."

Pell, goggle-eyed, cut in with an "Excuse me," and then departed. Dewey turned to his father. "Now look, Pa, none of us likes pimps, but they are paying customers. And you can't go throwing cans and slugging a paying customer."

"I'll slug 'em every time they make fun of my hat," said Grandpa. "And your friend Billy Wheeler is next on my list, if he don't look out."

The Billy Wheeler to whom Grandpa referred owned several cribs. The fact that his surname was the same as Grandpa's, with the false implication that the men were relatives, did not heighten the old prospector's regard for Billy. The landlord of the cribs was a quiet, self-possessed man with a passion for fine foods and the works of Rabelais. He introduced me to the tales of this master, but advised me not to tell just any blockhead about my reading of Rabelais' works.

I kept the borrowed classic beneath the seat cushion of the delivery wagon. Mr. Ott, with his genius for inspecting everything, came upon the book. He reported the circumstance to Grandpa. The old gentleman examined the book, saying, "I can't make head or tail out of it, but that damned Billy Wheeler's name is written in it."

Mr. Ott gave me to understand that Rabelais was a man of filth, but I had not observed this fault while reading the story, and I maintain that a great work of art never corrupts the young mind. The shoddy counterfeits may do so, as when I had been drawn into dark speculations by the piously worded articles in the Dr. Fowler book at the Sullivans'. The Dr. Fowler essays had roused in me grave thoughts. The accompanying diagrams had troubled me, particularly the chart which had to do with female anatomy; at first glimpse it looked like a drawing of the Labyrinth in which Theseus slew the Minotaur.

I was happy, when in possession of Billy Wheeler's Rabelais, to drive Bessie the old mare along the alleyways and read about Pantagruel or Panurge. On the day when Grandpa condemned the book because of its autograph, I mischievously asked him if he were a relative of Billy Wheeler. I stayed out of his reach for the next two days.

Although the Grand National stood among ramshackle buildings, with the Casa Bianca wine house on one side of it and a pawnshop on the other, there were many places of historic interest in this old part of the city. The once elegant Windsor Hotel was not far away on Larimer Street. That hotel now was on the downgrade, but its solid black-walnut doors, the marble pavement, the great mirrors, and other souvenirs of the days of the pioneers still remained in place. In the second floor suite, where Silver Dollar Tabor had died, was the town's first bathtub, the size of a child's coffin. The tub had been used by such famous visitors as Oscar Wilde, ex-President Grant, Charles Dickens, Mark Twain, Eugene Field, Rudyard Kipling, the Grand Duke

Michael, Robert Louis Stevenson, W. H. Vanderbilt, John L. Sullivan, Emma Abbott, Bernhardt, and Modjeska.

Uncle Dewey did not permit me to enter two buildings of the neighborhood: the Arcade, a gambling palace, or the Alcazar, a burlesque house. But business gave me access to many other places of forbidden grandeur. And perhaps the old mansion of gray stone with rose-stone trimmings at 1942 Market Street was best established in my romantic recollection.

It was there that I first met Trixie; and although she never knew a thing about it, she became my Dulcinea. I saw in Trixie the successor to the fabulous and beautiful darling of the pioneers, Sarah Jane Rogers, known to the generation before mine as Jennie. Madam Rogers had built this house and long reigned in it.

Market Street had been Holladay Street in the late eighties, a time when Jennie became the favorite of the western nose-thumbers of Commandment Number Seven. The provocative brunette had come from Pittsburgh, and soon afterward had built her mansion. Symbolic sculptures were chiseled in the rose stone. There was a horseshoe in a garland of flowers over the doorway. Among the other ornaments of the façade, there were five faces carved in relief. One was that of a smiling maiden. Another was the countenance of a woman of provocative lips, one eye closed in a sensual leer. There was a man's face, fat as if from gluttony; and an aging woman's, her lineaments suggesting a life assigned to worldly matters. The fifth face was that of an old man, and in it there were lines testifying to the folly of bought embraces.

As a fifteen-year-old boy peeking at the mementos of the mansion's scarlet past, I stole glimpses of the mirrored ballroom and the solid walnut banister of the stairway in the hall. Jennie's golden harp once had stood near the entrance to this ballroom. A grand piano now was there, and at night one heard music and the whispers of silk.

Memories of Jennie still were fresh in the minds of many

men. Her romance with Jack Woods was spoken of as late as 1905, the time when I delivered groceries at the back door of the mansion Jennie had built. It was recalled that she had found her greatest love one day in the nineties when out for a drive in her Victoria, a glossy black masterpiece. Her parasol, her accessories, her driver's and footman's liveries, the horses, all matched Madam Rogers' black hair. On this particular day, a brick wagon blocked the path of the madam's black horses. A broad-shouldered young man, his hair the color of his cargo, sat upon the buckboard seat of the brick wagon. He was whistling happily, and paid little attention to the stylish courtesan.

Soon after this chance meeting, Jennie managed to become acquainted with the handsome brick hauler. She recommended that he get an education, but he took a job in Colonel Bill Thompson's saloon instead. The Colonel, formerly Silver Dollar Tabor's bellboy in Leadville, had become the foremost saloon man of the West. There was no free lunch to be had in the Colonel's Denver saloon, but a drink of whisky there was an honest dram and not, as now, a trickle of atrocious spirits served in the flaw of a paperweight.

Jack fell in love with Jennie, who preferred him to the senators, judges, mining magnates, and all the rest of her suitors. Jack's was a roving nature, however. He prevailed upon Jennie to set him up in the saloon business in Salt Lake City. She placed the saloon in her lover's name, but prudently held the first and second mortgages on it herself.

Jack's visits to Denver became less and less frequent. One day Jennie paid a surprise visit to Salt Lake, where she learned that Jack was behaving in a frivolous manner. She walked into his saloon, shot at him, missed, then promptly foreclosed on the mortgage.

Having lost his bar and the most coveted beauty in the West as well, Jack went to Omaha to set himself up in business there. He talked in his sleep of "Sarah Jane," and when Colonel Thompson visited him, Jack was thin but still handsome. The Colonel returned to Denver and to Jennie's place and, while the wine was being chilled, Jennie inquired, "What kind of a visit did you have, Colonel Billy? Did you have a good visit?"

"Oh, I had a fine visit." Then he asked, "Rogers, why don't you ever write to Jack?"

She poured the wine and said with forced indifference, "Oh, you saw Jack, eh? Has he taken on any flesh?"

"He's still six feet of solid man."

"Well, Jack had a fine head of red hair. A good horseman too. Drove mighty well, even when he had the brick wagon. There was something about him, and the way he handled horses, that was distinctive. Well, I'm glad you had a good trip, Colonel Billy."

"I'll tell you frankly, Rogers," the Colonel said, "Jack spoke about you often. Asked how you were, and was your health good. He said he'd write to you, but told me, 'Colonel Bill, I don't believe she'd answer.' "

Jennie shook her head. "No, I don't think I would write back. That's all in the past now."

The Colonel called for another bottle of wine. "Rogers, let me tell you something. I'm going to make you a proposition."

"What is it?" asked Jennie. "I don't want to do anything foolish."

"Rogers, you write a letter. Just write any kind of a letter, only not insulting, of course; but just a plain letter saying 'How are you?' or some such thing, and give it to me to mail. If Woods don't answer it, I'll buy you a nice twenty-five-dollar hat. If he does answer, I want you to buy me a sealskin cap at Weber & Owens."

Colonel Bill soon afterward received a sealskin cap. Then one day Jack returned to Denver and called upon the Colonel. "Billy, I've got an important mission and I want you to help me. I want you to ride with Julia Newhouse [Jennie's housekeeper] in a carriage to the Windsor. I want you to pick me up at the Windsor, and drive out on the West Side where there's a certain preacher who's going to marry me to Sarah Jane, and I want you to be the best man."

Colonel Bill stood up with them at the wedding, and Jennie and Jack lived happily together for several years. When Jack died, Jennie buried him at Fairmont Cemetery and erected a fine granite monument over his grave.

Jennie Rogers employed twenty-four girls at her mansion during the early days, it was said, but I doubt if ever she had one as beautiful as Trixie. I first saw Trixie in the kitchen of 1942 Market Street. A kitchen is perhaps not the most romantic of places, but a kitchen was not merely a kitchen that day late in the fall of 1905. Two dogs in the backyard, huge and suspicious beasts, barked at me. The basket of groceries was heavy on my shoulder. I had to brace the basket against the wall as I opened the door myself, the cook not being at hand.

Then, as I went inside the kitchen to lay down my burden on a table, a woman's voice said, "Don't look!"

I wish I could be a gentleman. I wish a great many things. But why speak of decorum, of discretion, of anything when one's breast is full of jumping beans and fifteen years of life?

I did not know Trixie's name then. She had no name, it seemed to me, and she had all names. Other than a pair of high-heeled slippers, she had on no clothes. I did not know what had brought her to the kitchen, and I was not the kind of person to ask idle questions. Of one thing I was certain, and that was the way Keats felt when he first saw the Grecian urn.

Trixie hastened out of the kitchen, and I went to the backyard, completely forgetting to take the basket with me. The big dogs barked. I reached the wagon, my senses playing leap-frog. Then I drove Bessie with unaccustomed speed to the Grand National.

At the store, the efficient Mr. Ott observed, "You're one basket short."

"I guess I lost it," I stammered. "Must have fallen out of the wagon."

"Dot's kind of careless. Baskets cost money." He stood holding an ear lobe and studying my ill-ease. "You needn't take it dot hard. Just don't let it happen again."

I made it my business to learn the girl's name. She was beautiful and dark, and she had a way of walking into my skull at night. I could tell whenever she was coming into my skull long before I would see her in the moonlight. I could hear the sharp rapping of her slipper heels on the floor of my head.

All night long I would dream of Trixie, and all day long think about her. It seemed as though I would never see her again, for she apparently did not frequent the kitchen, and I was not permitted of course to enter the house by way of the front door above which the stone horseshoe stood against the rocky garland of flowers.

In the slender hope that I might come upon Trixie somehow during my deliveries, I resorted to such subterfuges as neglecting to take a whole order of groceries to her house on one trip. I would leave behind at the store or in the wagon a loaf of French bread, or perhaps a bundle of endive, then go back to the mansion on the pretext of delivering the mislaid package.

Mr. Ott soon put a stop to this practice. It was his unvaried procedure to check all the deliveries, twice inspecting each package in every basket or box, and comparing it with the description and price as entered on the bill carbon. After I had made an extra trip to Trixie's place for the third time in one week, Mr. Ott dressed me down for my carelessness.

He sent me into a panic by saying, "Vot is dis? Is it somebody you like to wisit at dis fancy place?"

I had almost despaired of ever seeing Trixie again when one day I was driving my grocery wagon and, in the manner of the late Jack Woods, crossed the path of a smart carriage in which Trixie was riding with her madam, Leona de Camp. But, unlike the fortunate Mr. Woods, I received no attention from the ladies. Still, I lived upon this vision for a week.

I became indifferent to the sordid aspects of the red-light district, so occupied was I by my dreams of Trixie. To be sure, I could see that the alleyways and the squalid backyards were still there, and that for the most part the women of the cribs, in their cheap, short dresses and with their painted cheeks and cigarette-stained fingers, were not a happy sort. But I moved in a condition of mind that denied what the eyes actually saw. Even the wax-faced mumblers in the bunks of the opium dens of "Hop Alley" did not arouse my natural curiosity. The noisy saloons, where the women and men danced the dances that afterward became commonplace gyrations in polite society, were passed by with scarcely a glance on the part of the enamored delivery boy. His horse was drawing a chariot through the regions of his own enchantment. I did, however, notice one thing clearly and as it really was, and that was at Christmas time, when a most melancholy hunger showed in the eyes of all the women of "The Row."

Of Trixie I dreamed through the long white winter, then on St. Valentine's Day of 1906 my plight became downright hazardous. I had wanted all along to send her a note, a poem even. But I remembered my bad luck on the day long ago when I had placed a note on a school desk. It was reasonable to assume that Trixie would not condemn me as Helga had done for being the son of divorced parents, but it would be wise not to risk Trixie's scorn, or, worse still, her laughter.

On Valentine's Day, I bought a somewhat ambitious creation with a winged cherub framed in a mat of paper lace and an outer ring of heart design sprinkled with flecks of gypsum. I did not sign my name to this token, to be sure. Instead, I printed the magic word, "Trixie," on the back of the valentine. I waited until after Mr. Ott had checked the basket that was to go to the mansion. Then I surreptitiously placed the valentine among the articles ordered for Trixie's house.

I hoisted the other baskets and boxes onto the wagon, then returned to get the one that contained my gift. I was unprepared for what I now saw. Mr. Ott was standing over the basket, the valentine in one hand, an ear lobe in the other.

"Oho!" he all but shouted. "A walentiner it is!" I said nothing, at least nothing out loud. Then the stern fellow barked, "Look at me! Vot is dis?"

I still pretended not to know what Mr. Ott was talking about. When I reached down to lift the basket, Mr. Ott said, "No hurry." He waved the valentine in front of my nose. "Your grandpa sent dis, maybe? Yah?"

"Oh, no," I replied, looking past Mr. Ott toward the front part of the store.

"Maybe I better go ask him," Mr. Ott said.

"I wouldn't do that," I advised.

"But, no?" and Mr. Ott's ear lobe was being plucked ominously. "Den maybe the uncle sends it? Ve vill ask him."

"Oh, I don't think he'd send anything like that."

"You don't t'ink so," and he mocked my voice. Then he turned to address the live alligator that Uncle Dewey kept in a shallow tank shielded by chicken wire. "Did you send de walentiner?" Mr. Ott asked the sleeping reptile. He affected great surprise when the alligator had no reply. Now, while I shriveled inside, he went to the cage in a dark corner, where Uncle Dewey's pair of white owls sat like dwarfed ghosts. "Did you fellows . . ." he began, then he wheeled about, marched up to me, his face a grim magenta. "Everybody says noddings. And it is de first time I find out ve sell walentiners in dis store."

"I better get started," I muttered over the basket, and my voice seemed to come from a far-off cave of despair.

"Hah!" Mr. Ott snorted. "Started at vat? Started at funny business?" He glared at me, then at the valentine, announcing, "Ve vill look into dis t'ing. Vot vill de uncle say to it? Vot vill the old grandpapa say? Yah! Vot vill the Madam Leona say ven I—"

"You're not going to snitch on me, are you?" I asked in great alarm.

"Dot's better," and he nodded. "You admit it! Vell! Vell!"

Then he said insinuatingly, "Tell me all about it, you and Trixie. Everyt'ing. Begin at de first."

"There's nothing to tell," I objected. "What would there be to tell?"

"Aha!" he exclaimed. "Noddings to tell, he says!" Then he became more grim than before and turned as if to go, the valentine in his hand. "Ve vill let de walentiner tell it."

"Mr. Ott," I almost howled. "It's the truth. I just bought a valentine, and that's all. Trixie doesn't even know I'm alive."

He came back to where I stood. He studied me closely, then said impressively, "I haff only dis to recommend, and it is for you to learn dat until you get old enough to wear long pants and go in de front door of a fancy place mit five dollars in hand, don't go in de back door mit only walentiners. Yah!"

"I won't," I said, putting out an unsure hand toward the valentine. "Will you give that back to me now?"

"*Nein,*" and he shook his head slowly. "I will just keep dis walentiner someplace. And for my saying noddings about it, you vill show me how good a grocer clerk you can become. I vill train you vot to do every day, and you do it, and no fooling. Dot's discipline like in de Old Country. And now you must say *auf Wiedersehen* to dis Trixie and all funny business."

In this manner I was blackmailed into becoming an alert, industrious, efficient, and capable grocery clerk as well as a dependable delivery boy. No one's horse ever received better care than mine. Although Bessie was but a dumpy, aging mare, I curried and brushed her gun-metal hide as if she were the charger of Lancelot. I was up at daybreak on market days, to go with Uncle Dewey or Mr. Ott to the open-air wholesale market where the farmers displayed their vegetables, eggs, and poultry beside the banks of Cherry Creek. I scraped the meat blocks, turned the grindstone to sharpen the knives and cleavers, polished the marble slabs, kept clean sawdust on the butcher-shop floor, learned to be polite even to Mattie Silks, the most testy-tempered of the madams. And all these labors were as nothing whenever I thought of Trixie—or remembered that Mr. Ott held over me the weapon of a winged cherub framed in a mat of paper lace and an outer ring of heart design sprinkled with flecks of gypsum. I tried vainly to find the hiding place of the incriminating valentine.

When summertime had come again, and there was talk of my re-entering high school in the autumn, I did not want to leave the vicinity of Trixie's house. Then one day I learned that Trixie had vanished from the mansion, but I did not find out at once where she had gone, or why. Had she died?

Although I mooned over the disappearance of my loved one, I must admit that my appetite, contrary to the usual history of young heartaches, remained huge. I managed to outwit Mr. Ott by smuggling goods from the store when he was in the basement brewing coffee for his lunch. Anyone who observed my eating habits never would have guessed that I was pining away.

One afternoon when the smell of burning leaves was in the cool air, I set out to deliver an order of goods to the home of a Mrs. Blank in South Denver. I found a small cottage that lay in a respectable although unpretentious part of the city. I did not know who Mrs. Blank was, but was given to understand that she had been a former customer of the Grand National.

When the back door was opened in response to my knocking, Mrs. Blank turned out to be Trixie. My confusion was great. She was plainly dressed in a calico wrapper, and she seemed extremely contented and housewifely. Trixie had on no rouge, and there were no high-heeled slippers on her feet. But Trixie was Trixie, dressed no matter how. It occurred to me that she now was married. A great, aching resentment boiled inside my breast. I felt that Trixie had been grievously unfaithful to me. Moreover, as she directed me where to set down the order of groceries, she gave no evidence of ever having seen me anywhere before, or caring to do so ever again.

Years afterward my uncle happened to say, in discussing the matter of courtesans entering wedlock, that Trixie had stayed happily married. I should imagine that in a world of change we never should be astonished or amazed at anyone's change of profession. Change also has come upon the old mansion built by Jennie Rogers, in the kitchen of which I first saw my love. That great house now is a Buddhist temple, where gongs sound and incense is burned. *Auf Wiedersehen.*

18

A MUSIC MASTER AND HIS SON

I WAS still reeling from Trixie's infidelity and the Teutonic discipline of Mr. Ott when I chanced to learn that one of my contemporaries was enduring miseries similar to mine. I refer to Paul Whiteman. Paul and I seldom meet these latter days, but whenever we do, we speak of Wilberforce J. Whiteman, his father, my friend of long ago.

I have been asked who was my best friend. My best friend is the one I am with, or he is the one of whom I am thinking. He may be far away, or perhaps he lives in the same town as I, the same block, or possibly the same house. Or again he may be with the vast democracy of the dead. My great friend is a member of a group, a somewhat large one I like to think, and as such he represents all friendship, and he stands neither first nor last. Is he poor or rich? It does not matter. Is he famous or obscure? That is of no import. Today I am thinking of Wilberforce J. Whiteman.

The son of this Rocky Mountain music master was well acquainted with my young years of window-shopping for a father; and Paul now agrees with me that Wilberforce J. Whiteman was the beau ideal. He did not think so, however, at the time when several girls and Wilberforce were making of his adolescence a seeming hell.

In conformance with the tradition of violinists, Paul Whiteman was unable to fix his mind constantly on any one girl. Each of his romances, however, was violent while it lasted and kept him in a condition of worried excitement. If I am remembering correctly, there were seven Whiteman heart hurricanes in 1906, the year of the San Francisco fire and the shooting of architect Stanford White. The young musician had nothing to do with either of these tragic matters; I make reference to them merely to indicate that the planets were restless. Paul's seven romances that year persuaded him that his troubles were seven times as many as mine, and Wilberforce's discipline seven-fold that of Mr. Ott's.

Young Whiteman played the viola. One evening in 1906 he was playing it with a four-piece dance orchestra. He escorted one of the young dancers home to sit on the porch swing. Paul placed an arm about the lass. A signal bell began to beat inside the girl's house. Lights flashed on. The sound made by heavy boots on the upper floor and stairway was heard. Thinking that he had set off some fantastic kind of burglar alarm, Paul ran to his motorcycle and rode off just as a huge man came on the run through the front door.

Paul afterward learned that the commotion had had nothing to do with his romantic designs. The father of his potential sweetheart, a fire department captain, lived at home near the fire house. An electrical connection was looped in from the main circuit to a signal box in the captain's bedroom.

Whiteman's second romantic frustration that year had to do with a chorus girl who was appearing for one week on the stage of the Broadway Theatre. Her admirer shadowed the stage door, Paul having read in a dime novel how a man of the world behaved during such a campaign; but sadistic employees of the theater interfered with the romance. On the first night of the company's Denver engagement, a practical joker asked Paul to go across town to the Tabor Grand Theatre, there "to borrow the key to the curtain, as we just broke ours."

Paul was detained for two hours at the Tabor Grand, then given a piece of iron junk weighing many pounds. He returned with this bogus key to the Broadway, to find that the performance had ended and his shapely loved one gone. During the remainder of that week, Paul similarly was blocked, duped, betrayed.

At this period of Paul's growth—and he was beginning to reach broad proportions—his home life was supervised with great wisdom by his father. My own interest in this father-and-son relationship was more than the exercise of childish curiosity. I was keeping an eye upon the fathers of my friends in the earnest make-believe that my own recluse parent, if he chose to do so, could come down from his high hill opposite Mt. Evans and excel in every respect all the other fathers whose talents I was appraising. I was keeping tally on Wilberforce Whiteman's relationship with his son, placing it beneath that most powerful of spyglasses, a child's eye.

The elder Whiteman, a native of Fairhaven, Ohio, had been the champion cornhusker of his state. Work in the fields had given him powerful forearms; he had, as it is said of certain boxers who punch hard, no wrists. The music master was as fastidious as a boulevardier; he wore a socially approved waxed mustache, and a gay boutonniere known in those days as a "Bob Hilliard." Like his son, Wilberforce ate heartily; but, unlike Paul, the father did not gain weight. He stood five feet nine inches tall, and seemed to weigh not more than one hundred and forty pounds. Actually he weighed one hundred and seventy pounds, all muscle and vigor.

An excellent boxer, he put on the gloves with his son every day except Sunday. "It will take off some of that fat," he would say.

One morning Paul observed a carbuncle on his father's neck. Paul hoped to escape pugilistic exercise.

"Oh, no," said the elder Whiteman, "we shall spar, as usual, but I'll ask you to look out for the carbuncle."

Paul had the extreme misfortune to jab the boil. He was given

the most effective lacing since the time Kid McCoy defeated
Tommy Ryan at Maspeth, Long Island.

Notwithstanding Mr. Whiteman's readiness of fist, his appearance was that of a curator of a Museum of Fine Arts. His courtly
airs stayed the same, were he boxing, hunting grouse, or leading
the choir at Trinity Church. Music commanded his thoughts, but
many other interests kept him from becoming lopsided of mind.
Wilberforce played both the violin and the organ for his own
private pleasure. To the western public he was known as a choir
master or chorus conductor, and director of music for the Denver
public schools, a post he held for more than thirty years.

This pioneer brought more than the precepts of musical art to
the young men and women of the Rocky Mountain West. He
taught them the value of systematic conduct and the rewards that
come of self-command. And I believe that his son, notwithstanding his own demonstrated talents, could not have attained such
lasting eminence in the world of modern music had it not been
for the fireside supervision which the boy rebelled against, denounced, resented, and now remembers with affection and gratitude.

Among my own recollections of the music teacher, there springs
to the foreground his paradoxical serenity on the day he knocked
out the toughest rowdy of Elmwood School. That grade school
was so dangerous to men teachers that even its burly principal,
Mr. Zirkle, had to keep in splendid physical condition at all times.
Mr. Whiteman met the ram-like charge of the tough pupil with
the same placidity that was his when bringing a pitch pipe from
his waistcoat pocket. The contest was over before one could say
Wolfgang Amadeus Mozart. A left hook, short and mallet-fast,
felled the champion of Elmwood. It seemed incongruous that a
slim professor in pin-stripe trousers and black broadcloth coat,
an owner of pitch pipes and tuning forks, possessed such speed
and strength.

Wilberforce J. Whiteman made weekly official visits to the
high schools, and knew everyone enrolled in them. It is my recol-

lection that he never missed a Monday morning assembly at West Denver High School, where eventually I had resumed my studies. Although I could not sing the notes of the musical scale, except in the Chinese version, I always looked forward to the hour when Wilberforce would bring the pitch pipe from his pocket with the flourish of a court chamberlain producing a snuff box, then lead us in songs as pleasantly stimulating as old wine.

On the first Monday morning of each new school year, Wilberforce would pass from desk to desk, at which the students sat in threes, to select a chorus to occupy the rostrum of the assembly hall. During the master's march along the aisles, pianist Sue Miller would play "America" over and over. Mr. Whiteman would pause briefly, now with a tuning fork instead of a pitch pipe in hand, diagnose a voice, leaning over a candidate like a specialist in lung diseases, to reject or accept the singer for the platform chorus.

The first Monday of school in 1906, he enraged my friend Sullivan, with whom fullback Henry Murch and I were sitting in assembly. Sullivan, as I already have said, had been the proud soloist of St. Joseph's parochial choir. He was an excellent tenor, and I may as well confess that I not only envied Sullivan his singing ability but also had a weird desire to be a tenor myself. What little talent I possessed vocally was located definitely in the bass register, but nevertheless I wished to be a tenor.

With the music of "America" sounding again and again, Mr. Whiteman leaned above me and my two friends. He endured my phrasing of "Land where my fathers died," then turned his attention to Sullivan, taking everything but his blood pressure. Then he crooked a finger, not at Sullivan but at me, and motioned for me to take a chair on the platform.

Sullivan's anger seemed acute, but he did not permit himself to be drawn into the kind of trouble that had befallen the Elmwood School tough. "I think that Wilberforce J. is tone deaf," the slighted Sullivan said to me soon afterward. "I have half a mind to get my father to write him a letter."

Emboldened by my new musical honors, I conferred with Mr. Whiteman in private. I wanted to sing tenor.

"Tenor?" and the music master twiddled the pitch pipe in his pocket. "Why, may I ask?"

"My mother always liked tenor voices," I replied. Then I asked, "You remember her?"

"Quite well," and he brought the pitch pipe from his waistcoat pocket. "Let us study your natural range." He blew the pipe, signaled, and what came out of my larynx might have been mistaken for a covey of startled quail. Mr. Whiteman shook his head, returned the pipe to his pocket, then placed a hand on my shoulder. "Bass is what you'll be asked to sing."

"How about barytone, Mr. Whiteman?" I said, hoping for a compromise. "Shall I try barytone?"

"Not today," he said, "but thanks just the same."

"Then do you think I'll ever be a bass soloist?" I asked.

"There is a saying," he observed mischievously, "that genius seldom reproduces. Do you suppose the philosopher had the sons of musical parents in mind?"

He was twitting me, but I was not offended, for it was plain to me that he was paying a tribute to the memory of Dodie.

At the annual festivals, during which the best singers from four high schools participated, he included me in the chorus. And on one occasion we were accompanied by no less an instrumental galaxy than the touring Minneapolis Symphony Orchestra. Perhaps Mr. Whiteman permitted me this undeserved honor in memory of someone he had admired and I had loved.

Paul Whiteman is known to his associates as an expert on business contracts, a faculty not ordinarily to be found in men of music. Where did he learn about the practical dealings between parties of the first part and the second? I shall tell you.

Wilberforce Whiteman and his son entered upon contracts as early as Paul's seventh year. Whenever Paul sought a favor his father would reply, "I want to think it over." Next day, the parent would have ready for signature a written agreement containing various clauses and stipulations. The contracts did not provide that the son pay any actual money to the father, but Paul had to agree in writing to fulfill specific promises.

For example, when the son asked for tools and materials to build a walnut desk, Wilberforce submitted the following contract:

1. Paul Whiteman, herein known as the party of the second part, agrees to take the best of care of all tools provided by the party of the first part, Wilberforce J. Whiteman.
2. Said tools will be kept sharp and clean and well oiled after each time they are used.
3. Said party of the second part agrees and promises to put tools away after use, sweep all sawdust and shavings from the bench and floor, look out for fire-hazards, and not waste nails, screws, or wood.

If an agreement were broken by the son, Wilberforce would not scold, but when Paul asked for another favor his father would say, "Wait until I look at our last contract."

After reading that document Wilberforce would rule: "No, I'm afraid we can't get you the new sled. It appears that you violated Clause Number Two of our last agreement. I am as sorry about this as you are, Paul, but a contract is a contract. The first thing to know about such a document is that it is something to be lived up to; otherwise there would be no point in entering into it in the first place."

Paul had his first fiddle, a small one, when he was five. The father permitted him to "play around" with the instrument as if it were just a toy, until the lad "got a feeling for it." When Paul was seven years old, he confided in Wilberforce that he wanted a larger fiddle, a viola, and would like to take lessons on it. Wilberforce thought it over, then drew up a contract. It was stipulated that sixty-five dollars would be spent on the viola by the party of the first part. The first party to the agreement also would pay for lessons during the year. As for Paul, he would owe his father one hour a day, and/or that hour was to be spent in practice on the viola.

After six months of fiddling, Paul became more interested in outdoor games than in exercising musically. "Well, Paul," said his father, "let's call the whole thing off; that is, everything except the contract." He produced the paper, then pointed out: "The agreement stipulates that if you fail to practice, you will owe me that hour each day. Now you actually don't have to practice, but you still owe me the daily hour. We can't get around something we both signed. I haven't quite decided what I want you to do during the time you owe me, so until then, suppose you spend it in your mother's sewing room."

Alone in the sewing room, Paul became restive. He looked out of the window at the summer scene and heard the voices of his playmates. When his gaze returned inside his prison, he became aware that his fiddle and some violin studies happened to be resting upon a near-by table. The party of the second part thought it odd that these things were in the sewing room; he had not placed them there himself.

Having nothing else to do at the moment, he picked up the instrument, tuned it, and absently began to scrape the strings. Then he suddenly became alive to the fact that his father must have placed the instrument and the lesson book in the sewing room, and was making an ass out of him legally. The enraged party of the second part broke the viola over the flywheel of his mother's sewing machine.

Wilberforce came into the room, glanced at the shattered fiddle and then at his son. "Well, my boy," and the party of the first part spoke matter-of-factly, "it seems we shall have to adjudicate this. I shall write off the viola lessons you have received so far, but it becomes quite necessary for you to pay back the sixty-five dollars the fiddle cost. Damages, you know."

The next day Mr. Whiteman presented his son with a lawnmower, a rake, a pair of sheepshears, and, of course, a new contract. "I've arranged for you to cut four lawns in the neighborhood at twenty-five cents each, and no doubt you yourself can negotiate some other lawns."

Paul cut lawns the remainder of that summer and all of the next to pay back the sixty-five dollars. In after years, when he had a farm of his own, Paul enjoyed all agricultural tasks except one, the mowing of hay. The smell of fresh-cut hay or grass always made him ill.

His early training taught him never to become excited about contracts. As an adult, and before he signed such a paper, Paul first made certain that the job he was undertaking was a good one. Then, the contract having been signed, he never moved to annul the agreement. He believed that if he fulfilled his written obligations, all things pertaining to his employment would be to his advantage.

It would seem that this conviction was sound. His New York debut brought him five hundred dollars a week at the Palais Royal Café, and his popular success was immediate. Rivals of the Palais Royal management urged him to break his contract and go with them. They offered him as much as four thousand dollars a week, as well as indemnity against lawsuits which might arise from contractual violations.

"No," said Paul. "I thought this was a good job when I took it, and I'm not going to be unhappy about it now."

That was during Prohibition times. One day the Palais Royal was "pinched," closed down. Certain other cafés where he might have played also were padlocked. Undismayed, Paul took his orchestra on a concert tour, his first notable one, during which the box office receipts amounted to $860,000.

Paul Whiteman's regard for the truth has been magnificently constant, a quality instilled in him by the remarkable Wilberforce. The father did not know how to tell a lie, and Paul himself simply cannot tell one, even when it might seem to his advantage to do so.

Concerning lies, Wilberforce once said to his boy: "First, it's a lot of trouble to lie; it makes you feel miserable, and it's a rather cowardly thing to do. Second, when you are found out, you have to go through ten times as much trouble to get your wires uncrossed than if you had told the truth in the first place. And third, if I ever catch you in a lie I'm going to beat your pants off. So, you see, the odds are three to one against it."

At the age of fifty years, Paul's father could run the hundred yards in thirteen seconds, at a time when the world's record for that distance was ten seconds. Notwithstanding his hale condition, he took almost as many pills and tonics as did Norman Wheeler. The spry music master constantly imagined that he was on the brink of some grievous illness.

One summer, Wilberforce decided that he was having a nervous breakdown. The Whiteman family went to the mountains so that Wilberforce might recuperate among the pines. The music master, with little to do in this solitude, became irascible, especially at breakfast time. The family tried to avoid doing anything that might excite the healthy sufferer.

One morning Wilberforce said to Paul across the table; "I don't like the way you're holding your mouth." The then twenty-year-old Paul made no reply. His father repeated in a reverberating tenor voice, "I said I don't like the way you're holding your mouth. Put it back the way it ought to be."

Paul rose to leave the room. "To hell with you!"

In passing, the young man gave his father a light push. Wilberforce sprang to his feet, picked up a camp chair and broke it across Paul's shoulders. The son, of course, did not strike back. Wilberforce called after him, "And don't think you'll ever be old enough or big enough to lick *me!*"

This instantly cured Wilberforce of his "nervous breakdown." He returned to town as fresh as the flower he wore each morning in his lapel.

Mr. Whiteman shunned strong drink until after he had passed fifty-five years, and then tasted it only because his physician recommended brandy four times a day instead of pills and other medicines. During Prohibition, and when brandy was not to be had in Denver, Paul kept his father supplied with the best liquor to be obtained from the cellars of New York. It amused Paul when Wilberforce measured out the brandy in a tablespoon, put a bit of sugar in it, then sipped it from the spoon instead of from a glass. Mr. Whiteman commenced to smoke cigarettes at sixty-five, but did not inhale the smoke.

A recent radio biography of Paul Whiteman portrayed his father as a maudlin parent sitting in a New York audience while his son led an orchestra, and calling out, "That's my son! My son!" Paul explained to me that the radio characterization of Wilberforce was well meant; but I cannot be that generous. The old gentleman simply was not a doting, prideful pudding-head.

What Wilberforce actually did say during the concert, in which his celebrated son introduced the *Rhapsody in Blue* and other modern works to a classic hall, was, "He can't conduct!"

Wilberforce liked all music other than jazz. Still, he knew a great deal about the popular rhythms, or lack of them, a fact that perplexed his son. "How come you know so much about a kind of music that you detest?" Paul inquired.

"I know about it because I'm not deaf," Wilberforce replied. "I listen to the radio; and the only people I ever associate with are young people, and they know all about jazz—unfortunately."

It was true that almost all his friends were young. "If you stay around old people," he would say, "you have to listen to their health problems. Second, they close their minds to everything."

When Wilberforce was seventy-eight, but still as sprightly as a gazelle, a radio agent invited him to appear with Paul on the air in a New York interview. The son met the train at Grand Central Station. "What kind of trip did you have, Pop?"

Mr. Whiteman breathed fiercely through his nose. "A miserable time. Perfectly damnable."

"What happened?"

"Oh, all the way across the country I had to listen to the health troubles of some old coot, a Judge Somebody or other. Talked my arm off. Told me all about his operations, his sinus condition, his rheumatism. Can't these old horses ever talk of anything else?"

"How old was the judge?" Paul asked his seventy-eight-year-old parent.

"Old as the hills," said Wilberforce. "He must have been all of sixty!"

The director of the program on which Wilberforce was to make his radio debut sought to advise the music master on what he should say during the broadcast.

"If you don't mind," replied Wilberforce, "I'll say exactly the truth as I see it."

At the beginning of the broadcast, Wilberforce made it clear that he regarded jazz as an atrocity. The interlocutor asked, "But what of your own son, who really created the modern jazz orchestra?" The western music master answered, "Oh, Paul does it better than most, but that still doesn't mean that it's music."

"What do you think of Bing Crosby?"

"I regard him as the most charming of young personalities."

"But his singing?"

"Do you mean to imply," Wilberforce Whiteman inquired resonantly, "that anyone in his right senses can judge this young man's voice to be better than that of Richard Crooks?"

With the sly hope of cornering Wilberforce, his son interposed, "Have you noticed any difference between the playing of Artie Shaw and Benny Goodman?"

Wilberforce replied with authority, "Mr. Shaw has a little more art, and Mr. Goodman a little more technique; but I do not care much for either of them—their music I mean."

During his young days, Paul played the viola in Rafaello Cavallo's symphony orchestra in Denver. He also appeared with orchestras that supported the school choruses his father so liked to organize and direct. Wilberforce frequently selected and trained a chorus for some special event, as in 1908 when William Howard Taft appeared at the new City Auditorium in Denver during his first campaign for the presidency.

A platform for the speakers had been erected in the center of the large building. This platform stood perhaps sixteen feet above the audience, the chorus, and the orchestra. The musicians were seated at floor level, and at one side of the flag-draped rostrum. Paul Whiteman was among the instrumentalists and I was in the chorus. Our musical director stood on the platform high above us, the better to lead the entire audience in "The Star-Spangled Banner" at the beginning of the ceremonies, and "America the Beautiful" at the close.

Mr. Taft, as many persons may recall, was a portly statesman. Perhaps he weakened the rostrum during his plea for revision of the tariff and justice for all. At any rate, Wilberforce Whiteman, baton in hand, had directed the audience in but four or five bars of the closing patriotic tune when that part of the platform on which he was standing gave way. He plunged out of sight as if through the trapdoor of Mephisto.

Paul was sawing away sleepily on the viola at the moment his father vanished. He looked up to catch the beat but failed to see the leader. Then the viola player almost fell with astonishment from his own chair when Wilberforce popped out from beneath the platform, bunting draped over his head and shoulders. "Are you hurt, Pop?" Paul called out. The dauntless Wilberforce shook his wand free of the bunting. "Never mind me. Don't miss the beat! Don't miss the beat!"

Mr. Whiteman's time sense seemed remarkable. He needed no alarm clock. He usually slept for a few minutes before lunch and dinner. If he were to say, "I'm going to nap for eight minutes," or "I'm going to sleep till six-nineteen," he would open his eyes on the dot.

Paul's mother, Elfrida Dallison Whiteman, was a gifted woman. Her contralto voice had both volume and quality; each year she went to Boston or New York to sing oratorios. Mrs. Whiteman was six feet tall. She was a person of great good nature, and Wilberforce adored her.

On Paul's twenty-fourth birthday anniversary, he overheard his father say to his mother: "It seems that our son has his mind set upon not amounting to anything. I've tried to see that he have a proper start. I've led the horse to water, as the saying is. But what do we see? A lazy fellow who indifferently plays a viola in a theater orchestra, and then drives a taxicab the rest of the night in the most immoral part of the city."

"He's only floundering until he can find his proper place in the world," said Mrs. Whiteman.

"Then his proper place is no longer here with us, Mother. We've done all we can for the boy. The truth is I don't want him around any longer."

When Paul overheard this pronouncement, he became greatly disturbed. His jovial manners, his careless, impulsive ways, concealed much pride. It did not occur to Paul that his father had taken pains to be overheard by the son to rouse him to his responsibilities. Time proved that Wilberforce was devoted to his boy, but he had the wit to perceive that the young dawdler never would find himself unless thrown upon his own resources.

Paul had no money that day when he overheard his parent's indictment; nor did he attempt to borrow any from his father. Wilberforce had definite views in regard to lending. He was a generous man and would make outright gifts to deserving persons, but he would not lend money; nor would he sign anyone's note.

"When a man borrows," he would say, "he feels relieved at the time he gets your money. But he soon has to change his whole frame of mind, his character even, because, if he finds it difficult to repay you, he must either hate you or feel that you are a bad person, so that he can justify himself in order to live comfortably with himself. Money lending is not my business; teaching music is my business."

Paul obtained five hundred dollars from his mother. "I'll be back some day," he said to her, "but not till I have something to show for what you've done for me. Pop is right."

Mr. Whiteman said good-by to his son without any flourishes. Several years after this, when Paul returned home as a celebrity, his father shook hands as if the son had been gone from home merely for a short holiday. Mr. Whiteman asked no searching questions, offered no comments on his son's popular success.

After dinner, Paul went with his father to the study, there to lay ten one-thousand-dollar bills upon the music master's desk. "What's this for?" asked Wilberforce calmly.

"It's the first installment," Paul replied, "on what I'm going to do to pay you back."

"You don't owe me a cent," said Wilberforce. "Nobody does. And besides, there are no outstanding debts mentioned in any con- tract we entered into."

"There'll be no more contracts," Paul said.

When Wilberforce had passed his seventy-third year, his son persuaded him to retire from professional activities. Then the family physician said to Paul, "You are behaving badly. Don't you know that a man of his kind will die if he isn't kept busy?"

Paul purchased a farm for his father just outside the city limits, and built a fine house on it. He persuaded Wilberforce to take up residence there under the pretext that his father manage the property for the creation of an estate for Paul's own son. When Wilberforce learned that Paul junior wanted no part of the farm or of farming, the grandfather became rebellious against life among the alfalfa fields. Then, when Paul's mother died, the senior Whiteman said, "No more farming for me. I'm a music teacher."

At the age of seventy-five years, Wilberforce J. Whiteman returned to the city, to resume his profession of teaching. His studio was on the fifth floor, rear, of the Knight-Campbell Music Company's building. There he presided over intimate luncheon gatherings on Tuesdays and Thursdays. The old music master was happiest when entertaining friends and students.

During a visit by Wilberforce to New York City, his son had him measured for an overcoat and a suit. Inasmuch as Wilberforce remained trim and wiry and constant in size, he could wear with- out alteration the excellent clothes cut to the measurements on file at the eastern tailor's, and sent periodically to Denver. Paul also placed a standing order with a Denver florist so that his father each morning might drop in at the flower store to receive a rosebud for his lapel, and on Saturdays a large box of flowers to take home.

In his eighty-fourth year, the music master suffered his first severe illness, pneumonia. His vitality was so remarkable, however, that he lived on for nine weeks but in a coma. Paul cancelled all his professional engagements to fly West. The old man was unconscious until shortly before the close of his life.

When it was seen that Wilberforce surely could not live another hour, Paul was unable to keep back his tears and outcries. Wilberforce roused, miraculously it would seem, to look at his weeping son and ask, "Now what have you done?"

Then, in a reasonably strong voice, this grand old man of music said, as if in response to some question: "I shall tell you why Toscanini is such a great conductor. It is because his orchestra never plays for Toscanini, nor does Toscanini reach out selfishly for the credit. First, Toscanini always conducts the music of Beethoven as if Beethoven himself were listening. And second, Toscanini wants Beethoven to hear it done correctly."

Wilberforce, his lecture and his long life done, went to sleep for the remainder of time.

19

THE UNCROWNED SQUATTER

AFTER a long and unexplained silence, Mr. Blake wrote to me concerning the importance of choosing a career. He said that a young man should fix upon his life's work as soon as possible and faithfully prepare for it, notwithstanding the common belief that success was a four-leaf clover, something one chanced upon while going to the fair.

I never again heard from the erudite tea-taster, and what became of him I do not know. The busy years find us neglectful of those wise counselors who influenced our early lives.

Notwithstanding my tendency to dream the other side of the moon, I became partly awakened by Mr. Blake's letter, and began to consider what I wished to become in the world of men. I had reached my second year at West Denver High School, moving at a laggard's pace that eventually might take me to college with an ear trumpet and a silvery beard. At seventeen I was six feet tall, weighed one hundred and seventy pounds, and looked like a Portuguese busboy. One of my teachers, Miss Lilian Newland, long afterward described me as having been "a lad of unbridled vitality."

The teachers of West Denver were for the most part fond of me. They called me a "promising young man." That was something I would continue to be: a promising reporter, editor, writer —and now about to become a promising ghost. At last I shall turn one promise into performance.

I took part in several branches of high-school athletics, but excelled at none. Although I was strong and fast on my feet, I had neither the time away from my various jobs after school hours, nor the disposition to train laboriously for the games. My one great talent went begging, and that was my ability to squat on either leg for as many as a hundred times in quick succession.

I had the legs of an Indian, lean and tireless. If there had been interscholastic races of upward of five miles, I might have been among the champions, for I never became winded or cramped from lasting action.

The drawback to my ability to squat on one leg was its lack of romantic appeal. In fact, I lost whatever chance I may have had to win the heart of Bertha, a dark-eyed enchantress, by trying to impress her with my one-legged virtuosity. Bertha sat across from me in two of my high-school classes, and I jeopardized my grades because I spent my time admiring her.

This alluring lass was in love with Ed Sullivan, whose good fortune it had been to concentrate upon piano playing, dancing, and fancy clothes, instead of squatting on one leg. Sullivan himself was in love with a girl named Dorothy. When it became apparent that Sullivan was heedless of Bertha's existence, she showed symptoms of accepting me as an alternate.

Her first smile—well, it was like being raised to the peerage. When she consented to go with me to the annual fraternity dance, I became so jubilant as to demonstrate my one claim to genius. I sank like a shot duck on one leg, and was up again in a flash. When I rose from the best squat ever seen west of the Mississippi River, Bertha cancelled our appointment for the ball. Moreover, she advertised me to her sorority sisters as being "completely crazy."

One day the physical instructor for the city's five high schools was standing on the circular platform which shielded a low steam radiator in the main hall of West Denver High, a hall in which we took our calisthenic drills. We had completed an exercise with wands that day, when, as if Fate herself decided to pay me a personal visit, the physical instructor put down his wand to announce that he would "demonstrate a difficult and tricky feat demanding balance and co-ordination." He proceeded to do five one-legged squats. Apparently that was his limit, for he said, "Of course I don't expect anyone here to do this even once, let alone five times."

I shook my wand to catch his attention, then flatly declared that I could do it. The instructor surveyed me with grave doubt; but I was undismayed, for almost everyone surveyed me with grave doubt.

"Fowler," the instructor drawled wearily, "they say you're a little too smart for your own good." Then he added, "All right then, you get up here and show everybody how clever you are."

I took a position on the radiator shield. My eye upon a plaster-of-Paris replica of Apollo Belvedere at the foot of the main staircase, I pretended to have some difficulty with the first squat. The instructor was leaning on his wand like an amused shepherd. Now I really went to work. I did forty-five or fifty successive squats. I was about to do more when the gaping instructor called it quits.

On my way to Professor H. B. Smith's class in English literature, I did not reply to the physical instructor's prophetic remark, "Fowler, some day you're going to get yourself into plenty of trouble showing off."

Mr. Blake's letter prompted me to consult various teachers at West Denver concerning my prospects for the future. One of my loved instructors was Sarah M. Graham, professor of Latin, a plump New Englander with a mind like Cicero's. Two of Denver's notable literary sons, Will and Wallace Irwin, had been her protégés.

Miss Graham recommended that I become an orator. Among the things that I could not do, and indeed never had the slightest wish to do, was to speak in public. But Sarah M. Graham hounded me until I composed an oration: "What Constitutes the State?" That speech embodied all the platitudes associated with the laying of a cornerstone.

As I took a chair upon the rostrum in the assembly hall on the night of the oratorical contest, a seam gave way in the blue trousers at a place Granny had overlooked when she mended my Sunday suit. I felt sure that the damage to my trousers was extensive, and that my home-made underwear was showing through the rent. This underwear, which I described in my book on John Barrymore, was made of flour sacks. The trade-name of the flour, "Pride of the Rockies," always occupied a place across the seat of these underpants.

As I sat among the contestants, awaiting my turn to describe the attributes of the State, my body seemed dead, my faculties inert. My heart, however, continued to beat loud and fast but uselessly, like an alarm clock in a cemetery. Then I saw Granny's confident face shining upon me. The platitudinous speech caught on fire. The judges awarded me the gold medal.

When we arrived home, Granny opened the small box in which the medal lay, to exhibit it to Grandpa. "It's the first time in our family history," she said, "that anyone ever got his hands on solid gold."

At this time we were residing in a pressed-brick house on South Emerson Street. Frank Fowler had made good his promise to buy a small cottage for us, with the understanding that my grandparents keep up the interest charges on the mortgage. This house had in it a bathroom with a built-in tin tub, electric lights, and a coal furnace instead of a base-burner. A dirt-wall cellar, larger than any we heretofore had known, underlay the kitchen. It had ample space for Grandpa's collection of mining tools, his shoe-mender's equipment, the musty ledgers, and patent-medicine literature.

The old gentleman made a bench for himself in the cellar, and sat upon it like a dusty prelate. The aging prospector ignored the one electric light which hung from a cord near the furnace. He read by the light of a miner's candle, the spike of its rusty sconce thrust into the dirt wall.

I now had a room to myself upstairs; and from my front window could see Mt. Evans and the silver plumes it wore.

"You know," Granny said one day, "I've changed my mind about having a telephone; but, mark you, we shouldn't become too ambitious."

"I'll get you a telephone," I assured her, "just as soon as I am settled in my life's work."

"In your *what?*" asked the old lady.

"My life's work," I replied. "I'm going to make thirty dollars a week one day. Then we'll have everything your heart desires."

She placed her arms about me. "My heart desires that you grow up to become a good man, and that you don't wander like the other males of the family. They have the dispositions of mariners who never bring their ships into port."

My ambition to earn thirty dollars a week had arisen from my observation of a Norwegian named Karl. He was head man of the delivery department at Hurlbut's grocery store, one of the largest and oldest establishments of its kind in the West. I now worked at Hurlbut's on Saturdays and during the summer vacation months. Uncle Dewey's Grand National had gone out of business and Dewey himself had obtained a position as head meat cutter at Hurlbut's. He found jobs there for Ed Sullivan and me.

Grandpa persuaded Herman MacCready to go with him to the mountains on a prospecting trip, which would be for the almost seventy-year-old Norman Wheeler his last sojourn among the hills of hope.

Mr. Ott had saved enough money to retire to the Old Country. I found his counterpart at the Hurlbut store in the person of Mr. Ruble, the general manager. The cool-eyed Mr. Ruble could be as gentlemanly as you please when implying that you were a wastrel, a cheat, a loafer, or all three. When making his rounds of inspection, there was no sound to his footfalls as he suddenly appeared among the bins at the very moment your mouth was full of merchandise. Mr. Ruble's sleuthing tactics encouraged strangulation and heartburn.

The Hurlbut store had been inherited by a pioneer's son, a free-spending sportsman. Owner Ned Hurlbut wore the first plus-fours that I ever saw. Attired in these golf pants, and carrying a bag of golf clubs, the wealthy young merchant would appear at the store each midday in fair weather. He would stay but a few minutes in his office, then briskly start out of the store to get into one of the first fine motor cars Denver had seen. On his way to the street, and without explanation to anyone, the dashing proprietor would pause each day at the cashier's booth. There he pressed the "No Sale" key of the cash register, helped himself to handfuls of currency or gold pieces. He never bothered to count what he had taken, or leave a voucher in the till. Then he would be off for an afternoon at the Country Club. As might be imagined, the cashier and Mr. Ruble were regularly confused as to the actual amount of the day's receipts.

Like Mr. Ott, Manager Ruble seemed painfully concerned over the appetites of the employees. Of the twenty young men in the order department, only one of them ever bothered to bring a lunch box from home. This spare-ribbed exception, Clarence Heffner, a diabetic victim, had to restrict his diet—a maddening circumstance, I should imagine, for one who literally sat inside the Horn of Plenty and watched the rest of us eat like furtive hogs.

The head of the wine and liquor department, Mr. Riddock, also gave Mr. Ruble much uneasiness of mind. The chief wine salesman sipped all day long from the stock barrels of Port wine in the cellar. He chewed such great quantities of cloves and Sen-Sen, however, that Mr. Ruble was unable to obtain conclusive evidence against him. Mr. Riddock never staggered, but had a tendency to move in a circle to his left. His left-sided circling and his devotion to the vintages of the valley of the Douro gave rise to the pun, "He's listing to Port."

It was said that certain of the drivers of the delivery wagons at Hurlbut's did business on the side, taking meat and other produce from the cold-rooms, and selling this plunder to their own private customers. Mr. Ruble sometimes ordered sudden shifts, sending the drivers on routes other than their accustomed ones; but he seldom "got the goods" on any of them.

Since it was impossible to charge Uncle Dewey with dishonesty or double-dealing, the manager set out to discover other defects in my brawny uncle's character. The principal flaw was a hot temper. One day when Mr. Ruble made the mistake of heckling him during the busy hours, Uncle Dewey submitted his resignation; that is to say, he knocked Mr. Ruble across a meat block, and left him sprawled there.

Mr. Ruble was on familiar terms with but one of his many employees, Karl, the industrious Norwegian. When Sullivan first informed me that Karl earned thirty dollars a week, I couldn't believe it. Sullivan and I received only a dollar and a quarter for a Saturday, working from eight o'clock in the morning until after the store closed at ten o'clock Saturday night. During vacation time, our pay was five dollars a week. Karl's thirty dollars seemed to us a salary unheard of this side of Wall Street.

Sullivan worked in the order department, where he munched shelled almonds all day long, and I was a "heavy," sacking potatoes, sugar, and rock salt in a cave-like chamber near the back alley. I also had charge of breaking up old boxes and crates, and disposing of them and other trash in the basement incinerator. This furnace room was next to the candy kitchen. Looking back upon those days, I wonder how much candy is required to kill a young man.

The diabetic Clarence Heffner used to visit the candy kitchen merely to look at the trays of sweetmeats on the long counters. Sometimes he would touch a sugar-coated roll of "log cabin" **or** a pan of nougat or even pick up a caramel fragment to hold it near his nose or eyes. One day Mr. Ruble caught him examining a piece of candy, and accused him of raiding the kitchen. It was the most damning kind of circumstantial evidence. Clarence seemed all the more guilty in Mr. Ruble's eyes when he cried out that it would be his "death warrant" if he ever swallowed a piece of candy. He was put on "probation," and ordered never to visit the candy kitchen again.

The trash-burning furnace smoked like a forest fire when the damper inside the flue was closed. Mr. Ruble's sensitive nostrils kept him at a distance whenever I created a smoke screen, and that was the time for me to raid the candy trays. One day I released too much smoke. The fire department responded. The firemen also liked candy.

During the afternoon lulls in business, Sullivan and I were assigned to the wine cellar. There we siphoned wine or whisky into bottles, then corked and labeled the spirits for sale upstairs in the retail liquor department. The purple-faced Mr. Riddock would come down the ladder-way into the bottling room at intervals to "sample" the wine. Then he would toss cloves or Sen-Sen into his mouth, and climb back on deck to be inspected by Mr. Ruble.

It was in this cellar that I resumed the experience of swallowing the contents of the rubber siphon, as I had done that night when I sucked wine at the drugstore of Lucian's uncle. Frequent contact with the barrels gave me a lifelong taste for drink. When I had taken aboard more than a sufficiency, however, I was unable to stomach alcoholic drinks next day. This idiosyncrasy, perhaps more than any other deterrent, kept me from becoming a drunkard.

Whenever I arrived home with alcoholic fumes rising from me, Granny astounded me by pretending not to notice the evidence of dissipation. When one of her nieces remarked one evening that obviously I had been drinking, the old lady said to her, "I'll ask you to leave the house, and never come snooping around here again."

When I inquired of Granny why she herself didn't take a drink as a tonic, as many other aging persons did, she replied, "Because I'm sure that I would like it."

Mr. Blake's letter, together with my desire to earn the fabulous sum of thirty dollars a week, caused me to think of the future. I was contributing to the school magazine, *The Heraldo*, and had edited it for two years. Several of my teachers urged me to try to become a writer, but it seemed to me just then that I should prefer to be a physician. A doctor was in a position to look at life and even see part way through the mysteries of being.

One of my good friends, Al Waters, was preparing to study medicine. It was of much interest to me to observe that Al Waters' father applauded his son's decision to enter a profession which he afterward practiced with distinction.

Al's father was an undertaker, a large man of charitable good nature, and one of the best-liked citizens of Denver. The handsome F. B. Waters belonged to so many fraternal organizations that his lodge regalia was as colorful and extensive as the wardrobe of Sultan Abdul-Hamid.

The Waters house in West Denver usually was filled with guests. The hospitable undertaker owned the most extensive collection of phonograph records in our part of the city, the cylindrical kind that antedated the disks. One afternoon Al and I attempted to record our own voices. We heated the wax records in the oven, let them reharden, then placed them successively on the machine, using the regular needle as a stylus. We began to shout into the big horn. While we were conducting this experiment, Bob Landon, a somewhat older person than ourselves, called at the Waters home to see Al's sister Glennie. Bob tried out his own voice in the big horn. His efforts and ours were not as successful as Edison's. All that we accomplished was to change the voices of Italian and French opera singers into those of Arapahoe medicine men.

Later on that evening, Mr. Waters was entertaining members of the Elks lodge. He slipped one of the records onto the holder-roll, then began to doubt his own sanity. An extraordinary gibberish vibrated the horn. Mr. Waters tried to play several other records, then stormed out to the backyard where Al and I were sleeping in a tent. Bob Landon emerged from the porch shadows to announce that the blame for tampering with the records was entirely his. This seemed a magnificent gesture of self-sacrifice, but Mr. Waters had a quite opposite opinion.

"Well," he shouted at Bob, "I can't say that I relish the idea of getting the world's biggest dunce for a son-in-law."

Mr. Waters' geniality, however, seldom left him for long at a time, although, to be sure, he stayed properly sad during funeral services. He had installed a private bowling alley and card room underneath his mortuary chapel. He permitted his son's young friends to use this play-place in return for keeping the bowling alley in good order. Our outcries and the crashing of the big ball against the ten-pins frequently startled the mourners assembled overhead.

We reached the bowling alley by means of a trapdoor in the floor of the embalming room. The necessity to pass some lifeless human figure sheeted on a slab gave me a tight feeling across the chest. Sometimes we saw a coffin in the embalming room with a corpse in it, and once there was a small white box containing a dead child. Mr. Waters' assistant was putting rouge on the cheeks and lips of the still girl. Death, I thought, did not know how to play fair.

Late each afternoon, Mr. Waters paid Al and me a dime to drive two obese and stolid black horses to the West Side livery stable, where they and the undertaker's black wagon were kept. Often on these occasions we would play "fireman," galloping the habitually sedate animals past the homes of our friends. Sometimes we put on the high silk hats which belonged to the morticians.

Once we drew up before the house of Al's best girl, opened the rear doors of the black wagon, dragged out the undertaker's long basket, and carried it on the run up the steps of the front porch.

The girl's mother now was turning the street corner on her way home from a shopping errand. Her arms full of groceries, she did not immediately recognize the porters of the grisly container. Parcels slipped from the mother's hands as she began to sway and clutch at a fence paling. Mr. Waters suspended us from all bowling-alley privileges until Al's apologies were accepted by the girl's mamma.

I decided to obtain the confidential view of Ed Sullivan's father as to my choice of a career. When I called at his home early one Sunday morning, the great Hibernian had just returned from mass. He placed his rosary in the top drawer of the highboy in his room; then, while waiting for his breakfast, began to compose a letter of denunciation addressed to the members of the City Council. The letter, he explained, had to do with a fountain and statuary group designed by Sculptor Frederick William Mac-Monnies for the Civic Center. The city, Mr. Sullivan went on to say, had commissioned the noted pupil of Augustus St. Gaudens to celebrate in bronze the many virtues of Colorado's pioneers. The memorial group would cost the taxpayers seventy thousand dollars.

The sculptor evidently had resided in France too long to know much about the sensibilities of western settlers. When he placed an Indian high above the effigies of pioneers at the base of the fountain, he not only offended Mr. Sullivan but also enraged many other "old-timers." The elderly Scout Wiggins was crying out that the MacMonnies Indian was an outrage. Another frontiersman, Dad Caldwell, one-time mule whacker for General Custer, had come down from Wyoming, wearing his old knives and pistols, and as Granny said, "was armed to the false teeth."

Caldwell represented himself as "the only survivor of the Custer Massacre." He had "survived" that military debacle simply because General Custer himself had ordered him to the guard-house the day before the troops rode off to the Little Big Horn. General Custer charged his mule driver with intemperance and insubordination. Until the day of his death at the age of ninety-six, Caldwell would describe his "survival" as a great joke on Custer. But the MacMonnies desecration was no joke in Cald-well's opinion. He agreed with his friend Norman Wheeler that shooting was too good for "that thar tenderfoot."

Granny alone defended the right of an artist to express his own ideas freely, "providing, of course, that the figures are prop-erly clothed." She accused Grandpa of being so prejudiced against Indians as to see nothing good at all in them.

Mr. Wheeler thereupon made the only remark ever delivered with any noticeable effect upon his wife. "I'll say this for the Indians: they know how to handle their womenfolks. There never was a henpecked Indian."

On the day when I solicited Mr. Sullivan's advice as to a career, he said, "Don't be too impatient about what you aim to do. Just keep your shirt on. A terrible thing happened to me, all because my parents got too dad-burned impatient to get to America."

"What happened?" I inquired.

"Blessed be the saints!" He shook his head and whispered hoarsely, "On the way to the ship, I was born."

"Well, now," I said. "I think it was wonderful that you were born, Mr. Sullivan."

"So do I." Then he made the sign of the Cross. "But I was born in Liverpool—on English soil!"

As for the pioneers' statue, Sculptor MacMonnies jolly well revised it, changing his Indian figure to that of the great trail blazer, Kit Carson.

"I have little regard for a man who has no mind of his own," Granny said of the sculptor's surrender to public opinion. "But I suppose this MacMonnies is getting along in years; and old men, like old books, grow weak in their spines."

Mr. Sullivan took full credit to himself for having "rescued" the monument from the Indians. His success in this campaign caused him to write scores of letters to various public officials in regard to the bonding of Montclair Park, the erection of a public bath house, the library, and other matters of moment.

"If I was younger," he said, "I'd go in for politics." Then he advised me, "If you went into politics, my boy, you would soon get your thirty dollars a week."

20

THE BELL TOWER

Y SHOES were tight. The swelling of my feet increased as the new Interurban car carried me from Denver to Boulder among the hills thirty miles away. The fancy shoes were beautiful but tight. I knew no one among the rah-rah young men or the giggling girls on the train or at the station. I tried to appear stoical, but the shoes had been copied from instruments used during the Spanish Inquisition.

These shoes had cost five dollars, an exorbitant price for footwear in 1911. It had been the last five dollars of a hundred advanced me by Miss Mary White, a philanthropical teacher of English at West Denver High School. She had advised me to spend the hundred dollars wisely, but thrift and Fowler never were bedfellows. After paying twenty dollars as a matriculation fee at the University of Colorado, I visited George Wilke's pawnshop. There I purchased among other articles a leather valise and a set of practice boxing gloves said to have belonged to the retired heavyweight champion James J. Jeffries. Then I visited Tom Holland's crowded saloon for some beer and free lunch.

As I busied myself at the free-lunch counter, Charlie Epworth, the cynical guardian of the sausages and other dainties, commented upon my appetite. Accepting this as a slur on my purchasing power, I bellied up to the bar to address Mr. Holland with a slogan made famous by Buffalo Bill and John L. Sullivan: "Drinks for the house!"

This bravado entitled me to enormous helpings of free lunch, but it left me with only five dollars and little more than carfare to Boulder. On my way home, I saw the two-tone shoes in the window of Weiner's store. They didn't fit, but they were the largest of their kind that Pop Weiner had in stock.

When Grandpa saw the shoes he said, "Don't ever ask me to half-sole *them* things."

The next morning, as I got off the Interurban car at Boulder, I had but fifteen cents. The cold dew of torture on me, I reflected upon stories of great men who had begun their education with severe handicaps. In emulation of them, I must begin life on the campus in a penniless condition. So I purchased five cents' worth of gumdrops at Fonda's drugstore, then boarded the town's one streetcar for a ten-cent round trip into the near-by hills. Now I was bankrupt indeed.

The car climbed to the Chautauqua grounds among the pine trees, where William Jennings Bryan used to shake what was left of his mane and belittle monkeys and cry out for the betterment of the human race. I wondered if the Great Commoner ever had tight shoes.

After I had left the car near the campus, I found myself at the gate of a small cemetery. I decided to retire for an hour to the graveyard, there to remove my shoes and convalesce in privacy.

A rusted iron chair stood beside one of the granite memorials. I sat down in it, envious of the strangers sleeping so comfortably below ground. As I unbuttoned and wrenched off the shoes, my mind held rows of asterisks. I wished that I had enlisted in the Foreign Legion.

After the pain began to lessen, it occurred to me that I had no buttonhook with which to lock up my feet again. While thinking gloomily about buttonhooks, the poverty of great men in their youth, and the inadequacy of gumdrops to stay hunger, I heard the notes of a flute. I looked up to see a preoccupied musician coming through the gate. He was as slender as a sacristan's reed, and was hatless, with a fine head like that of Erasmus. And he was playing a skirling melody on a silver piccolo.

When the flautist caught sight of me, he left off playing to ask, "You're new around here, eh?"

I nodded, not too affably perhaps. The flute player put his instrument away in an inside coat pocket. Then he sat down on a stone slab near by and began to study the inscription on the granite monument nearest my chair.

"Tom Horn," he read, "November 21, 1860–November 20; 1903." Then he said, "Hm! Just missed another birthday."

I reacted to the mention of Horn's name. Tom Horn was well known to my people. He had been interpreter for Geronimo, and the Apache chief had called him "Talking Boy." Afterward, he served the cattle barons of Wyoming as a detective during their war against the sheepherders.

In 1902 he set out to "eliminate" a sheepowner named Kels Nickell. He went secretly to the Nickell ranch, armed with a Winchester rifle. Horn lay in ambush two days and nights. A rainstorm came. Then, at a distance of three hundred yards from Horn's hiding place, Nickell's sixteen-year-old son appeared in the doorway of his father's ranch house. He was wearing Kels' raincoat. Mistaking the son for the father, Horn fired. The boy fell dead. Horn was arrested, tried, and finally hanged.

While I was thinking of Horn and looking at his grave, the flute player inquired, "You're not related to Horn?"

I shook my head. "No, I just came in here to think."

"It's the best possible place to think," he said. "What were you thinking about?"

"I was thinking how sore my feet are," I said. He nodded sympathetically as I went on, "Then I was thinking how Charlemagne was buried in a sitting position on a marble throne, with the Gospels in his lap."

"Is that a fact?" The stranger seemed genuinely astonished.

"Yes, he sat there for three hundred years before he was disturbed. And did you know that there are three keys to the nest of coffins of Napoleon?"

"No," he said, "but information such as that comes in right handy." There was a twinkle in his blue eyes as he added, "Or does it?"

"I'm full of useless information," I said. "I always draw upon it to anesthetize my skull when I'm in trouble, such as now, when my feet hurt." His friendly manner caused me to go on. "But I was thinking most of all about pleasant walking when you piped yourself on board."

"Well, well," he said, "it's funny you'd be thinking it pleasant to walk when your feet hurt."

"It's not that," I said. "I was thinking about the most wonderful walk there is. I take it many, many times."

"Tell me about it?"

"Why not?" I said after sizing him up more carefully than before. "This walk I'm speaking of leads through a rising lane of great trees. I'd say they are oaks. There are vineyards, too, on the hillside beyond the grove. At the end of the lane among the trees —it's a trail really—there may be seen the outworks of an old castle and an octagonal bell tower."

"Castle?" and the man squinted. "Not around these parts, I take it?"

"No." I said, "not around here. But in the place I'm speaking of it's always autumn, and the leaves are always golden brown. There's an old fellow stooping over to gather twigs. I don't really know his name, but I call him Hans. I nod to him whenever I go up the hill, and he politely nods back; we've never actually spoken to each other. Then, just around the bell tower, which you reach after entering the courtyard, there's a girl. Her hair is like the autumn, and she is slim and lovely."

"Say, now," my listener cut in, "that's great! Is she *your* girl?"

"In a way," I replied. "I don't know her name, either, but I call her Gloria."

"Where is this place?" the stranger asked. "I'd like to go there."

"The place is Heidelberg," I replied. "And the castle overhangs the east of the town and the Neckar River, where it enters the plain of the Rhine. It's on the Jettenbühl, and—"

"You've been there? You say you take that walk often? See the girl? Gloria, I mean. But how—"

"It's only a picture hanging on the wall of my grandmother's bedroom," I said. "And when I'm all alone, I look hard at it. And that's how I go there."

He rose from the slab and came close to me. "Say, fellow, you're lonesome and homesick. It hits everybody, I guess. Come with me to the Delt house for lunch."

"The Delt house, eh? Then you must know a friend of mine, Ed Sullivan."

"I sure do," the man replied. "Too bad Ed didn't return to school this year." He offered me his hand. "Let me introduce myself. The name's Lockhart. Ferd Lockhart, but I'd rather you'd call me Jim. My father's name was Jim, and that's my middle name. I prefer to be called Jim."

So here was another fellow who had name trouble! I told him my name but did not reveal that my father's name was different from mine. And I agreed never to call my new acquaintance Ferd.

"Well, now," he said cordially, "Ed Sullivan used to talk a lot about you. What's happened to Ed?"

"He's on the road selling cornflakes," I replied. "He just sold a whole carload to some trusting fellow in Pueblo. First time it's ever been done."

"Sullivan could sell stilts to a giraffe," Jim said. "It's his personality." Then he snapped his fingers and exclaimed, "So *that's* where all those cornflakes are coming from! I've been wondering about it all week."

"What cornflakes?"

"Why," Jim explained, "three big crates of cornflake samples arrived at the Delt house last week, and another three cases just yesterday. Is Sullivan supposed to get rid of his samples that way?"

"He's not a conventional fellow," I said. "Are you connected with the University?"

"Yes," Jim replied simply, then blurted out, "I detest cornflakes!"

"I could use a crate of them right now," I declared. "You see, I neglected to bring any pemmican with me on this expedition."

"Sullivan told me you had the biggest appetite since Henry the Eighth. You wouldn't think it to look at you."

"That all Sullivan said about me?" I asked.

"No. He said a lot of fine things, but he said to look out, because if anybody named something, you'd do it."

"He was just talking," I said. "Actually I am a very shy person."

"That's not what Sullivan said."

"You don't happen to have a buttonhook, do you?" I asked.

"No," he said. "Newspapermen don't usually carry buttonhooks. Corkscrews occasionally, but no buttonhooks."

"You're a newspaperman?"

"Yes. *The Kansas City Star*, the Associated Press, and a lot of others."

"But you said you were connected with the University."

"That's right. I'm the professor of journalism."

I began to draw on my shoes. "You don't look like a professor," I said. "Where's your beard and your copy of Horace?"

"I play the piccolo instead. Do you want to know something?"

"If it's completely useless," I replied.

"It is," Jim replied. "I own a small ranch near Ordway, where I take my vacations. In the early evening, I take my piccolo outdoors to play on it. The first time I did this, hundreds of jack rabbits came from all around. They formed a circle, then sat on their hind legs to listen to the piccolo, their big ears up in the air. They did this every time I went out to play. One day I tried playing the regular flute. But the jack rabbits never showed up for the big flute. No, sir, they liked the piccolo."

"What was their favorite number?" I inquired.

He answered me at once with, "The piccolo part from 'The Stars and Stripes Forever.' In fact, they appreciated anything that Sousa wrote."

I took an immense liking to this man, and although his manner was quiet and gentle, there was a Pan-like quality to him. On the way to the Delt house—where soon I was to be blackballed as a prospective member—he spoke of his pets at the ranch, especially a terrapin.

"This terrapin was a big fellow, as western turtles go," he said. "Nine inches in diameter. I first met him at a picnic. I had a piece of watermelon preserve in one hand and the turtle in the other. While I was toying with the turtle, he snapped at me. I held out a piece of preserve and he snapped at it. Then, as he tasted it, he grew mellow. I took him home. He didn't like the piccolo, but at nine o'clock precisely each morning he would come out from a trash pile to get some watermelon preserves. After a while I ran out of watermelon preserves and gave him quince instead. The turtle went wild over quince. I rode my horse to town to get some more watermelon preserves, but the turtle wouldn't take any of it; he wanted the quince. So I fed him quince every morning at nine, on the dot. When I went to the ranch last vacation, he had vanished; perhaps to enter a monastery or to write his memoirs."

Jim again spoke of his father, saying that he had been a great horseman, a harness race driver, a rival of Pop Geers. "I was brought up with horses, but my father wanted me to get a real education. I wanted to obey my dad, for he was a grand man, but I got sidetracked. I came in contact with some newspapermen. When I got to know them well I had a call, like some fellows say they hear when they enter the ministry. Newspaper reporters have minds, and they speak them and write them. They learn one great thing: that everyone is only human. They stand in awe of no one, and they are alive. And when a newspaperman turns in his last story, he dies happily ever afterward."

Jim had lost his puckish manner and now looked like an evangelist as he concluded with, "I'm a fine judge of horseflesh and of newspapermen, and I'd like very much to have you enter my class in journalism. What say?"

"I was planning to become a doctor of medicine," I replied. "That is if I can hold out long enough here."

"The death rate is too high as it is," he said. "A fellow like you belongs in the newspaper business."

"What makes you think so?"

"Because," he said, "that's the business where you'll see life firsthand. And besides, it's where you'll come across castles, and Glorias, and many other things."

The next day I registered for Jim Lockhart's class in the basement of Old Main, the first big building erected on the beautiful campus. Old Main was a brick building held together by star braces and huge rods. There was a big bell in the tower, and when Jim talked to us, Old Main became the castle on the Jettenbühl. It was a time of grand illusion, even though the professor permitted such earthy practices as the chewing of tobacco during class.

Instead of lectures, Jim told anecdotes pertaining to newspapermen and their profession. He supplied me with a new list of heroes, among them Steve O'Grady and Charlie Blood of Kansas City, and Roy Giles of Denver. Jim's stories roused the Dean to advise him not to make a vaudeville show of the class. But Jim had the newspaperman's defiance of hidebound rules, and when the Dean paid a surprise visit to the basement of Old Main one morning, Jim went right on chewing tobacco and telling a story about Kirby McRill.

"Kirby had bushy whiskers that he dyed a fiery red," Lockhart was saying as the Dean entered the classroom. "He had about a bushel-basketful of whiskers, and his hair grew down even with his collar. . . . Sit down, Dean. Glad to have you with us. . . . Kirby dyed his hair red until it made him shine like phosphorus in the dark. He was a long-distance walker. Claimed to be the greatest walker in the world. . . . This is a true story, Dean, and I hope you're enjoying it. . . . Kirby McRill claimed he never had been kissed. He worked in a pet store and slept with the dogs. He always made deliveries in a wheelbarrow. He'd deliver ten cents' worth of birdseed in the wheelbarrow even if it was five miles away. Kirby boasted he'd never trim his beard till he'd found true love. Then, he said, when he found the right girl for him, she would be given the honor of trimming it. He fell in love with Susie Bell, and sent her to Mohler's Barber College to learn how to trim a beard. There she fell madly in love with an Italian instructor and eloped with him. When Kirby heard the news he said, 'Well, I never believed in higher education anyway.' "

Jim crossed from his desk to one of the narrow windows to get rid of some tobacco juice. He had to raise his sights to spit up and over the high sill of the basement classroom. The Dean, a frown on his classic forehead, wordlessly left the room.

Unperturbed by this mark of disapproval, Jim went on: "Kirby McRill was a believer in free speech. When asked by the Chamber of Commerce what he thought of a town in which he couldn't buy a drink on Sunday, he said, 'If I had a home in hell and a place in this town, I'd sell the place here and go home.' "

It was a stimulating year at the university's class in journalism, with but a single exception, the textbook. When I complained about that book Jim asked, "What's your chief objection to it?"

"The book's insufferably dull," I replied. "If the newspaper world produces dusty-minded clods such as this author, I don't want any part of it."

"Not so fast," Jim said. "You mustn't judge a whole profession by one of its lackluster members."

"Well," I countered, "do *you* like this tedious book?"

"I can't say," he replied. "I simply don't know."

I was amazed at this indecision on the part of the teacher. "Haven't you any opinion at all about it?"

"None," he said calmly. "Absolutely none."

"Well, I'll be damned!" I snorted. "Have you read it recently?"

"As a matter of fact," he rejoined, "I've never read it at all." As my mind did a back flip, he went on, "You see, that book was wished on me by the Dean. I presume that he found a kindred joy out of the author you think so commonplace. We have to have a textbook for appearance's sake. But have I ever referred to this book by word or deed? Do I ever quiz you on it?"

Come to think of it, Jim never did refer to a textbook which had been concocted by the biggest horse's behind since the wooden one of the Trojan war.

One of Lockhart's principal charms was his ability to make the journalism course seem like mighty play, a purposeful play to be sure, but the kind of activity that caused a man to love in advance a profession that was to be his livelihood. And here, I thought, was the ideal professor, an expert in his own right, a man who had made his own living in the field unhindered by flamboyant theories and bookish vacuities. Furthermore, this unpretentious sage nurtured the careers of his former students, procured jobs for them in newspaper offices all over the land, and gave them advice during the early years that find a newspaperman floundering and yearning.

The seeming trifles that attend the birth of a career become landmarks in memory. I often think kindly of tight shoes, a small cemetery, and a wonderful, Pan-like player of the piccolo.

21

WAITING FOR THE CAT TO DIE

ONE of the most practical things that Jim Lockhart taught the prospective reporter was to listen patiently to the other fellow's troubles. Everyone has at least one trouble, he said, and stands in momentary readiness to preach upon the sad text. If no one else is within range of a hey! hallo! hist! or soho! a troubled man talks to himself, a hazardous practice indeed. Anyone who talks to himself invites proof that he is the biggest bore since the first tiger hunter returned from Bengal to Dorsetshire.

Were I given to punning, I might say that listening has been for me a sound investment. Among other things, I learned that social barriers disappeared whenever human beings catalogued their woes. You may say that I was not the first philosopher to recognize this common denominator of the aching heart, but I shall reply that I was the first to discover it for myself.

Early in my newspaper days, I listened to the plaints of Harold Henwood as he cooked beefsteak on a gas plate in the jail cell where he was staying during his two trials for having slain a rival in love. At his first trial, Henwood had received a life sentence. He appealed the case; but instead of improving his position, was sentenced to be hanged. His comments upon the stupidities of juries, the cynicism of judges, and the sheer folly of having been born lasted for hours. Several months later he went insane, and in that way avoided the gibbet.

Thirteen years afterward I heard Queen Marie of Rumania recite some of her sorrows as the mother of a wayward son. Why persons so widely removed as were Henwood and Her Majesty in terms of time, sex, and station should confide in reporters was something I do not know, but I recall one thing clearly, the mood of the luckless slayer matched that of the thwarted queen.

Mr. Lockhart's teachings and my large ears made of me an ideal listener. If only I had hearkened to good advice as readily as I did to the clatter of breaking hearts, I might have become a pillar of society.

As I floundered about during the months that followed my departure from college and from the class in journalism, I frequently thought of Lockhart's gospel of patient ears. "Just take your bump of curiosity back to town," Jim had said, "and conquer the place."

"How will I begin?" I asked.

"By keeping a weather eye out, and listening," he replied. "That's what people do at railway crossings. The trouble is, they often quit looking and listening the minute they leave the vicinity of the tracks."

As I remembered my one year in college, I felt that I had been a failure. Among other things, I had failed as a "businessman." One of my fruitless ventures had been a laundry route handed down to me by Sullivan and "Bull" Stirrett. It collapsed because of a smallpox scare among my cash customers and the nonpayments of bills by those who literally left me holding the bag. I also had undertaken the milking of two cows belonging to an ex-coal miner, but I simply could not learn how to milk. It made me feel self-conscious and futile when a cow turned her head to see what I was or was not doing to her. Even a correspondence course with an expert, my grandmother, did not make of me a dairyman.

If it had not been for a gentle gray spinster, Miss Galloway, I might have suffered a year of famine. Miss Galloway was the cook at a sorority house where I washed dishes for my board. The bountiful cook prepared almost as much food daily for me as she did for all the Greek-letter girls for whom I dipped the chinaware and silver.

I became something of a Greek myself when the Alpha Tau Omega fraternity rescued me from a leaking tent where I had been residing at the rear of Mrs. Venable's boardinghouse. At the fraternity house, I slept in the hull of a one-time double-decker bed. My roommate, John Barbarick, a young man of my own size, lent me articles from his somewhat large wardrobe.

There was another fraternity member as indigent as myself, Kenneth "Cac" Kennedy. His skill as a boxer inspired me to suggest bouts for him at near-by coal-mining camps. As Cac's manager, I obtained matches at club smokers at a fee of three dollars.

During the Christmas holidays, neither Cac nor I had carfare to visit our homes in Denver. Instead, we tramped to the mining town of Marshall, where Kid Eggert, a professional pugilist, beat Cac's ears down, cut his brows, broke a rib, but could not rub out Cac's wonderful smile. Our three-dollar purse went to the doctor who dressed my champion's wounds.

Years afterward, Kennedy became vice-president of a transoceanic airlines company. The last letter I ever received from this stouthearted little fellow referred to a large brass spittoon which I appropriated as a souvenir at the Elks Club the night of our defeat. Soon after Kennedy's letter reached me, I read in the newspapers that he had disappeared during a trans-Pacific flight; and I am sure that he went down smiling.

I had managed to support myself in school, but could send no money home to my grandparents. I learned toward the close of the school year that all was not well with them; nor were their usual benefactors, Frank and Uncle Dewey, now in a position to assist them.

All I had been able to send home were assurances that my marks were good. This had seemed an empty show. I had had no difficulty in respect to college grades, but somehow I never was able to regard marks as a true revelation of a man's potentialities. It seemed to me that anyone could get good marks if he set out to do so. But can you eat marks? Can you keep warm with them? Can you make love to them?

Except for the class in journalism and the psychology course of Professor L. W. Cole. I had been unable to find satisfaction in academic life. This, of course, was not the fault of the excellent college of liberal arts. The fault lay within me, within my confused and dreaming nature. I still sat, in fancy, in the mulberry tree, and held onto the belief that if I had a father, all confusions would be miraculously resolved.

After I had come home from college, I spent each night in the basement of the Telephone Company Building, where I worked as a signal clerk for the American District Telegraph Company. It was my monotonous business to record on charts the many bells that banged out numbers whenever night watchmen rang signal boxes during their isolated rounds in warehouses, banks, factories, lumberyards, or amusement parks.

The banging of the bells almost routed one's sense of hearing. Above the discord, however, I could hear in fancy the words of Jim Lockhart: "You're meant to be a newspaper reporter, and you'll come across castles, and Glorias, and many other things."

There were six clerks in the signal ring, among them Strat Martin, a sprightly ex-quarterback of the West Denver High School team. "Seems I was born to call signals," he said. The first night Strat came to work, he mastered the great list of bell boxes, memorized all of them, not only their numerals but the characteristic sound each bell made in the clanging chorus on the quarter hour, the half, or the hour. Martin's amazing proficiency with the signals gained him the praise of Foreman Strohm, an overseer not easily moved to admire subalterns. All night, and for twelve hours each night, with a half-hour intermission for lunch and beer at Tom Holland's saloon, we listened to the bells.

These chimes frequently got out of order. Whenever the bells sounded, "tickers" simultaneously punched the corresponding signals onto paper ribbons. The mechanisms were obsolete, the punch pins defective, and the records emerged in a sort of bastard Braille.

There was also a master machine, a drum which revolved like a prayer wheel. It recorded all the box numbers on a large roll of paper. We had no access to this register, for it was sealed inside a case in the office of Superintendent Keim. We worked in terror of this machine, this cynical God that spied upon us. If we omitted from our charts signals which had been sounded, or, far worse, set down the ones which had not been sent, Superintendent Keim next day was able to descry the error on the master machine. And the man who had committed the blunder might find employment elsewhere.

The master machine also was a weapon used against us by the association of fire and burglary underwriters, under whose specifications we were qualified to serve their policyholders. About once each month, sleuths for this supreme court appeared unannounced among the insured factories or yards to order a watchman to omit a box, or sometimes neglect a whole row of them, to try to catch us napping or soldiering.

We devised a method, however, to fight the fire underwriters with fire, as it were. We conspired with certain watchmen in widely separated parts of the city to apprise us when the underwriters were riding the night. These friends warned us by means of sending in prearranged signals five minutes before their regular rounds, and then repeating them five minutes after a designated time. In return, we permitted the humanitarians once each week to skip an entire round of signals for purposes of sleep, saloon visits, or other natural delights. This courtesy, of course, had to be extended on the night before Superintendent Keim's

day off, Sunday, so that he would not be on hand next day
to check the record of the master machine.

I had listened to the bells for several months when Foreman
Strohm one night announced that I had merited a two-dollar
raise in wages. This meant twelve dollars a week instead of ten;
but twelve dollars was not my objective. I wanted to earn thirty
dollars. That had been my goal ever since the days at Hurlbut's.

I wrote to Jim Lockhart, who was playing the piccolo to the
jack rabbits on his Ordway ranch, to remind him that the bell-
ridden nights were far removed from newspapers and my dream
of thirty dollars. To watch one's life slow down, I wrote, was
a serious version of the childhood game of waiting for a swing
to come to a standstill; of "waiting for the cat to die."

"Look around City Hall," Jim wrote back. "You're bound to
come in contact there with some helpful gentlemen of the press."

I began to rise earlier than usual, at about two o'clock in the
afternoon, to look for newspapermen at City Hall. But it was at
Tom Holland's saloon that I met my first journalistic hero, Roy
Giles of *The Rocky Mountain News*. I gathered that Mr. Giles
was not entirely happy this day. He was reciting his complaints
to proprietor Holland and Charlie Epworth, the free-lunch custodian. I listened in, and afterward pieced together some of his
experiences as a newspaper reporter.

Mr. Giles' tour of duty was at police headquarters. He worked
for Editor Henry D. Carbery, one of the most energetic journalists of the West. Mr. Carbery was a just man but had a quick
temper. His face would turn vermilion during sieges of anger,
as at an editorial conference on an April Monday in 1912.

Among those present at this news conference was telegraph
editor Jack LaHines. Mr. LaHines was the least demonstrative
of sub-editors, forever unflurried and self-possessed.

On the afternoon of this April Monday, Carbery complained
to his editorial board: "Now look, gentlemen. The paper is getting dull. Our first page is beginning to look like something out
of the *Congressional Record*. Can't we breathe a little life into

it? Haven't we any stories today with lace drawers in them? We really need some lace drawers to stimulate our men readers and interest the women."

He looked across the conference table at the expressionless LaHines. "Jack, are there any lace drawers hanging on the telegraphic lines today?"

LaHines glanced up from a sheet of cable flimsy. "Well, Henry, here's one bulletin that might be interesting. Something might come of it."

Carbery brightened. "Lace drawers?"

LaHines pursed his lips. "No, hardly lace drawers; but suppose I read you the bulletin. It says here, 'The new luxury liner *Titanic* is reported sinking by the head, and the *Carpathia* is nearing it for possible rescue work.'"

Carbery leaped to his feet, overturning his chair, and began to shout, "Everybody on the job, quick! It's the biggest story since Noah's Ark!"

The unperturbed LaHines was still eying the shipwreck bulletin as Carbery leveled a finger at him. "No lace drawers, eh? You stoical bastard!"

The reporters in the basement of the City Hall had telephone extensions to their respective city desks. One afternoon Carbery called Giles over *The News* extension: "Now look, mister, you haven't had a story for a week. You're going to have one in tomorrow morning's paper, by cracky! and it's going to be an exclusive story; and if it isn't on page one, and exclusive, you can look for a new job as of five o'clock in the morning."

Before Giles could reply, Mr. Carbery hung up. The worried reporter appealed to all his official friends for news, but even his most reliable source, Detective Pete Carr, said, "Roy, it's the deadest day in my whole experience as a cop. There's not even a case of wife-beating on the blotter."

Giles went into Larimer Street to get some fresh air. Someone called his name, and he turned to see an acquaintance, "Bad

News" Hawkins. "I was on my way to visit you," Mr. Hawkins said. "They just let me out. And the minute I got through with a little business deal I been planning with a certain party, I came right down to thank you for your kindness to me."

"Forget it," Giles said.

"No, I won't forget it, Roy," said Bad News Hawkins. "Those cards made my days in the nut house more bearable."

It was Hawkins' custom to play poker with underworld cronies. After losing a bet, he would passionately insist upon examining the next cards of an undealt deck to ascertain what he *might* have drawn. Hawkins would look at the card or cards he might have drawn and mutter, "Bad news!"

One night Hawkins had just wagered and lost a set of silverware to some friends and was looking through the dead deck when Detective Pete Carr pounced upon him. Detective Carr charged Hawkins with housebreaking and burglary. But Hawkins' resourceful attorney, Judge O. N. Hilton, convinced a jury that any man who looked at undrawn cards was a mental case, and hence not responsible for a crime. The jury refused to convict. And the presiding judge sent Hawkins to the insane ward of the County Hospital instead of to the penitentiary at Canyon City.

In less than an hour after he had entered the hospital, Hawkins began to deal himself poker hands on his cot. When Reporter Giles learned that Bad News Hawkins wore out a deck of cards the first day and had no means of replacing it, Giles each morning thereafter sent to him from the Press Club the packs which had been used there the night before.

On the evening when Editor Carbery delivered his ultimatum to Giles and Hawkins was released from the hospital as "partly cured," the friends shared a bottle of whisky in the pressroom at City Hall. Giles felt too sad to play cards, so Hawkins dealt himself hands and inspected the next cards that might have come up. He also kept looking at the big clock of the pressroom, and twice made low-voiced calls over the coin-box telephone on the wall; but the only thing he was overheard to say was, "That's fine. Call me here right away." Then he gave the telephone number.

When Hawkins sat down to his bottle and his cards again, Giles asked him, "How can I snatch a first-page story out of thin air?"

"The Lord will provide," said Hawkins.

In about an hour the telephone bell rang. A reporter rose to answer it, but Hawkins politely intervened with, "If you don't mind, I think it's for me." He winked as he prepared to lift the receiver. "I been a long time without a dame, you know." Then he said into the instrument, "This is Hawkins, honey." He listened, pursed his lips, then said, "I'll be there, dear. Of course I love you."

Bad News Hawkins put his cards in his pocket, had a nightcap from the almost depleted bottle, said good evening to the other reporters, and invited Giles to accompany him to the street.

On their way past the office of Detective Pete Carr, Hawkins whispered to Giles, "Roy, you've got that page-one scoop right in your hands."

Giles shook his head. "Don't rub it in."

"Go to some outside telephone," Hawkins said, "and send in this story to your rewrite desk: 'The mansion of Marvin L. Hudson, mining magnate and capitalist, on Logan Street, was burglarized. The intruder entered through a dining-room window, took the silver from the buffet, then opened Mr. Hudson's safe and removed $2,420.80 in cash, and a diamond ring, two earrings, and a brooch.' No one else knows a thing about this excepting you and me, Roy, and a certain other party. Now just put it in your paper exactly like I've told it to you but don't use my name, naturally."

Giles was somewhat worried about this unofficial news. "This isn't one of your hospital dreams, is it?"

"I'm dealing you a royal flush," said Hawkins. "It's up to you to bet on it."

Giles went to Undertaker Bob Rollins' near-by funeral parlor, was admitted after ringing the night bell, and whispered the story into the telephone on the mortician's desk. Giles assured Mr. Carbery that the story was exclusive. The editor said that he would place it on page one, final home edition.

Toward eight o'clock the next morning, Millionaire Hudson arose cheerfully in his Capitol Hill mansion. He went outside to breathe the fresh Colorado air, and to pick up his favorite newspaper from the grass. The capitalist glanced at the front page casually over his coffee, then gave a start. Large red-ink headlines informed him that his house had been burglarized while he slept.

This seemed a preposterous announcement, but it occurred to him that he should investigate the presumable hoax. He decided first to examine his safe. He found the heavy door open, and the strong box rifled. The diamond ring, the earrings, the brooch also had been taken, just as the newspaper had disclosed. Next he learned that his silverware had vanished from the buffet. The capitalist was enraged.

Mr. Hudson called up the newspaper, but no one except a telephone operator was on duty at this early hour. Next he called Henry Carbery at the editor's home. Mr. Carbery endeavored to explain to his excited caller that he did not know who had given the news of the robbery to Giles. Mr. Hudson then charged that someone on the paper must have been "in on the job." He said that he was coming to *The News* office for a showdown.

Senator Tom Patterson, owner of the paper, also attended the indignation meeting, and two police representatives were present. The police officers were righteously offended because the burglary had come to their attention only in the columns of the morning newspaper. An emissary of Mr. Carbery located Giles in the steam room of the Glenarm Turkish Baths, and summoned him to *The News* for cross-examination.

"This is an unusual situation," Giles remarked to all parties concerned. "I'm still in a sweat from the baths."

"You'll be in a bigger sweat," said Senator Patterson, "if you don't explain certain things."

Mr. Hudson asked, "Where's my silverware?"

"Silverware?" asked Mr. Giles. He turned to his editor: "I'm still overheated. Didn't have time to get in the cold shower."

"I'm not interested in your hydrotherapy," said Mr. Hudson. "Who robbed my house?"

"I haven't the faintest idea, sir," said Giles. "You surely don't think *I* did it?"

Mr. Hudson addressed the Senator. "Somebody knew the precise amount taken from my safe." He brought a slip of paper from his vest pocket, and turned to Giles, "It was thoughtful of you to leave my memorandum behind. It says $2,420.80."

"Do you care to tell us where you got the story?" asked the Senator of Giles, "or would you prefer to be fired?"

Giles appealed to Editor Carbery. "Mr. Carbery, you threatened to fire me yesterday if I didn't get a page-one exclusive story. I got it for you. Now the Senator is going to fire me for getting it. Mr. Hudson is a heavy advertiser, so I guess I'll just retire and play cards with a friend until I'm indicted."

"A man can't be fired for doing his duty," the just Mr. Carbery said to the group. "A newspaperman must never betray a confidence."

"That's all very well," said the Senator. "But Mr. Giles at least might try to get Mr. Hudson's valuables back."

"Well!" said Mr. Hudson. "If that's all you're prepared to do, I'm canceling my subscription to *The News*. And don't ask me for any more advertising. Good morning, gentlemen."

At the pressroom in City Hall, Giles found Bad News Hawkins dealing four hands of poker to imaginary opponents. "Hawkins," Giles asked, "could you use your great influence to return all or part of the swag?"

Hawkins was examining his own poker hand. "I don't know what you're talking about, Roy." Then he frowned over a card from the undealt portion of the deck and muttered, "Bad news! Bad news!"

When I first met Mr. Giles I asked, "How did you happen to go into the newspaper business?"

He appraised me over a stein of beer. "At a time when I was completely out of my head with a high fever and yellow jaundice."

"I'd like to get into it myself," I said. "I mean, as a reporter."

"God forbid!" he all but shouted. "It's a harlot's life without the gaieties."

"Would you tell me the best person to see for a job?" I asked. "Maybe Mr. Carbery?"

"My boy," said Mr. Giles, "I wouldn't introduce my worst enemy to an editor. And if I had a son of my own, which is mathematically possible, I'd rather see him in Potter's Field than in a newspaper job."

"Then tell me why do *you* stay in it?" I inquired, unmindful that I was setting off a charge of explosives.

"Good God of Hosts!" shouted Mr. Giles. "This callow stranger asks why I stay among the pastepots and the stinking presses. Let me ask you something, my boy: Why does a galley slave stay at his oar? Why does a dope addict stay with his bottle of snow? Why does a tired husband stay with his wife?" Then he pounded the bar fiercely. "I'll tell you why: Because we're all chained to our hateful destiny."

Mr. Giles blew the foam from a fresh glass of beer, and said, "You put awfully big collars on these, Tom."

Giles' denunciation of the newspaper business perplexed me, and when Jim Lockhart resigned as a professor and came to town the next week to go to work at an editorial desk on the Associated Press, I reported Giles' remarks to him.

"They all talk that way," Jim said. "You'll hear their cries in every city room in America: how they hate the whole business, how they are going to get out of it to write a book, do a play, or become press agents for Anna Held. But they go on, year after year, crabbing, snarling, working, and loving every minute of it." Then Jim said, "I've talked to James R. Noland. He's city editor of *The Republican*. And he's promised to interview you for a job as cub reporter."

I could barely speak. "You mean it?"

"Yes. But you'll have to start out at only six dollars a week. That is, if Jim puts you on."

"I'd start out for nothing," I said reverently.

"I hope your grandmother won't object," Jim said. "Good luck."

With characteristic impulsiveness, I quit my job among the bells on the Saturday before the Monday when I was to have my momentous interview with City Editor Noland. This optimistic action caused Granny to say, "Don't you think you may be taking too much for granted?"

"No, ma'am," I replied. "Soon I'll be making thirty dollars a week."

"Indeed," and the old lady peered at me dubiously. "Then may I ask how much you are to receive at the start?"

"That's beside the point," I said. "You start at a nominal wage, but you go up like a skyrocket."

"Well," she said, "I hope you don't come down like one. Nobody pays much attention to a rocket when it falls; in fact, you can't even see it." Then she persisted, "Just how much is this nominal wage which you are to receive, maybe?"

"Oh," I said, "six dollars is the general rule."

"And you have just thrown away a twelve-dollar job to take a six-dollar one that may or may not be open?"

"It'll be open all right," I said. "Jim Lockhart has paved the way."

"Son," she said quietly, "I want to confide in you."

"I know, I know," I said impatiently.

"You are not, shall we say, an expert at figures. Now, mark you, I never have taken you to task for being backward at arithmetic, but there is something you simply should be told. Believe it or not, twelve dollars is more than six. Incredible as you may think it, twelve dollars is exactly twice six. Furthermore—"

"I'm getting bell crazy," I interrupted. "And I'm tired of waiting for the cat to die."

"Bells? Cats?" and the old lady seemed perturbed. "I'm speaking of dollars and common sense."

"My mind is made up," I said. "You'll stand up and cheer when I bring home thirty silver dollars."

"No," she said, "I'd have to sit down from the excitement."

I went to the cellar to tell Grandpa of my great decision. The old prospector was examining a dusty ledger. He listened to my excited words, then, when I closed my speech with, "I'm going to be a newspaperman," all that he said was, "You air?"

I slept but little during that night. I lay awake thinking of the excellent and fluent speech I would make to Mr. Noland. I thought of the day of the interview. All other days of my life, the ones that had been lived and the ones that were to come, stood in the calendar like mere courtiers waiting upon tomorrow, the monarch of all days.

At times thoughts of Granny intruded, of her doubts, her worries over my exchange of a twelve-dollar job for a six-dollar one. She loved me, and to have her love was a comforting thing. She always had been there when needed, and she was a symbol of faith and reliance. It was like putting down one's feet in the darkness, but with the sure knowledge that one's bedroom slippers were there on the floor at a particular place. I loved her, and I would not hurt her, but now I was determined to put my feet into the shoes of my choice, and not in comfortable bedroom slippers.

I waited breathlessly for the coming of tomorrow. As I refashioned and rehearsed my speech of self-nomination again and again, I seemed more eloquent than Disraeli.

22

THE LIONS' DEN

AS I stood early next afternoon in front of the old gray-
stone building in which I was to meet City Editor
Noland, the nearness of the interview thinned my
starch. To keep up my spirits, I began in a low voice
to say the speech I had prepared. But I shut off this recitation
when several passers-by turned their eyes in my direction.

Until today it had seemed to me that I had known the many
faces of the townsmen, a mass face composed of the features of
all the two hundred and thirteen thousand inhabitants of this city
of the plains. Daily I had moved as if among loved companions
and with a feeling of communal ownership of the ground upon
which I walked. That always had been my attitude toward any
enjoyable place, a concept of ownership and unquestionable possession. A park became mine merely by my having seen and admired it. Anybody's church, anybody's house, anybody's anything
—except anyone's sweetheart perhaps—belonged to you or to me
if you or I enjoyed contemplating it. In this fashion I came to
own two circuses, six original paintings by Franz Hals, and Mt.
Evans. This kind of dreaming may be high folly in the opinion of
realists, but it rids the pilgrim heart of greed, envy, and self-pity,
and it is tax exempt so far.

But today, as I stood on the sidewalk in front of the newspaper building, a challenging loneliness bore down upon me. The faces of the townsmen suddenly became those of strangers seen through the mists of troubled sleep. Fragments of thought strewed the conscious mind with the fossils of forgotten hours. From the unbidden past there sprang a word of an old ballad which my mother had sung, the word "forsaken." . . . Then I heard in flashing retrospection the clamor of a train as it wheeled upon the trestle near Monkey Tree. . . . Then there came a sudden mind's-eye view of the hillside next to Red Mountain, bleak from an ancient forest fire; the trees, long-killed, upthrust their bayonets of black and gray from the steep field of snow.

I roused from this nightmarish miscellany of sounds and scenes when a stray dog appeared at my side, rubbed his body against my leg, and looked up at me. He was a burly black mongrel with soiled white targets on his flanks. His tongue lolled out like a brakeman's flag, and his eyes were the kindest since those of the good King Wenceslas.

He followed me to the alley entrance of the newspaper office. The rear door of a saloon stood opposite this editorial portal, a convenient arrangement if ever I observed one. During the years, the boots of the many bearers of news had grooved the threshold stone of the back entrance to the newspaper office until it seemed the nether stone of a grist mill.

The dog at my heels, I crossed over the stone, and began to climb a flight of venerable wooden steps that reached the editorial rooms on the second floor. As I opened the door marked "City Room" at the head of the stairway, the sounds of the early afternoon assignment hour gushed in my face. The jumbled conversation, the katydid beats of a telegrapher's instrument, the laments of chairs in friction with the bare wooden floor—this was the voice of the newspaper issuing from the mouth of the door.

My heart began to pound. Should I turn back? No, the call to become a reporter, fainter now perhaps than before, still sounded from afar like the enchanted horn of Roland. And, besides, the dog was pressing against me, herding me forward as if to justify his fractional heritage from a shepherd grandsire.

Inside the littered city room, perhaps thirty men were at work with scissors and pencils, typewriters and pastepots, or conferring at desks and tables, or moving to and from the side offices, galley sheets in their hands. No one looked in my direction; no one came forward to ask what my business was. Each newspaper-man seemed intent upon his own work, as though it were the most important thing in all the world. To look upon this scene for the first time at close view was an exciting privilege, but the small swinging gate of the reception pen, in which I now found myself with the dog, proclaimed me a friendless alien in a strange port.

A scarred pine bench stood against the undecorated wall inside the reception pen, where I stood as if paralyzed by indecision. The half minute during which I gaped with gawking self-consciousness stretched out like an elastic band. Then I sat down on the bench. My eyes took in the dingy ceiling from which electric lights hung like the hats of dead cardinals.

The dog suddenly barked. I froze as the men swiveled their heads. The animal woofed again with unreasonable confidence, then got up on the bench beside me and insisted upon sitting in my lap. I endeavored to convince him that he was not a lap dog. At length he agreed to a compromise, and sat hugely beside me on the bench and daubed my cheek with his tongue. I kept a restraining arm about him, and waited to be thrown out. After peering none too approvingly at me and the dog, the newsmen returned to their respective tasks.

And now another caller entered the reception pen, a soldierly man of advanced years. He carried a black walking stick with a silver handle; wore a square-crown derby hat, and had a gray goatee. A rosette, the size and color of a brussels sprout, occu-pied one lapel of his Prince Albert coat. At first glance I believed this man to be some illustrious editor; but he paused at the low swing gate to call out to a passing newspaper worker, a stout

gentleman with silver-rim spectacles and a scrub-brush mustache:
"Mr. Dickensheets, has Joe come in yet?"

Mr. Dickensheets replied in a polite though reproving tone,
"No, Colonel Jamieson, Mr. Ward happens to be out."

"He may be 'Mr. Ward' to you," said Colonel Jamieson stiffly,
"but he's just plain 'Joe' to me. I'll wait here for him."

The Colonel turned toward the bench, frowned at the dog,
appraised me suspiciously, then spread his coattails and sat down
as far away as possible from me and my friend. He brought out
a cigar case from his breast pocket, chose a cigar, sniffed it as
if it were a fine Havana, which it was not, then fired it with
much ceremony.

No one paid further attention to the Colonel or to me. After a
time I ventured to say, "I beg your pardon, Colonel Jamieson,
but which of these men is City Editor Noland?"

The Colonel slowly removed the cigar from his lips. "Have I
the honor of your acquaintance, young man?"

"No, sir," I replied, "but your name is well known to everyone."

"Quite true," was the Colonel's response to this tribute. "I
suppose you are familiar with my campaign to rid this city of
flies?"

I wasn't, but I nodded, and in this lying manner became the
sounding board during the next hour—and, for that matter, the
next several years—of a man regarded by numerous critics as the
biggest bore in the Rocky Mountain West.

While anxiously trying to identify City Editor Noland among
the busy men, I sat squirming on a numbing buttock, and not only
heard the Colonel's plan to kill off houseflies to prevent the spread
of tuberculosis among the citizens but endured the story of his
gallstones. He carried these surgical trinkets in a small bottle. The
Colonel also went into his career as a soldier in the Union Army,
and for good measure discussed his pioneer baseball days in Phila-
delphia.

During this recital, it suddenly occurred to me that the Colonel was the fabulous blade once known among the ladies of Market Street as "Bouquet Jimmy." My interest in him became more pointed than before, and served to offset some of my anxieties concerning the job I was seeking.

Colonel Jamieson neglected to refer to certain ancient phases of his career, such as events during his term long ago as engineer at the County Jail. He had quit that job in a huff, it was said, when someone claimed that he had lost his temper and thrown a cat into the jail furnace. Nor did the Colonel volunteer the fact that he had been a mere corporal in the Union Army, and afterward promoted himself from year to year, an amiable quirk of old soldiers. He was supposed to have died of wounds in 1864, and displayed a photograph which he carried with him at all times, the picture of a tombstone bearing his name together with an epitaph that didn't give him any the worst of it. I listened with one ear to his autobiography and with the other to the commotions of the city room.

In the early nineties, Colonel Jamieson, then only a self-breveted captain, had come to Denver after a relative had died and left him two thousand dollars. The heir did not trust banks, but fashioned his bequest, two one-thousand-dollar bills, into a rosette which he wore as a boutonniere. When circumstances induced him to change the banknotes into bills of lower denomination, he made new rosettes of hundred-dollar bills. During lean times, he wore rosettes of tens and fives.

By the time he had decided to become a major—a promotion which occurred at the turn of the century—Jamieson had become known as "Bouquet Jimmy." He earned this nickname, one which he deplored, because of his practice of carrying flowers to cafés on nights when he chose to squander a rosette or spend his pension payment.

He invariably went out alone on a night of pleasure, to sit in some café with an eye out for a happy young couple. Having found such a pair, he would send a waiter to them to offer the bouquet to the young lady, together with his calling card and the written inquiry if he might have the honor of buying a bottle of wine for beauty's sake. The wine having been accepted, the witless ones would invite their benefactor to share the champagne. From that hour on until closing time, the victims had no romantic privacy but spent the remainder of their precious evening peering at gallstones and the photograph of the Jamieson grave, and listening to baseball memoirs and all the rest.

The Colonel always selected a café in which an orchestra or vocal entertainers performed, like the Mozart Cabaret where Bill and Paul Frawley sang. Bouquet Jimmy would attract attention to himself almost every half hour by bringing a small silk American flag from his pocket and attaching it to silver clasps on his walking stick, then waving it. At this, the musicians would cease playing Strauss waltzes and strike up "The Star-Spangled Banner." The customers, forced by patriotic tradition to rise again and again, secretly would ask God to strike Bouquet Jimmy dead. Jamieson subsidized the orchestra with a dollar for each rendition of the work of Francis Scott Key.

In 1902 Bouquet Jimmy finally commissioned himself as a full colonel. He decided to celebrate this promotion by attending a fete organized by the pimps of Market Street. The procurers called their social "The Broadsmen's Ball," and gave it at Reddy Gallagher's Coliseum. The newly created Colonel arrived there with a large bouquet of pinks and a boutonniere of hundred-dollar bills. When his eye and his intentions fell upon a vivacious little chippy, he detached a banknote at once from his lapel. He sent the bouquet and a card to her, and before long she was dancing among the wine glasses on her admirer's table.

The stimulated Colonel climbed upon a chair to permit the girl to kick a five-dollar bill out of his silk hat, which he gallantly held high for her. He was about to let her earn another five dollars with her twinkle-toe when someone threw a wet beer towel across his mouth. Bouquet Jimmy did not think highly of this gesture, but restrained himself, dried his face, then again held up his hat for the lady to kick it. Another beer towel, a really soggy one, struck him in the face. At this the Colonel forgot the dignity of his honorary eagles and leaped onto the table to announce that he would lick the low so-and-so who had thrown the towel. No one came forward.

The next night the Colonel, carrying another bouquet, and once again handsomely garbed in silk hat, fried shirt, starched wing collar, and detachable cuffs, visited the cigar store of Burt Davis in the Tabor Grand Block. The shop of this tobacconist served as headquarters for sportsmen, actors, and newspapermen. The Colonel himself was not particularly welcome at Burt's because he would rummage among the stock of expensive cigars, damage their wrappers, and finally purchase merely a few Cremos, a five-cent brand of the period.

While the Colonel was moving like a dignified locust among the costly cigars, smelling them, massaging them out of shape, and keeping Clerk Gene Kaiser from waiting on more desirable customers, a short and surly man entered the store. He walked up to the Colonel and accosted him with a tough voice: "So you're Bouquet Jimmy, eh?"

The Colonel pushed aside a box of Perfectos to say, "I don't believe I've ever had the honor of an introduction to you, sir."

At this the other man blurted out, "Well, you cheap old bastard! I'm the fellow who threw the beer towels at you last night for stealing my girl."

The Colonel stiffened, then in a courtly manner but without wasting time, placed his stick and silk hat on the counter beside his bouquet. Next he removed his Prince Albert coat and waistcoat, but allowed his fried shirt and cuffs to remain in status quo. Then he went to work with his fists.

The Colonel was an unusually good boxer for his years, which were then about fifty. Ordinarily Burt Davis or Gene Kaiser immediately stopped all fights that began in their store, but this one was too good. The Colonel now had maneuvered his stocky antagonist into a corner farthest away from the glass showcases, and was jabbing him smartly. Suddenly the shorter man got in a chance blow that rocked the Colonel to his shiny black boots. Instead of pursuing this advantage, however, the fellow ran toward the door and disappeared.

The Colonel meantime was holding a hand to his mouth and calling out in a strangled manner, "Help! Help!"

"I don't think you need any help now, Colonel," Burt Davis remarked. "Quit squawking!"

It so happened that the chance blow had knocked three of the Colonel's artificial teeth down his throat. When a police surgeon had removed the teeth from a place near the victim's windpipe, the Colonel drew on his coat, put on his hat, and began again to manhandle a number of the store's best cigars.

At a much later date, some years after I met the Colonel at *The Republican,* he was standing at the counter of Burt Davis' store. He now had become bailiff in the court of United States Judge Lewis, and because of this exalted office did not welcome certain references to his Bohemian past.

"Colonel," Burt said, "you've been mangling my Havanas for at least twenty-seven years. I like to have you come in, and I appreciate all you've done for baseball and the florist trade. But couldn't you manage to choose a five-cent cigar without breaking up whole boxes of twenty-five and thirty-cent ones?"

To this the Colonel replied: "I have been offended many times, sir, by your scurrilous remarks during a quarter of a century and more. I remember distinctly that when I was having a slight altercation with a thug in this very place twenty-four years ago, you were slow in coming to my rescue when I suffered a dental accident."

"Oh," said Davis, "you mean the fellow who hit you with the beer towel for stealing his girl?"

This reference to an undignified past enraged the bailiff of the United States Court. "Burt Davis," he said, "I shall never enter this place again. Never, sir! You have my solemn word."

Several years passed, and the Colonel caught cold one night when at the florist's. He died the following week of pneumonia.

Some days after the undertaker had plucked the Colonel's rosette as payment for services rendered, a well-dressed man of middle age entered Burt Davis' store to purchase some pipe tobacco. He had with him a package which he put down upon the counter.

"How nicely wrapped that package is," observed Gene Kaiser.

"Yes," the man agreed, "they did a good job on it in every respect. The contents are the ashes of a man named Colonel W. A. Jamieson. Maybe you knew him? I'm taking his ashes back East to his people."

Kaiser mystified the stranger by saying, "I knew he would come in here again some time."

If I may be permitted to recall Colonel Jamieson from his urn long enough to go back with him to the offices of *The Republican*, I should like to say that my listening to him that day and on subsequent days served me well in three respects. In after years he provided me with numerous news "beats" by informing me what was occurring, or about to occur, in the court of Judge Lewis. The judge was a brilliant but testy man, who disliked all reporters and would never give them any news whatsoever. The Colonel also served me as a model for a character in a novel that pleased me much more than it did the public. But, best of all, on the day of our first meeting, it was the Colonel who pointed out and identified for me the men of *The Republican* staff as they moved across what seemed a mighty stage.

"That's Arthur Chapman," he said as I gazed popeyed, "the poet who wrote the immortal 'Out Where the West Begins.'" Again he indicated such luminaries as "Spencer the cartoonist," or explained that "Mr. Dickensheets was a close friend of Eugene Field, who worked on this paper when it was *The Tribune*. I knew Field well."

· But the men who interested me most were the reporters. The great Richard Milton came up the stairs like a wind. He conferred hurriedly with a cynical fellow in shirt sleeves, who was, the Colonel said, Arthur MacLennan. I watched Milton closely.

This mighty graduate of *The Kansas City Star*, his derby hat pushed back on his red head, sat at his desk, rolled a Bull Durham cigarette, stared at his typewriter accusingly, then began to beat out a sonata like a two-fingered Paderewski. How I envied him! How I still do!

As the pageant of reporters arrived to receive news assignments for the afternoon, the Colonel spoke to one and all as they passed. Almost everyone smiled knowingly when responding to his greetings. A woman reporter, the red-haired Millie Morris, one of the best of her day, stopped for a moment to chat with Colonel Jamieson, but escaped through the gate when he reached as if for his gallstones.

It would seem that this newspaper had a preference for red-haired reporters, for now a third person of that coloring came through the outer door. He was Herbert Belford, the Colonel said, the best political observer in the West, and brother of Francis Wayne, noted writer on the staff of *The Denver Post*.

The name Belford contained celebrity and tradition. Herbert's mother was Frances McEwen Belford, Colorado's foremost woman citizen and one-time friend of Abraham Lincoln. His late father had been James B. Belford, an eloquent, impulsive man, pioneer judge and leader of the territorial bar. As a member of Congress, the senior Belford had been known as "The Red Rooster of the Rockies." The Belford home was always open to all the waifs of the western world, to the downhearted ones and the browbeaten ones, and the visitor there received more than bread. With parents such as theirs, the wonder was not that the Belford children were so bright and vital; the wonder would have been had they been anything less.

The dog that had followed me to *The Republican* city room proved a fickle companion. Perhaps the Colonel's stories bored him. At any rate he leaped down as Herb Belford came in, and tried to take advantage of the open door. Just then a tall man appeared in the doorway and almost fell over the dog, which got out and past him.

And now the Colonel said, "There's your man!"

The tall gentleman was well dressed, but there was one incongruous note to his garb, a green eyeshade instead of a hat. He looked neither to right nor left, and muttered to himself, "Oh, damn it all!"

"How do you do, Mr. Noland?" the Colonel said, but the tall gentleman didn't respond. He went swiftly through the gate and toward a cluster of desks at the far side of the room.

"Go right in and introduce yourself to Jimmy Noland," the Colonel advised me. "Now's your chance."

I was undecided what to do. Mr. Noland seemed in no mood to hear a speech such as the one I had rehearsed. Besides, I had completely forgotten it. As I sat debating with myself, I saw Mr. Noland angrily throw his eyeshade to a desk. Then he turned toward a wall peg to take from it a fedora hat. He spoke briefly to the man previously identified by the Colonel as the assistant city editor, Art MacLennan, then left in great haste.

As Mr. Noland again passed by the reception-pen bench, I rose to speak to him, but before I could say anything Colonel Jamieson stepped to bat with, "Jimmy, this young man has been waiting over an hour to see you."

"Tell it to MacLennan," said Mr. Noland tersely, and then went out.

My heart was in a lemon squeezer as the door closed upon my great opportunity. Then I experienced an amazing turn of spirits, a grim but solid resolution to go into action. My courage, as it were, got its second wind.

I opened the gate and walked directly to MacLennan's desk. He was standing on one foot, the other one propped on the seat of his chair. While in this contorted posture, he was gazing solemnly at something in his hand. I was rude enough to observe what it was that occupied his attention: the photograph of a woman clad in nothing but her earrings.

"Mr. MacLennan," I said as he almost regretfully lifted his eyes from the photograph, "I want a job."

"Doing what?" he asked.

"Well," I replied, "I was supposed to see Mr. Noland. But he said to see you."

"And you took him seriously?" inquired Mr. MacLennan, and he indeed seemed cynical and sardonic.

"Mr. Lockhart arranged it," I replied. "James Lockhart of the School of Journalism at Boulder—"

"Good Lord!" said MacLennan. "Surely you're not another one of *those* fellows? School of Journalism! Hah!" He took down his hat and coat from one of the wall pegs and continued, "It's time for me to buy myself a drink. If your problem is not too long or morbid, I'll listen to it in the saloon."

I followed MacLennan past the reporters' desks and past Colonel Jamieson who said, "It's a nice day, MacLennan," to which MacLennan replied, "That's your opinion," and we went out of the door to the stairway. As we walked down the stairs we met a dumpy, red-faced man on his way up. He wore eyeglasses, a short-cropped mustache, and had a mouth that turned severely downward at the corners.

"Oh, Mr. Ward," MacLennan called out to him, "Colonel Jamieson's upstairs."

Mr. Ward stopped in his tracks, or rather in his treads. "The hell you say!" he exclaimed in a high-pitched, rasping voice. "Can't he bother someone else with that damned campaign of his to swat the flies?" Then Mr. Ward turned to go back downstairs, saying, "I'll be at Tortoni's. Telephone the office to inform Colonel Jamieson that I just had a stroke and was taken to St. Anthony's Hospital."

"All right, Mr. Ward," said MacLennan.

I was so impressed by seeing the celebrated editor Josiah M. Ward in person that I paused at the saloon door to look after the retreating, fuming, dumpy little firebrand of western journalism. The stories of his wrathy conduct as an editor did not support his present state of flight.

"What's holding you up?" MacLennan was asking.

"I was wondering," I said as we went inside and to the bar, "how a great man like Mr. Ward—"

"I know," MacLennan interrupted, "you mean, why is he running out like a rabbit?"

"Yes."

MacLennan ordered two rye whiskies without asking me my choice of drinks, then said, "Every great man has a great weakness. Mine is listening to starry-eyed fools who want to get into the newspaper business."

"You wouldn't ever think that Mr. Ward had a weakness," I said.

"Mr. Ward's weakness," and MacLennan tossed off his whisky, "is for pioneers. He's rough and tough and ruthless with everyone else, including babes at the breast, but he simply can't offend a pioneer. And Colonel Jamieson is a pioneer bore, in fact, the Daniel Boone of all boredom."

The job was uppermost in my mind. "Do you hire many new men?"

"Mostly those with experience," he said. "The newspaper game is not a Maypole dance."

"I had a year in the school of journalism," I ventured.

"You don't mean to tell me?" and MacLennan's sarcasm was sulphuric. "In that case we'll put you in charge of the paper."

I weathered this to ask, "Didn't *you* start at the bottom?"

"It's all bottom and no top," MacLennan said, "like the fat lady in the sideshow." He paid for the drinks, then continued bitingly, "Never mind about me and where I started, or where I stopped. Just mind your own affairs, if any. You're going to have your own worries. You'll be kicked around, hooted at, and I personally will try to break your heart. Then, if you can stand a year of it without cracking up, hating everyone including yourself, and murdering your family in their beds, you can consider yourself on your way to being a newspaperman."

My excitement made me hoarse. "You're putting me to work?"

"I'm recommending you to Mr. Noland," he said. "He does the hiring. I make it possible for you to get fired, and I'm not fooling about *that*."

"Lockhart says that Mr. Noland is the ideal newspapermen." Then I asked, "Say, what was he so mad about when he came in?"

"He'd forgotten his hat," said MacLennan. "He always does. Every day he goes out with his eyeshade on instead of his hat; the most absent-minded fellow I ever saw. Always comes back for his hat, madder than hell. One day he tried to find a telephone number in the office dictionary."

"Oh," I said. Then I asked almost gingerly, "When do I report for work? And may I buy you a drink?"

"No, you can't buy me a drink," said MacLennan sharply. "Report for work tomorrow afternoon at one. Meantime, I'll speak to Noland. And after tomorrow you and I are strangers. Understand? No palling around. No familiarity."

"I understand," I said. "So long, and thanks."

When I arrived home, I found Granny churning some butter by means of shaking the cream in a large mason jar. She did not like store butter, and regularly made her own butter laboriously.

"Well," I said to her importantly, "you are now looking at a real newspaper reporter."

"I'll try to get used to it," she said. "How much are they paying you?"

"I forgot to ask," I replied, "but that will be taken care of."

She handed me the improvised churn. "Suppose you take care of this while I get things ready for supper."

Apparently she could not regard me as an adult about to engage in a great career. I wondered what Horace Greeley's grandmother had said to him the day he decided to become a newspaperman. Then, as I shook the jar to clot the cream, I thought of the adventurous days to come; of castles, Glorias, and life seen at firsthand.

It wasn't MacLennan but the absent-minded Mr. Noland who put the first dent in my heart. Mr. Noland did this inadvertently, to be sure, for he was a splendid person and an excellent craftsman. After I had worked for a week upon the trivia that a cub reporter attracts, but worked hard and with an abiding fear of the written word, I waited for the paymaster to give me one of the small stout envelopes which he was distributing among the other men.

There was no envelope for me, none at all. Mr. Noland had completely forgotten to enter my name on the payroll.

When I tried to explain the lapses of the city editor's mind to Granny, she remarked, "I trust that Mr. Noland will not cut your salary any further next week."

Jim Lockhart told me not to worry about a thing, that he would speak to Mr. Noland at once.

"Better put it in writing," I said, "or he'll forget it."

23

BRINGING IN THE SHEAVES

ALMOST everyone, I should imagine, has a year which
seems peculiarly his own in memory, a year enshrined where bright and fragrant candles ever burn.
My year was 1912–1913, during which time I experienced a feeling of self-importance which I never again possessed.

The newspaper world may best remember 1912 as the year of
war in the Balkans, the wreck of the *Titanic*, and the assassination
of gambler Herman Rosenthal by New York gangsters. But those
events seem less real in my own recollection than the unsung happenings of a provincial yesterday.

To me it was the year of the last illness of old Scout Wiggins,
protégé of Kit Carson; the motorization of the fire department
and the retirement of Tom, the celebrated white horse of the
"Old Fives" pumper team; the promotion of the dauntless John
F. Healy to the post of fire chief. Those bits of local history
were symbols of a change that was sweeping the West and all
America as well. It was good-by to old ways and hail to the
machine.

Not only did the assortment of scouts, firemen, and fire horses forward my career and move me toward the dreamed-of thirty dollars a week, but a remarkable Roman Catholic priest, Father Hugh L. McMenamin, chanced to take a fancy to me. This handsome, fluent clergyman was completing his building of the Cathedral of the Immaculate Conception, of which he was the rector.

Whenever Father Mac had an important speech to make, it was his habit to seek pointers from Father O'Ryan of St. Leo's Church. Father O'Ryan was eloquent and wise and well loved by everyone. His fellow-priests conceded his oratorical talents but sometimes wearied of the O'Ryan sermons because of their length.

One day in 1912 Father Mac decided to consult Father O'Ryan in regard to an address to be delivered to a group of American university women. At St. Leo's he found a funeral service in progress and the priest preaching on the immortality of the soul.

"Will he be long?" Father Mac asked the sexton.

"You can't tell," the sexton replied. "Sometimes he's long—and sometimes he's longer."

"Well," said Father Mac, "I'll go in and wait for him."

Father O'Ryan now was saying from the pulpit: "Then I went out, and I gazed upon the mighty mountains lifting their giant peaks into the blue of the everlasting sky, and I said, 'O mighty mountains, the day will come when you will pass away, but not so I.' And then I went out and gazed upon the beautiful valleys, the valleys rich with grain to feed the starving millions, and sweet with the scent of a million flowers, and cooled by the mist of hidden streams, and I said, 'O beautiful valleys, the day will come when you too will pass away, but not so I.' And then I went out and gazed upon the vast ocean heaving those mighty billows, with its thunderous waves bearing messages from far-off lands, and I said, 'O mighty ocean, the day will come when you will dry up, but not so I. . . .'"

Father Mac took the speaker at his word, rose and went outside. As he passed the newspaper reporters at the door, Father Mac whispered: "He never said a truer thing."

When Father Mac induced Bishop Edward J. Hanna (afterward Archbishop) of San Francisco to grant me an interview, I earned the right to cover the dedication ceremonies at the cathedral. The only one I did not impress with my new importance as a recorder of Roman Catholic events was Granny. "I don't know what you see in these papists—and vice versa," she said. "You're beginning to smell of incense."

During the week of the dedication ceremonies, Father Mac kept an eye on me. Indeed, he has kept an eye upon me these thirty-four years. When I last saw him a year ago at this writing, he wore the purple collar of a monsignor. The still keen-minded priest referred only to the good I had done, which was little enough to escape most men's notice, and said nothing of the rest.

"Well," said Father Mac, "I remember that you had a hearty appetite and that you cut quite a figure among the young ladies. Of course," he added, "you are more settled now—let us trust."

Perhaps the good father was referring to my memorable year, which began in 1912 and ended in 1913, and which contained high romance. As my passions grew, so did my determination to achieve that weekly thirty dollars. Such a magic sum, I felt, would open all gates; and as I moved with bouncing spirits toward the monetary goal and toward romance, Assistant City Editor Mac-Lennan heckled me. Himself a darling of the ladies, notwithstanding his cynical and superior manner toward them, MacLennan took pleasure in hexing the love lives of reporters. I often wonder how newspapermen can in later life become so fond of editors who formerly distressed them.

The first of MacLennan's onslaughts occurred at about the time when the absent-minded Mr. Noland finally got around to putting me on the payroll. As a six-dollar-a-week cub, I made nightly calls among the "lowers," the secondary hotels on Seventeenth Street near the Union Depot. While returning newsless to the office late one evening, I heard the music of a Salvation Army band. The marchers were leaving the place of a street revival in the red-light district to go to headquarters in Larimer Street. They were playing and singing an evangelical hymn well known to me, "Bringing in the Sheaves."

Among the group of newly redeemed sinners following after the band, I saw none other than Grandpa's one-time antagonist at the Grand National, Diamond Louie. Material as well as spiritual changes had come upon him. His clothing was frayed and when he opened his mouth I observed that the jeweled tooth was missing. The spiritual rebirth of this now-seedy procurer struck me as a news event of considerable interest. So I joined the small parade of penitents and went to the mission hall, hoping presently to hear Diamond Louie tell how misfortune had overtaken him and his studded tooth and brought him into the fold. But instead, Captain Sledd of the Salvation Army directed one of the girl members, a trumpeter, "to play taps for our late comrade, Sylvester." Captain Sledd explained to us newcomers that Sylvester had been the bass drummer, "a worker for the Lord" who had died only two days before. The Captain went on to say, "Sylvester's place will be hard to fill, both at the drum and in the vineyard."

I didn't hear the rest of Captain Sledd's words of praise for the late tympanist, for now I was looking breathlessly at the girl who was to play taps. Here, I thought, was the prettiest creature I had ever seen, a rosy-cheeked brunette, on whose head the blue poke bonnet of the Salvation Army became an enchanting piece of millinery. This girl made of my heart a tambourine, which shook and rattled and hummed. When she blew taps on her battered cornet, I felt that Gabriel couldn't have done a better job.

Captain Sledd now beamed a "Thank you, Hettie," then asked for a moment of silent prayer for Sylvester. When Hettie closed her big blue eyes and bowed her head, her hat brim hid her features. I waited in a kind of anguish until she lifted her head and showed once more that face so like a fresh bouquet from an old-fashioned garden.

At the conclusion of the services, I interviewed Captain Sledd and asked if I might play the bass drum some time soon.

"Have you had any experience?" the Captain inquired.

I was looking at Hettie. "Not much, but I'm a Methodist."

The Captain, obviously mistaking love for religious fervor, seemed impressed by my earnestness. He said that I might appear with the band on approval the next Saturday night, and offered to lend me an official cap. When he disclosed that Hettie was his daughter, I had certain formless forebodings; the Captain was a muscular fellow with a granite eye. I held Hettie's hand a moment too long. She withdrew it and blushed.

"Hettie's the apple of my eye," the Captain said.

"Apple, forsooth," thought I. "Rather a whole orchard in bloom."

My breast was full of bees. When my bees and I swarmed into the newspaper office, MacLennan said, "Not that we can't go to press without you, but you're supposed to get back here the same night. This is not a weekly newspaper."

I recited the news of Diamond Louie's reformation, but Mac-Lennan merely shook his head and began to check the first copies to arrive upstairs from the pressroom.

"You seem mighty excited," MacLennan said shrewdly, "over seeing just a down-and-out pimp."

I kept thinking of my Saturday night appointment to play the drum at Hettie's side. Then, when Saturday night arrived at last, MacLennan called me to his desk to say, "Never mind the lowers tonight. Here's the weather report. See what you can do with it in six lines."

"But," I objected, "I was planning on a human interest story about the Salvation Army. Captain Sledd has arranged for me to beat the drum."

"Go beat the typewriter instead," MacLennan commanded. "When you get big enough and good enough to give assignments to yourself, I'll notify you." Then he went on to say, "The weather forecaster is getting worse every day, and I'm gunning for him. If you can figure out some way to make his predictions look sillier than they already are, I may assign you to a Salvation Army story."

My heart was a bass drum. Could MacLennan hear it? Would Hettie ever hear it?

I had just begun to write the "short" on the weather when MacLennan again summoned me to his desk. "Didn't I hear you bragging the other day that your people knew Scout Wiggins?"

"My grandfather and he are old friends," I replied.

"All right, then," said MacLennan. "I've a tip that Wiggins is dying; no outsiders are allowed to see him. Run out to his home on Larimer Street, talk your way in, and get a deathbed statement."

The wheels of the streetcar on which I rode far out on Larimer Street were singing, "Bringing in the sheaves. . . . Bringing in the sheaves. . . . We shall come rejoicing, Hettie, my great love in your pretty blue poke bonnet, bringing in the sheaves."

Scout Oliver P. Wiggins, the almost ninety-year-old protégé of Kit Carson and our earliest surviving settler, lay in a room off the small parlor of his niece's home. Five years before this time he had suffered a paralytic stroke which had caused his retirement as bailiff at the courthouse. Now he was dangerously ill from a gangrenous condition of the left leg. He had carried a rifle ball in that leg for sixty years, the reminder of a battle with Indians.

His physician did not want anyone to disturb him, but when he overheard me say that I was the grandson of his old and valued friend Norman Wheeler, he demanded that I come to his bedside. I tried to forget about Hettie and keep my mind on the deathbed of Scout Wiggins.

It was my first experience at soliciting a last philosophy from a dying man. So I began far afield, mentioning that just recently I had read that Buffalo Bill had visited the Scout, pressed his hand, and talked of old days. It was my garrulous misfortune to say that I regarded Buffalo Bill as the greatest frontiersman since Kit Carson.

The sick pioneer got up to his elbows on the bed. "Just don't mention that faker's name in the same breath with Kit Carson," he commanded me.

The doctor came into the room to order me from the dying man's presence. On my way to the door I blurted out confusedly, "What kind of weather will we have this week, Scout?"

"Never mind the weather," the doctor interposed. "You've upset Major Wiggins enough as it is."

"Wait a moment," the Scout said suspiciously. "Is Cody shooting off his big mouth as a weather expert?"

"No, sir," I replied, "but the weather forecaster claims we're going to have a week of clear skies."

"He does, eh?" said the Scout. "Well, I got an old wound here that never fails as a barometer." He flexed his sore leg carefully, then said, "It will be fair tomorrow, cloudy next day, and the next day after that we're going to have the damnedest cloudburst in years; and you can tell all the citizens for me, except Cody, to keep out of the way of Cherry Creek."

The urge was upon me to stop off for Salvation Army duties on the way back to the office. I had failed to get the deathbed statement, and MacLennan would not like that. But what more could he do or say if I were late at the office again? I had a handful of nothing as it was; at least I could brighten my doom with an hour in Hettie's presence. Then I decided not to succumb to temptation but go to the office, confess failure, and—after MacLennan fired me—hasten to the mission hall to enlist.

When, as a passing remark, I mentioned Wiggins' weather forecast, the editor gave a happy start. "This may be our chance to show up the weather bureau," said MacLennan almost jovially. "If the Scout is right, I'll see to it that you get to play the drum."

During the next days I watched the sky like a man adrift on a raft. The first day was fair, as the Scout had predicted. Clouds formed the next day; and then, on the third day, the black bowl of heaven dropped all it had, and Cherry Creek became a destructive torrent. The flabbergasted officials at the weather bureau called the storm a "freak variation of low barometric pressures."

The next Saturday night MacLennan once again stood between me and romance. "They say the Scout is sinking fast," he declared. "Suppose you go out for the deathbed statement, and perhaps another weather report."

Once again the Scout rallied at the mention of Colonel Cody's name, and then issued a second weather report. Thinking of Hettie all the while, I asked the Scout if Kit Carson ever had been deeply in love.

"Oh, my yes," he replied. "His one great love was his wife, Josefa, daughter of Don Francisco Jaramillo of Taos. I was thinking only today of his two funerals. He was buried the first time at Fort Lyon, Colorado, in 1868, a month after his wife died. His brother-in-law Tom Boggs moved both bodies, like Kit had wished it, in a wagon to the American Cemetery in Taos where Carson's bones were buried for a second time. And after the earth was put onto the grave, a woman took some artificial flowers from her bonnet and strewed them there."

The Scout's second prediction concerning the weather was in exact opposition to the scientist's in the Federal Building. And again the frontiersman was correct.

Upon MacLennan's recommendation I received from Mr. Noland a six-dollar raise in wages. Now I could look Granny in the eye, and also think more confidently of eloping with Hettie. I hoped soon to reach the thirty-dollar goal, whereafter I need never again worry about matters of finance.

In recognition of my gaining the Scout's almost clairvoyant weather forecasts on several successive Saturday nights, MacLennan permitted me to appear with the Salvation Army band, but on Wednesday evenings only. As a drummer, I do not believe that I quite measured up to the late Sylvester. But I knew the hymns by ear, and I knew Hettie's charms by heart.

I spent the Wednesday nights of August at the Salvation Army drum. But I had little chance to speak to Hettie for long at a time or privately, for the Captain kept his granite eye upon his apple. When I did have an opportunity, one warm romantic evening, to whisper to Hettie between hymns, I asked her if she would admire me the more were I to invest in a full uniform. At this she behaved as if I had made an indecent proposal. I was afraid that she was going to report me to her muscular father.

When Hettie regained her composure she said, "You mustn't speak of worldly things." But I kept on thinking of them just the same.

Now the unseen hand of MacLennan throttled my romance.

From a remark I dropped at the Press Club concerning "the most beautiful girl in the world, a great musician too on the silver cornet," the alert MacLennan smelled out my secret.

One Wednesday night while I was hammering away at the drum and yearning for another chance to say worldly things to Hettie, I observed Harry McCabe, a police reporter of *The Rocky Mountain News,* standing at the curbstone. Harry was leering at me and moving his brows up and down. It should have occurred to me at once that MacLennan had put McCabe up to this low Irish trick, for the men were close friends, but love had obscured my reasoning powers. Besides, my heart pangs had caused me to take three solid jolts of liquor on my way to the sacred concert, and my blood was hot. When McCabe again leered and grimaced, I slipped my shoulders from the drum straps. I set the instrument down against a lamppost. Then I advanced toward the leering McCabe and was about to belabor him when Captain Sledd and other soldiers of the Lord intervened.

"I'm afraid that you are not meant for this work," the Captain said. He sniffed and continued, "Besides, we do not countenance strong drink."

This ouster and this rebuke were as nothing compared to the look of farewell on Hettie's face. Two weeks afterward I went to the mission hall where she was serving hot coffee to a group of flophouse bums and managed to speak to her, but to all my entreaties she only shook her bonnet. I even promised to learn to read music; but nothing could influence her to readmit me to the fold. She gave me an extra helping of sugar, however, and there was a tear in her big blue eye as she turned from me. I never played the drum again.

Scout Wiggins did not die until December. Before that time, he would rally each Saturday night when I resorted to the new device of mentioning Colonel Cody's name.

"I'll outlive that faker!" he would exclaim, and we'd go on from there.

The Wiggins' weather forecasts had become so popular that MacLennan now printed them regularly alongside the bureau's reports. This pleased the old scout but not the official weather prophet, who called in person to beg MacLennan to cease publishing the Scout's predictions. This he urged on patriotic grounds; the government itself was being brought to ridicule.

The old frontiersman would permit no anesthetic when surgeons operated to remove the ancient bullet. "Huh!" he said. "What would Kit Carson think if I couldn't stand a little pain?" After the operation, his disturbed wound became unreliable, and his talent as a weather prophet lapsed.

One Saturday night in December I did not go to the Larimer Street house for the weekly deathbed statement and weather report. MacLennan sent me to a fire instead. That night the Scout died. When I heard the news I felt as though one of the high peaks had vanished from the great mountain wall to the west.

The fire to which MacLennan assigned me on the night Scout Wiggins died burned down a large livery stable. The new chief, John F. Healy, was directing the fire fighting and the rescue of the screaming horses from the stalls. I had followed this remarkable Irishman to fires ever since I could remember. Oftentimes he had booted me in the pants to send me away from the lines. Now it was different. I was a reporter, a comrade; and because of his consideration I received another six-dollar raise. The story that earned it concerned the retirement of the fire horse Tom. That white Percheron lived to the incredible age of thirty-nine years, worked for the nuns at the Convent of The Little Sisters of the Poor, and died on the same day as that of Chief Healy's own funeral.

As an eighteen-dollar-a-week man, I felt that my next inamorata would be unable to withstand me. But where should I find anyone as blossom-like as Hettie? Who else could wear a bonnet with such charm? Sometimes I stood on the sidewalk at a distance from the revival services and envied the bums who received Hettie's words of spiritual encouragement and the accompanying beatific smile.

If Hettie saw me, she gave no sign. And the granite eye of Captain Sledd looked stonily past me. I wrote Hettie a note, revealing that I now was making eighteen dollars a week. I enclosed a two-dollar bill, explaining that it was a tithe. There was no reply.

That autumn after I completed my assignment for the dedication of the Cathedral, the friendly Father Mac wrote Editor Joe Ward a letter in which he proclaimed my work the best of its kind outside of Irish journalism. City Editor Noland, returning for his hat in exchange for his eyeshade, spoke to me cordially, and my mentor Jim Lockhart predicted that another raise was in the wind.

During all my flutters over Hettie and my excitement over my own importance as a journalist, I thought often of Granny and of how best to share my forthcoming wealth with her. For one thing, I would have a telephone installed; and for Grandpa I would finance a prospecting trip.

My grandmother now was seventy-one years old, and Grandpa seventy-three. The years were beginning to make their shoulders droop, but their spirits never. Soon would come their golden wedding anniversary. The old couple themselves didn't seem to regard the fiftieth year of their union as a noteworthy occasion, but I made secret plans to celebrate.

MacLennan permitted me to write a short story about the

golden wedding day. When I handed it in he said, "Now don't get swell-headed, and always remember that you are just one of the help around here. But the cashier may have something special for you."

When I opened my pay envelope, all the dreams ever dreamed by man came true. A twenty-dollar gold piece and a ten-dollar gold piece! Thirty dollars! The thirty dollars I had so long been waiting for! The most money in the world. Not all the money I would ever earn would seem as much as was in this little paper pot of gold at the end of my first rainbow.

I reeled dangerously, but managed to ask the cashier in a tone of bogus serenity to change my gold into silver dollars. The cashier obliged me. If the pieces of silver had not weighed me down, I think I might have risen to the skies to sing with our state bird, the lark bunting. A surge of generosity came upon me. One must do good with one's resources. Where to begin? Why, at home, according to the words of Sir Thomas Browne, and according to my own heart.

It would be a joyous golden wedding day, albeit several hours late. But silver dollars—they were not appropriate. I asked the cashier if he would mind taking back the dollars and returning the gold pieces.

"What in hell's got into you?" he inquired. "Didn't I just—"

"Never mind," I interrupted him resignedly.

Shortly after the first edition rolled off the press, MacLennan permitted me to go home. I took a copy of the paper with my story in it and read and reread it on the South Broadway "owl" car, but glanced up casually to inform George Pell, who was the conductor, that I was now making thirty dollars a week.

"When I write your father about this," he said, "he'll be the happiest man alive."

This was the first time I had heard that Pell, or anyone else, had written about me to my father. At first I was disposed to be indignant, thinking my privacy violated. So that is why Pell always asked so many questions when we met! But in a moment my new wealth and proven importance raised me above small resentments. "Tell my father," I said to Pell, "that I'll never be dependent on him for support."

This remark distressed Pell. "Why," he said, "Charlie would be glad to back you up in all ways. Only he's had a tough struggle; and besides, your grandmother—"

"I'm not criticizing my father," I interrupted. "And I don't think he's much worried about me."

"Gee, but you're wrong!" Pell said. "So wrong." Then he suggested, "Why don't you write to him yourself, and tell him about your luck?"

"Not till he writes to me," I said. "And besides, Mr. Pell, it's not luck. It's ability that got me the big raise."

"I suppose so, I suppose so," he said dubiously as I left the car at Alameda Street to walk up the long dark hill.

I let myself in as quietly as the clanking dollars would allow, turned on the light in the parlor, and stood for a time looking at the trophy cabinet with its pitiful memorials to all that my family had been. The painted china tea set brought remembrances of Dodie. She had seemed so close to me, yet so remote, like a loved spirit. The sea horse was there, a question mark that peered out from the little box. Where was Mr. Blake? And would he be proud of me? And I wondered what Frank Fowler would say. Would I still be a "peculiar cuss" to him? And the glass shaving mug that Papa Sullivan had given me. I must not forget to tell him my news. So the trophies stood as they long had stood, memories of yesterday with faces pressed against the glass, looking out at the present and perhaps at the future as well.

As I turned from the cabinet, I saw the eye of the old Bible looking at me. That eye never slept. Looking back at it, I seemed to hear the warning verses that denounced worldly riches. And yet how comforting was the feel of the round silver dollars!

I removed them from my pockets and placed them one by one on the edge of the green Wilton carpet to frame the tile hearth of the mantelpiece. I rearranged them, spacing them apart so they would make an orderly line along the tile apron. Then I rose from my knees and went to the foot of the stairs.

"Granny! Granny! Come down! Grandpa, get up and come downstairs!"

There were stirrings upstairs, the creaking of bedsprings, the slow slithering uncertainties of elderly feet in the darkness. Granny was first to appear, with a shawl like Lincoln's draped over the shoulders of her canton flannel night dress.

"What in the world?" and she peered down at me. "Can't you let a body sleep?"

"It's your golden wedding!" I shouted. "Come on down."

She began to descend. Then Grandpa came. He wore a red bandanna handkerchief tied over his head, and was holding up his trousers which seemed to have been hastily put on over his long woolen underwear. He was in his sock feet.

"What air you up to?" he asked.

"Just you come down and see!" I called out. "It's your golden wedding!" First I showed them the newspaper article which told of their fiftieth anniversary. "I wrote it myself," I said with grand unconcern as I handed the paper to Granny.

The old lady adjusted her eyeglasses nearer to her eyes, stared in amazement at the story, then gave the newspaper to Grandpa. "Look, Pa. Our names are in it. See? Right there. Both our names are in the newspaper."

While Grandpa was inspecting the story, Granny spied the silver-dollar frame of the mantelpiece tiles. "Well, well, now!" she exclaimed. "What have we here? What on earth?"

I placed my arms about her. "It's a present. A golden wedding present."

"No!" she said incredulously. "Not for me, surely?"

"Yes," I replied; then I turned to Grandpa, "It's wealth for all."

"I really will have to sit down," Granny said through her tears. "Son, you shouldn't do this."

As I was about to reply, I observed that a sad, beaten expression was in Grandpa's eyes. He was managing to smile, but he seemed hurt about something.

Suddenly I knew what was wrong. This good, serious, hopeful old man had worked and searched and striven for "wealth for all," yet never in his long life had he earned more than eighteen dollars a week as a regular wage. He was happy over my success, not the least doubt of that, but it sharpened the edge of his own failure.

I put an arm around him. "You know what this means? It means that you and Granny made it possible for me to get ahead. Don't you see? And it means that I'll send you on a great prospecting trip, so you can make us really rich."

A new light—rather, the light of other days—came to the old man's eyes. He straightened his shoulders, nodded confidently, and almost forgot to hold up his pants.

24

GLORIA

PERHAPS no one was more genuinely interested in my new financial status than Colonel Gideon B. McFall. This charming gentleman was an associate member of the Press Club. There he served as banker of a poker game which, with few interruptions, had been going on for years. The Colonel encouraged the legend that he came from the South; but it happened to be South Iowa, where it was said, but never proved to any newspaperman's satisfaction, that he had been in the "book business."

The Colonel had one of the two finest heads of silver hair in the city; the other one belonged to Coroner William P. Horan. He also had an eye of sweet, pellucid blue. I suppose that Colonel McFall was about fifty years old at this time. At any rate, if you played cards against him for longer than an hour, you became much older than he in every respect.

Colonel McFall was entirely honest at cards, but his skill was such as to keep many of us in straits. He seldom lost, and we should have known better than to play against him. Still, we almost begged him to fleece us again and again; and I never knew another man who made losing seem such a pleasure.

The Colonel had but one annoying trait, and even in that respect stood well within his rights. If he lent you money with which to continue losing to him, and then if you had a sudden turn of fortune and seemed on your way to get even for the night, the Colonel would reach for your stack with a "Do you mind?" Then he would help himself to enough chips to satisfy your debt. He could pinch off the exact number of chips owed him and never make a mistake.

This method of collection brought cries of denunciation, but the Colonel gravely would say, "I'm not doing any too well myself at the moment. Besides, I object to playing forever against my own money." By this procedure, he kept a debtor's bankroll within such niggardly bounds as to forestall big bets when high cards belatedly commenced to fill an opponent's hands.

Although I was a wretched poker player, and had a face which reflected every good card I ever held, the Colonel never once remarked my lack of skill. Indeed, he even defended me to MacLennan. That critic had announced that if anyone could convince him that I so much as knew one card from another, he would publicly eat all the gaming devices this side of Monte Carlo, and then swallow the Kittredge Building, in which our club was, for dessert.

"MacLennan," said my silver-haired defender, "I grant you this young man is not a Canfield, but he has many sharp qualities."

"Well," said MacLennan, "horse sense is not one of them. And I want you to quit taking him, as well as his gullible friend Lee Casey, over the jumps."

"I shall ask you to respect my white hairs," said the Colonel. "This is a gentleman's club."

MacLennan deputized the Chinese steward, Jim Wong, to study the Colonel's play. But the steward, a Cantonese cynic, was unable in all Chinese honesty to make out a case of malpractice against our banker.

"Colonel just plain good gambler," Wong reported to Mac-Lennan, "and Casey and Fowler just plain nuts."

Lee T. Casey was my first newspaper crony, and his brilliance at everything except cards amazed me. He had been a *Kansas City Star* man, of itself a guarantee of journalistic excellence, and had come to Denver under a medical sentence of death from tuberculosis. He brought with him a copy of Gibbon's *Decline and Fall of the Roman Empire*, a work which he almost knew by heart, and a gracious little mother who played the piano beautifully while young reporters ate everything to be found in her icebox or on the cookstove.

Casey didn't die. Our town knew many such men who had made liars out of the medical wizards of other cities. Casey was too brave to die, and I trust that I do him no harm with his present-day readers when I say that he was almost as wayward as myself, except for a well-balanced show of realism—sometimes.

I loved and admired Casey, and we had much in common. Among other matters, Colonel McFall shared both our salaries with us. And MacLennan also heckled us, afterward explaining that he did so "to bring out the iron in us." With MacLennan bringing out the iron and Colonel McFall extracting the gold, Casey and I were always at the smelter's.

I confided freely in Casey as to my mighty dreams of love and journalism. When I revealed to him one day in May of 1913 that I intended to buy some "real" clothes, he not only applauded my intentions but said that he would accompany me to the tailor's to order a suit himself.

We considered all the tailor shops that extended credit, then decided to honor Ben Lebovitz on Welton Street with our business. This was my first visit to a maker of custom-built suits. Indeed, it was the first time that I took much interest in clothes, a fact which leads me to believe that love and plumage are as closely related as a disease to its symptoms. I selected from Mr. Lebovitz's stock a checkered pattern upon which the chess masters easily might have played ten games simultaneously in the dark.

"Well, now," said Colonel McFall when I appeared in my new

suit at the Press Club, "allow me to congratulate you upon your seeming prosperity and your excellent taste."

MacLennan was less enthusiastic than the Colonel. "Are you taking a job in a cat house?" he asked. Then he added professionally, "Look here. We're starting a campaign to advertise Colorado roads and the Automobile Club. The paper is sponsoring a road race to Morrison. But it's not to be a race of speed. Understand? It's to be run in the interest of safe-and-sane driving. You'll motor with a committee from the Auto Club tomorrow over the Morrison route, secretly to determine the safe-and-sane rate everyone should drive on the open road."

He ran his hands across his eyes, saying, "God! That suit of clothes is striking me stone-blind!" Then he continued with his instructions. "The time it takes the committee to drive to Morrison will be sealed in an envelope in the Mayor's office; he's a trustworthy fellow, up to a certain point. Now, a week from next Saturday, everyone with an auto, gasoline, steam or electric, is invited to enter the race. And there will be loving cups awarded respectively to the five motorists in each class to come nearest to the safe-and-sane time secretly determined by the committee."

He studied me for a moment, inclined his head with mock humility, then said, "If you will be gracious enough to take time off from your regular business with Colonel McFall, Editor Joe Ward will deeply appreciate your handling the details of this race."

"I'll do it as a special courtesy," I said, endeavoring to match his sarcasm.

"I knew we could count upon you," he said with full irony. "You can't always judge a man by the clothes he wears."

The safe-and-sane contest was a popular event in which many "society" men and women participated. These Rocky Mountain "bluebloods" treated me with unexpected cordiality, a fact which quite turned my head.

At the finish line, and as the cars trailed in, I arranged the loving cups for distribution among the winners. I was standing there with Tiffany grandeur when an automobile dealer, the local agent for the Baker Electric, tugged at my checkered sleeve.

"I wonder if you'd do me a little favor?" he inquired.

"I'm pretty busy," I replied.

"Well," he said, "it'll only take a moment." Then he went on to explain, "One of my customers misunderstood the rules of the race; she thought the first one to finish would win a prize."

"I can't help what she thought," I said. "We've had stories that it wasn't to be a race of speed, and printed the rules all week long."

"But my customer is terribly upset," he persisted. "This young lady drove the first electric car to finish. And her heart is fixed on a loving cup."

"Then," I said, "suppose you buy her one. I didn't make the rules."

He astonished me by saying, "It so happens that I brought a nice silver trophy with me in my own car. All you need do is publish her name as 'a special speed winner,' and I'll have the cup engraved at my own expense."

"Say!" I exclaimed. "Do you think I'm crazy? Why, Mr. Ward would fire me for doing that."

"Well, then," he said, "would you just meet this young lady, and square me with her and her family?"

Against my better judgment, I went with the automobile dealer to mollify the young lady. She was standing beside a big rock. Here was Gloria! Her name wasn't Gloria, but she was the one I had dreamed of seeing each time I had looked at the picture of the forest lane on the hill near Heidelberg. And Gloria is what I always called her to myself.

She was blond and seventeen. When she turned her smile on me I forgot safe-and-sane driving races, loving cups, newspaper ethics, and even Hettie.

"I really don't expect a prize," she said, and I began to dissolve. Then she devastated me by adding, "What an attractive suit you're wearing, Mister . . . Mister . . ."

"Fowler," I supplied. "But you may call me Gene. I'm terribly sorry that you misunderstood the rules."

"Oh, you mustn't break the rules," she said. "I wouldn't let you."

I tottered for a moment between love and duty, then fell on the side where my heart already lay bleeding. "I'm going to award you a loving cup," I blurted, and knew that I was a fool for saying this. And I knew that a fool and his newspaper were soon parted.

She gasped prettily. "Oh! But *have* you an extra one?"

"By the greatest coincidence," I said, turning accusingly to the automobile agent, "your enterprising friend brought a loving cup. Probably thought he'd get thirsty on the road."

At this she laughed wholeheartedly, and then confessed with great candor, "I knew it all along. It was a conspiracy. But I don't want you to get into trouble."

"It's worth it," I said, taking her by the arm. "And I want to discuss something with you." I looked toward the agent to add, "Alone."

He seemed worried by my sudden personal interest in his beautiful customer. He began to hem and haw and speak of Gloria's mother. "Do you want the loving cup," I asked him, "or don't you?"

As we walked along the base of the rock, and away from the ring of cup winners, I said to Gloria, "Suppose we never go back?"

"But what do you mean by that?"

"Let's never go back to the others at all," I said. "Let's just go on, and on, and on . . . together."

Gloria seemed impressed by my ardor. "But aren't you just a reporter?"

"Yes," and then I concocted a braggart's lie to round out my day of dishonesty, "but I make forty-five dollars a week!"

The falsehood almost stuck in my throat. But it got out and past my teeth, and it was too late to call it back. It always is too late. If thirty dollars not long ago had seemed all the money in the world to me, then why should I now make it forty-five?

Gloria did not seem awed even by the mention of forty-five dollars. Then she said, "I'd like very much to have you call on me sometime at my home."

"When?" I almost shouted. "Tonight?"

"Oh no," Gloria said. "It's too late."

"Tomorrow night, then?"

"But don't you work at nights?"

"I'll resign," I said hotly. "I'll quit my job and get another in the daytime."

"No," she said. "Don't quit such a remarkable position."

"But you just said I'm only a reporter."

"I didn't know you were such a great reporter." And she left her hand in mine. "But I know it now." I could say nothing, nothing at all, and then she asked, "When is your night off?"

"Monday," I managed to reply.

"I'll speak to Mother," she said, "and let you know if Monday is all right. She's very strict." Then she said, "Please don't give me that cup. I didn't win it fairly."

"No," I said heroically, "nobody can keep me from giving you that cup. I'll print your name in tomorrow morning's paper. And I'll have Harry Rhoads, our photographer, take your picture. It'll be the prettiest picture they ever had."

When Josiah M. Ward saw Gloria's picture next day and read of the "special award" to her, it was thought that this time he really would go to the hospital with a stroke.

"Mr. Ward wants to see you in his office," MacLennan announced next afternoon at assignment hour. "And I may say that my heart really goes out to you this time, you God-damned stupid ass!"

But I was a knight now with a plume in my helmet. I feared neither sarcasm nor loss of position. I had a first mortgage on the world. And it was my intention to foreclose next Monday night.

When I entered the office, Editor-in-Chief Josiah M. Ward

was putting out a pan of breadcrumbs on the windowsill for the sparrows. I stood looking at the back of his bald head, which was set low on a pugilistic neck. He seemed in no hurry to attend to me.

At length he turned from the window, glanced at me over the rims of his spectacles, then sat down at his paper-strewn desk. He picked up a galley proof and read it for what seemed an hour. I began to feel small and worried and lost. Then he examined a story sent in from the city desk for his approval.

Suddenly he exploded. He seized a pair of long-billed scissors and began to snip the air with them. "Can't anyone on this damned newspaper spell names correctly?"

Now he turned his fierce eyes upon me, as though I were responsible for the misspelling. "A man's name is one of his most priceless possessions," he cried out. "A man works year after year to make his name mean something. Then along comes some careless reporter to misspell the man's name, and we have another enemy for life."

In his present choleric state, I thought that Mr. Ward was about to stab me with the scissors for my crime of last night. Instead, he asked, "I suppose you have some high-blown excuse for what you did? Or don't you know what you did?"

"I know what I did, Mr. Ward," I replied. "I did it because I liked the girl."

"Hmmm!" he intoned. "A girl, eh? All the worst crimes are committed in behalf of petticoats."

I bridled. "She's not a petticoat, Mr. Ward!"

I stood ready to be either stabbed or fired, or both, but Mr. Ward unexpectedly grew cool. "Sit down, young man."

I sank into a chair that creaked. Mr. Ward looked at the birds on the windowsill for a long moment, and then he said: "I want to tell you what a newspaper means. It's a serious, sacred business. The least smell of corruption, fear, or favoritism must not creep into its news columns. What you did last night was only a little thing, when judged by rule-of-thumb, but it really goes deeper than that. To some persons it will seem as though we owed a favor to the important and wealthy family of your young lady. And a newspaper, like Caesar's wife, must be above suspicion. Avoid even the appearance of evil. Never again do anyone a favor which might compromise the newspaper you are connected with. To get the news, you may kill, steal, burn, cheat, lie; but never sell out your paper in thought or deed. A newspaper doesn't belong to the men who run it or to those who own the plant. The press belongs to the public, to the people. It is their voice, their shield, their champion. And to keep it free, we ourselves must stay free, sincere, honest. What you do in private with your own life is nobody's business, if you don't get caught. What you do as a newspaperman is everybody's business and everybody's concern. So go back to your desk, and decide not to make another mistake—and for Christ's sake, spell names correctly!"

The smell of lilacs was in the air as I waited the long hours until time to call on Gloria. Mt. Evans wore an Elizabethan ruff, and the sky was royal blue. I pressed my checked suit on the kitchen table until the trousers took on creases like the edges of Uncle Dewey's meat cleavers. I debated whether to wear a felt hat or a straw one on this formal mission, then decided to wear the straw, for the felt hat of last year made me look like an organ grinder whose monkey was a mediocre businessman.

During this long afternoon, the telephone company man came to install our first telephone near the stand on which the old Bible lay. The eye of God on the back of the Bible watched him do this, and so did Granny and I. The old lady was so excited, although she tried to appear unconcerned, that she fumbled the receiver when putting in a call to Uncle Dewey's new store on West Third Avenue. When she had hung up, I called Gloria's number.

A servant answered the telephone, and then Gloria's sweet voice came to me. I became unmindful that Granny was in the room, listening sagely to my part of the conversation and reading the emotions behind the question: "Gloria, do you mind if I call a little bit earlier than we had planned?"

I turned from the telephone to see Granny standing beside the big Bible, one hand resting upon it, and her eyes wide with censorship. "Well," I said defensively. "I'm grown up now."

To this she replied, "So I understand."

Gloria lived on Capitol Hill, where the mansions of the elite stood with austere façades. I had been inside but one authentic mansion before this time, the château-like residence of Mrs. Crawford Hill, wife of the owner of *The Republican*. That had been an unhappy experience. The social leader berated me for entering her great hall with muddy shoes on a rainy day when I called to interview a one-armed general during a tea of the *Alliance Française*. Shoes always were a problem in my life. If they were not tight, they were muddy, or otherwise unsightly.

As I got off the streetcar on Capitol Hill to go to Gloria's house, I found that I had forgotten to put blacking on my shoes. When a manservant opened the big door of the red-brick mansion, I fancied that he was reading my pedigree in the unshined shoes.

The servant commandeered my hat, then conducted me into the drawing room. The rug was as deep as a field of clover. The chairs were carved and cushioned and gilded. I never was so scared in my life, before or since, and I began to wish that I had not let myself in for this.

I suffered additional qualms when the equivalent of a marchioness entered the drawing room. I rose in my unshined shoes to hear her say, "Gloria will be here presently. I am her mother."

She motioned for me to be seated, then sat opposite me as if to hold an audience at St. Cloud. Her face somehow seemed familiar, but it was not until some weeks afterward that I puzzled this out: she looked like a composite portrait of Martha Washington and Colonel McFall.

"Gloria tells me that you are an executive editor on *The Denver*

Republican," she remarked. "I had expected to see an older man."

"Well, ma'am," I stammered, "I hope to be editor soon."

"Oh," she challenged, "then you are *not* an editor?"

"Only in a sense," I said, hoping for a way out of high society—a way out of sudden doom.

"In *what* sense, may I ask?" she persisted.

Now I was on the witness stand. My shirt became clammy against my shoulder blades. "At the moment," I said, "I am a reporter." Then I added, "But that is only one step short of an important desk."

She looked at me with a district attorney's eye, but before she could offer a further impeachment, her daughter danced in like a breath of columbines. Gloria had on a lovely blue dress that whispered of silk and lace. And now I didn't give a damn what her mother or anyone else thought of me, so long as Gloria cared. And apparently she had cared enough to tell her mother a preposterous untruth about my newspaper position.

I thought the mother never would leave us. But she eventually rose and ironically urged Gloria not to keep me up too late to attend to my "important newspaper work." Then she retired like a cloud that holds back its thunders for another day.

It may be that I ordinarily was timid with women, but then I wasted no time. I took Gloria in my arms and kissed her. And it was like a confluence of rivers that join to go to the sea.

That summer and into the autumn, I called upon Gloria each Monday evening. Occasionally I had dinner at her house; but it was clear to me that the marchioness regarded me as cordially as she would the smallpox. If it had not been for Gloria's father I probably would have been forbidden the home. The old gentleman had a twinkling eye, and I think that retirement and riches and high society bored him.

I don't believe that he actually knew how deeply we were engrossed, Gloria and I, for once I overheard him say to his wife, "It's only puppy love."

Gloria took me for drives in her splendid electric automobile, a black brougham model with a silvered steering bar. It was like trundling along the avenues in a showcase. When MacLennan chanced to see me riding with such elegance, he lifted his hat with an overdone flourish. And next day he made a point of saying in front of the other reporters, "We have the rare privilege of knowing a male Cinderella."

Each noonday before I left home to go to work, I regularly telephoned Gloria. I tied up the ten-party line for as much as three-quarters of an hour. Gloria also telephoned my house whenever she could escape the watchfulness of the maid who reported all her activities to the marchioness.

"Are you quite sure you had the telephone put in for *me?*" Granny asked one day.

Whenever Gloria telephoned, I was lucky if I reached the instrument before Granny did in response to our party-line signal, one long ring and three short ones. The old lady would make disparaging comments into the transmitter if Gloria was on the line. I explained to the perplexed girl that Granny was quite a wag in her own way, and urged her to pay no attention to acid remarks, such as the one, "I hope that you are not just another one of my grandson's whims."

The night hours of the newspaper office interfered with my seeing Gloria more frequently than once a week. I seldom got off before midnight, and then I would go to the Press Club to play cards with Colonel McFall and his group. It became increasingly difficult for me to support myself, the Colonel, and my grandparents, and then buy flowers for Gloria.

Fortunately I met Colonel Jamieson at the florist's one afternoon, and he explained to me that carnations were a fine gift and much cheaper than roses. So I sent carnations to Gloria each Monday, convincing her that they were my favorite and that under no circumstances could I bear to change to other flowers while the carnation season lasted.

One Monday afternoon Gloria expressed a desire to call upon

my grandmother. So we rode in the electric automobile to our home on South Emerson Street. As we drew alongside the curb, there were flurries of window curtains, and several neighbors came out-of-doors to do chores in their yards or go on errands.

Granny was unexpectedly gracious, and made tea. True, as the old lady poured it she said, "Our gold teapot has been mislaid somewhere," but otherwise behaved herself. And when Gloria invited Granny to go with us for a ride in the electric automobile, my grandmother resisted what must have been a great temptation. Then she said the truest thing ever uttered: "No thanks; young persons shouldn't be bothered by old ladies."

As Gloria and I went away from our house, the girl said, "I like her very much."

To this I replied, "I love her," and Gloria looked at me with some astonishment, as if it were an odd thing for one to love a grandparent.

Soon after this visit, Gloria's mother began to describe to her the horrors that befall one who "leaves a palace for a hovel." Then Gloria would come to our meetings in tears.

Gloria's father died that autumn, and now I was left without a champion in the Capitol Hill mansion. I was quick to notice the open hostility toward me in Gloria's home, although she herself gallantly insisted upon seeing me there.

The mother declared a long period of mourning. During this time of black garments, the daughter was forbidden most social events, my own calls being classified as such by the widow. Gloria and I met secretly, or reasonably so, whenever she could get out for a stroll. Then she would come to the newspaper. And now even MacLennan relented somewhat (for, after all, he was Irish and sentimental beneath his cynical veneer). He permitted our meeting in a dusty room where old clippings and bound volumes of newspapers were filed.

October came, and the leaves turned brown and gold, and Mt. Evans was all white. And my love for Gloria was white and wonderful, and nothing else mattered.

25

AS A MAN THINKS

SOON after the death of her father, Gloria and her mother went to reside at the Brown Palace. I looked forward to making an appearance in dinner jacket and black tie at this celebrated hotel, a man of the world, with Gloria sitting opposite me at table. With this triumph in mind, I consulted Colonel Jamieson on the finer points of decoding a bill-of-fare as complicated as the Rosetta Stone.

The Colonel promptly scribbled a note on a sheet of stationery of the society-shunning Judge Lewis, requesting a Brown Palace menu card. The maître d'hôtel sent an entire week's supply of cards, and the wine list as well, by special messenger to the Judge's chambers. The puzzled jurist promptly sentenced the bills-of-fare to the wastebasket, where the Colonel recovered them to chart my maiden voyage as a gourmet.

I visited Colonel Jamieson the next noonday during court recess. He began at once to discuss an item on the menu which, after its rescue from the French, meant "pressed duck." A fly settled on his nose. With what seemed unreasonable fury, he began to hammer at it with the menu card. When his anger cooled somewhat, the Colonel explained that during the Civil War he

323

had lain six months in Libby Prison, unable to move, while flies kept crawling over his face and hands, almost driving him mad. He never forgave them for this.

"Suppose," said the Colonel, coming back to the menu, "that we solve your problem by *my* going with you and the young lady to the Brown Palace for dinner?"

"No thank you, Colonel," I said, leaping away from the trap.

"But," he persisted, "I would provide flowers and wine. It would give a touch of old-world elegance to the event."

"Colonel," I said flatly, "I'd rather eat a dish of chili beans with her alone than have all the ducks that ever were pressed, or drink all the wine that ever was bottled, if a third party looked on."

The Colonel grudgingly accepted defeat.

After much wheedling by Gloria, her mother consented to her dining with me at the Brown and afterward attending a performance at the Broadway Theatre across the street from the hotel. But my other colonel friend, the silver-haired McFall, so consistently depleted my finances that I had to postpone my society debut two weeks in succession. On both occasions, I gave as an excuse the fact that an impending coal miners' strike kept all news men at their stations.

Eventually I had the good fortune to obtain the promise of a pass for a pair of orchestra seats for Monday night of the week when John Mason was to play in *As a Man Thinks*. I rented a dinner jacket, but lacked sufficient dinner money. So I hurled myself upon the mercy of Colonel McFall.

He examined the pages of the little red morocco notebook in which he kept a record of sums owed him by club members. Then he raised his eyes to study a moth-eaten polar-bear rug which the Arctic explorer, Robert E. Peary, had given the club, and which now hung by the heels on the wall opposite the bar. Presumably, the bear gave some oracular sign in my behalf. For the Colonel produced a sheaf of currency from his pocket, selected from it a ten-dollar bill, and handed the greenback to me.

He entered the ten-dollar loan in his red book, remarking, "That makes nineteen-fifty you are into me." Then he telephoned the headwaiter at the Brown Palace Hotel: "Mr. Fowler wants a table for two. A little to one side, and private-like, if you please, Georges."

When Colonel McFall had done me this mighty favor, he appraised me with his eye of sweet, pellucid blue. "Do you know?" he said. "You ought to carry a stick. Nothing marks the gentleman so much as a walking stick when at the theater or in the lobby of a fashionable hotel."

Having said this, he again brought out the sheaf of currency, peeled off a five-dollar banknote and handed it to me. "Here you are. Go to Gano Downs and tell them I said to provide you with a smart malacca; but be sure it has a silver-plated knob." He entered the additional five in his book, then continued, "And the next time I happen to reach onto your stack, my boy, please refrain from ungrateful remarks. Good luck."

At the haberdasher's, I found a light-complexioned walking stick, but its price was six dollars and a half. The cane not only had a silvered knob but also a thong of leather for a wrist loop. I hesitated to pay such a big price for it, but the salesman assured me that it was an exact replica of the one carried by the well-groomed war correspondent, Richard Harding Davis, at the Battle of Mukden. That was argument enough to win anybody's six dollars and a half.

After my acquisition of the splendid stick, I strutted to the newspaper office to pick up the pass slip left in the mailbox by the drama editor. Then, while leaving the building, I encountered MacLennan as he came out of the saloon across the alley. He pretended to be pleasantly overcome by the magnificence of the stick, then remarked, "Nothing is as handy as a cane to keep the dogs away from your leg."

The dinner at the Brown Palace was not the ordeal of etiquette I had anticipated. For one thing, the headwaiter and his assistants knew Gloria and gave courtly attention. The headwaiter assumed the burden of ordering the dinner, although he generously made it appear that I was doing the executive work. Moreover, Gloria was not to be bullied by the French phrases of a menu card—the soundest reason I ever encountered for a girl being sent to a fashionable school.

When I failed to partake of the meat course, the headwaiter politely raised his brows. "Is it not cooked to your taste?"

"It's just fine," I replied. "But I don't happen to want it now."

When he had gone, Gloria said, "You know, my mother once spoke of your not eating meat at our house."

"Did she?" I asked. Then I said, "I don't care a lot about meat. Does it worry you?"

"No," she said, and afterward I remembered that there was a far-off look in her eyes, as though something really did trouble her.

I might have explained to Gloria that my boyhood job at the taxidermist's had sickened me, and that somehow I connected the sights and smells there with the butchering of animals and the eating of their flesh. But I didn't go into the matter. I so seldom explained anything to anyone; it was against my nature to ask for explanations of a personal sort, and it was against my will to give them.

Perhaps her black dress of mourning accented her fleeting black mood. "How much longer must you wear black?" I inquired.

"Mother won't say," Gloria replied. "Don't you like me in black?"

"Black itself is all right," I answered. "The thing I object to is the idea behind the barbarous show. The bombast of funerals is a gesture to ward off the reprisals of furious ghosts, who see us for the hypocrites we really are."

"I don't know what you mean," the girl said somewhat helplessly. "Do you mean that I shouldn't wear black for Papa?"

"I mean," I blurted out, "that he was too fine a sport to be bored and bullied into a mausoleum, and then mourned."

"He was sweet," the girl said.

"Black," I conceded, "makes your face lovely and ethereal."

She was happy again, now that I had absolved black.

We had coffee in small cups, in keeping with the instructions of Colonel Jamieson. I didn't like coffee in a small cup, and I never would; and my antipathy to little cups of coffee should have convinced me at the start that I was not earmarked by Fate to be a society man.

After dinner we went across the street to the Broadway Theatre. There I endeavored before curtain time to impress Gloria with my vast experience with the drama and my wide acquaintanceship with its greatest practitioners. Perhaps I may be forgiven for love's sake for having spoken with assumed authority about my theatrical contacts. They were but a few months old, and consisted merely of the following:

An interview with E. H. Sothern backstage; it was the first time I ever saw the other side of the footlights. I had made a remark, intended as a compliment to Mr. Sothern, on his physical agility in *If I Were King*, notwithstanding what seemed his "ripe years." At this he thundered a rebuke to "a fool who should know that I am active enough to jump over the moon." My monstrous reply, "Do you give milk?" caused my ejection from the star's dressing room.

The next week Wilton Lackaye had come to town with an all-star cast in Eugene Walter's play, *Fine Feathers*. Mr. Lackaye, a sardonic wit of much repute, had heard, as had several other artists, of my "milk" retort to Mr. Sothern. Lackaye almost adopted me, so great was his joy upon learning of Sothern's rage. He gave me Scotch whisky from his own dressing-room bottles, and became my friend for life.

Next I interviewed playwright Eugene Walter, a former police reporter on *The Denver Republican*. I asked Mr. Walter if it were true that he had risen, penniless and cold, from a bench in New York's Bryant Park, to beg enough money to buy paper and pen and write the stage success, *Paid in Full*, within a mere week. To this he replied, "I wrote the play on paper in ten days, but I had been writing it for ten long years in my head."

Until now, these had been my only intimacies with the theater and its people. But as I sat with Gloria beside me, I enlarged upon these experiences until they seemed as weighty and as huge as those of Critic William Winter. And Gloria encouraged me with worshipful blue eyes. It suddenly occurred to me that I was becoming a consummate liar; but I kicked my conscience back where it belonged and went on to establish a new world's record for bragging to one's girl.

Suddenly I leaned nearer to her to whisper, "You are a princess," and I was not lying now. And just then the curtain went up on the play.

I do not remember too vividly what the Augustus Thomas work was about. There was a Dr. Seelig in a silk hat and Inverness cape; the distinguished John Mason played the role. And between acts I heard people saying that Mr. Mason was talented. I also remember that somewhere in the play the actor declared that the whole structure of modern society rested upon man's faith in woman's virtue. . . . But I could think only of Gloria as I sat there. The touch of her young hand, and not the play, was the thing.

The stage occurrence which I remembered best, and long remembered with poignant clarity, was a song played and sung incidentally during the performance, "Just a Little Love, a Little Kiss." And until Gloria and I parted, which would be too soon, that would be our song.

Toward autumn a feeling ran through the newspaper office that some ominous event was impending within the organization. Nothing was said by our superiors to verify this foreboding, but we felt it and spoke of it at the Press Club. Colonel McFall wore a knowing frown, as though mindful of the prospect of losing a prized comrade or two. The Colonel mentioned visiting his friend, Crawford Hill, "to learn the true state of affairs."

Few of us ever had seen Mr. Crawford Hill, the owner of our newspaper. He had inherited *The Republican* from his capitalist father, the late ex-Senator Nathaniel P. Hill, founder of a reduction and smelting process to treat refractory ores. Other than to hire Josiah M. Ward "to breathe new life into the old lady," the younger Mr. Hill soon lost whatever interest he may have had in the editorial welfare of his newspaper.

And now one afternoon early in October 1913, Josiah M. Ward did not appear at his desk to snip the air with his long scissors or to curse someone for having misspelled a name. The chubby little fire eater did not come to the office the next day, or the next. Then we learned that Mr. Ward had resigned.

The reporters spoke of this loss with concern, not only for themselves but for their newspaper. For a man comes to love his paper as a member of a crew does his ship. There is something intensely personal and intimate about one's love for one's newspaper. When a newspaper is ill, her sons are unhappy; and when she dies, they grieve, and they receive the sincere sympathy of the sons of all other newspapers. Then almost everyone gets drunk, and there is a wake.

Men who inherit a newspaper sometimes give no sentimental thought to the great, living thing they see sicken and die. Frequently they are men with numerous business enterprises other than publication of a newspaper. Oftentimes they merge one paper with another, and sell the hyphenated property to some fellow-magnate. And they dismiss any inquiries with, "It was a business necessity." But the men who have worked through the long night hours to gather news, and who have seen their paper fall ill and die, sometimes revisit the silent old building to look at the doorway through which they once passed in and out when life was new.

After Joe Ward's resignation, the aged and mild-mannered Fred Dickensheets assumed the managing editorship. This colleague of Eugene Field had been our Sunday editor, a comparatively quiet station in which an elderly veteran might study the works of Thoreau between times when selecting articles mailed each week from *The New York Herald* syndicate. Mr. Dickensheets had been a distinguished journalist. But his sudden recall to arms, together with the unsettled atmosphere of the office, dismayed and confused this worn-out Cincinnatus of the Fourth Estate. If it had not been for the dynamic MacLennan, I doubt that the paper ever would have reached the streets on time.

It was during this period of uncertainty that Colonel Jamieson paid me a call at the newspaper office one October afternoon. He whispered that he was bringing me a news "tip" of great importance. He had overheard in court chambers that the coal operators soon were to hold a secret meeting with Governor Ammons. The corporation heads were going to demand that the Governor send troops to the Trinidad district to subdue the striking miners in the southern coal fields.

MacLennan told me to follow up the tip. He advised me to see one of his acquaintances, a coal operator named Brown. I went to Mr. Brown's office to ask, "off the record," if the meeting were to be held, and if so, where and when.

To my pleasant amazement, Mr. Brown said, "I'm on my way to it right now. Come along."

"Won't the others object?" I asked.

"It's to be in a hotel suite," Mr. Brown replied. "I'll leave you in the bedroom, and we'll not bother to say anything to the others."

I knew little enough of how industrial war was waged. My only experience with labor was labor itself as a personal, perpetual task. And my one experience as a capitalist was my thirty dollars a week. I knew that most Americans worked, and that they must work to live. I did not believe that work lessened the dignity of man, but I could see that too many persons had too little bread. Of politics I knew nothing, although I was beginning to glimpse what I afterward saw as a melancholy truth, that politics is the science of promises.

To me at this time of the dawn's early light, a governor of a state, no matter what his political party or his views, seemed a great man, a person set apart from lesser mortals, a being who could do no wrong. I had seen our then governor, the Honorable Elias M. Ammons, but a few times, and then only at public functions. He actually was a tired, wrinkled little man. The voters knew him mainly as an ex-rancher, "chosen from among the common people," and a "friend of labor." Labor, if one is to believe the speeches and the eulogies of office seekers, has more friends than Jesus ever had—and almost invariably suffers the same fate as He did.

But the title of Governor was upon Mr. Ammons, and to my hero-ridden mind, the magic label made him seem tall and fearless.

Mr. Brown and I were the first to arrive at the meeting place. In the bedroom of the hotel suite, I tucked notepaper inside my upturned cap on the night table. Then I heard the great men as they came into the parlor for the conference. They exchanged pleasant greetings while waiting for the Governor to appear, and spoke of golf and fishing and the Supreme Court. After a time I was able to identify three voices other than Mr. Brown's among the eight voices overheard by me.

One of these voices was that of a former deputy in the office of the District Attorney. I frequently had met this able attorney when covering the West Side Criminal Courthouse. The two other voices belonged respectively to Mr. Osgood, an aggressive capitalist, and to the forceful Jesse F. Welborn, head of the Colorado Fuel & Iron Company, a Rockefeller subsidiary. Mr. Osgood changed the subject from trout streams to say that the Governor must be compelled to declare martial law. And Mr. Welborn announced that he and Mr. Osgood would do the talking.

The Governor now arrived. Everyone greeted him cordially, then Mr. Welborn got down to business. He bluntly requested that troops be sent to subdue the striking miners. The Governor answered that he could not comply, adding that the laboring men of the state had helped elect him. At this Mr. Osgood began not only to threaten the Governor's political future but also to call him names.

To hear the Governor cursed was an unthinkable thing! I became ill at the stomach, and I wanted to punch someone in the nose. Then, when the tirade was an hour old, the Governor wearily surrendered to his browbeaters. He promised to dispatch members of the National Guard to the Trinidad fields on October 28.

And now the door separating me from the conferees opened. The attorney for the coal operators entered the bedroom on his way to the toilet. He recognized me, and forgot his physical necessity.

"How in hell did *you* get in here?" asked the lawyer.

"How do you suppose?" I said.

The counselor hastily went back to the parlor. Within a few moments the Governor's conquerors appeared at my side to hurl epithets at me. The Governor himself stayed in the frame of the doorway, like a portrait of defeat painted in ochre and sallow green. He was more wrinkled than I had ever seen him before, and he worriedly plucked at his cuffs.

I pocketed my notes, and Mr. Osgood said, "Why, you God-damned, sneaking bastard! I'll—"

I rose to interrupt him. "You'll what?" And then, before he could reply, I said close to his face: "I've heard you call the Governor names, and I'm ashamed of him. You'd never call Theodore Roosevelt names! And what's more, if you call me names, you pompous old bastard, I'll smack you on the chin. I didn't sneak in here, and I've got a story that will make the whole country sit up."

With that, I walked toward the door. I heard Mr. Welborn ask, "Who let *him* in here?" and I heard Mr. Brown's frank but worried reply, "Why, I did."

As I left the place, everyone except the harassed Governor was shouting at Mr. Brown, calling him names.

I ran all the way to the newspaper office, the biggest story in the world, or so I thought, in my pocket. When I leaped up the old stairs and dashed into the city room, I found Mr. Dickensheets drooping over the telephone on his desk. Apparently he had just hung up the instrument. MacLennan was standing beside the old man, offering him some water from an improvised drinking cup made of folded copypaper.

"I've got a scoop!" I cried out.

"Yes," said MacLennan. "So we just heard."

"Heard?" I said. "Who told you?"

The old editor looked at me with a special kind of horror in his eyes. "You can't go around calling important people like Mr. Osgood names!" he said almost petulantly. "You simply can't do it! My gracious!"

"But he called the Governor names, Mr. Dickensheets," I said. "And he called me names. But the point is, I've got a great story. The state troops—"

Mr. Dickensheets interrupted me with a gesture: "We're not printing the story. That's final."

"My God!" I blazed. "You mean to throw away this scoop just because old Osgood or some other coal operator telephoned you? Would Joe Ward do that?"

"Mr. Ward," said the palsied editor, "is no longer here."

"Then, by God!" I said, "you'd better send for him, quick!"

"Come on," MacLennan said, taking my arm. "Let's go down to the saloon for some lemonade."

At the bar I almost wept with rage, but MacLennan said, "Forget it—if you can. I hate to admit it, but we're on a sinking ship. Don't blame the old man. The world has passed him by. I'd print the story in a minute, but we have to be soldiers."

He poured himself a drink, then pushed the bottle toward me. "It's a big story, and what it leads to is big and tragic and wrong. And you could take your scoop to another newspaper, and get a swell job and a raise. Had that entered your mind?"

"Hell, no!" I replied. "Joe Ward wouldn't think much of me if I did that. Would you?"

MacLennan now became demonstrative—the first time I had

ever known him to be. "I want you to know," he said, "that you've got a place on any paper I ever work for, no matter where."

This statement by the cynic touched me deep down. "Gee! That's pretty nice of you!"

"I'm the flower of chivalry," said MacLennan, then added, "but let's go back to our old relationship. You're just one of the help, so don't get folksy. Understand?"

"Yes," I replied.

"That's the way it'll be," said MacLennan. "And just keep your mouth shut about the big scoop you didn't get."

On the way out of the saloon, MacLennan said through his teeth, "Christ! If I ever get so old that I lose my guts, I'll dodder up Pikes Peak and jump off."

On October 25, 1913, Gloria telephoned me at the newspaper early in the evening to say that she was calling under great difficulties, and that her mother had ruled that I never see her again. As if that were not enough to unhorse me, Mr. Crawford Hill later that same evening appeared in person at *The Republican* with black tidings. He announced that John C. Shaffer, Chicago traction magnate and proprietor of *The Chicago Post*, had purchased *The Republican*. Mr. Hill added matter-of-factly that Mr. Shaffer also had purchased Senator Patterson's morning and evening newspapers, *The Rocky Mountain News* and *The Denver Times*, and would merge *The Republican* with *The News*.

"Tonight," Mr. Hill concluded, "is the last edition of *The Republican*."

With this, he handed a typewritten statement to Editor Dickensheets, who then saw him to the door. Mr. Hill left the silent, stricken office without thanking anyone for long service. He was a handsome, pleasant-mannered man, but I now regarded him as a direct descendant of Pontius Pilate.

Mr. Dickensheets turned from the door to hand the typewritten sheet to the head of the copy desk. "Mark this for a two-column box on page one," he said. It was the obituary notice of the newspaper.

As the old editor went from the copy desk to his office, he looked as if his own life's work was done, as indeed it was. He stayed a few minutes inside his office, then came out, his hat and overcoat on, and addressed the city editor: "Mr. Noland, will you please take over for the night? I shall be at the Denver Club if you wish to reach me. Good night, gentlemen."

The editors and reporters now returned to work on the last issue of the newspaper which had for so long been a part of the Rocky Mountain West. The men said nothing about this being their final night together; they worked even harder than usual. The absent-minded Jimmy Noland forgot his hat three times in succession, instead of just once, and went each time in his eye-shade to the saloon.

When the antique press began the last run, and the "Good nights" were being said to dismiss the reporters, MacLennan came over to my desk. "Mr. Fowler, I'd like to ask you a very personal question."

"What is it, Mr. MacLennan?" I asked.

Then he said with mock gravity, "Why should the spirit of mortal be proud?"

"I'll let you know sometime," I replied.

I went to the Press Club, got drunk, and stayed that way for two days.

I awakened under peculiar circumstances. At first I heard familiar noises through a swirling fog. Then my eyesight decided to return to me. I was sitting at a reporter's desk. There was a typewriter under my nose, and a sheet of copypaper in it. And on the paper I saw several lines which seemed the merest drivel, through which there ran repetitiously the phrase: "Swat the fly! Swat the fly!"

Good Lord! I thought. Is delirium tremens finally overtaking me?

I slyly looked around. I observed Harry McCabe and several other *Rocky Mountain News* reporters at desks. If this were not just an alcoholic dream, I myself was sitting in the editorial rooms of *The Rocky Mountain News*. As a precaution against exposure to alienists, I unrolled the sheet of copypaper from the platen of the typewriter. Swat the fly! Good God!

And now MacLennan, in shirtsleeves, came over to me from the region of the city desk. "Well," he said, "are you going to get out that copy, or aren't you?"

What copy? I thought. Was I a member of *The News* staff? If so, when had I been hired? And was MacLennan now one of the editors? My mind was riding a carrousel, and was trying to clutch the brass ring.

"I just wanted to think up an appropriate lead for this story," I hedged, hoping to get a hint from MacLennan as to what the story might be.

"The hell you say!" MacLennan snorted. "I think you're still pie-eyed. Are you? If you are, just be big enough to take me into your confidence."

"Well, then," I replied, "I'm not only corked, but I think I've gone nuts."

"I guess I made a mistake," MacLennan said. "But last night, when I found you stretched out on the Press Club couch with the bear rug over you, I thought you could sober up in time to handle the swat-the-fly campaign."

"What?" I called out with great relief. "Is *that* what I've been trying to write?"

"Aha!" said MacLennan. "So cockeyed you don't even remember coming here with two staggering pallbearers."

"But how did the swat-the-fly business get into *this* office?"

"Your bosom friend, Colonel Jamieson," MacLennan said, "after failing to hornswoggle Joe Ward for the last two years, finally sold Henry D. Carbery on the mighty project. Now get busy."

On the evening of October 28, and in confirmation of the scoop I had failed to get past the desk of Mr. Dickensheets, the Governor ordered one thousand and one hundred members of the National Guard to the southern coal fields. MacLennan assigned me to go on the troop train to cover the story.

A large-bodied oculist, Adjutant General John Chase, was in command of the National Guardsmen. A place was assigned to me in the General's coach, one of twelve cars of the first of two sections of the troop train. Almost at the outset of this slow journey, I entered the General's bad graces.

We were traveling with running lights dimmed, for there was a report that strikers were planning to fire upon the train and perhaps place bombs on the tracks. As a precautionary measure, a pilot engine ran half a mile ahead of the troop train. Suddenly our engineer set the brakes in response to the red flare of a railway fusee on the road bed. The General ordered everyone to stay calm, but he himself began issuing loud and conflicting commands. He said, among other things, that if and when the battle began, the men were to return fire from a prone position beside the tracks, but *were to stay inside the railroad cars*.

After much excitement and delay, another report reached us that the pilot engine merely had struck and killed a cow. When I laughed out loud at this, the General dressed me down. I penciled a story concerning the cow, and at the next station gave it to the despatcher to telegraph to my newspaper. When the General learned that I had sent this story without first seeking his approval, he denounced me and threatened to place me in military custody.

At Trinidad we spent the first cold night aboard the train. The next day the guardsmen put up tents. I occupied a pup tent with Don McGregor, crusading staff correspondent of *The Denver Express,* a Scripps-McRae newspaper. Our tent was pitched near an old tree where, it was said, General Lew Wallace had written a chapter of *Ben Hur* while waiting to change trains.

McGregor and I obtained clear-cut evidence in the town that a number of gunmen strike breakers had put on militiamen's uniforms. These professional sluggers and snipers were members of the notorious Baldwin-Felts organization, specialists in strike breaking, imported without the Colorado Governor's knowledge from the West Virginia coal fields.

When I tried to get this news past the General's censorship, he went into a rage and called me a "damnable socialist." I stood my ground. I offered to supply proof. And when the General said that he was in a position to know everything about his troops and see everything, I replied, "You are an oculist, General, and I respectfully suggest that you test your own eyes."

This remark caused such a furore that the General demanded that my paper recall me from the field. Under the rules of martial law, MacLennan could not do otherwise than withdraw me and assign in my stead a more diplomatic young man.

Don McGregor saw me to the train. "Never mind," he said as we shook hands, "I'll carry on from here. It's a bigger movement than anyone can know. The working world is coming of age."

When, next April, the troops machine-gunned the Ludlow tent colony where many of the striking miners had their quarters, and killed four men, three women, and eleven children, McGregor put aside his reporter's notepaper and his pencil for all time. He joined the strikers and carried a saber at the head of a band of miners in the battle of the Hog Back. Afterward, he was indicted for murder and disappeared. I was told that McGregor died in Mexico at the side of Pancho Villa.

There was a stop-gap administration of *The News* editorial staff pending the advent of the new owner's appointees from Chicago. The hard-hitting Henry D. Carbery continued to act as editor-in-charge, but it was understood that he would resign whenever Mr. Shaffer said the word.

Until now I had been of the opinion that Mr. Carbery was an aloof disciplinarian of inflexible, stern purpose, notwithstanding his desire to see "lace drawers" in the newspaper columns. One night, after Mr. Carbery and the other editors supposedly had gone home, I discovered a box of apples outside his office. The paper long ago had been put to bed. The shipping label on the box disclosed that the fruit had been sent to Mr. Carbery from the ranch of Governor Ammons.

I decided to open the box and share Mr. Carbery's gubernatorial apples with the other late lingerers. After we had eaten several apples, I suggested that we throw the remaining Jonathans to test our marksmanship. We hurled apples until the city room began to smell like a cider press. Squashed fruit lay on the floor and splotched the walls. I was winding up to toss perhaps my twentieth apple when my colleagues suddenly scurried toward their desks.

As I turned to see what was causing the stampede, Mr. Carbery himself thundered from the main doorway, "What in hell is this, may I ask?"

"Mr. Carbery," I said, "we are throwing apples for a nickel a bull's-eye. Would you care to join sides?"

The ruddy-faced executive placed his derby hat and his cigar on the copy desk, removed his coat, and said, "Hand me an apple!" The excellence of his aim, his speed, and his delivery astonished us all.

Mr. Carbery next day raised my salary to thirty-two dollars a week. But he unwittingly did me a bad turn soon afterward by telling Gloria's mother that I did not make forty-five dollars a week. The marchioness had been trying to deflate my forty-five-dollar boast for some months. And now when she met Mr. Carbery at a social function, she cunningly drew the truth from him.

Gloria's mother used this as evidence to prove that I was a lying scoundrel and should not even speak to a resident of Capitol Hill. But Gloria made such scenes that her mother eventually consented to permit her to attend a formal dance given by my college fraternity in the grand ballroom of the Brown Palace.

The dance chairman agreed to have the orchestra play "A Little

Love, a Little Kiss" late in the program. And until time for the ball, I waited for Gloria and the playing of the song.

The girl advised me in a restrained note not to call for her at her suite on the night of the dance. Her mother once again was using "the mourning for Papa" as a pretext. Nor would she allow Gloria to lay aside her black dress for an evening gown. She further decreed that the girl must not be disrespectful to her father's memory by dancing with me. Gloria, attended by the chaperoning maid, was merely to meet me outside the ballroom for a few moments, then retire.

On the night of the formal ball, I danced with no one. And it seemed that Gloria never would appear. Toward eleven o'clock I left the ballroom to telephone her apartment from the lobby, but the marchioness had left orders for no one to disturb her. I hastened back to the ballroom, fearful that Gloria might have come and gone during my absence. Then I began to pace along one of the balconies which formed the sides of a great, deep well above the lobby.

And now the music of "Just a Little Love, a Little Kiss" came from the orchestra in the ballroom. I tried to think of other things than Gloria. As I looked down upon the lobby, I tried to think of the great men and women, my own heroes among them, Buffalo Bill and Scout Wiggins, who often had walked that marble floor, their admirers gathered around them. I endeavored to think of the legends and the history of this ducal hotel. At one time in the early eighties, the wild grass grew over its neglected foundation stones. Pessimists had scoffed at the builder, Henry C. Brown, for having listened to the visionary William Bush. That believing man had persuaded Brown to rear this stone flatiron on the mile-high table of the barren prairie. Now it stood handsomely in the midst of many other buildings. In its lobby and among the bronze-railed galleries, the city's heart pulsed. And my heart beat with my own great big little life until I could no longer keep my mind on old legends. I could not shut out the melody from my ears, the song I had been waiting to hear, but did not want to hear alone.

The song ended. Gloria had not come. There was a clapping of hands by the off-scene dancers; muted clapping, as if made by distant, muffled drums.

Then I saw Gloria and the maid on their way toward the ball-room. She was dressed in black. As I came close to her, I saw that she had been weeping.

"What is it?" I asked. "Do you care to tell me?"

"Let's sit here some place," she said as her maid looked past me.

"But," I said, "can't we have the last dance? They'll play it soon. I thought you'd never get here. I danced with no one."

"I promised not to," and she turned appealingly to the maid. "Would you mind sitting over there a little while?"

"I shouldn't," the maid said. She hesitated, then said, "Oh, well!" and moved out of earshot.

"The last dance is about to begin," I said.

She didn't reply to my entreaty, then said slowly, "I'm afraid this is good-by."

"Oh, bosh!" I retorted. "That's getting to be an old story."

"No, this time it's really good-by." She paused, then went on as if reciting something from the Book of the Dead, "I'm going to be married."

I don't remember what reply I made, if any, to that announcement. Then she mentioned the name of a man known to me only by reputation, which was an excellent one.

"I want to ask you something," she said, "and I've been meaning to ask you several times." And this is what she asked: "Do you take drugs?"

"Oh, my God!" I cried out. "How can you say such a damned fool thing as that?" When she did not reply, I became quite angry. "Did your mother say that I did?"

She still did not speak, and I gripped her arm. "You surely don't believe it? What makes you believe it?"

"I didn't want to," she said eventually.

"But you do. I can see that you do."

She twisted a small kerchief edged with black. She made a ball of it, and she undid the little ball and then made another ball of the black-banded kerchief. There was a peculiar, stricken expression in her eyes, and in flashing retrospection I found the clue. That was the same look she had had during dinner that night when she had asked why I didn't eat meat.

I tried to speak gently, not to be angry or resentful. "Did someone point out to you that drug addicts seldom eat meat?"

She replied almost in a whisper, "Yes."

"Do you mind telling me what else the story is based on?"

It was with considerable difficulty that I drew from Gloria the charge that I had frequented Market Street houses of ill-repute, and also the opium dens of "Hop Alley." Of course I had gone to those places many times until a recent reform movement had closed the brothels. My knowledge of the tenderloin, my acquaintanceship with underworld characters during the days when I was a delivery boy for the Grand National, had become of value to me as a reporter.

My knowledge that I was still a virgin, and the fact that I never had taken even the mildest sedative in all my twenty-three years, urged me on to offer a defense. Instead, I fought a brief battle upon my own private field of pride, and I compelled myself to laugh out loud. And I think that the laughter seemed a confession.

After Gloria had gone, I stayed on the balcony until the orchestra began to play "Good Night, Ladies" and "Auld Lang Syne."

Sic transit Gloria. . . .

26

THE BIG STORM

I THOUGHT of my father. Of the lone man I thought, and of his white mountain, and of winter winds, clean and cool.

A sickness possessed me, and its name was loneliness. Some men go with their wounds to the mountains or to the wilderness. Others go to the devil. That winter I entered upon a period of caprice, of drinking, of swashbuckling, and promiscuous ways. I turned my eyes away from Mt. Evans. Perhaps I was afraid to look at the far-off peak, or ashamed.

One Saturday evening in November, MacLennan assigned me to relieve Police Reporter Harry McCabe at City Hall. After supper at the free-lunch counter of the Black Cat Saloon across the street from the newspaper office, I went to police headquarters. On my way there, I felt that someone was following me. I performed the orthodox tricks to trap a shadow, but could see no suspicious figure among the stragglers.

At City Hall I mentioned my imaginary follower to Paris B. Montgomery, an authority on matters of this nature. The veteran police reporter looked up from his typewriter to shout, "It's your conscience! That's what dogs you." He astonished me further by crying out morosely, "O God! O God!"

"What the devil?" I asked. "Are you sick?"

He made frenzied motions above a sheet of paper in his machine. Then Harry McCabe came to the pressroom for his overcoat.

"What's wrong with him?" I asked McCabe in an aside.

"Hah!" he snorted. "Monty's been writing a suicide note all afternoon." At the doorway McCabe sang out, "His suicides are beginning to bore me."

During the last two years Paris B. Montgomery had made several "attempts" at self-immolation. Whatever it was that prompted these actions, I cannot say. He was a crack reporter, well liked, and reasonably solvent most of the time. Each tussle with the bottle, however, inspired thoughts of death in him. The favorite place for his last farewells was at the Press Club during early-morning hours when his colleagues were engrossed with cards, games of Kelly pool, or listening to the player-piano beat out "La Paloma." It was Monty's morbid pleasure to emerge from the washroom, his mouth foaming, then stagger to the couch and collapse. The jaws of the polar-bear trophy instead of the jaws of death grinned down upon his simulated convulsions. Nevertheless, someone was sure each time to summon Police Surgeon McGillivray and the stomach pump. The weary McGillivray would announce that once again the false-alarmist had gargled a solution of bicarbonate of soda and powdered soap.

These bogus death throes upset the members of the Press Club, especially Colonel McFall. "It is difficult for me to keep bank with such goings-on," he complained. "I suggest we enter a gentlemen's agreement to pay no attention the next time Monty swoons. Now, let's see; whose deal is it? And please ante up, Mr. Casey. They used to shoot men in Cripple Creek when they neglected to ante up."

On the night when Montgomery sat slumped over his suicide note in the pressroom of City Hall, I wasn't feeling gay myself.

But Monty's distress seemed mightier than my own; and, besides, I actually believed him each time he announced his doom.

I removed the sheet of paper from his machine and tore it to bits. At this, Monty rose with raging disapproval. "Have you no decency?" he cried out. "Reading a man's private papers?"

"I didn't read it, Monty," I replied. "Let's send out for some black coffee."

He aimed a long swing at my chin, but I easily deflected it and held him up. "What's all this about?"

Monty began to speak thickly. He made contradictory remarks about "the unimportance of owning a violin," and "the terrible sorrow of never having had one."

"If that's all that worries you," I pointed out, "you can get a fiddle at George Wilke's pawnshop first thing Monday morning."

"I'm tired inside," Monty said.

"What of it?" I said. "I'm tired myself, inside and outside too; but that's no reason to walk the plank."

The ambulance signal box above the door of the pressroom began to chatter. I frog-marched Monty along the corridor and up the stone steps of the basement exit to board the motor ambulance. When the black van rolled out of the morgue building across the street, reporters Jack Carberry and Diedrich von Stacklebeck appeared on the scene. We laid Monty on the floor of the ambulance, for he kept falling from the side seats.

As the ambulance traveled a curve into Market Street, where the call had originated, the rear doors flew open. Monty slid like a torpedo from the tail end of the vehicle. I cried out for the driver to stop, but Police Surgeon McGillivray overruled me.

"We're on a suicide case," he said, "and besides, Monty is too relaxed to be hurt much."

Our destination was a secretly operated house of ill-fame which so far had escaped Police Commissioner George Creel's order closing the red-light district. Inside this cheaply furnished burrow, we came upon a partially clothed woman sprawled across an iron bedstead. The bed seemed long ago to have despaired of fresh linen. An uncorked bottle labeled "Carbolic Acid" lay empty on the floor. There were acid burns on the woman's mouth and chin. She was not a pretty sight, but she had the most beautiful blond hair I had ever seen.

On the way to the County Hospital, Carberry held a flashlight while the police surgeon operated the stomach pump. Reporter von Stacklebeck, a tall, skinny pessimist from the Fatherland, stared at the woman through lenses as thick as paperweights. "Gott!" he said. "Vot hair has the voman on her head!"

Reporters served as stretcher bearers whenever orderlies were slow to meet the ambulance at the hospital entrance. I gripped one front handle of the stretcher, and von Stacklebeck the one opposite me. The near-sighted Dutchman stumbled on the hospital stairs. The jarring of our burden caused the woman's beautiful hair to pop off, revealing a completely bald head.

Jack Carberry wrote the incapacitated Monty's stories that night. The police surgeon taped two fractured ribs of the human torpedo, who showed his gratitude by calling Dr. McGillivray a stinking ghoul.

Sometime afterward at the Press Club, Monty had another suicidal urge. He grumbled about "violins," but I paid little attention, for on this occasion I was ahead in the poker game for the first time since April first.

On that day of All Fools, I had been some forty dollars in the clear when Ronald Millar, a Dartmouth alumnus of much erudition and muscle, decided to pummel Morris Legg, a fellow-reporter. The poker table went down with Mr. Legg. My chips cascaded to the floor, there to mingle with the markers of other players.

"Let the chips fall where they may," Colonel McFall ruled, to the consternation of the winners. "We shall begin play again from the beginning, gentlemen. Everyone starts even."

Now, on my second night of good hands, and with Christmas but a month away, I was about sixty dollars ahead. My luck seemed so roseate that even the Colonel hesitated to call my bets.

Then, just as I had filled in a King-full, after drawing to a pair of Jacks, Paris B. Montgomery called out from his place on the sofa beneath the polar-bear skin, "Here goes! This is it!"

With that, he partook of what seemed a Sedlitz powder from a paper sheath. He rolled off the sofa to the floor. The thud disturbed the players, and Colonel McFall rapped with his knuckles on the table. "Gentlemen, remember our agreement. We are not to pay the least attention to humbug Montgomery. I believe you opened, Mr. Fowler? It's your say."

Steward Jim Wong was bending over Monty to lift him to the couch. The police star on Montgomery's belt reflected the ceiling light. I heard the Colonel say, "Well, are you checking the bet, or what? Let us proceed."

"I think we should ring for the ambulance," I said.

"Nonsense," the Colonel replied. He addressed MacLennan across the table, "Mac, I have half a mind to prefer charges. This is a gentlemen's club."

"Quick!" Jim Wong called out. "Monty got blue face!"

MacLennan left the game to telephone headquarters. When the police surgeon arrived, he said that Monty's troubles were over for all time. "It was cyanide," said Dr. McGillivray.

"Gentlemen," the Colonel said, "I was only jesting, of course, about the charges. And I move that we call off all play for the night out of respect for Monty. Furthermore, I propose that we give the cash in tonight's bank toward a funeral fund. There are to be no winners and no losers among us." Then he said reverently, as he looked toward the sheeted figure, "I am wrong. There is one loser—Monty."

"Maybe," said MacLennan, "he's the winner."

Whenever I rode in the police ambulance, I thought much about life and death. There were births in the narrow, rough-riding vehicle, and there were deaths. It was a traveling library of personal histories from which one might draw analogies to one's own unfinished chronicle. Among the last chapters that unfolded before one's eyes there could be read the hopes, the fears, the tragedies of all men's lives. The belled black wagon seemed a caravan for strolling players, who performed on instant notice one of the old morality plays. An afflicted mortal, upon entering the night's play, became Everyman.

Again, the ambulance seemed an hourglass on wheels. Its sands spilled tales of many men and women, old and young. The sands ran alike for the nameless ones and the named—alike for all, rich or poor. A man found no prestige or favoritism at the tribunal of Time; in Death, no aristocracy.

There was one elderly workman who had been loading a steel safe onto a railway flatcar. The cable he had been manipulating parted, and the one-ton kite made splinters of his bones. The old man stayed conscious in the ambulance for some time. He had but one complaint as he lay dying: "I'll be late home for supper, and she'll worry."

At another time we dug out a Negro from beneath a scaffolding. He was grotesquely coated with plaster and lime. From his broken chest and crushed throat came only hymns and hallelujahs as he died.

How then could a spectator help but despise his own coddled troubles? How could the young reporter stay inside the shell of real or fancied pain when dying men thought only of being late to supper, or sang spirituals?

One saw examples of simple faith which shamed the transgressor who had been taking false refuge in the regions of doubt and obstinacy. But the habit of careless living now was upon me, and I was drifting. It is at a time such as this that a man's career, his pattern of living even, is either saved or lost beyond reclamation.

Granny looked on but said nothing. Grandpa also maintained silence. Frank Fowler saw in me only an "up and coming fellow," and suggested that he and I together engage in publicity campaigns to advertise his new schemes.

But Uncle Dewey took me aside to say, "Look here. I'm only a meat cutter, but I'm not impressed by you or anyone. I was terribly fond of your mother, and I used to think that you were all right. I've got no criticism if you take a drink or go with the girls; no one is expecting you to act like a sissy. But you'd better make up your mind pretty soon to pull yourself together. Nobody else can do it for you."

On the night of December 3, 1913, the skies were starless, and Colonel McFall said to Lee Casey and me, "It doesn't take the skill of a Scout Wiggins to foresee that we shall have a slight flurry of snow. Why don't you boys come out to my cottage and be my guests for the night? I have Bourbon, a crackling fire, and a snack in the cupboard."

The Colonel's invitation came at a time when Mr. Casey and I were trying to persuade Jim Wong to cash our weekly paychecks. The practical-minded Chinaman explained that to oblige us he would be compelled to strip the club's till of ready cash.

"Put your checks right back in your wallets, boys," the Colonel advised. "In my home there'll be no need to use them. You are my guests."

The Colonel would not permit us to ride the streetcar. No. A horse-drawn cab, he said, was to carry us in style to Park Hill, where his cottage was. The hospitable Colonel also invited Police Reporter Jack Carberry to join the party. As we rode along Seventeenth Street, the snow flurry began to gather volume and voice. Soon it was a blizzard, and the horses barely made headway against the wind and snow.

"Colonel," said Jack Carberry, "I'm going with you against my better judgment. I've seldom ventured more than six blocks away from the police station, and I can get almost anything my heart desires on Larimer Street."

The Colonel was peering through the storm. "Aha!" he called out. "Hold up, cabby!"

Through the swirling curtain of snow there appeared the face of Charley Carson, foreman of the stereotype room. He had been waiting for a streetcar, he explained. And then he offered the somewhat presumptuous inquiry, "You boys going to a hook-shop for the night?"

The Colonel lifted a frosty hand. "If you please, Charley, my white hair doesn't merit your low insinuation. We are en route to my home for a social time. Will you join us?"

"I ought to go on to my own home," Charley replied.

"Bourbon awaits you at my cottage," said the Colonel. "Bourbon, a snack, and a roaring fire."

"Maybe you need another hand at cards," said the suspicious Charley. "Anyways, I ought to take my paycheck home this once."

"All right then, Charley," the Colonel said. "Suppose you stay on right there in the snow and think up some more low jokes. We are on our way."

"Well," said the foreman, "I've run out of liquor at my house, and no telling when the car will get here." He climbed into the cab. "But don't expect me to play any cards."

At the Colonel's cozy home the fire, the Bourbon, the snack, all seemed fine and free and heartening. The storm roared on outside. The good Colonel was seated like a kindly squire in a Morris chair. A pair of red morocco bedroom slippers, which exactly matched the binding of his little notebook, were on his feet. While reaching for some tobacco to fill his meerschaum, the Colonel chanced upon a deck of cards on the fumed-oak table at his side. When he riffled them, it was like a moose call.

We began "just a sociable game." At daylight Mr. Casey reported that the snow was three feet deep outside and still coming down. I wasn't interested in the weather, for by now I had lost my paycheck to the Colonel and was down in his notebook for another twenty dollars.

By noonday Casey also had lost his paycheck. Carberry was almost ready to say farewell to his. But Charley stayed about even, and the Colonel complimented him upon his conservative play.

We were due at our offices soon, but when we attempted to

get the front door open we could not budge it. Casey telephoned
MacLennan to advise him of our plight. MacLennan said that he
could spare Casey and Fowler, but needed the foreman of the
stereotyping department. Then, just as the editor was making
another nasty remark, the telephone went dead. The lines had
collapsed beneath the heaviest snowfall since the time Buffalo Bill
rode the Pony Express.

We played in relays with a stripped deck of cards, and took
occasional naps and occasional nips. By nightfall the snow was
five feet deep, or so Casey reported.

A rescue squad of circulation department men arrived on snowshoes at nine o'clock in the evening. They shoveled their way
into the Colonel's home to succor the foreman. That made the
game eight-handed.

We stayed four days and five nights at the Colonel's house,
still playing in relays. At the conclusion of the ordeal, I had lost
the equivalent of three weeks' pay, and Casey two. Carberry was
more fortunate; he lost only one paycheck and in addition suffered a mere five-dollar notation in the Colonel's book. Charley
had continued to stay even with the board, a remarkable fact
which the Colonel applauded in the manner of a good sportsman.

As we said farewell to our money and to the Colonel, Casey
remarked, "I am exhausted but proud. We have proved our ability
to withstand the rigors of nature."

How far I might have gone on my downhill way, I do not
know. A nail-hard physique, the gift of pioneers, was both my
good fortune and my bad. My youth and toughness withstood the
sleepless nights, the driving work that a reporter had to accomplish or be fired, and the assaults of dissipation. That was good,
the fact that the body could bear this burden. But it was also
bad, for it encouraged my asinine bravado.

Then one night MacLennan assigned me to interview a celebrated young woman, Miss Fay King.

"We've got a tip," the city editor said, "that Miss King left her husband flat during their honeymoon."

Fay King was one of the few women cartoonists in the newspaper world. She wrote articles to accompany her drawings, and both her art and her editorials had a freshness and a simple originality which revealed their creator as an extraordinary person. She was the daughter of an old-time trainer of athletes in Seattle. Many champions had seen her grow from childhood to young womanhood, and regarded her as their mascot. Just recently she had married Oscar Mathew Battling Nelson, lightweight champion pugilist of the world.

When I arrived at Miss King's hotel suite to ask if she were leaving the man known among sports followers as "The Durable Dane," I was unprepared to come upon so much vitality in such a small package. She was playing with nine canary birds. They were fluttering about the room, sometimes alighting upon her head and shoulders. They seemed charmed by her cries and her laughter.

It was the first time I had seen Fay King. I observed that she was dark-complexioned, with very large dark eyes, and that she wore numerous pieces of jewelry which chimed like bells as she played with her birds. There were gold hoops in her ears, and on one forefinger she wore a heavy gold band to which was affixed a cartoon effigy of herself.

In her published drawings, Miss King caricatured herself as the possessor of large feet and other exaggerated features. But she was a petite, lively girl. She was part gypsy.

"Shut that door!" Miss King called out. "If one of my little birds got away, I'd be sure to die. What's your name? I didn't catch it over the telephone. I hope it's not Schultz."

I told her my name, and when she asked what it was I kept staring at, I replied, "Those earrings."

"Don't you admire them?" she asked.

"I'd like to chin myself on them," I said. Then I became businesslike. "Is it true you left Battling Nelson the first week of your honeymoon? Is there to be a divorce?"

"Yes," she said frankly, "but I wish you wouldn't print it."

"And why not?"

"I don't like to make him feel sad," she said. "Whenever anybody feels sad, I want to cry too. I don't like to cry; it makes my mascara run."

"Well," I said, "you'd better outfit yourself with a big supply of handkerchiefs."

"You mean you'll print it?"

"What else? You're both public figures. Have you filed papers?"

She amazed me by asking, "Do you like corn on the cob? I mean after it's cut off and piled high on the plate?"

"I like it that way best of all," I replied. "Is that what caused your divorce? Whether corn should be cut off the cob?"

"No," she said. "But let's go down to the cafeteria."

"Fresh corn is not in season," I reminded her.

"I know," she replied, "but we can have some canned corn. When I crave something, I must have it right away."

As if she did not have on enough jewelry already, she found some more bracelets. And by the time she was ready to start out for the street she was more ornate than an admiral's arm. She liked gay colors also, and when she had assembled her various scarves and sashes, she reminded me of the mountain flowers of August.

"I am simply mad about cafeterias," she said, then announced matter-of-factly, "I think I'm going to like you. Do you mind?"

"Not at all," I said. "I'm one of those fellows who likes to be liked."

She looked at me and said, "Oh."

We had canned corn that night at the cafeteria. And when summer came, we had corn cut from the cob. And we also shared laughter and great affection. In this completely honest and honorable person I found one of those friends who never die.

Fay had an unreasonably high estimation of me, and I tried—at times—to live up to it. I began to return from the dark places where I had strayed.

Our principal bond was laughter, and our attraction, one for the other, arose from the circumstance that two wild-natured creatures found companionship, honesty of expression, and instant understanding. Loneliness went away.

We differed in several respects, of course. Beneath the carefree, gypsy personality of this girl, lay the inflexible soul of a moralist. One could not justifiably call her a prude; still she had a puritanical code which she revealed only to those who knew her in private life. She herself was abstemious, yet uncritical of the indulgences of others. She did not endeavor to reform me in the usual ineffectual manner of well-meaning persons who think that bridles, saddles, spurs, and quirts can tame desire. Rather, she undertook an educational campaign to make me believe what she sincerely thought herself, that I had within me the materials of manhood and achievement. So earnest was her belief in my potentialities that I began to believe in them myself.

It was difficult for me, however, to wear blinders when exposed to romantic issues. In respect to my extreme fondness for the ladies, Fay remarked: "When men like you and Columbus discover something, you go overboard with delight."

This girl and I, both lately wounded by a careless Cupid, together laughed our way through spring and summer, and once again I could look off at Mt. Evans. And once again I thought of my father.

I confided in Fay concerning my long-time yearning for a father. I said that perhaps one day I would go to see him. "He will come to see you," she replied. "And when he does, be sure to welcome him as if the long separation never had been."

I thought her clairvoyant, for there were numerous times when she successfully foretold events. And when she said with conviction that my father and I would meet one day, I believed her, and the belief comforted me.

Although she seldom showed a solemn face to the world, Fay at times would fall silent when we were alone. Her extraordinary dark eyes would glow, and she would whisper things that had to do with the future.

One day when I chanced to mention my feeling that I had been followed by some mysterious person, she said, "It's your father."

"You mean he is thinking of me? Telepathy?"

"I mean," she said, "that he comes down here to see you. He comes here to look at his son from a distance, and then he goes away."

This announcement startled me.

Then she quite suddenly put off her Delphic mood, for she was as volatile as a little wind of summer, and she began to laugh and sing. Then she announced that she wished to do a pastel sketch of me. She often made sketches of me; sometimes when she sketched, she would say above her drawing board that I would go away soon; that I would have children of my own, and in that way find my greatest happiness.

"But we shall always be the best of friends," she said. "Each of us has work to do."

27

THE DAWN'S EARLY LIGHT

THE young years seemed a time of beating the sea with a hammer. So many questions. So few answers.

I worked nights and Fay King worked days. The young cartoonist's editors objected to her late hours in my company, but she had a way of charming them, especially Harry H. Tammen, co-owner with Frederick G. Bonfils of *The Denver Post*. Fay and I together attended the baseball games and prizefights, for now I was writing of sports as well as other events. Because of her girlhood among the champions, as well as her analytical mind, she was an excellent appraiser of athletes and their games. She was the only woman I ever knew who fully understood the fine points, such as the fact that a short punch actually originates in a boxer's legs and is much more effective than a showy, swinging blow that has little behind it but the torso and shoulder. When I began to referee the professional fights she would review my mistakes with the stern eye of a critic, and I was happy indeed that she didn't publish these opinions in her newspaper.

When I set out upon my first tour as a baseball reporter with the Denver "Grizzlies," she advised me to give attention to the human interest stories among athletes rather than write of statistics and technical matters. I afterward learned that she had instructed my roommate on the tour, Pitcher Carl Zamlock, and the manager, Jack Coffey, to see that I behaved.

This tour of Western League cities was the first extensive journey I had made. Athletes seemed to me the best of traveling companions; they valued the correspondent as both friend and historian. To associate with members of this minor-league club was a revealing experience. I was privileged to hear the contrasting testimony of older men on their disillusioned way down from the big leagues, and that of heady young dreamers of fame.

Among our pitchers was left-handed Clarence Mitchell, the protégé of none other than Colonel Jamieson. Not content with the glory of discovery, the Colonel began to bombard the managers of metropolitan baseball clubs in the East to hire his prodigy. Sometimes I mischievously interpolated my own comments in the letters I typed to oblige the enthusiastic Colonel. In one of these, I had the Colonel accuse the hot-tempered John McGraw, manager of the New York Giants, of being "a slowpoke Englishman posing as an Irishman for the sake of popularity." McGraw took the letter so seriously as actually to burn the Union Jack in the fireplace of the Lamb's Club.

Mitchell was a Nebraska farm boy. On this, his first professional baseball tour, he inquired concerning the usage of the small hammocks which the porter strung at night in Pullman berths. An ex-big leaguer replied that the hammocks were a convenience for ballplayers to rest their throwing arms. Mitchell slept the first night on the road with his left wing in the netting. Next day he was too stiff-armed to start the game against the Wichita Club.

He soon, however, became a star in the National League; and his mentor, the Colonel, almost apoplectic with pride, saw him off at the Union Depot, the silk flag fluttering at the peak of the Jamieson walking stick.

On our first night in Wichita, I asked Manager Coffey to permit five of my friends, all pitchers, to accompany me to the amusement park. The head keeper of the Grizzlies consented to this, but exacted a promise that I not lead his valuable twirlers into temptation, and most important of all stay off the roller coaster and other rickety devices.

At the park we came upon one of those throwing games in which one tosses cheap little baseballs at pyramids of wooden objects shaped like bottles. If a customer knocked over all six bottles with one ball, he not only won a dime but received his nickel back and was allowed a free ball. My five precisionists not only could bowl over these bottles at short range but could have hit the dime prize itself. When they opened fire the concessionaire almost lost his reason. I don't think any of the five sharpshooters missed even once. After the owner of the booth had paid out perhaps ten dollars, he shut up business for the night and began shouting "Crooks!" as we went away.

The next day, however, four members of the pitching staff were successively knocked from the box. They had "thrown out" their arms the night before because they had hurled the light balls without warming up. Wichita tanned the Grizzly hides that day with a score of 19 to 3, and Manager Coffey said to me, "If it weren't for Fay King, I'd send you home."

When I returned from this tour I thought of applying for a job on *The Post*. About a year or so before this time City Editor Eugene Taylor had asked me to join his staff, but I had declined. There was a well-founded belief that anyone who spurned such an invitation never again would be so honored. My refusal occurred before I met Fay King, and I had been reluctant to leave my colleagues on *The News*. Besides, our paper had taken on a crusading spirit which appealed to my love of action.

The then editor of *The News*, William Ludlow Chenery, was a man of personal charm and ability. He afterward became editor, then publisher, of *Collier's Weekly*. At the outset of John C. Shaffer's ownership of *The News*, Mr. Chenery persuaded him to undertake a policy of espousing the interests of "little people." The coal strike, with *The News* championing the Colorado coal miners' position, was the first major issue of journalistic concern to us.

Mr. Shaffer appointed William Forman, former sports editor of *The Chicago Post*, as managing editor. Arthur MacLennan was much too capable to be overlooked by anyone in his right mind, so Mr. Forman promoted him to the city editor's desk. Mac-Lennan lashed us with the scorpions of his sardonic wit. However, he defended us against all outsiders, including Chief of Police Felix O'Neill, whose official automobile Jack Carberry and I stole from in front of City Hall and then wrecked on a railway crossing.

Ours was a fine, fighting organization, and we feared no one except the auditor who pruned our expense accounts. Our news editor was Frank Farrar, a quiet little veteran who knew more about type than Gutenberg. And at the head of the copy desk sat a deaf-and-dumb genius whose name I forget, because he always was referred to merely as "The Dummy."

The Dummy was probably the greatest copyreader this side of New York, although Casey was his equal for speed. He detested ladies of the evening, because one of them had taken his watch during a time of dalliance. Still, on the night when I wrote of the bald-headed prostitute, a look of compassion came to The Dummy's eyes as he captioned the story: "Let Him Who Is Without Sin."

The crusading spirit of *The News* and the presence of the gifted Chenery on the editorial page attracted as visitors to our office an array of celebrated writers from the East. Among these were Upton Sinclair, Norman Hapgood, John Fox, Jr., and John Reed. To my dismay, I failed to see Julian Street, whose prose style as well as his superior reportorial eye had aroused my admiration. Street was now making a cross-country survey of the American scene for *Collier's Weekly*. Perhaps he hastened away from Colorado because of a premonition of what the town of Cripple Creek was going to do to him.

Street had stopped over at Colorado Springs where a friend

invited him to take a trip to Cripple Creek on the Short Line. They traveled in a heavy steel private car, the weight of which delayed the little train on the steep grade. This curtailed their Cripple Creek visit to less than an hour before the train went back down. The high altitude bothered Street, so he merely walked around the block nearest the station. This aimless stroll led him through the town's red-light district, which had on one side a deserted dance hall with broken windows and doors swinging in the wind, and on the other side a row of cribs with the names of inmates painted on the windows like the names of little stores. One name was Madam Leo, and as Street was passing by this place, a poor, half-witted trollop came out and gave a lecture on how bad business was.

Street thought this a grisly spectacle. He had not meant to write about Cripple Creek, but did so. The horror he expressed for that part of the town he had seen made the citizens of Cripple Creek feel like beating him over the head with their mining shovels. Street received many scurrilous letters, and a Cripple Creek newspaper suggested that the author had been in the red-light district for no good social purpose. When the Chamber of Commerce demanded a retraction from Mark Sullivan, then editor of *Collier's*, he replied that if the town hadn't kept its red-light charms next to the railroad station his correspondent would never have chanced upon them. That view failed to comfort the townsfolk. To them Street was just a lowlife who, instead of writing about precious metals mined long ago by Gold King Stratton and other stalwarts of the West, had gone out to interview a wicked and decrepit Moll Flanders.

The revenge of the Cripple Creek populace brought enormous hilarity to newspapermen everywhere; the civic fathers changed the name of their shoddiest thoroughfare from Myers Avenue to Julian Street. Street has since told me that it took him three days to see how funny this was.

The successful authors I met during my wide-eyed time of questing were neither too big nor too busy to reveal to the young stumbler where the literary hazards lay and where the fair fields might be found. Among those who arrived to study the strike in Colorado coal fields was John Reed. He was a young man of great personal charm and courage, was over-contentious with the police and all millionaires, but graciousness itself to reporters of the provincial scene. Julian Street, who disapproved of Reed's eventual activities, described the gray-eyed nonconformist during his earlier days as being "full of fun and visions," and "a mischievous boy throwing snowballs at the world's silk hat." Now in 1914, as Street also observed, Reed was "putting stones in the snowballs."

Reed was sitting on the pool table of the Press Club when I first met him. Our club just recently had moved into new quarters above the Denham Theatre, owned a new player-piano, new glasses, but the polar-bear rug was still with us, and philosopher Jim Wong remained our faithful steward.

"Success in writing," John Reed said, "is the sum of industry plus talent. There's no shortage of talent, and there's no shortage of industry. There *is* a shortage, however, of the combination of both talent and industry in one person. You can have either one or the other and be a complete failure. You need both to succeed." Knight-errant Reed then added, "I have been speaking of public success. As far as one's personal private success is concerned, there are two other elements needed: guts and concern for the betterment of the underdog."

In less than a year the crusading spirit of *The News* began to flag. The owner of the newspaper, as a traction magnate of the Middle West, gave ear to the complaints of powerful critics. His journalistic surrender chilled our spirits. Chenery went East, then other editors began leaving.

Mr. Shaffer assigned Frank Farrar to *The Chicago Post,* and

Colonel McFall decided that we give a farewell party. The members of the Press Club set aside enough money from the poker-game pots to purchase a watch from pawnbroker George Wilke. On the night of farewell, I was made custodian of the watch, to hand it to the orating Colonel, on cue, during his presentation speech.

After drinking in Frank's honor, I fell asleep. When the Colonel uttered my cue: "And now as a token of our great esteem for a precious ornament of the Fourth Estate," I awakened to find the watch had mysteriously disappeared.

The Colonel repeated his cue line, then asked outright, "Well, where in hell is the—er—the you-know-what?"

"Colonel," I replied truthfully, "I don't know."

"I beg your pardon!" the Colonel said. "You don't know? Why, you had it in your hand not ten minutes ago."

"I fell asleep," I said. "And now it's gone."

"Gone, you say? This is no time to play some low jest. Come, now! Where is it?"

"I tell you, the watch just disappeared," I sang out.

The deflated Colonel again addressed the guest of honor: "Frank, we have a splendid timepiece to give you, twenty-two jewels—when we locate it."

After an hour of searching the premises, Jim Wong found the watch inside a large brass cuspidor. It didn't tick now, for the works had been damaged by submersion. The Colonel shrank from touching it, and announced that Wong would take it to the "jeweler's" for overhauling and forwarding to Mr. Farrar in Chicago.

The Colonel turned to me with quiet scorn, "And I always thought this was a gentlemen's club!"

MacLennan was the next casualty at *The News.* He too went to Chicago to become one of Mr. Shaffer's outstanding editors. And now I reluctantly said good-by to my crony Lee Casey and quit my job. I walked over to *The Post* on Champa Street, took off my hat and coat, and sat at one of the typewriters in the city room.

"What do you think you are doing here?" asked City Editor Taylor.

"I'm accepting your cordial invitation to join *The Post* family," I said.

"I know," Mr. Taylor replied, "but that was more than a year ago. We are not so cordial now."

Notwithstanding this pronouncement, Mr. Taylor conferred with the excellent newspaper editor, William Shepherd, and I began my four lusty years of service on that audacious and colorful newspaper, *The Denver Post*.

Among other duties, I became assistant sports editor to Otto C. Floto, who himself had begun his career as a bill poster. That gallant sports authority overlooked my numerous madcap antics and I sometimes wondered why he never fired me. His vivacious wife Kitty wondered the same thing. Kitty formerly had been the most capable woman bareback rider in the circus world, where she had been known as "The Lady in Red." Her opinion of me was that I was wilder and more untractable than any horse she ever had met, including the bronco Steamboat.

Years afterward Otto told me that he always had wanted a son above all other things, and that in me he had found a reasonably good substitute for one.

A man of the world, Floto knew many celebrated persons of the stage as well as those of the sports arenas. Because of Floto, I had an opportunity to make friends of these public idols, learned firsthand that the great men among them actually were the simplest in their private lives and the most approachable.

Many down-and-outers and sports world has-beens also visited our office. Otto always had time and dollars for such drifters as the blind Negro "Birdlegs" Collins, a former boxer, or Leadville Liz, who was said to have been the belle of the mining camps in 1880. Otto would make jokes as he gave away his dollars, so as to lessen the sting of charity. He would claim that certain mysterious persons had authorized him as their agent to pay old debts, saying, "Here's a dollar that Captain Muff of the Glass Ship bequeathed you as he dived from the bridge," or, "Here's your share of the earnings of Alonzo the stud crab."

Certain critics have lamented my propensity to write sometimes in terms of the sports world. Still, there are philosophies to be drawn from men whose slightest mistake invites a smashed jaw. I do not believe that Emerson could have stated more interesting truths than Bob Fitzsimmons', "The bigger they are, the harder they fall," or Sam Langford's, "Never bet on anything that talks," or John McGraw's, "Kid winners, but never kid losers." And I think Otto's last words, "After a while," a phrase which can mean so many things.

At the time when I began work on *The Post*, I renewed an acquaintanceship with the then little heard-of Jack Dempsey. He was five years younger than I, and those of us who knew him at all called him Harry, for his name was William Harrison Dempsey. He was a sensitive, restless chap, who boxed here and there for his beans.

Notwithstanding his later legend of rip-roaring aggressiveness, he actually was a shy person of acute sensibilities. It was almost impossible to hurt him during the fury of combat, but so easy to wound him otherwise. And when a supposed friend did him a bad turn—and how frequently that happened—he retired further inside himself. He never complained of any misfortune, large or small, and no one could carry tales to him and still keep his respect.

It entirely escaped my notice that the modest and then slim young Dempsey had fistic genius. But I did see in him from the first a deep and brooding quietness which introspection brings. The public came to believe that Dempsey was purely a fighting machine, one of the greatest the world has ever known; but he also had an inquisitive and retentive mind, much as he himself sought to belittle its good qualities. He understood the essence of many things because he had clarity of thought. He knew the good things from the mediocre, and that I believe to be important.

In the ring Dempsey was merciless and savage and careless of the rules. Out of it he was a gentle sentimentalist. In some ways he was naïvely credulous, as when he first stood with a huge cowboy hat on his head at the corner of Broadway and Forty-second Street and asked a policeman, "Say, partner, would you tell me where the Great White Way is located?" And when the officer asked pityingly, "Well, well, where did you come from?" Jack replied with quiet candor, "From the West, and I'm going to be the next heavyweight champion of the world."

Dempsey seems one of the important men in the gallery that is my America. In him, as in Fay King, were embodied many nationalities; but instead of gypsy, he had a dash of Indian blood. He went from the little Mormon town of Manassa, Colorado, where he had been born, to the sugar-beet fields of Utah, and then back to Colorado to be a mucker in the gold mines of Cripple Creek. He learned to fight with his fists because he had to, and then was amazed to learn that he could be paid for fighting. He sometimes relied upon faulty counselors, suffered the jeers of the crowd, but got up again to move toward his goal and reach a popularity such as seldom follows a man beyond retirement as a champion. He was both wise and credulous, both furious and gentle, both realist and dreamer.

On the hot afternoon when he battered down the hulking Jess Willard at Toledo, he was slow to appraise his triumph or grasp the full meaning of victory.

After that fight, the crowd of back-slappers and self-appointed friends trooped to Jack's dressing room. Few persons, however, attended the beaten Willard in the ex-champion's quarters, for defeat, it would seem, is a contagious disease, and no one wishes to risk exposure to it. The vanquished man's jaw had been broken, his cheeks were out like eggplants, his eyes almost closed. Willard laboriously dressed himself in his big baggy street clothes, and nobody gave him more than a passing glance as he shambled half-blind along the fence, looking for an exit. Reporter Charles

MacArthur recognized him and took him in a taxi to a hotel.

But in Dempsey's quarters the demonstration was so riotous as to prevent his taking a shower or having a rubdown. Jack still was somewhat dazed from the bout; it had not been as easy as it looked to beat the Man Mountain. The hot crowd in the dressing room on the hot afternoon further confused him. He needed sleep, but the public does not willingly permit a new champion that privilege.

At about eight o'clock that evening, Dempsey managed to escape his well-wishers to go to his hotel. There he persuaded the manager to assign him a room as far away as possible from his regular quarters.

He removed his clothes and lay down. His was not a carefree sleep, however, for hostile dreams assailed him. At about one o'clock in the morning, he dreamed that he was being knocked out by Willard. Jack got up in the darkness, went to the bathroom, turned the light switch and looked in the mirror to see dry blood on his face. Now he was positive that he had been knocked out by one of Willard's uppercuts and then deserted by former adherents.

He drew on his trousers and a shirt and got into his shoes without bothering to put on socks. In the hallway outside his room, even the elevator man was not in evidence. Jack walked down a back staircase, then hastened through the lobby to the street. The night clerk, checking the room-service slips, did not glance up.

In the street outside the hotel, a lone drunk looked blearily at Dempsey and made unintelligible sounds. At the corner a newsboy was sorting the morning papers.

"Who won the fight, son?" Jack asked.

The newsboy looked up from the papers. "Why, ain't you Jack Dempsey?"

"Yes," Jack admitted, "I guess I am."

"Who you think you're kidding?" the newsboy snorted. "Don't you know who won?"

"No," Dempsey said, "I honestly don't."

The boy handed him a newspaper. "Just in case you're not kidding."

Dempsey read in the front-page headlines that he had become the new world's heavyweight champion. "I haven't any money on me," he said to the boy, "but I'll leave a dollar with the clerk first thing in the morning."

"You don't owe me a cent, Champ," said the newsboy.

The outstanding reporter on *The Post* was Courtney Ryley Cooper, whose name also appeared in magazines, a circumstance which in those days gave a journalist an exalted status. Early in life Coop had run away from home to become a clown in the circus. Afterward he worked as a reporter on *The Kansas City Star*, and now was a member of *The Post* staff. He traveled sometimes as press agent for the Sells-Floto Circus, one of the many enterprises conducted by Messrs. Tammen and Bonfils, proprietors of *The Post*.

Cooper was a sprightly, colorful chap, skinny and balding in his late twenties, a dancer of surpassing grace, and full of wit and the juice of living. Besides, he was an idolator of Buffalo Bill, who at this time was fretting away his old years as an "attraction" with the Sells-Floto Circus.

The personable Cooper many times smoothed down the white mane of the old Colonel when he growled against the terms of his contract with Harry Tammen. The almost seventy-year-old wild westerner, after seasons of misfortune and distress, had pawned his show and his celebrated name by borrowing money from Tammen. Then Tammen foreclosed. At the auction sale in South Denver, Buffalo Bill said farewell to his old white horse Isham and to his last hope of happiness in the arena.

The still handsome plainsman, disillusioned though he was, held his head high, continued to speak in loud, 4th of July tones even in private conversation, and always looked twice at a pretty face. Cooper's newspaper articles helped sustain the ego of Pahaska, the long-haired one. The Colonel also found solace in his mighty love for his foster son Johnny Baker.

Cooper told me that Baker, when but six years old, used to follow Buffalo Bill about Dodge City (how many of us were like that in our boyhood!) and, when Cody tied his horse to the hitching post in front of the tavern, Little Johnny would wait until the Colonel had gone inside and then untie the reins and stand there, sometimes in the rain or snow, holding them in his hands until the scout emerged from the saloon. This happened so many times that Cody at last was touched by the hero worship of the lad, and took him into his show. He taught him to ride, shoot, and finally adopted him. If ever a boy's dream came true, this was it.

A third man to hold a place in the harassed Cody's old heart was Major John Burke. The Major had been with Buffalo Bill for forty-four years, in fair weather or in foul, and now stayed on after the days of near bankruptcy. In moments of temper, Cody piled abuse upon the Major.

For some reason unknown to me, I always have attracted the attention of sorrowing old men like Colonel Jamieson or Major Burke. And it was no matter of astonishment when the Major frequently visited my office in the sports department to mourn, "Cody is taking it out on me again. He threatened to kill me today."

I, too, idolized Buffalo Bill, and perhaps I listened to the Major's long recitals of his own woes the more attentively because he would speak of "the old days" and tell of men who had been part of the America that seemed my heritage. He had tales of Ned Buntline, of Sitting Bull, of General Custer, Yellow Hand, Rain-in-the-Face, Annie Oakley, Wild Bill Hickok, and the Pinkertons. He would speak with the freshness one has of yesterday morning's happenings of the Pony Express, the Deadwood Stage, Wells-Fargo's beginnings, the building of the Union Pacific, the Battle of Wounded Knee. Of travels the world over the Major also spoke, of meeting crowned heads, Victoria, the Kaiser, and Pope Leo XIII. Then he would return to his sorrows of the moment, actually shed tears, and say, "To think that Bill would call me a whisky-soaked old idiot!"

The Major was a dumpy fellow who looked like an elderly W. C. Fields with sideburns. He smelled of uric acid and sour-mash whisky, but somehow still remained a darling of the ladies, among them Lulu, who secretly operated a house of call.

The Major had begun his career as a circus acrobat, and soon afterward became a drama critic on a small newspaper near Washington, D. C., a demonstration of Darwin's law of evolution in reverse. Burke had never seen an Indian outside of a circus enclosure or a reservation, or smelled powder other than that of the blank cartridges of the Wild West show or on a lady's face. But he claimed to have been a hero of the Ghost Dance War. Soon after meeting Buffalo Bill, the Major commenced to wear his hair long.

The Burke tresses were not as luxuriant as those of Pahaska. When not on parade, the Major wore his hair done up in a kind of washerwoman's bun tucked underneath the crown of his Stetson hat. He did up his hair twice a day, and wore three hairpins to staple the bun in place.

One day the Major came to my office to recite his woes and, as he sat doing up his hair, great tears rolled down his cheeks. "Cody has gone too far this time," the Major said. "He accused me of having been in league with his wife to poison him way back in 1900. Everybody knows that poor old Louisa wasn't trying to poison him. She only put a drug in his coffee to cure him of drinking. Somebody told Cody that she was feeding him dragon's blood to make him love her again, but it wasn't dragon's blood. It was a patent medicine to make him sick the next time he took a drink."

"Did it work?" I asked.

"It gave Bill a big bellyache, and now after all these years he claims I went out and bought the medicine for Louisa to slip in his coffee."

"Well, Major," I advised him, "keep your buckskin shirt on. The Colonel is not himself these days."

Major Burke had lost a hairpin. "Now where did it go?" Neither of us could find it, and the Major dried his eyes with his red bandanna and said, "No matter. I'll get another one from Madam Lulu."

I interceded with Buffalo Bill himself that day; but the hero seemed astonished when I suggested that the Burke heart was at the breaking point. "Now, now," the Colonel said resonantly, "he's getting childish. Why, I never spoke crossly to John in my life, except maybe the time I found him supplying liquor to Sitting Bull. Sitting Bull just couldn't carry firewater. He got out of hand, whooped it up and mistook me for Custer. Besides, it was against the law. Tell John I'm sorry. Hell, I'll speak to him myself."

I sometimes ate with the Major and Ryley Cooper when the circus was in town or had taken up winter quarters south of the city. At one of these pleasant get-togethers, Cooper said in an offhand manner, "I just bought a house at Idaho Springs." Then he asked me, "Doesn't your father live there?"

This question made me ill at ease. "I guess he does."

"You guess?" Cooper inquired. "Don't you know?"

"Why are you asking?"

"Oh, no particular reason," Cooper said, and I permitted the matter to drop. Besides, the Major was now expansively describing Buffalo Bill's "one hundred and ninety-three wounds." The Colonel actually had but one scar, if the subsequent testimony of his wife and the undertaker could be believed, but the Major was not one to minimize anything that concerned his hero.

Again that same month Cooper indirectly brought up the subject of my father, this time in the presence of Colonel Cody.

"I ran away from home," Cooper said, "but afterward I kept in touch with my parents." Then he asked Buffalo Bill, "Colonel, what is your idea of kids who go out in the world? Should they keep in touch with their folks?"

The Colonel always liked being consulted about anything, except going on the water wagon. "Well, now," he said, in his ever-resonant voice, "Johnny Baker never lets a day go by without sending me word."

This seeming violation of my privacy made me fight shy of Cooper's company for some time. Not until later years was I to know what prompted his interest in my personal affairs.

Partly from mischief, and partly from pique at Buffalo Bill's stentorian implications that I was a careless son, I played pranks upon the celebrated plainsman. One of them was to pretend that I suddenly had gone deaf. Whenever I interviewed him, I urged him on to louder and louder repetitions of his replies to my questions. Mr. Tammen one day came from his office to say, "Can't you take that God-damned loud old cuss somewhere else to talk?"

One day in 1915 a friend of mine, Jack Kanner, a promoter of boxing contests, asked me to go with him to City Hall.

"The Health Department," Kanner explained, "is kicking about some technicalities. Afterward we'll relax at the Russian baths, where I'm to meet Oakland Frankie Burns and Vic Hanson to arrange matches for them."

At the Health Department I glimpsed an unusually bright-eyed girl at one of the desks. I thought she smiled at me, but when I smiled back, she immediately busied herself at the telephone. Kanner observed this, laughed, and said, "You know something? That's the girl you should marry."

"I don't even know her," I replied.

"But you will," he said confidently.

"What makes you think so?"

"I have a matchmaker's eye," he said. "It's my business to know a good match when I see one."

He spoke of the girl several times as we baked out with Frankie Burns and Vic Hanson at the baths. Finally I grew irritable and said, "I haven't the slightest idea of marriage, ever."

"But you're so nuts about kids, and how else. . . ."

His remarks were interrupted by a brief but furious fight between Burns and Hanson. Hanson had been sitting naked on an upturned tub on the floor of the hot-room. His good friend Mr. Burns slipped up behind the meditative Hanson to pour a bucket of ice water down his back. The two men began to slug it out. The violence of battle in the stifling room soon overcame them.

The subject of my potential marriage was dropped.

I kept thinking of the girl I had seen in the Health Department. I learned her name, Agnes Hubbard, and that she was a friend of Mayor Henry Arnold's daughter. One day I decided to visit her at her office.

The bewitching lass became solemn when I announced to her that it was my intention to take her to the altar of any church of her own choice. When she retreated from her desk I followed after her into the main corridor. Now she began to run. I ran along behind her, crying out my matrimonial purposes, including a promise to make parents of us both.

Visitors may have been startled at my slogans during the chase among municipal halls, but I cannot say as to that, for my mind was on the girl. She ran into the office of her friend and patron, Mayor Arnold. I was at her flashing heels. She dashed past the Mayor's secretary, Miss Benson, and into the executive sanctuary. There His Honor was in conference with officials of the Burlington Railroad. In I went after the girl, and the angry Mayor began to threaten me with his police powers.

Several times after this I lay in wait for Agnes. I would pop out from behind corners in City Hall, or from doorways in the street, to shout, "There's only one way to put a stop to this!" or, "Do you want to drive me to drink?"

The only intelligible reply I got from her at this time was to my second inquiry. She tossed her head and retorted, "I don't think you have to be driven very far, from what I hear."

Granny was the first to fall ill. A gangrenous infection of the feet kept her in bed. She suffered great pain all the while, but was as stout-hearted as old Scout Wiggins had been. On the day she died, and when the doctor sought to administer a hypodermic to lessen her pain, she said calmly, "No, thank you, doctor. It is my intention to meet my Maker with a clear head."

After Granny died, Norman Wheeler sat in the cellar and said nothing. He sat for two weeks among the musty ledgers and the old iron tools, and then suffered an apoplectic stroke. At the hospital he rallied somewhat, and at length was able to talk haltingly. He wanted to go home.

Aunt Etta took Grandpa to her own house, and there kept him in bed. One morning, just before daybreak, Grandpa called out to indicate that he wanted to get up to sit at the front window.

"But you shouldn't," Aunt Etta said. "Anyway, it's still dark, and you couldn't see outside."

The old man was obdurate. Aunt Etta's son Delford lifted Grandpa from the bed and carried him to an easy chair, and turned the chair around to face the window. Grandpa motioned with the one unparalyzed hand for my aunt to raise the window-shade. She obeyed him and tiptoed away.

When sunrise came, my aunt looked in upon Grandpa. She thought him asleep. He was asleep forever, his eyes fixed upon the distant snowcaps of the hills he had roved so many times.

"What do old men think about when they look off and do not speak?"

"They think of things that will not come again."

"Oh," I said, "so you care enough to look into my spotless past?"

"It's not so spotless," she said and moved on.

What an adorable little baggage she was, and so independent, too.

I said nothing to Fay King about my new interest. But somehow I felt that she knew all about it, for she would look at me and smile as if she were a reader of hearts.

There was another person to whom I said nothing of my new love, my grandmother. She kept a sagacious gray eye upon me at the dinner table, and on one occasion said, "I am a sharp observer, son. To hide a secret from me is like trying to smuggle daybreak past a rooster. What are you up to?"

"I'm up to my ears in work," I evaded.

"Hm!" she snorted. "And they are big ears, too."

My three colonel friends, McFall, Jamieson, and Cody, came to my assistance, as it were, in this earnest affair of the heart. Colonel McFall one night permitted me to win sixty-three dollars at cards, saying. "There's no truth to the adage, 'Lucky at cards, unlucky at love.' Buy her a fine present, laddie buck."

My second colonel, Jamieson, early next morning helped me select flowers, but was aghast when I insisted upon buying sixty dollars' worth of American Beauty roses, saying, "Two dozen is the absolute limit of good taste." I withheld the other three dollars of my winnings to pay the fare for a taxicab, in which I piled the blossoms. And now my third colonel, Buffalo Bill, saw me as I was getting into the flower-filled cab.

"Who is dead?" Pahaska inquired. "Someone I know?"

When I explained to the great man the meaning of my floral mission, he shouted with authority, "When all other maneuvers fail, one must take a fair one's heart by storm. That's strategy, son. A frontal attack. Strategy!"

Thus encouraged by my three colonels, I delivered the cargo of red roses to Agnes's house. Her father, a plain-spoken Kentuckian, said that either I was drunk or a damned fool, or both.

However, my many roses made an impression upon the hitherto skittish girl.

She telephoned her thanks to me at my home one noon. I barely saved myself from catastrophe by seizing the receiver from Granny's hand, after she had said over the telephone, "Who is this? Another of my grandson's laundry queens?"

I never talked so earnestly or persuasively in my life as I now did to repair the impression my grandmother had made on my potential sweetheart.

In June of 1916 Fay King left Denver for Kansas City. As she said good-by to me the gypsy look came to her eyes. "If you get married before I come back," she said, "I'll not be surprised."

"What!" I said. "Are you predicting it?"

"I've seen the girl," she replied, "and I think she is wonderful for you in all ways."

In July, I married Agnes Hubbard.

I persuaded a Free Methodist minister, the Reverend James Thomas, former mule driver in the coal mines and ex-wrestler, to perform the marriage ceremony out-of-doors among the high Red Rocks south of the city. Jack Kanner served as best man. He borrowed a car from a professional gambler known in the West as "Cincinnati." The obliging Cincy himself acted as our chauffeur. He drove his car at a rate of speed which caused the Reverend Thomas to ask for Divine Guidance.

Out of gratitude to the minister, I published a picture of him in fighting pose, stripped to the waist to show what a rugged foe of the devil he was. His parishioners were about to ask him to resign his pulpit because of undignified publicity, but reconsidered when business began to boom at his church. He was a great little man.

It is my feeling that to tell the story of Agnes would require the dimensions of another book. Besides, it is a story that pertains to the years in the great, strange city of New York.

I shall never forget Jack Dempsey's solicitude for me during the first week of my marriage. Due to my patronage of Colonel McFall and other expensive follies, I had been unable to buy a new overcoat. My old one seemed to have been salvaged from the trash bin of the Volunteers of America, so I simply didn't wear one. Dempsey, however, had the most splendid overcoat I ever saw, before or since that time. It was his first tailor-made garment, a bright cinnamon-brown creation, double-breasted, with pearl buttons as big as moons, and had cost the tremendous sum of $125.

"It's a mighty cold afternoon," Dempsey said one day, "so suppose you borrow my overcoat."

"But don't you need it yourself, Jack?"

"I'm not on my honeymoon," he said, "and it would be terrible if you got pneumonia at a time like this."

When I arrived home Agnes stared unbelievingly at the bright brown coat and the pearl buttons. "My goodness!" she said. "Well, my goodness!"

When I explained that it was Dempsey's coat, she said worriedly, "But of course you'll give it back to him right away?"

"Oh, yes," I replied, "but it's the finest coat I ever saw. I'd like to have one like it."

"Who is Dempsey?" she asked. "One of your gambler friends?"

"Oh, no," I replied. "He's a young prizefighter I happen to know."

She again stared at the coat with wide eyes, and she looked at me the same way. And she has been looking at me with wide eyes for thirty years, except for the many times when she closed her eyes to my errors and my faults.

Uncle Dewey died from an injury to his liver in 1917. Now the old couple on Emerson Street sat as if waiting their own last call. That call did not come until 1918, after I had gone to New York.

28

MINUTES OF THE LAST MEETING

A WESTERNER saw in the New York subway-station stampede reminders of other days. One closed one's eyes as the trains clamored on the underground iron of the tunnels and tubes, and one heard echoes from the far-off plains of home.

The thing that stayed on in my mind after I began my New York career was the Cheyenne story—the annual Frontier Days celebration at the Wyoming capital. One remembered the dusty thunder of the steers, roped or wrestled down by iron-hard men who leaped from their horses into the hazardous cradles of horns. One remembered for a long time the tumult of the broncos as they bucked out of the chute; and one thought back to the shrill-voiced challengers who performed with artistic violence in the saddles. A rider kept his hands free of leather, fanned the laid-back ears of a wild horse with a big hat, and alternately scratched both flank and shoulder of his mount with the saw-teeth of his rowels. A man pivoted on his buttock as his outlaw horse screamed like a woman in labor, wheeled, sun-fished, or came down with stiff-legged frenzy. Sometimes the man sailed off like a faulty rocket and skidded along the ground. One rode life in the same precarious manner, or was thrown by it.

The soldiers from near-by Fort Russell, the sham battles between the last scouts and the Indians from the Sioux Reservation,
the nights spent at the Plains Hotel with one's friends of Wyoming, T. Joe Cahill, George Carroll, Percy Hoyt, Harry Hynds
and his wife Nellie: all these things and people were remembered
as part of the western pageantry. But what stayed on and on in
memory was a happening of the night before that week of carnival: the chanting of Indians and the weird solo in tom-toms of
Chief Pipe-on-Head, the Sioux medicine man.

On a July afternoon the day before Cheyenne's festival in 1917,
I traveled northward from Denver in a car driven by Jack Kanner. The Colorado highlands lay to our right, slicks of water in
the gullies, and obstinate patches of snow on high ground. We
rode among windrows of red-rock outcroppings, then across
cobbled trails and past alfalfa fields and the singing rakes of the
hay-makers. We came to the wide plain where gray earth showed
beneath the buffalo grass. Dry tumbleweeds lay against the slatted
snow fences or trapped by the barbed wire of the railroad right-
of-way. We left behind us a scattering of rural schoolhouses and
small brick churches, and dairy barns which were Dutch in hip-
roof design but reassuringly American with advertisements of
Carter's Little Liver Pills painted on the shingles. We rode into
the Wyoming range where many thousands of white-faced Here-
ford cattle grazed like solemn politicians.

The sun left a pastel remembrance in the sky, and then it was
night, cool and voiceless except for a locomotive whistle beyond
a prairie rise and the purgatorial yelpings of coyotes along the
arroyos and the dry creek bottoms. It also was strangely silent
when we came to the town of Cheyenne.

Here we heard no shouts or laughter to introduce us to a week
of carnival. Cowboys were standing at the curb in silence except
for their low-voiced "howdies" and the jingling of spurs at their
high heels. The bowed legs of the cowmen made wishbone sil-
houettes against the light of the hotel doorway. From somewhere
beyond the Plains Hotel there rose a monotonous and melancholy

chanting and the beating of tom-toms. The solo of a medicine man then carried over, his falsetto voice rising and falling to the rhythmic accompaniment of tribal drums.

T. Joe Cahill greeted me with unaccustomed gravity, then asked me to follow him to a near-by street. There in the light of a small campfire, we saw perhaps eighty Sioux Indians, both young and old, assembled near an undertaker's place of business. The body of Floyd Irwin, son of the Wyoming rancher, Charlie Irwin, lay inside the undertaker's place, Cahill explained. The young man, the best trick rider of the West, had fallen this same day while practicing his rides.

"A saddle girth parted," T. Joe said, "while Floyd was passing underneath the belly of his horse at full gallop. The flying hooves fractured the skull."

The medicine man was playing a solo with the leg bone of a wild turkey on the horsehide drumhead of a tom-tom. In his song of mourning, I heard a good-by to the West, a good-by to youth, and in this valedictory I began to find a meaning of my own young years.

Cahill now introduced me to former Governor A. W. Barber, who was standing among many other citizens at the wake of the red men for the dead white boy. Governor Barber knew the plains Indians well and spoke their tongue well. He had been a friend and adviser of Owen Wister when that novelist was assembling material for his western story, *The Virginian*. Governor Barber translated for me the priestly chant of Pipe-on-Head and the words intoned by the chorusing squaws.

The tribeswomen sat upon their haunches, their blankets cowling their heads. They sat as if in a witches' ring and rocked forward and back as they sang in reedy, primitive drones:

"Where has the young buck gone? Tell us where the long ride ends; say to us where the young buck has gone?"

The medicine man, his lean face streaked with white-clay symbols, beat upon his tom-tom. Now his owlish voice rose above that of the other chanters in ritualistic elegy:

"From La-no-wa, the rider rides for the last time. The young buck rides away swiftly from the prairies and the streams. Our young brother goes afar."

The Governor explained that "La-no-wa" meant the valleys, the mountains, and the plains—the land of the road to the Sioux Paradise.

The firelight, the keening voices of the chanters, the snaggle-tooth grimaces of the cowled squaws, the nearness of death to life, the beating of the bird bone against the hide of the willow-wood tom-tom. . . . The sudden close of youth's bright time. . . . Was not youth itself a solo in tom-toms?

Again the chorus of the old women rose in wailing cadence:

"Where does the young buck sleep? Tell us where the young buck is sleeping after the long ride? Say to us, where is the place for his rest?"

Again the tom-tom sounded in the night like a naked heart. The old Indian sang his response:

"In the sky you will see his campfire. The young buck lies down beside the fire. He has made his fire among the uncounted lodges in the sky of night. See his fire, all people. Our young brother sleeps afar beyond the blue Tetons and the yellow river. He is brave with dreams."

The tom-tom, I thought, was the heartbeat of all young men and women. It suddenly became my own heartbeat. Its eerie telegraphy addressed me with a message of authority and truth. The message seemed clear and strong: "Youth is a dearest thing, and beyond it one is to find faith."

Now in New York City, as I awaited the coming of the father I never had seen, I again heard the solo in tom-toms playing within my own breast.

When Charles Devlan and I eventually met in 1920, the awkward newness of our personal address hindered an immediate exchange of confidences. Our difference of surnames also imposed a shadow which fell like a forgotten debt from the past.

When I asked the stranger if the name of my adoption troubled him, he replied, "Not now. Not if you can get used to the idea that I'm your father, and not a very good one."

"There is no good or bad about it," I replied. "It's a matter of biological fact."

There would be seventeen more years of questions and answers before we could fully comprehend one another's story. There would be many meetings and much correspondence between Charles Devlan and myself. One did not assemble the pieces of the puzzle with one clever flurry. Perhaps one or two pieces became lost forever, but the main pattern might be discerned.

Charles Devlan, it became plain, was a man of little learning; he had gone to school hardly at all. The hermit had read little else than the newspapers. He could not spell easily, and knew he lacked many other accomplishments. These defects made him self-conscious. It was with difficulty that he set down his thoughts on paper. His speech, however, was pleasantly direct, and the quality of his voice excellent and manly. He was not a talkative person, to be sure, but we held long conversations, and he eventually lost all restraint when with me. At times he even grew somewhat eloquent.

What had happened inside my unpretentious father? Just recently he had come from a self-chosen sanctuary of mountainside and wilderness where one competed mostly with natural forces. Now at the age of fifty-two years he was returning to a world where men and their ideas were arrayed in endless, noisome rivalry. His slightly troubled manner, his shyness, his sad smile—were these the evidences of an inner emptiness of spirit? Had he made a great mistake when he went away? Was he making another one now by coming back?

Notwithstanding his long resistance (or was it a fierce embrace?) to the snows and solitude of thirty years among the hills, he never voiced self-pity or regret. But sometimes his eyes seemed to say that a mortgage lay upon his spirit.

Self-sufficient as he had proved himself in the mountains, now it seemed that he suddenly had acquired a need to depend on me as a guide. And I thought that he, and not I, was the child.

His need for someone of his own blood in whom to release the pent-up story of the lone years seemed so much greater than my own. My youthful groping, my thirsting desire for a father, my quest now was at an end. I had quit guessing about Charles Devlan. His quest, however, really never would end this side of the place where he long ago had buried his heart.

On the evening of Sunday, December 12, 1920, I was notified, while reporting a murder case in Weehawken, New Jersey, that Agnes was about to have a child, our second one. Even a New York city editor, and particularly the former Denver journalist Martin Dunn, permitted a reporter an obstetrical recess.

As I left the ferry slip on the Manhattan side, I quite unexpectedly saw Ryley Cooper as he was hailing a taxicab. We exchanged greetings so noisy and demonstrative as to make bystanders mistake us for Texans. Then I confided in him that I was becoming a father for a second time, and I mentioned that my own father was visiting me.

"That's great," Cooper said. "Give the old boy my best regards."

"You know him pretty well?" I asked. "Or don't you?"

"Oh," Cooper said, and I thought him somewhat evasive, "we run into each other in Idaho Springs on occasion."

As my father and I sat that night waiting for the baby to come, I mentioned having met Cooper and inquired, "How well do you know him?"

"Well," he said uneasily, "I know Ryley Cooper pretty good." Then he seemed to decide that candor was expected. "Cooper used to come to Idaho Springs to tell me how you were doing, how you looked, what you said. And once or twice each year I'd go down to Denver to wait till you came out of the newspaper office."

"I felt that someone was following me several times. Do you believe that?"

"I believe it," he said. Then he inquired anxiously, "Was it wrong to keep track of you?"

"No. But I wish Cooper had told me. I used to get kind of uppity with him, and with George Pell, too."

"I asked Coop not to say anything to you," my father disclosed. "I was afraid it would put a stop to my visits to town."

We stayed up all night waiting for the baby to arrive. "I never was around a baby before," my father said, as if apologizing for some fault. "It's kind of wonderful."

"Well," I said, "you've seen newborn calves and colts?"

"Sure," he replied. "And wild animals, too."

"It's about the same thing," I said, "only babies are much more helpless."

"I guess everything that's born is helpless," he said.

The baby, a girl, finally appeared in the world the morning of December 13. When I had seen her, I said to my father, "Do you think she looks normal?"

His eyes blazed. "Well, by God! Don't you say a thing like . . ." He broke off when he saw that I was only joking. But I had learned in a flash that he had a temper, and a pride of grandfatherhood, and that our blood line was authentic and strong.

My father had sold his homestead acreage on the side of Squaw Mountain. As I afterward learned, he received less than twenty thousand dollars, which he soon lost in investments of the kind so dear to old Deacon Green of snake-barrel fame.

He spoke of his farewell to Squaw Mountain as "a possible mistake." I had waited until now for him to volunteer the detailed story of his thirty years of solitude. That narrative came from him in fragments and without regard to chronological sequence. Eventually I assembled it in my own mind in the order with which I have sought to write of it. He spoke of the days of his visit to the church, of hearing the song outside the memorial window, the honeymoon trip aboard the cable car, the cup of coffee, and the rest of the ancient happenings. Hesitantly, he spoke of the visions seen against the white side of Mt. Evans, and of standing at the graveside of my mother, and of the scream that escaped his throat that day in March of 1903 upon his return to the hills.

He spoke of having cleared trees from the hillside, of building a dam, and of learning from the study of government pamphlets how to make a source of electric power for his timber-saw. He had built a blacksmith shop and forge where he shod his horses, repaired his wagons, and coopered the barrels for storage of vegetables in winter.

Then an opportunity to build a great house presented itself. My father's words, as best I recall them, were as follows:

"My nearest neighbors are members of the Evans family. They have separate homes, and they are fine people. There is Miss Anne, the daughter of Governor Evans. And there's his grandchildren, John, the president of the First National Bank, and Margaret, wife of Roblin H. Davis of the Denver National Bank. I've done work for all of them and they are friendly and kind, and their grandfather was a great man."

"I know that," I said. "He was Lincoln's friend. And I used to look off at Mt. Evans every day."

He studied me wordlessly for a time, then went on to say, "I always wanted to build a big house; not to live in myself, but just to show I could do it. I'd picked out a place on a ledge eight hundred feet above where the beavers build in the basin. The house I kept seeing for the ledge would be a kind of proof that I could give your mother a fine home. But of course that was a crazy thing even to think about."

"I don't think it crazy at all," I said.

"You don't?" and he seemed relieved. "But she was dead."

"Anyway I don't think it crazy. It was a memorial."

"That's right," he said. "That's exactly what I mean. How did you know? But I had no money. Then one day Mr. Leonard Metcalfe of Boston—he's a big civil engineer—visited the Evans people and saw my place as he rode along the trail. He wanted to buy it, but I wouldn't sell. He kept offering me more and more money. But I wouldn't sell. Squaw Mountain was my whole life. Well, no, I kept thinking of you all the time. I mean—"

"I know what you mean," I interrupted. "But you finally sold to Mr. Metcalfe?"

"Yes. You see, he said he'd put a lot of money into a house of native stone and timber, and he'd let me build it, and stay on as caretaker. I could put my own ideas into the new house. That's what he promised, and he kept his word. I'll show you."

My father left the room to get something out of a suitcase. He returned with several photographs of the most beautiful mountain lodge I ever had seen.

"Did *you* build this?" I asked incredulously.

"Yes," he said. "I pretended that I was building it for her to live in." He asked almost timidly, "Don't you ever pretend something?"

"Yes," I said. "Perhaps too often." Then I asked, "Tell me what you really think of your life; I mean what do you think the answer is to your own years?"

"Oh," he replied, "I'm not smart enough to say."

"I think you are," I said. "Men have written of solitude and of a world well lost; but you've lived it. What did you learn?"

"I got so's I knew a little about the woods and mountains, the ways of wild game; I guess I know something about that, maybe."

"That's not what I want to know."

His gray eyes were on me as he said simply, "You mean was I a coward to go away?"

"That's a serious word to toss around," I replied. "I'm not accusing; I'm asking."

He nodded. "And I've asked it of myself lots of times. Sometimes I thought it was a brave thing when the winter snowed me in and the wind blew across the Bishop's Razor and the Blacks. Then in spring when the thaws came and the flowers were out, I thought I was the biggest coward in the world."

"What made you think that?"

He stayed silent for some time, then said in a tone so low that I barely caught the words: "I hadn't made a fight to keep somebody I loved."

"Why didn't you? Because you were just a boy?"

"I didn't think she wanted me," he said. "And I guess I've got the wrong kind of pride."

"Then let me tell you something," I said. "I was only thirteen when Dodie died, but I know that she loved you."

He seemed far away in thought.

"Didn't you hear what I said?" I asked. "She always loved you, and nobody else."

"It's nice of you to say so," he replied.

"Nice, nothing. She did."

"But you were only a child. No, I was no good; and a woman can't love a man who's no good. How can she?"

"If that's what you think," I said, "look at me! The champion no-good of the century."

This remark seemed to hurt him. "Why," he said, "you're the finest—"

I interrupted him. "Didn't Cooper tell you the way I carried on? Maybe you yourself saw me coming out of—"

He cut in quietly, "I never paid much attention to where you came out of."

Unable to persuade my father to see my faults, I asked, "What do you remember best about Dodie? I mean what happy thing?"

"Well, well now," he said with almost childish eagerness, "it was the time we went to Professor Stevenson's concert at Trinity Church in 1889. Yes, it was a Friday night in May. And do you know? When the concert was over, and all Dr. Stevenson's fine singers were standing there, and all the people standing up to join in 'The Star-Spangled Banner,' do you know what happened?"

"No," I said. "How could I?"

"Well, Dodie's voice rose over all the others. And everybody turned to look at her." He nodded his head in wonderment at this recollection. "I guess that was the proudest moment in all my life. I know it was."

We saw each other several times between 1932 and the last time in 1936, both in New York and in Denver, and we exchanged letters.

Then, in 1937, one of those things occurred which I always dread putting into print, for to do so invites letters which suggest that I am either demented or a spiritualist.

I was living with my family in a house owned by my actor friend Roland Young in Beverly Hills, California. Perhaps an excerpt from a diary which I kept during that year best describes the event of which I would speak:

"At three o'clock this morning, I awakened after a harrowing dream, the contents of which are not easily recaptured. Upon awakening, I found myself in a sweat. I said to Agnes, 'Something has happened! Something terrible!' I arose and turned on the lights, considered dressing and driving to the sea. After some minutes I lay down again but could not sleep. An hour afterward there was a knocking at the front door. I answered the knock to receive a telegram. It informed me that my father, Charles Francis Devlan, had died of a heart attack at four o'clock. Allowing for the difference between Pacific Coast and Rocky Mountain time, that would fix the time of my father's death at the hour when I first awakened from the dream. . . . I think that my father's life was a great innocence."

When I review my long quest, I become convinced that in my father I found quite another goal. In my scrutiny of many men as candidates for a make-believe parent, the uncelebrated ones and the celebrated ones as well, I found my own definition of what America is and will always be.

My youthful reveries had given way to a realistic picture of America, and the heartening fact that Americans are "people." In the characters who had passed my questioning heart and eye, I heard and saw and felt an expression of the heartbeats of my country, the passions, the charities, the faults as well as the virtues of America, its failures as well as its successes. This grand march of the Americans made me feel warm and good and worthwhile as I looked on. And I wished to become a part, however small, of this brave procession.

Even the alien-born among my proxy fathers, such as Blake, the profound Englishman, and Lord Ogilvy of *The Post*, were a part of the national pattern. Were we not all aliens, once or twice or three times removed? Americans were people, human in all respects, garishly remiss at times, creatures of impulse, but always on the grand march to the future.

My pioneer grandmother, **poor** in worldly goods yet rich of mind, was American in terms of self-reliant courage. In her there were to be found the prejudices and obstinacies that America sometimes shows to the consternation of her neighbors. Granny's dislike of England and of Roman Catholicism was no more commendable than the biased views of many other men and women of the land. Still, the priests of Denver admired her, and Blake and other Englishmen admired her for her unflinching honesty of thought and expression. And she herself seemed aware of the many sidedness of our national ancestry when she paraphrased an adage to remark, "It takes all kinds of worlds to make a people."

Grandpa, too, was an element of America. Unlettered and ineffectual as he may have been in many ways, the doughty old herald of "Wealth for All" had a stubborn optimism that is our country's heritage.

Even the pompous Dr. Parr, the tricky peddler of Magico-Sulpho and spurious etchings, had a place in our national design. Were it not so, we should be denied the great pleasure of listening today to the miraculous virtues of patent medicines and beauty restoratives as advertised on our radios. And the suave and altogether enchanting Colonel McFall, and the boresome Colonel Jamieson, have their counterparts in almost every community.

And in the warm boasts of Papa Sullivan, I found America with its seasoning of Irish temperament and fly-off-the-handle moods, as the time when Papa Sullivan, now too old and unreliable in the eyes of his family to be trusted with money, filched his own snap-purse, the one in which he had stored old coins when but a boy. He spent his hoard on little follies, and then got into a fight with a man at the barber-shop for singing, "The Green Grass Grew All Around." Papa Sullivan construed the song as a slur on persons of Irish ancestry.

The fortitude of Scout Wiggins and of Buffalo Bill and Ivy Baldwin, the dignified behavior of "Silver Dollar" Tabor and of Stratton "the gold king" in times of sorrow, pain, and disillusionment was a part of my America. The editors Joe Ward and Art MacLennan, Otto Floto, Jim Lockhart, and the many other men of the western newspaper world seemed recording angels of a national epic.

So many great men and women walked the land. Judge Lindsey, denounced by powerful enemies, never took a step backward from a foe or from his own ideals. The story of the boys' lives he influenced and the good he always did for young Americans never will die.

In the young men whose lives touched mine—Paul Whiteman, Jack Dempsey, Damon Runyon, Ed Sullivan, and Lee Casey—there was a spirit and a daring which made one believe that everywhere in our land there lived other such contemporaries.

The Land itself was both one's father and one's mother. No American was an orphan.

"Honor thy father and thy mother, that thy days may be long. . . ."

Dreams dreamed in a mulberry tree are precious things, and each young man of America can find himself somewhere within the broad reaches of his hopes, his loves, his faith in mankind.

"Tell us where the young buck is sleeping after the long ride?"
"In the sky you will see his campfire. . . . See him, all people.
. . . He is brave with dreams."